You Can Do It!

A Beginner's Introduction to Computer Programming

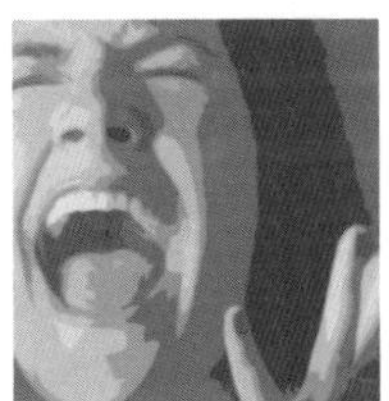

Francis Glassborow with Roberta Allen

You Can Do It!

A Beginner's Introduction to Computer Programming

John Wiley & Sons, Ltd

Telephone (+44) 1243 779777

Email (for orders and customer service enquiries): cs-books@wiley.co.uk
Visit our Home Page on www.wileyeurope.com or www.wiley.com

Reprinted January 2004

Other Wiley Editorial Offices

John Wiley & Sons Inc., 111 River Street, Hoboken, NJ 07030, USA

Jossey-Bass, 989 Market Street, San Francisco, CA 94103-1741, USA

Wiley-VCH Verlag GmbH, Boschstr. 12, D-69469 Weinheim, Germany

John Wiley & Sons Australia Ltd, 33 Park Road, Milton, Queensland 4064, Australia

John Wiley & Sons (Asia) Pte Ltd, 2 Clementi Loop #02-01, Jin Xing Distripark, Singapore 129809

John Wiley & Sons Canada Ltd, 22 Worcester Road, Etobicoke, Ontario, Canada M9W 1L1

Wiley also publishes its books in a variety of electronic formats. Some content that appears in print may not be available in electronic books.

Library of Congress Cataloging-in-Publication Data

Glassborow, Francis.
A beginner's introduction to computer programming : you can do it! /
Francis Glassborow.
p. cm.
Includes bibliographical references and index.
ISBN 0-470-86398-6 (Paper : alk. paper)
1. Computer programming. I. Title.
QA76.6.G575 2003
005.1 – dc22

2003020686

British Library Cataloguing in Publication Data

A catalogue record for this book is available from the British Library

ISBN 0-470-86398-6

Typeset in 10/11pt Joanna by Laserwords Private Limited, Chennai, India
Printed and bound in Great Britain by Biddles Ltd, King's Lynn, Norfolk
This book is printed on acid-free paper responsibly manufactured from sustainable foresty in which at least two trees are planted for each one used for paper production.

Dedication

This book is dedicated to the many colleagues and numerous students who moulded me into a better teacher. In particular my first Head of Department, Gerry Astell, who taught me never to teach something that I knew I would later retract. False simplicity is never helpful to the student in the long run; it just makes a poor teacher's life easier for a moment.

Contents

How to Use This Book

In my school days I used to read my science textbooks cover to cover in about a week to ten days from the time they were issued to me. On the other hand, math textbooks took many months to read. Later in life I found when studying a book that was pushing the boundaries of my knowledge that I usually stopped reading after about six or seven chapters and took a few weeks, or even months, off before resuming my study by quickly re-reading the first few chapters and then pushing on with the material that had been overwhelming me first time round and moving on to new material, which would again eventually overwhelm me. I would repeat this process until at the third or fourth shot I would finally finish the whole book.

I suppose that with more self-discipline I would take everything more gently and give myself time to absorb new ideas before pushing on; it just isn't my way. I am always impatient to move on and master new things so I proceed more like the hare than the tortoise.

Which way you learn does not matter as long as you do not suffer from the illusion that acquiring new skills is just a few days' work. Factual textbooks such as those I had for science can be read in a few days or weeks but we are unreasonable to expect to read a book that is designed to help us acquire a new skill in just a couple of weeks.

Another feature of books introducing skills is that they have to assume the reader will practice. It is no good reading a book about playing a flute if you wish to become a flautist. It may be technically possible to read such a book in a few days but that would not turn you into any kind of musician. A single book on flute playing takes many months to read effectively and at every stage you would read the book with your flute readily to hand. You would practice and listen to good flautists.

This book is about acquiring a skill and so I have designed it to be used with a computer to hand. I have also designed it to be studied at whatever pace you feel comfortable with. However I have designed the first seven chapters to work together as a single block. The acceleration from Chapter 1 to Chapter 6 is quite high and most readers will find that they need to take time to digest that material before continuing their studies. I have written Chapter 7 as a natural break before you proceed with the rest of the book.

Each of the next six chapters (8 to 13) is a unit adding some new material and some new ideas. Many readers will find that they want to take breaks after some or even all those chapters. During those breaks you will want to use what you have learnt. Some readers will happily plough straight through in much the same way that they read the first six chapters. That will be fine as long as you set a pace that gives you time to absorb each of the new ideas and practice using them.

During the study of this middle part of the book you should take time out to think about how what you are learning can be used to achieve tasks that interest you. That thinking time is best done away from the book and the computer (much of my thinking is done waiting for buses, enjoying a hot bath or while eating a meal).

Chapters 14 to 16 are different because their main objective is to consolidate your knowledge and skills and show how what you have learnt can be put to use to do things that may look difficult. Roberta comments that she felt that these chapters treated the reader as if they were now a programmer. She is right, and by that stage in the book you definitely are a programmer, just an inexperienced one. These chapters both show you what can be done with what you know and provide you some useful extras that you can use in your own programming.

The last chapter has the same title as the first exactly because you will have come full circle. You start as someone who has the potential to be a programmer and you finish as someone who knows they can program.

Whether you move from Chapter 1 to Chapter 17 like a hare or a tortoise or in some other way, getting to the end is a new beginning and one where you will truly be able to declare "I can do it, I can program."

Study Elements

There are various elements built into this book, all but one of which require your active participation. The exception is that there are places where I give you an anecdote or an analogy to help you with your understanding or motivation.

I use two ways of introducing you to new code. Sometimes I work through developing some code writing about what I am doing at each stage. The purpose is to show you how programs come into existence on a bit by bit basis. During that process I will expect you to work alongside me and create your copy of the program by following in my footsteps.

Sometimes I will give you a finished piece of code and ask you to type it in and correct any typing errors so that the program works. After you have done that I walk you through the code explaining what the pieces do and how they work.

Why the two ways? Sometimes experiencing what a program does greatly aids in understanding how it does it; at other times it is more important to learn how programs come into existence by actually following the thought processes that lead to the finished program. Both ways are valuable to you.

During the course of working through this book you will come across items that are marked as "tasks". These are things that you should do before going on with reading. Sometimes they will require you to write a program; sometimes they will simply require that you do something exactly as described. However they share the property that I consider doing them to be an inherent part of successfully reading this book. Sometimes you may eventually have to look at a solution that I have provided but you should think of them as hurdles that you should seriously try to cross without knocking over.

I have also provided exercises. I have tried to choose these so that doing them will help you develop your programming skills without asking you to write dozens of repetitive programs that lead nowhere. In general doing the exercises will be good for you but missing a few will not be a disaster. Your personal pride should motivate you to do the exercises unless they have been marked as ones for specialists (there are a few marked as "for mathematicians").

There are some places where I explicitly invite you to try something for fun. These are only a reminder that you should be trying the ideas you find in this book and it should be fun. You should be trying things that you want to show to others. You may be lucky enough to have an appreciative family, friends or colleagues but if you haven't (or even if you have) I want others to see your work and I invite you to send me things you are proud of so they can be made public via the book's website. Your best work will deserve a wider audience so do not be too shy to put it forward.

End of Chapter Elements

Every chapter, bar the last, has an end of chapter section that contains one or more of the following elements:

Roberta's Comments: In which my student author contributes whatever she feels like writing about the chapter in hand. They are an example of something you might consider for yourself: keeping a diary of your experiences. I hope that they will sometimes give you the consolation of discovering that someone else had problems too, and sometimes allow you to feel superior because you didn't. However do not feel too superior because the text you have is greatly improved over what she learnt from, largely because of the effort she made to criticize my work in a positive way.

Hints: Sometimes I provide a hint for a task or exercise to help you succeed in doing the work yourself.

Solutions: Unlike most books, reading the solutions is not a way of cheating. I expect you to read the solutions when they are provided. Studying the solutions is part of the correct use of the book. Not just reading the solutions or trying them out, but understanding why they work and perhaps why they are different from yours.

Summary: This is broken down under three headings. Key Programming Concepts contains the elements of the chapter that are independent of the programming language. They are the general principles of programming. C++ Checklist gives you a quick summary of the elements of Standard C++ (i.e. the common core of C++ available everywhere) covered in the chapter. And finally there is the Extensions Checklist which summarizes elements that I have added to C++ via the library I provide for you.

End of the Book

I could have added 100 pages to the end of this book by including printed appendices summarizing the C++ language and library, my library, and details of the way the programming style of this book differs from common C++ programming styles. Instead you will find a single printed Appendix A which lists common errors that test readers had when trying to get their code to work.

The other four appendices and the glossary are on the CD that comes with the book. You can print those out if you wish but they will not assist your early efforts when most of their contents will be of no practical use to you.

You may find that there is a greatly extended glossary on the book's website because I plan to add to it in response to questions raised by readers such as yourself. If you meet a term that is puzzling you, check the latest version of the glossary and if it is not there or it still puzzles you, email me and I will do my best to respond promptly and helpfully.

The CD

The CD that comes with this book contains two elements. The first is the software needed by the reader. I will put that more strongly: you should not use programming software that I have not provided either on the CD or on the website; if you do then you are on your own. There are many excellent commercial programming tools available but they are professional tools and as such they are designed to be used by professionals.

The second element is the appendices and glossary. These are provided as Microsoft Word and HTML files. That means that you can print them or use them electronically. The former allows you to add your own annotations and the latter makes it easy to search for a word or phrase.

Installing software from the CD: Unless you have switched off the auto start feature of Windows, the CD should automatically start and lead you through the process of installing all you need. By default it will offer to install in C:\tutorial. If you want to install to another drive just change the drive letter. You can install to a different directory but I would encourage you not to do so. It will make it much easier to follow help provided by others if you have everything in the standard form provided on the CD. You can manage with about 100 megabytes of disk storage but around about 250 megabytes will make it more comfortable and save you from having to clean up intermediate working files from earlier chapters as you progress through the book.

Why fgw?

In many places in this book `fgw` is used as an identifier or prefix. Roberta wondered why, was I dyslexic? This is an example of a little thing that can nag at the back of the mind when we try to do something new. Once we know the reason, however trivial, the irritation goes away. My initials are FWG but I always use fgw to identify my work. The reason is that the school where I taught for almost twenty years identified staff by the initials of their first and last names. Where that left ambiguity the final letter of the surnames was added. There were three members of staff whose initials were FG so I was FGw. I came to feel most comfortable with using fgw as my initials.

Introduction

Before Purchase

If you are trying to decide whether to buy this book please read far enough to reach a conclusion. I will do my very best to help you reach the right conclusion for you because delighted though I would be to have vast sales figures I do not want you to waste your time and money buying something you later regret.

This is a unique book on the subject of computer programming because it has been written for ordinary people and it attempts, I believe successfully, to make programming accessible to anyone with a computer (at this stage, one running some version of Microsoft Windows), some curiosity about what programming is and the willingness to spend some time satisfying that curiosity by learning to program.

This book is a collaboration between me as a technically knowledgeable and experienced teacher and Roberta, whose qualifications were exactly those that a reader will need. Roberta's contribution is small in textual content and vast in helping me to write a book that can be used by someone whose computing skills are just enough to load a program, use a word processor, use email and surf the Internet. When she started as the student half of the authorial team, despite having used a computer for a decade she still had not grasped the concepts of directory structures and the like. Her study of mathematics ended at 16 and her mathematical skills more or less stop with simple arithmetic and those skills needed to keep a set of company accounts.

She had two positive qualifications; she wanted to discover what programming was about and she was willing to trust me to show her. Both those are important. If you use this book you will need both those qualifications. You need to be willing to put in time and effort to discover the rudiments of programming and you need to trust us, Roberta and me, to help you achieve that ambition. However given those qualifications we promise you that you can learn to program and that long before you finish this book you will have written programs for yourself. As long as you have some imagination some of those programs will be uniquely yours. Roberta had written her first entirely original program before she had finished Chapter 6 and by the time she had finished her studies she had written several programs for her grandchildren as well as at least one following her own interests.

I tell you these things because I am certain that anyone who wants to can learn simple programming. I also believe that many people will find programming rewarding in many ways. One of those is the tremendous sense of achievement that any programmer gets whenever a program finally works and does what it is designed to do.

`If you browse through the pages of this book you may wonder if you could ever cope with the weird things written in this font`. There is no need to worry, you will soon find that all that text is just a way to express intentions in a way that a computer can use, and that it isn't at all weird. It isn't English though there is a scattering of English words in it. It is a computer language called C++ (pronounced cee plus plus). Friends, relatives and colleagues who know something about programming may give you dire warnings on hearing that this book uses C++. Believe me, they are well intentioned but mistaken.

Why C++?

Let me ask you a different question, "Why English?" Well you know the answer to that; it is a language you speak. Think a little further, what is the most widely spoken human language? Chinese is the mother tongue for more people than any other language, so why am I not writing in Chinese? On the other hand languages like Spanish and Swahili are far easier to learn than English so why am I not writing in one of those?

As you know, English is not only the mother tongue of a few hundred million people but it is also the second language for immensely more people. If you were an alien visitor to Earth I doubt that you would think twice about which human language you should start with. For all its complexity English is overwhelmingly the first choice language for those who want to move outside their own community.

C++ is very like that in the computing community. It is a rich and complex language with dark corners and traps for the unwary. But it is also the most widely used general-purpose computer programming language. Few people, if any, ever master the whole of English and few people, if any, master the whole of C++. But we do not need mastery of the whole of English nor do we need mastery of the whole of C++. This is not a book about C++ and when you finish it you will not be a C++ programmer. What you will be is a programmer who can use C++ to express solutions to problems and to write programs that meet real needs.

Why C++? Exactly because C++ does not get in the way of my showing you how to program. Other programming languages may be simpler but too often I would find myself frustrated because they would prevent me from showing you simple answers to programming problems. I have been able to pick and choose from the richness of C++ to empower my readers with powerful tools that match powerful ideas.

C++ has one small failing in that the basic language lacks tools for graphical work. That was easily fixed because I could write those tools in C++ and make them available to you. I needed some specialist help with those tools because of the quirkiness of computers: they have different graphical facilities, numbers of colors on the screen, etc. Using C++ allowed me to specify what I needed and have a colleague (Garry Lancaster) turn those specifications into tools that will work on all MS Windows machines. Eventually (maybe even before you see this book) I will find others who can turn that C++ into identical tools for other machines but until I do, we have to put up with an artificial limitation in that programs you write using my tools will only work on machines running some version of MS Windows.

The last element I needed was some simple tools for you to use to write programs and manage the various technical details of turning what you write into something the computer can use. Those tools were provided by another writer, Al Stevens, who gave me permission to distribute Quincy, which is his tool set for newcomers to programming.

The work of people like Garry Lancaster and Al Stevens demonstrates the very best of the computing community, good work freely shared. The consequence is that you have in your hands everything you need (other than a computer and your time and energy) to learn to program.

The choice is entirely yours, if you want to learn to program and by doing so learn a bit about how other people's computer programs work, you can. Roberta and I have spent nine solid months writing this book for you (that does not mean it will take you nine months to read it – she had the added burden of persuading me to improve the text so that others would find it easier). For the first time you have a real choice about learning to program. We have done our bit, the rest is up to you.

Getting the Best from This Book

Now you have decided to buy this book let me give you some advice on how to get the best use out of it.

Ideally you should not study alone. Note that I wrote "ideally", in practice you may find that you have no choice other than to study by yourself. However, avoid that option if you can. With that in mind the following is offered as, I hope, helpful advice rather than as some requirement for studying this book.

Two things will help you, a partner and a mentor. The partner should be someone of similar ability and someone with whom you are happy to learn, someone with whom you can share your mistakes as well as your successes. The process of learning includes making mistakes. Mistakes are nothing to be ashamed of; they are the way we learn. We should feel comfortable with sharing our mistakes with a partner in learning. Sometimes we may laugh at our idiocy, and sometimes we may be impressed at the insight of our study partner. What we should never do is laugh at someone else. The mistake may be cause for laughter but the person making it deserves respect for letting you learn from their mistakes.

If you do not have someone you know who wants to learn with you, it is worth seeing if you can contact someone via the Internet. Please check the book's website where you will find links to potential sources of study partners. To get to the book's website use the file on the CD (copied to your hard-drive when you install it) called "Link to Website.html". For success, you should be comfortable with your study partner and broaden the base of the relationship so that you do not just communicate about technical programming issues. Regular human contact even if only via email is more important to learning than most people realize. The other person needs to be considered as just that, a person.

I am also providing you with a virtual partner, my assistant author. She is the person who was first to read every word that is here as well as many that were omitted because she found them unhelpful. Her comments and experiences with each chapter are included. Sometimes her questions and my answers have been included as well. At the end of this introduction she will add a short section introducing herself and from then onwards she will be that vital second set of eyes that every technical writer should have. If this book is easy to read, you have her to thank. If you still find some of it hard going remember that she has been there ahead of you making the path a little easier.

The second person to help you, a mentor, should be an expert who can correct you when you stray off course, encourage you to persevere and compliment you on your successes. A good mentor is an invaluable resource; a bad one is a disaster.

You will identify the bad ones pretty quickly because they will want to tell you all kinds of things that are not in the pages of this book. The poor ones will want you to start from where they are or have you learn the way they did. A mentor who does not give helpful correction and reassurance as to your progress is a waste of time. One quality of a good mentor is that they are willing to learn from your work as well as to guide you. In other words they are true experts, always hungry for new ideas, new viewpoints and new insights. I loved teaching not only for what I could teach my students but also for what they could teach me.

If you cannot find a suitable mentor, try the book's website again. You can also try doing without (certainly better than having a poor mentor) and using such resources as model answers (provided in this book, or on the book's web pages) or a newsgroup such as alt.comp.lang.learn.c-c++. But be careful because you will find a great mixture of good and bad in such newsgroups.

Many modern books seem to be written on the basis that the reader needs instant gratification and will only read the text once. That means that we get solid doorstops in which the new information per page is very low. Authors try to find a dozen ways of saying the same thing because they expect the reader to only read a page once. I do not. I expect you to study and that means re-reading as often as is necessary to reach an understanding of what is going on. Take time over it. It took me nine months to write and it took Roberta nine months to understand it. Maybe because of the improvements Roberta has helped me make, it will only take you six months but do not expect to master the contents in much less time. However, you will be programming long before you finish this book.

I expect you to work at each chapter and return to earlier chapters as your understanding deepens. That is one of the great strengths of a book as opposed to a training course. The second advantage that a book has is that you can set your own pace. Some things you will grasp quickly, others will take you more time. The things that you understand quickly may well be things that someone else struggles with.

I expect you to work through most of this book with your computer in front of you. Just reading will not be enough; you will need to *do*. I will assume that you type in the code that I am writing about even when I do not nag you into it. One thing Roberta says fairly early on is that, with hindsight, she made a mistake by skipping some of the code when she was working through my text. Believe her, I rarely if ever waste a student's time with make-work exercises or code that has no value.

Someone with some knowledge of programming casually browsing this book could well be very surprised by some of the material they see in the early chapters. They are used to long, tedious and repetitious tomes that proceed at a snail's pace.

I hope that what you will find in this book is something different. This book aims to explain programming and challenge you to write programs with a limited set of C++ tools. As you progress you will acquire more tools, but the challenge to you to program will be a constant theme.

What You Will Achieve

Everything that you achieve will be built from simple parts (Standard C++ together with my library). I think you will be surprised how much can be done with simple resources. I certainly find myself playing with Playpen and hardly a day goes by when I do not think of something else I can do with it. That is a key point; what you do with your programming is only constrained by your imagination. For example, it is not that hard to program a computer to play chess, just very hard to write a program to play sensibly, which is why we leave it to experts to write chess-playing programs.

You will also learn techniques to produce simple animation, elementary data processing and numerical work so that your programming basics will be fully rounded out. The main theme of this book is to achieve competence with simple programming and learn that, in essence, it is much simpler than some experts like to make out. Yes, there are arcane corners, weird traps and bizarre features but you do not need to go near them to achieve something that you can be proud of.

Programming should be a rewarding experience. If you do not find it so then either it is not your thing or you have been badly taught. I hope that by studying this book you will discover that you can do it and that you like doing it.

Notes for Students

Never give up, but learn to ask for help. Have the wisdom to understand the difference between getting help and being lazy. If you do not understand a problem ask for more information but only just enough to point you in the right direction.

If you ever get someone else to write a program for you because you are going to miss a deadline, at least be honest enough with yourself to work at understanding the other person's work. You will already have lost a good deal by not doing the work yourself; do not compound that by not understanding what has been done for you.

Notes for Instructors

This book is based on many years of classroom experience coupled with over thirty years of programming. Keep focused on what your students require. Impress your students with your qualities as a teacher. That includes the willingness to listen to your students and a desire to understand what they are asking. They do not expect you to know all the answers but they do have a right to expect you to be honest. If you do not know an answer to one of their questions, say so and then take the time to find it.

Please do not destroy the spirit of this book if you use it as a course text. This book is designed to introduce programming basics as a voyage of discovery. The reader is invited to explore what they can achieve with the tools they have been shown rather than constantly hunting for more tools.

Understand that it takes skill and insight to do things in a simple way and appreciate the complicated solutions your students will first offer. But encourage them to look for simpler solutions. It is not enough that a program runs and produces correct solutions; it should also be a clear expression of the solution to a problem.

Do not burden your students with unnecessary requirements. Things like comments should be used constructively and not as some requirement by which you judge the quality of a student's work. If you think a student is under-commenting their work, wait a couple of weeks and then ask them to explain the program. If they can do so, the comments are probably adequate to their needs. The best documentation of code is the code itself. The more it needs the support of comments the more you should doubt its quality.

Personal Introductions

From the lead author

We are going to be spending many hours together so I should introduce myself. You do not have to read this but you might enjoy satisfying your curiosity.

I was born in 1942 (3rd June for those who like such trivia) as a first child of six. In 1949 my father went to work in the Sudan and sent his children to the local mission schools in the belief (correct in my opinion) that living in a foreign culture was worth much more than any English primary school education. The school I attended had 2000 pupils, used three teaching languages and there were never more than six pupils there whose first language was English. I had to learn Arabic and Italian. By the time I was nine I was preparing to return to an English prep school so I was also learning Latin from a private tutor and French from my mother who was a fluent French speaker (having been educated in a French convent school).

I started at an English prep school in September 1953 where I added classical Greek to my language studies. I went to Downside – a leading Catholic public school – in April 1956. In October 1960 I went to Merton College, Oxford. There I read a degree in Mathematics, and obtained a third class honours degree. As my tutor said to me several years later, the degree was disappointing but what mattered was that I had got a lot of other things from Oxford such as representing the University at Judo in the annual match against Cambridge in 1961, 1962 and 1963. In 1962 I was president of the Oxford University Judo Club.

I went on to teach mathematics in the early years, becoming Head of Mathematics at Cherwell School, Oxford before taking responsibility for computing in the school. By then I had taught myself to program and had produced several programs for use by my students. In 1982 I implemented the Forth programming language to provide portable programming resources for my students so that they could write programs that ran on their own Sinclair ZX Spectrums as well as the school's Research Machines 380Z. A colleague of mine designed and built hardware to link a Spectrum to a 380Z and I designed a protocol to allow the machines to exchange information over that link.

In 1988 I retired from teaching because the stress of supporting my colleagues with their computing needs had damaged my health. In that same year I joined the C Users Group UK, which later became ACCU. I was Chair of that organization for most of the 1990s as well as editor of its principal publication from August 1990 to December 2001.

In 1990 I became involved in the BSI's panels for standardising C and C++. From there I went on to represent the UK at the ISO/IEC SC22/WG14 (C) and WG21 (C++) committees. During the last few years I have been head of the UK delegation to those workgroups.

If you are interested, I am also an RYA Senior day boat instructor and I play competition Contract Bridge. I have two children as well as a beautiful disabled granddaughter (born in May 2001).

All I know about you is that you want to try out in my world of programming. Welcome, I hope it enriches your life because it has done much for mine, not least allowing me to meet many intelligent and entertaining people. Without those people this book would never have come to be written.

From the student author

I was born, bred and educated in Oxford and I'm still here. I left school at 16, married young, and had a son and a daughter. During the early years I juggled a wide assortment of part time jobs to fit in with my family commitments; these included telephone operator, barmaid, playgroup leader and working as a butcher's shop assistant in Oxford's wonderful covered market.

When the children were both settled in school I decided to further my education and went to Westminster College as a mature student. Initially I intended to take a teaching degree but I changed to theology. I was thrilled to get a first class honours degree.

After this I joined my husband in his plastic injection moulding factory as a company director and I was responsible for the administration, sales, quality department and general management. This is where I first met Francis who was our company's computer consultant.

When we had built a competent management team I felt that I could return to my studies and I went to Manchester College and took a diploma in theology mainly to learn the Greek and Hebrew necessary for more in-depth biblical studies. I spent the next couple of years specialising in John's Gospel and wrote a book that I have not attempted to get published.

Over the years Francis has continued to help me with my many computer problems. I am not exactly a technophobe but I am rather in awe of the dreaded machines. However, I love the Internet and have found it invaluable for both research and fun. I hope to have my own website eventually and I am slowly designing a website to publish my book and other pieces of writing.

As a development of my interest in all things spiritual I have recently become interested in more esoteric subjects including astrology and kabbalah.

My hobbies over the years have been as eclectic as my work experience and have included ballroom and Latin dancing, archery, gardening, badminton and more recently Tai chi and belly dancing (because now I am 50 I intend to grow old disgracefully) and last but not least having fun with our three grandchildren.

When Francis asked me to be a C++ student I thought he was rather insane. I am scared of computers and useless at math. However, I am sure that if I can learn to program with Francis' help then anyone can, so perhaps I am a good choice after all.

Acknowledgments

A book is the product of many people in addition to the named authors. An attempt to give an exhaustive list only leads to a feeling of having been slighted by those who have been left out. However there are always a number of individuals who have contributed above and beyond the calls of duty and friendship. In that context I want to publicly acknowledge and thank the following:

Al Stevens (al@alstevens.com) for writing the Quincy IDE and modifying it to better meet my needs even though this book might be considered to compete for some of the potential readership of his book (Teach Yourself C++, 7th edition, 0-7645-2644-8).

Garry Lancaster (glancaster@codemill.net) for all the many hours he spent implementing Playpen without ever grumbling that it would have been much easier had I given him a complete spec to start with instead of coming up with new items as the work progressed. Garry is among the best MS Windows programmers I know.

Anthony Williams (anthony_w@onetel.net.uk) who carefully tweaked the installation code for the CD so that it would make the reader's life as easy as possible.

I also thank all those on the editorial side, most particularly Gaynor Redvers-Mutton who tolerated my fiercely individualistic approach to writing a book.

Finally I should acknowledge the tolerance of my wife, Dulcie, and Roberta's husband, David, without which this book would never have been finished.

CHAPTER 1

You Can Program

In this chapter I will introduce you to the essential programming tools and show you how to use them to write your first program. You will find that this chapter is packed with screen images. In so far as is possible these are exactly what you should see though I cannot promise that future versions of Windows will not introduce minor variations. I place immense value on ensuring that if you do what I say you will see what I see.

I will also try to give you a sense of what programming really is and show you that you can already program though not program computers. By the end of this chapter you should be able to write a very simple program for yourself that will build more complicated images from an instruction to place a colored square in a window at a place of your choosing.

What Is Programming?

Many people think that computer programming is an arcane art. In truth it is just another form of something that most people can already do. When you are asked how to get to the local library, you respond with a program even though you probably call it ''giving directions''. Your instructions might not work because you forget a turning, or do not count an alley as a street though the person you give the directions to does. Computer programmers call that kind of mistake a ''bug''.

Knitting and embroidery patterns are programs; indeed they can often be converted into a machine-readable form by punching the instructions on a card or tape.

A musical score is another form of program with special symbols that have to be placed correctly in two dimensions. A music program (score) can also be converted to some mechanical or electronic format so that devices such as modern keyboards can play them automatically (and devices such as piano rolls provided such automation long before electronic computers were invented).

Computer programming is just another way that an exact set of instructions can be given in order to achieve an objective. I am sure that you have both followed and provided some form of program at some stage in your life – it just wasn't a computer program.

TECHNICAL NOTE

Program v programme

Note that the word for a list or details of an event (such as a play, football match, etc.) is spelt "program" in the USA and "programme" in the UK (with other English-speaking countries making their own choice). The term for a set of instructions for a computer is "program". That is the only correct spelling in English (though it was not always so).

Almost all forms of programming have special terms and symbols. I sometimes suspect that those that can "program" deliberately maintain the mystique of special terms to make themselves seem somehow special and to make it easy to identify the outsider. But the more likely explanation is that they have simply forgotten how confusing the terminology can be the first time you hear it.

Before you read any further please take a sheet of paper and write a set of instructions (a program) for blind guests in your home that will tell them how to get from the dining room to the guest bedroom. (OK, it can be any two rooms, preferably ones that involve climbing stairs when going from one to the other – you will find out why the stairs in the next chapter.)

Let me guess that you have been very careful in getting the instructions right. However they are useless to your blind guests because a blind person will be unable to read them. The program you have written must be converted into some form that is suitable for the user. Please think about this and we will come back to it after you have done a small practical exercise. This involves a computer program, a very simple one that I have written for you but which you have to pass to your computer.

Introduction to Your Programming Tools

You will need a few tools for your work. I have provided them on the CD that comes with this book. Please resist any temptation to use tools from elsewhere. They will be excellent when you have gained confidence and fluency with programming. However, their complexity will overwhelm you while you are struggling to learn to program. It is enough to try to do something new without also trying to do it in an unnecessarily complicated environment.

You also need something to manage these tools with rather than having to remember every detail for yourself. Programmers use things called IDEs (Integrated Development Environments), which are rather like carpenters' workbenches. Those that come with commercial compilers, or even the free ones that are used by experienced programmers, have a multitude of options that will simply get in your way and lead to confusion. (No differences here, then; professional work environments are rarely suited to the newcomer.) So I have chosen a very simple IDE written and maintained by Al Stevens. He calls it Quincy and it provides just what we want: enough to work with but no frills to get in the way.

If you have followed the instructions for installing the software you will have installed Quincy somewhere on your system (perhaps on the C drive, but possibly somewhere else; I have my copy on my E drive). You should have an icon of a cat's face on your desktop. Click (or double-click, depending on how your system is set up) on it to open Quincy. You should see:

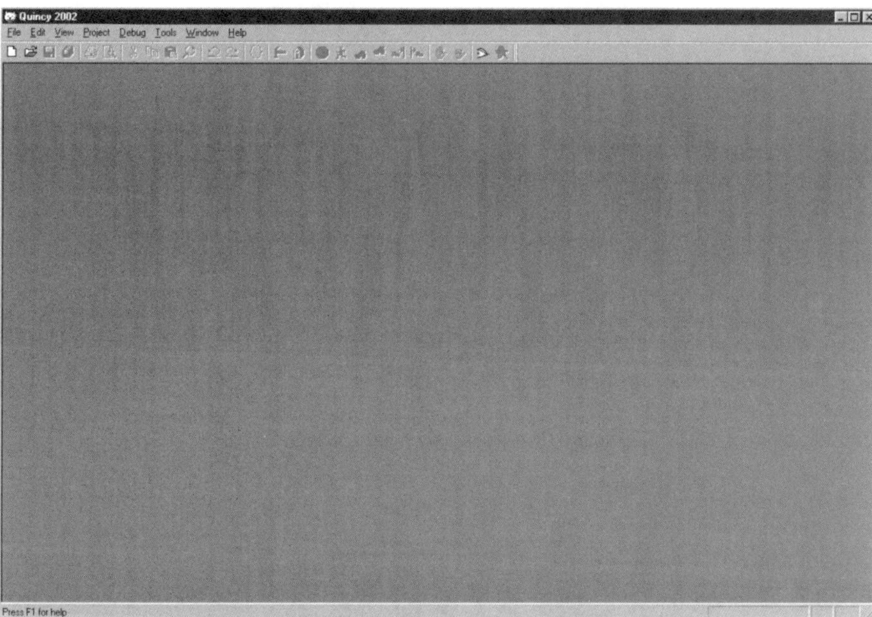

There are some things that you need to do every time you prepare to write a new program. I am going to walk you through them this time with images from my screen to help you. Until you get used to it, come back to this section each time you start a new program and follow through these steps.

1) Create a new project

Left click on the File menu and then the New option:

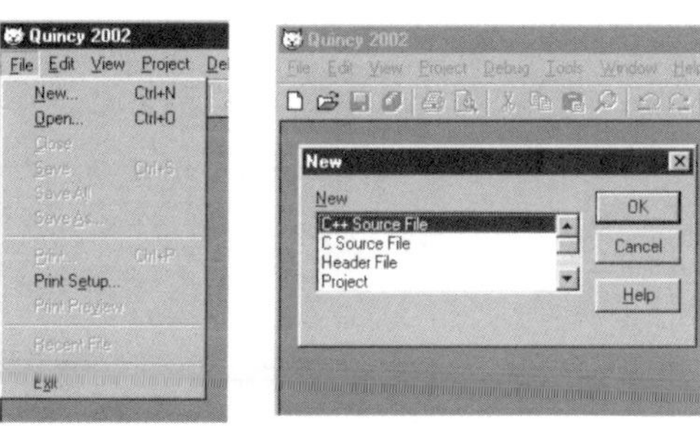

Select ''Project'' by double-clicking on it (or click and select ''OK'').

Type ''my_first_program'' (get into the habit of giving descriptive names to projects and other files) in the Target name box. Use the browse button to find the sub-directory named ''Chapter 1''. You should find that in the directory called ''tutorial'' on the drive where you installed the tools from the CD. When you have found it, left click the OK button in the browse dialog box. Check that the ''Type of Build'' selected is ''Console application''.

The dialog box should look like this:

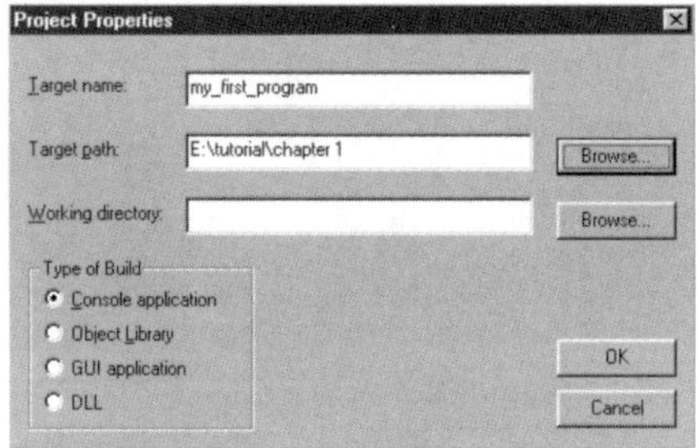

Left click on the OK button and you should see:

2) Set the project options

Select the "tools" menu and choose options. You should see the image at the top of the next page. Make sure that the boxes have been selected as in this image. Then use the browse button beside the Includes box to find the sub-directory called "fgw_headers". That should be one of the other sub-directories in the same place that you found "Chapter 1". Click OK in the browse dialog and then click OK in the Options dialog box.

3) Get the special libraries

Much of the programming you will be doing relies on two special files. Do not worry about exactly what they are; they contain resources that one of the programming tools will need. You have to find these two files and include them in the project.

Click on the Project menu and select ''Insert Files''. You should then use the drop down menu in the dialog box to find the fgw_headers sub-directory. You should then see something like this (the exact file list may be different, but the two important files fgwlib.a and libgdi32.a should be there. (If they are not in the sub-directory, your installation from the CD is faulty. Copy the contents of the fgw_headers directory on the CD to tutorial\fgw_headers.)

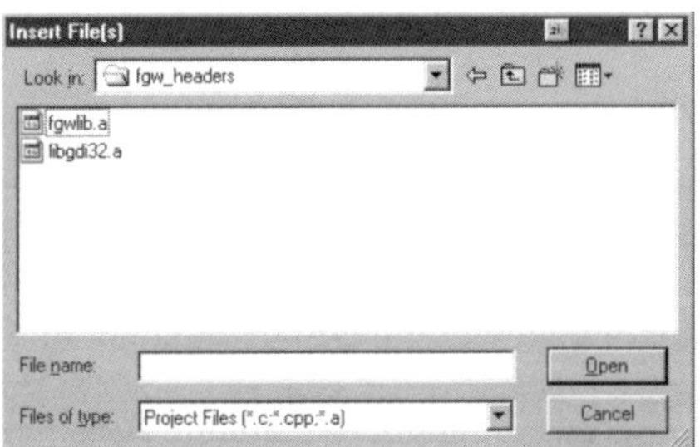

Now you need to be careful because you need to get the files fgwlib.a and libgdi32.a into the project in the correct order. Hold down the Ctrl key on your keyboard and first click with the left mouse button on libgdi32.a and then on fgwlib.a (the selection will list them in the reverse order when you have done that) and click on the ''Open'' button. Quincy may ask you if you wish to copy the files to the project directory: click on yes. If it asks you about replacing an existing copy, accept that as well.

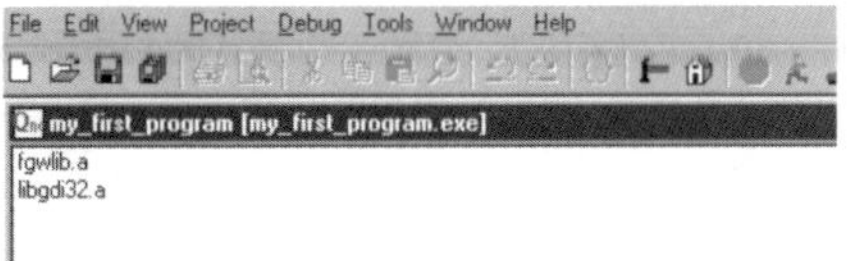

If you have done everything correctly you should be looking at the image on the right.

4) Save the project

Go to the File menu in Quincy and save the project.

Our First Program

Let us write a program together. First go to the File menu and select New. (I won't keep telling you to use your mouse to make these choices.) Four kinds of new things will be visible (there are three other file types if you scroll down, but the only ones we will use are three of the top four and, later, the ASCII Text file type). Choose C++ Source File.

Creating the source code

Type the following into the editing window:

```
// first program typed in by
// on
#include "playpen.h"
#include <iostream>

int main(){
  fgw::playpen paper;
  paper.display();
  std::cout << "press RETURN to end program.";
  std::cin.get();
}
```

Add your name at the end of the first line and today's date at the end of the second, otherwise type in the above text exactly (you do not need to worry about extra spaces). We will shortly look at what each line of the above is doing but, for now, focus on getting this program working.

Saving the source code

When you have finished typing you must save your work. Go to the File menu and select Save. STOP! Check where you are about to save your work and by what name. Unfortunately sometimes the defaults will be wrong. Use the controls on the Save dialog box to find the sub-directory called Chapter 1. Now change the File name entry to Empty_Playpen (because that is what this code produces) and click on Save.

When you do this some of the words above will change color. Do not worry: Quincy uses color-coded syntax, which means that Quincy uses color to help you distinguish such things as comments and the basic words of C++ from the rest of the program. If you do not like the chosen colors you can change them by using the "editor" tag in the Tools\Options window.

How easy the next part is will depend on how meticulous you have been with my instructions. If you have done exactly what I asked you to do then the next step will be easy. However if you have mistyped anything you are going to get error messages, and some of those can be pretty obscure.

Compiling the source code

Press F5. You will see a small window open with a long one-line message in it. Do not worry; Quincy is just reporting what it is doing. In this case it is using a tool called a compiler to convert your program into something that can be used with pieces from the libraries to make an executable (a program that can be run all by itself).

After a short time (how short depends on the speed of your computer, but it is six seconds on mine) you should see a second message *Successful build*. If you are unlucky you will see several more lines of messages followed by *Unsuccessful build*. At this stage all that those extra messages mean is that you mistyped something. Go back and look through your **source code** (that is what programmers call text that is going to become part of a program) and see if you can spot where it is different from the version I provided above. Make your corrections and try again.

What you have done so far is to use a simple text editor to create some source code. You saved the result in a file called Empty_Playpen.cpp (Quincy supplied the .cpp for you) and then you converted it into a form that the computer can use to create a program. That last stage happened when you pressed F5: a tool called a compiler converted the source code into something called **object code**. The process is like taking your instructions for a blind visitor and converting them into Braille. The object code would be pretty arcane if you tried to read it but it is just what is needed for the next stage.

TECHNICAL NOTE

Creating programs

You might be wondering why I did not make life easy for you by placing the source code on the CD. I would not be so cruel as to destroy such an important opportunity for learning. You need to start experiencing typical errors as soon as possible so that you will learn what they are whilst your code is still only a few lines long. This is like the falls that a young child experiences while it learns to stand up and then to walk. Mistakes are opportunities to learn.

Programming is largely a skill. That means that you need regular practice, and that includes practice at handling mistakes. Try making a couple of simple alterations to my source code (such as omitting a semicolon or misspelling `playpen`) so that you can see the resulting error messages when you compile it by pressing F5. Do not try to understand them in detail but try to get a feel for them and what causes them. Note that double-clicking on an error message will often locate the place that the compiler is complaining about. However the actual error might be in an earlier line of source code. All the compiler can do is tell you where it first detects that it has a problem with your source code.

Including the program in a project

Now go back to your project window (re-open my_first_program.prj, if you closed it) and use the Project menu to insert your empty_playpen.cpp source code file into the project. You do this in the same way that you added the two library files earlier but this time the file should be in the "Chapter 1" directory. At this stage your screen should look something like that on the right here.

The list of files can be in any order with the single exception that fgwlib.a must come before libgdi32.a. This limitation to the order in which files are placed in a project is very unusual and is the result of some of the things I had to do to allow support for a simple program style suitable for those learning to program while using a modern Windows style operating system.

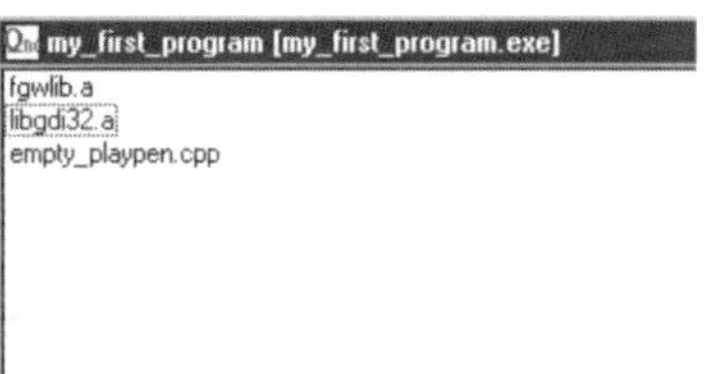

Creating and running an executable

Now Press F9. You will get a message saying that my_first_program does not exist. Click the Yes button and Quincy will create the program for you and run it. This program will hardly take a prize for originality but it has a special place in your life because it will be the first C++ program you have created by typing in some source code, compiling, linking (the process of creating a program from object code and other resources such as the fgwlib.a and libgdi32.a that have been provided) and running it. You will see two windows: one is a standard console type window (like the ones you get when you run MS-DOS programs from Windows); the other is a large empty white square with a border and a banner naming it "Playpen". Here is what your screen might look like:

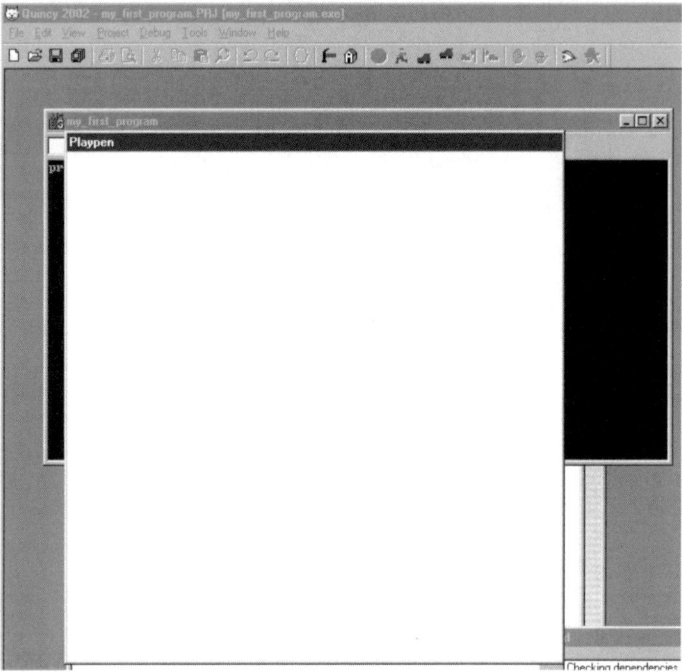

The white square window with ''Playpen'' in the window's banner is where we can display graphical material. Underneath it is a black console window that will have the name of the program in its banner. In this case it is my_first_program. The graphics window is unusual because it is a static window, which means that you cannot resize it (and on some versions of Windows you cannot move it either). The console window is a normal MS-DOS type window: it can be moved and resized, but you should not try to close it unless you are left no options (i.e. your program has locked up and will not end normally).

If you look at the task bar (normally at the bottom of your screen) you will find that each window has its own task button. The easiest way to switch between the windows is to click with your mouse on the one you want. Experiment a little to get the feel of working with the two windows.

Use your mouse to bring the console window to the top. You will see the message ''Press RETURN to end program''. Do so and the program ends.

Well, not quite. After the program ends and the Playpen window closes, Quincy wakes up and keeps the console window open until you press return again. Quincy is trying to be helpful and possibly succeeds in being confusing. We should not blame it because Playpen is very unusual and was specially designed to help people learn to program. I cannot remember having seen anything that works quite like it anywhere else.

Congratulations, take a break and then I will walk you through the source code and explain a little about what it does.

Walking through the Empty_Playpen code

Those first two lines, which start with ''//'', are comment lines. Whenever we want to write something in C++ source code that is intended purely for human readers, we write it as a comment. Comments start with // and continue to the end of the line they are on. Some authors, instructors, etc., seem to think that source code should have lots of comments. Nothing could be further from the truth. Comments should only be used when they add information that cannot be provided by the source code. Choosing good names and programming structures removes the need for many comments, just as writing good text reduces the need for footnotes in a book.

All source code files should have comments to identify the author and the date of creation. They should also include the date of the last modification if this is different from the creation date. If you are working by yourself that might seem unnecessary, but it is a good habit to get into. If you are responsible for a file of source code, put comments with your name and the date at the top (or if you prefer, at the bottom) of the file.

It is easy to underrate the value of making sure that a file contains its last modification date and its author's name. It is all too easy to finish up with identically named files in different places on your computer and not be able to determine which is the most recent version. Some programs such as Microsoft Word track the date of the last change as part of the information it stores when you save a file. Professional programmers use a tool called a version control system that requires files to be checked out and checked back in. For now you should try to ensure that your source code files contain their creation date and last modification date.

The next two lines of our program are instructions to the compiler to tell it that it will need to look up information somewhere else. We call these other places "header files" (I guess because they come at the head of a file of source code). Header files generally have a .h extension, except the ones that belong to Standard C++ which have no extension (and are usually just called headers). A second difference is that the names of the Standard C++ headers are placed in angle brackets and the names of the others are placed in quotes. That matters: if you get it wrong, the compiler may not be able to find the right files.

There is also a small issue of good style. Place the ordinary header files first, in alphabetical order. Place the Standard C++ headers afterwards, again in alphabetical order. The compiler will not care about this but other human readers may.

The contents of the header files and headers will be copied into your file on a temporary basis (we call this **pre-processing**). If you look at the contents of a header file (you can find the ones for my library in the fgw_headers directory), they might look pretty strange. There is nothing mysterious about them; they are like tables of contents for a book except that a header file documents what can be found in a corresponding C++ library or source code file. C++ library files (such as libgdi32.a, which provides graphics support for Microsoft Windows, and fgwlib.a, which contains the special support material I have written for this book) have a .a extension in this IDE; C++ source code files use a .cpp extension by convention. The compiler (the tool that translates source code to object code) needs to know what the linker (the tool that links, or joins together, your code with other code to make a complete program or executable) can expect to find in other object code files and libraries. Header files give the compiler this essential information.

In this case the playpen.h header file provides the information the compiler needs to know about what it can find in the fgwlib.a library. That includes everything that comes as part of the Playpen facility (more later). The second header file, iostream (notice the use of angle brackets) is a C++ Standard Library header that provides information about basic input and output facilities provided by the C++ Standard Library.

C++ provides a sophisticated mechanism naming things. It is among the most sophisticated that I have come across. It allows programmers to provide information about where names are declared and the context that adds to their meaning. This should not be a strange idea because we use something like it in everyday conversation. When you hear an art teacher talk about *drawing a gun* you do not expect that to be followed by firing it. However if you hear a police officer use the same phrase, you would be surprised if he then went on to describe the use of charcoal for the purpose.

At this early stage in your programming I do not want to have to explain the mechanisms for providing short names in context so I have provided the full names for the things I am using from the C++ Standard Library (those that start with `std::`) and my library (those that start with `fgw::`). Names are important in programming and I will have a lot more to say about them as we progress.

Mostly, programmers do not worry about the contents of header files, they just include them where needed. Sometimes they will look in a header file to make sure they know how the names being provided have been spelt and the details they need for correct use.

The next line, which starts "`int main(`", is special. It tells the compiler where your program will start. Every program needs exactly one line that starts "`int main(`". In this case our program does not need any data from outside when it runs so the line is in the simplest form: "`int main(){`".

The next line is called a declaration and definition. The declaration part is because it tells the compiler about a new name (`paper`) and what type of thing it will refer to (`fgw::playpen`, i.e. a `playpen` type of thing from the `fgw` library). The definition part is because writing that statement in this context will result in creating (the C++ term is "constructing") the `fgw::playpen` object that we will refer to by the name `paper`.

We will deal with objects and types quite a bit. In many programming languages the idea of **type** is an essential component of the language. In general, a type is a combination of storage for information together with a specification of how that information may be used or altered. That will seem a bit vague at the moment but as we progress I hope that the concept will become clearer.

All objects of the same type behave the same way though they may be different in some details. Just as when we say that Fido is a dog, we know that we mean that "Fido" is a particular dog, the compiler knows that `paper` is a particular instance of the type (breed) called `playpen`.

The next line "`paper.display();`" is the way that we tell the object named `paper` to exercise the `display` behavior of a `playpen`. (Rather like saying "Fido, beg".) That causes many things to happen behind the scenes but the result is that a white `playpen` window is displayed on your screen.

The next two lines are there because without them the program would end and close the Playpen window belonging to `paper` before we have time to realize that anything has happened. Take a moment to try that, by adding // at the start of each of those last two lines. (This technique is called "commenting out" and is used when you want to suppress a line temporarily.) Recompile (F5) and relink and run the program (F9) to help you appreciate the need to know how to pause a program.

As you might guess, `std::cout << "Press RETURN to end program";` causes the message to be displayed in the console window and the next line waits for you to press the Return (or Enter) key.

`std::cout` and `std::cin` are the names of two more program objects, this time provided by the C++ Standard Library. `std::cout` represents the console output in your program, so that when we want to do something to our console output window we send it to `std::cout`. << is an operator that is used in this context to send information ("`Press RETURN to end program`") to the screen. `std::cin` represents the console input; in our case, that is the keyboard. So `std::cin` is the name of the object that provides a mechanism by which we can obtain information that has been typed in. `.get()` results in the program extracting one key press from the keyboard.

However the keyboard does not normally hand over anything (including the code for Return) to a program until you have pressed Return (or Enter). You could type in a whole lot of things and the program will see none of them till you press the Return (or Enter) key (from now on I will just call it the Return key).

Elements of C++ Programs

A few other details before we take a break for more experimenting. Programs are mainly made up of statements (the equivalent of sentences). Simple statements end with a semicolon. There are several other kinds of statement; we will come across them later.

Statements are often organized into blocks (equivalent to paragraphs, except that they can be nested inside each other). A block starts with { (read as "open brace") and ends with } (close brace).

C++ programs are composed of words and symbols. Most of the words are of one of four kinds. There are keywords, about six dozen of them (see Appendix B on the CD for a complete list of operators and keywords), which are the basic words built into the language. In the default setting Quincy identifies these for you by displaying them in blue. We have several dozen operators (things like + and −) most of which are represented by symbols or sometimes two symbols together (such as << in the source code above) rather than letters and numbers though a few operators are spelt out. Next we have literals. These are mostly ordinary numbers such as 3 or 2.4 or −8. We also have character literals which are placed in single quotes such as `'a'` and string literals which are placed in double quotes such as `"Press RETURN to end program"` in the above source code. Lastly we have names that are used to identify programming entities. Mix up and spice with a little punctuation and we have the bulk of the C++ language.

Names are important because they are the things that programmers create to help express their intentions. Names are made using 63 symbols (26 lowercase letters, 26 uppercase letters, the ten digits and the underscore ("_")). A name cannot start with a digit. That is an absolute rule. The other rules are subject to exceptions:

- Do *not* use two or more consecutive underscores (which has special significance).
- Do *not* start a name with an underscore (which also has special significance).
- Ensure the names you invent have at least one lowercase letter unless they are for the pre-processor.
- Ensure that names for the pre-processor do *not* include lowercase letters.

At this stage those rules will not mean very much. Do not worry; stick to the simple positive rule that names should make sense. If you need to add a comment to explain why you chose a name then it was probably a poor choice.

There is a second important aspect of names, which is when a particular name refers to a particular entity. It is too early to cover this in detail but you need to know that a name (like `paper` in the source code earlier in this chapter) that is declared within a particular block (remember that a block is a set of statements enclosed within braces) only has that meaning within that block. Because names have strictly limited locality, we do not have to spend time checking if some other part of a program uses a name we want to use. If it is a different place, then it refers to a different entity.

Do not try to understand this completely; as you progress you will be able to flesh out your understanding of the way names work in C++. Keep in mind that, just as you probably have several names, nicknames, etc., each of which is recognized in a particular context, entities in C++ can have several names each used in its own context. And just as other people can share your name, a name in C++ can refer to different entities in different contexts. There are various ways of selecting which entity a name refers to if there is any ambiguity.

Enough theory for now; time to do some more programming.

A Playpen Doesn't Have To Be White

We are not restricted to using white squares. At any one time we have a palette of 256 colors available. I know that your machine can probably put millions of colors on the screen at once but 256 are more than enough for our purposes and using more will just get in the way. If you have your computer set up to display in high color or better and you are using only 256 screen colors, Playpen may affect the rest of the screen, but not permanently (and it doesn't on my hardware).

During the course of study we will want to handle red, green and blue elements of color separately (if you are more used to mixing paint you need to know monitor screens work by mixing light; the rules are different for light, giving priority to those three colors). In order to make this relatively easy, the `fgw::playpen` type has a carefully tuned palette option, which it uses by default (i.e. you get it when the first `fgw::playpen` object is created in your program).

There are the two extremes, black and white. Then you can create colors by mixing three shades of pure red, two shades of pure green, two shades of pure green and turquoise that doubles up as both a shade of green and a shade of blue.

I have provided a special type called `fgw::hue` to handle the palette. The numbers 0–255 identify the 256 palette codes (note that programmers usually count from zero, we will have more about that in the next chapter). I have provided names for the pure colors provided by the default palette together with special versions of + and – to allow you to mix those colors. The names are `red1`, `red2`, `red4`, `green1`, `green2`, `green4`, `blue1`, `blue2`, `blue4` and `turquoise`. `green1`, `blue1` and `turquoise` are synonyms.

Those names have been chosen to provide a logical relationship between shades of the same color. `red1 + red2` will give a shade that is between `red2` and `red4`. However be careful because `fgw::hue` uses its own rules for addition and subtraction. These mean that, for example, `red1 + red1 = red1` (adding a color to itself results in the same color, which is what you would expect if you think of adding as representing the process of mixing; mixing something with itself results in what you already had).

In theory (if we had the intensities exactly balanced) `red4 + green4` would give you a medium yellow. The brightest red available is given by `red4 + red2 + red1` and so on. Addition is straightforward and on most screens will be close to what physics knowledge would predict.

Subtraction might give you some surprises. If you try to subtract a color, it will remove elements that are shared. So if we have `shade1 = red4 + red1 + green2 + blue4`, and `shade2 = red4 + red2 + green4`, then `shade1 - shade2` results in (`red1 + green2 + blue4`). In other words subtraction is done on each of the eight primary shades separately and you cannot take away what is not there. I hope that does not confuse you too much. It actually has little to do with programming as such but relates to a common mechanism for encoding things like colors.

You only need a couple of other tools to start experimenting. The first is that you can change the color of your Playpen window (I will just call it a Playpen in future when I want to refer to the window on the screen, and use `playpen` when I want to talk about the source code side) by using the `clear()` function. You can write:

```
paper.clear();
```

That changes the Playpen to all white. Well at the moment that is not exactly useful because it is already white. You can place any one of the primary shades (`red1`, `red2`, etc.) or the result of adding together primary shades in the parentheses following `clear`. Writing `paper.clear(red4 + blue4);` will result in a magenta window. If you want to be obscure you can use the numerical codes directly by using any number between 0 and 255 inclusive. So you could write `paper.clear(243);` which gives a nice warm pink on my monitor.

You can also create a colored Playpen by adding a color code in parentheses after the name when you declare it. A little experimenting will make that a lot clearer.

Try modifying your program so that it looks like this:

```
// experimental program 1 by
// on
#include "playpen.h"
#include <iostream>

int main(){
  fgw::playpen paper(fgw::blue2 + fgw::green4);
  paper.display();
  std::cout << "press RETURN to clear the screen";
  std::cin.get();
  paper.clear(fgw::red4 + fgw::green4 + fgw::blue4);
  paper.display();
  std::cout << "press RETURN";
  std::cin.get();
}
```

Now compile it (F5) and when it compiles successfully, run it by pressing F9. Try different color mixes and numerical codes to see how you have a variety of different colors to use. Much later we will find that we can change the way the numerical values map to colors.

When you start experimenting with an existing program by changing the source code you will almost certainly make the same mistake that I do. I run a version and then I am so keen to make a change and test it that I forget to end the previous run (the program is still on the task bar). When I do that I get a bundle of error messages. Effectively they are telling me that I cannot build a new version while an old one is still active. I just go back to the console window for the running version and finish the program. Now I return to Quincy and press F9 again. Everything should now be fine, barring any typos.

Did you get irritated by having to type in all those `fgw::` prefixes to names from my library? Well, even if you did not, I did. We can avoid the need to add those prefixes by telling the compiler that we are using a particular namespace (the context of a library). The required program statement is:

```
using namespace fgw;
```

for my library and:

```
using namespace std;
```

for the C++ Standard Library.

You need to be careful that you only write those statements in your own source code files and never place them in header files which will be shared by other people (or even yourself). I will use this technique in the rest of the source code that I provide but use the full name when I need to identify which library a name belongs to.

You already use names like this. My friends call me ''Francis'' and only add ''Glassborow'' when they need to distinguish me from some other Francis. C++ names work almost exactly the same way.

Plotting a Point

Just being able to change the color of a large square window is not going to get us very far so next I will show you how to plot a point. By default the Playpen behaves like a sheet of graph paper with the origin in the center. Do not worry if you have forgotten those math lessons about plotting points because the program will do most of the work. There are lots of colors available but let me stick with black and white for now. If you feel adventurous you can replace my black and white with color mixtures or numbers (I will call those palette codes from now on).

Create a new project, like the one you did before but call this one first_plot. Just a quick reminder as to how to do this:

1) Open Quincy.
2) Go to the File menu and select New.
3) Select Project.
4) Make sure that you are going to put it into the Chapter 1 directory.
5) Change the name from the one Quincy guessed to first_plot.
6) Set the options as we did above.
7) Now insert the two library files (libgdi32.a and fgwlib.a) making sure they are in the right order in the list: fgwlib.a first then libgdi32.a.
8) Save the project file.

Next start a new source code file. Call it plot. Now copy in the following source code and compile it (F5). When it compiles successfully add this file to the project and press F9. You should get a white playpen with a tiny black dot in the middle. Yes, it really is tiny, small enough so that 512 of them would fit side by side across the Playpen.

```
// point plotting program
// on
#include "playpen.h"
#include <iostream>

using namespace fgw;
using namespace std;
```

```
int main(){
  playpen paper(white);
  paper.plot(0, 0, black);
  paper.display();
  cout << "press RETURN";
  cin.get();
}
```

Notice how those two `using` statements (correctly called "`using` directives") simplify what we have to write subsequently. You may wonder why we provide the prefixes if we then promptly remove them. The answer is that, just like our family names, they are there when we want or need to be more specific.

Wouldn't it be nice if we could make that black point bigger? Well you could patiently add the following lines immediately after `paper.plot(0, 0, black);`

```
paper.plot(0, 1, black);
paper.plot(1, 0, black);
paper.plot(1, 1, black);
```

If you are anything like me you would prefer not to do all that work, even if most of it is done by cut and paste. If you want to make the point four times wider and higher you would have to plot 16 points. That seems excessive. There is a better way; you can change the scale of the display with the following statement:

```
paper.scale(2);
```

You can use any number from 1 to 64 as the scale. If you try numbers outside that range they will be ignored. Changing the scale changes both the size and the position at which a point is plotted. So when you use a scale of 2, the pixel is twice as high, twice as wide and twice as far from the origin compared to using a scale of 1.

Instead of plotting black points you can choose any palette code from 0 to 255. By convention 0 is black and 255 is white.

Create a new project for the following small program. Please do not skimp by reusing the one you have. You need to become fluent in starting a project so that the process becomes second nature, including checking that you save files where they belong.

```
// point plotting & scaling program
// on
#include "playpen.h"
#include <iostream>

using namespace fgw;
using namespace std;

int main(){
  playpen paper(white);
  paper.scale(8);
  paper.plot(0, 0, black);
  paper.scale(4);
  paper.plot(0, 0, white);
  paper.display();
```

```
  cout << "press RETURN to end";
  cin.get();
}
```

Please remember to get the source code to compile by using F5 before you add the file to the project. This is just a good habit and helps you focus on one thing at a time. Once it is in the project you can still edit the source code, but you know that it has compiled successfully. If it stops doing so you know that it is something you just did that caused the problem.

Now experiment with this program (remember the warning I gave earlier when experimenting; make sure you finish a run of a program before you try to build – F9 – a new version). Use some different scales, some different palette codes or color mixes and some different coordinates for the points instead of the `0, 0` that we have been using.

You should notice that when you plot at other places the two plots may no longer overlap. Actually you will not even see the second one if you continue to use white for it because you will be plotting a white pixel on a white background.

Mixing Colors

The designer of the `playpen` type arranged that when points are plotted their color "mixes" with the existing color in one of four ways. These are called plot modes. The plot modes are:

- `direct`: the new color replaces the old.
- `additive`: the new color mixes with the existing one. For example, if you plot a bright green point on a red screen in this plot mode you will get yellow (it might be greenish or reddish but basically it is yellow). Did you forget that we are mixing colored light not paint?
- `filter`: if you use this mode you will get something equivalent to using color filters. If you put a red filter in front of a mixture of colored light only the red part gets through. In effect you will only see the color produced by the primary elements that are found in both the current color and in the new one.
- `disjoint`: this one may seem strange to you, but it is probably the most useful mode after `direct`. It combines two color values to make a new value by removing any shared primary elements. For example, if the screen color is `(red2 + blue4 + green2)` and you plot a point that is `(red2 + blue2 + green2)` the result will be bright blue `(blue4 + blue2)` because `red2` and `green2` appear in both the screen and the plot colors and so cancel out. Unlike in the other three plot modes, plotting the same point with the same palette code a second time makes a difference in the `disjoint` plot mode. It undoes the effect of the first plot. In the other plotting modes, repeating a plot makes no further difference.

Modern Art?

I will not insult talented artists by suggesting that the following program does anything resembling real art. However if you have an artistic streak in you, you might be able to produce something with merit by exploring the potential that you already have.

Here is my program:

```
// point pseudo modern art by Francis Glassborow
// coded on 23 November 2002
#include "playpen.h"
#include <iostream>

using namespace fgw;
```

```
using namespace std;

int main(){
  playpen paper;
  paper.clear(224);
  paper.scale(32);
  paper.plot(0, 0, 19);
  paper.setplotmode(disjoint);
  paper.scale(24);
  paper.plot(1, 1, 28);
  paper.scale(64);
  paper.setplotmode(additive);
  paper.plot(3, -2, 113);
  paper.plot(0, 0, 37);
  paper.plot(-2, 0, 49);
  paper.setplotmode(direct);
  paper.plot(-3, 3, 187);
  paper.setplotmode(disjoint);
  paper.scale(23);
  paper.plot(-6, 8, 231);
  paper.display();
  cout << "press RETURN";
  cin.get();
}
```

I have deliberately used palette codes in the above program so you can see how such numbers result in obscure source code. Can you tell me what color the background will be? Now had I written `paper.clear(red4 + red2 + red1)` you would know that it was going to be bright red. Programmers refer to numbers used like that in derogatory terms, as "magic numbers". I introduced those eight primary color elements exactly so I could avoid magic numbers. I hope that makes sense to you now.

You do not have to type in my program but you might like to use it as a starting point for your own version. Have fun and if you send in your effort I will place it on the book's website so that others can admire your work.

Tasks, Exercises and Fun

Each chapter includes one or more "task" sections where you are given a programming problem. The problem can always be solved with no more than you have learnt from studying this book. Do not go and get answers from elsewhere because they almost certainly will use features that you have not yet studied.

Please do not cheat yourself by skipping these tasks. I have never believed in setting repetitive "make work" tasks, so everything I ask you to do has been chosen with a purpose.

I will sometimes provide the solution that my student partner produced and her comments on both the exercise and the difficulties she had with it. Often you will also find my solution. The purpose of my solution is not to pour scorn on yours but to set an example of what good code looks like. Remember that I have spent many years programming so my code should be better than yours. If you think it isn't better or if you are puzzled by any solution of mine, first check the book's website and then, if necessary, email me (assuming that you do not have a mentor who can answer your question).

I expect you to work through material that is presented in the main text and try all the items labeled as tasks. If you are unable to complete a task you should try to find someone who can help you understand whatever it is that is causing a problem.

There are also exercises in many chapters. These are provided to give you something to practice with. Programming is a skill and needs regular practice. It is not essential that you complete all the exercises but I think you will become a better programmer if you attempt most of them. You should check my solutions when I provide them because these often include further points that will help you become a better programmer.

Then there are suggestions of things that you can do which should be fun as well as contributing to your programming skills. In this chapter you can spend time experimenting with the various aspects of color, scale and plotting modes. Not only should that help with your programming but it will also give you a better grasp of the fundamentals of using color on a computer screen.

Write a program that places a black cross at the center of a white Playpen. All the other details are up to you. Please do not start Chapter 2 till you have succeeded in this task.

ROBERTA'S COMMENTS

When I read through Chapter 1, I was quite excited by the prospect of creating a work of art so early in my programming career. So I wanted to rush through and get to the fun bit.

*Unfortunately I got stuck. I had problems with plotting a point. It refused to build (compile) and the error message said that **paper** was undeclared. I was convinced that I had typed it in correctly. In desperation, I phoned Francis and felt very stupid when I discovered that I had indeed left out the dot between "**paper**" and "`display()`" in `paper.display()`. By the time I got to the fun bit I was quite used to error messages. My most common mistake was typing a comma instead of a point.*

I typed in Francis' program to begin with to see what he had produced – artistically speaking I thought just maybe I could do better. It's rather amazing what you can achieve with such a simple thing as plotting a point. After a while I felt quite familiar with Quincy and Playpen. However, I couldn't understand how the colors worked.

After all the fun of producing a masterpiece I thought the idea of producing a black cross on white paper was rather boring. I didn't have any problems producing a cross but was frustrated by the fact I had to plot each individual point to produce a line. I was certain there must be a simpler way to do it.

Summary

Key programming concepts

- A program is written in a programming language such as C++. The human readable form is called source code.
- We use a simple editor to write source code. Program editors are specialized to help produce source code. Modern program editors use color and layout to help programmers see the structure of the source code.
- Source code is converted into a form called object code by a tool called a compiler. A compiler will provide us with error messages if it cannot translate our source code. It may also issue warnings if it is suspicious of our source code even though it can be converted to object code.
- A tool called a linker combines object code from one or more source code files. It then searches for any missing pieces by looking in special files called libraries that contain collections of object code for common activities. If it finds all the required pieces it creates an executable program.
- There are other programming tools, such as a debugger (which helps to find errors in programs), that are designed to support us when we are programming.
- We generally use an Integrated Development Environment (IDE) to help organize the tools we are using and to provide communication between the tools.

C++ checklist

- Every C++ program must have a single block of source code that is used as the starting point. The name of this block is `main`. Though there are several variations, we will be using the form:

```
int main(){
  // insert program source code
}
```

- A C++ compiler also needs to know the names and some details of things that will be provided elsewhere. This information is provided by special files called header files.
- The compiler is instructed to access a header file by lines that start `#include`.

- `iostream` is the header that provides C++ names of input and output facilities.
- C++ provides a facility so that we can add comments to our code. Comments are for human readers and will be ignored by the compiler. A comment starts with // and continues to the end of the line. All files should, at a minimum, include comments naming the writer and date of writing. Other comments should be added as necessary to help other people understand the source code.
- C++ programs use objects and variables that have a type. Knowing something's type tells you what you can do with it. Types are named and the only named type you have used so far is `fgw::playpen`.
- The principle ingredients of a C++ program are the keywords, operators, names (those provided by C++ such as `std::cout` and `std::cin`; those provided by third parties such as `fgw::playpen` and `display()`; and those provided by you as a programmer such as `paper`) and literals (sometimes called values) such as 2, 3.5, 'a' and "Press RETURN". There is a small but essential amount of punctuation of which the semicolon is the most obvious.
- We use the ingredients of C++ to write statements that are often grouped into blocks that are marked out with braces.
- Objects generally have behaviors. We can ask an object to do something by appending a period followed by the behavior name followed by any necessary data in parentheses. The parentheses are required even if empty.
- `std::cout` is a Standard C++ object that, for now, represents the screen. Messages may be sent to `std::cout` with the << operator.
- `std::cin` is a Standard C++ object for the standard input (by default, the keyboard). `std::cin.get()` extracts a single symbol (letter, digit, symbol, etc.).
- Programs are broken into blocks by using (curly) braces. Names declared inside a block are only significant in that block.
- C++ provides a mechanism for placing library names in context. This mechanism is called a namespace.
- This book uses two primary namespaces: `std` for the C++ Standard Library names and `fgw` for my library.

C++ provides a mechanism to allow programmers to use library names without providing the namespace prefix. For example, the following directive allows use of names from the C++ Standard Library without the `std::` prefix:

```
using namespace std;
```

Extensions checklist

In this book you will be using a set of extensions, written by the author with the help of others, to write programs that produce graphical results in addition to the pure textual and numerical results for which Standard C++ provides the tools.

- `fgw::playpen` is a type that provides the principal graphics resource. This graphics resource is not part of the Standard C++ language but is written in Standard C++ in so far as that is possible. Deep under the hood it has to use system-specific features, so you can only use it on systems where it has been implemented. At present that means that you can only use it on a computer using Microsoft Windows (95, 98, ME, XP, NT4 or 2000).
- We create (construct) an `fgw::playpen` object by declaring a name for it (`paper` in the code in this chapter). Note that `fgw::playpen` is the name of the type, while `paper` is the name used to refer to a specific Playpen object. (Just as "dog" is the name of a type of animal whereas "Fido" might be the name of a specific dog.)

- We can choose a background color by placing a number from 0 to 255 or a color mix in parentheses after the name used in the declaration.
- The following is a list of the named palette codes:

```
white  : 255
red4   : 128      red2      : 64      red1   : 32
green4 : 16       green2    : 8       green1 : 1
blue4  : 4        blue2     : 2       blue1  : 1
black  : 0        turquoise : 1
```

The eight primary palette codes (`red4`, `red2`, `red1`, `green4`, `green2`, `blue4`, `blue2`, `turquoise`) encode an 8-bit binary number. `red4` is the high bit (128) and `turquoise` is the low bit (1).

- If you do not understand this point, do not worry. However, if you know about binary numbers, the `additive`, `filter` and `disjoint` modes work by using the binary representation of the palette codes. If you write two palette codes as binary numbers and then compare them place-by-place the result is generated by the rules given by the following table:

	additive	filter	disjoint
0+0	0	0	0
0+1	1	0	1
1+0	1	0	1
1+1	1	1	0

So given palette codes of 134 (10000110 or `red4 + blue4 + blue2`) and 69 (01000101 or `red2 + blue4 + turquoise`), we get 199 (`11000111, red4 + red2 + blue4 + blue2 + turquoise`) in `additive` mode, 4 (00000100, `blue4`) in `filter` mode and 195 (11000011, `red4 + red2 + blue2 + turquoise`) in `disjoint` mode.

Do not worry if binary math is a mystery; just enjoy the results. The computer will do the work as long as you tell it which plot mode to use. We do this with the `setplotmode()` member function of `fgw::playpen`.

- The possible things that we can ask a `fgw::playpen` object to do or tell us are provided by its member functions:

`clear(n)`	clears the Playpen window to the specified color (n is a palette code from 0 to 255).
`setplotmode(pm)`	determines the way that the palette code of a new plot mixes with the existing one (pm is one of `direct`, `additive`, `filter` and `disjoint`).
`plot(m, n, h)`	plots a point (m and n are the coordinates of a point to be plotted and h is the palette code to be mixed with the current shade).
`scale(n)`	determines the width and height of a single point in pixels to be plotted (n is a number from 1 to 64).
`display()`	causes the results of your instructions to the `fgw::playpen` object to appear on the Playpen window.

CHAPTER 2

You Can Loop

One of the most fundamental guidelines for good programming is to avoid writing something more than once. Programming languages provide a variety of mechanisms to help you to avoid repeating code. The most basic of these is the concept of looping. In this chapter, I will introduce you to one of the ways that C++ supports looping.

Drawing a Cross

When you did Task 1 at the end of the last chapter you probably felt that there must be a better way to do it. However if you stuck within the limits of what you had learned from this book you would have written a program something like:

```
#include "playpen.h"
#include <iostream>

using namespace std;
using namespace fgw;

int main(){
  playpen paper;
  paper.scale(3);
  paper.plot(0, 2, black);
  paper.plot(0, 1, black);
  paper.plot(0, 0, black);
  paper.plot(0, -1, black);
  paper.plot(0, -2, black);
  paper.plot(2, 0, black);
  paper.plot(1, 0, black);
  paper.plot(-1, 0, black);
  paper.plot(-2, 0, black);
  paper.display();
  cout << "Press RETURN to end";
  cin.get();
}
```

If you feel there must be something not quite right about a block of almost identical `paper.plot()` statements then your instincts are right on the ball. Good programmers do not like repeating themselves or even almost repeating themselves. Quite apart from pure laziness there is the issue that if you discover a way of improving code you will have to find every place you wrote the same thing in order to change it. Any time that you have a sense that you are repeating something you have already written, stop and ask yourself if you can arrange to write it only once. There are various program elements designed to reduce writing the same code. We are going to look at one of them in this chapter.

If you look at the above code you will see that the points being plotted break into two subtasks, plot a set of points vertically and plot a set of points horizontally. You probably thought in terms of drawing two lines, one horizontal and one vertical. Put that view to one side for a moment; it is useful but we must learn something else first.

Look at the plots that produced a short vertical line. Notice how they are almost identical except that the second number changes from 2 to −2 in steps of one. There are five points to plot. Effectively you have to repeat something five times with a minor variation. There is an idiom for repeating something a fixed number of times based on a mechanism called **looping** or **iterating**.

for-Loops

Think back to the task of getting your blind guest to the bedroom. Along the way he has to negotiate a set of stairs. You probably did not tell your guest to take each step of the staircase individually. You might have written something like: "You are now at the bottom of the staircase. There are 20 steps." Your guest would start at the bottom and count the steps until he reached twenty. Then he would stop.

The process might go like this:

```
Stand at the bottom of the staircase (and, almost unconsciously, ask:
   'Have I counted to 20?' 'No, so continue.')
Climb a step. Count '1'. In other words we do not consider the floor to be
   the first step. ('Have I counted to 20?' 'No, so continue.')
Climb a step. Count '2'. Now you are on the second step. ('Have I counted
   to 20?' 'No, so continue.')
Climb a step. Count '3'. That is the third step. ('Have I counted to 20?'
   'No, so continue.')
...
Climb a step. Count '20'. ('Have I counted to 20?' 'Yes, so stop.')
```

Think back to the start. Which step were you on when you were standing at the bottom of the staircase? If you count backwards from "1" you get "0". In other words, before you climb any steps the count stands at zero. Many people are surprised by this idea because they have an image of counting from 1, but that is not the case. Let us see how we can write something like that in a program-like style.

```
       start a count at zero;
again: have I reached twenty? if yes, stop
       if no, climb another step
       increase the count
       repeat from 'again'
```

Programmers quite often write things like that while they are trying to get a handle on a problem. We call it **pseudo-code**.

If you look at those statements you will see that there are essentially four of them:

- Set up the start conditions
- Check if we have finished
- Do some action
- Increase the count and go back to check for completion

This general structure is so common in programming that most programming languages provide a special structure for expressing it. In C++ it is a `for`-statement and looks like this (this still contains a little pseudo-code – *`climb_a_step`*):

```
for(int count(0); count != 20; ++count){
  climb_a_step;
}
```

The sequence of the four parts has been modified by moving the action part to the end because there might be several things to do each time we repeat. The structure is introduced by `for`, which is a C++ keyword. That means it is a word that has a built-in meaning that is the same everywhere it is used. `for` is always followed by an open parenthesis and then three expressions that are separated by semicolons. Any or all of the expressions can be empty (technically called a **null expression**). In this case, all three expressions actually have some content.

The first expression, the **initialization** expression, gives the starting point. In this example, I have written `int count(0)`. That creates a **variable** (an object with a value that can vary) called `count` whose type is `int`. The 0 in parentheses is called an initializer and it provides the initial value for `count`, zero in this case.

Because `int` is one of the built-in C++ types (provided by the language), Quincy displays it in blue (the names of the built-in types are keywords). An `int` variable can store a whole number from a limited range of values. C++ guarantees that the range will be at least −32767 to 32767. That range is enough for many purposes. Later we will see what we can do if we must have a bigger range.

The next expression in our `for`-statement, the **continuation condition**, uses one of the C++ special operators, !=, which stands for "not equal to". It gives the condition for continuing with the `for`-statement. As it has just created `count` with a value of zero, `count` is not yet equal to 20 so the program continues. It does not continue with the third expression (`++count`), but with what comes after the closing parenthesis. So it executes *`climb_a_step;`*.

The part immediately after the closing parenthesis of the `for`-statement (*`climb_a_step`*, in my pseudo-code example above) is called the **controlled** or **action statement**. The action might be a simple statement (even an empty or null (do nothing) statement) or it might be a compound statement enclosed in braces (which might still be a single statement – some programmers meticulously use compound statements for controlled statements). The program completes that action and then returns to the last of the three expressions in the parentheses.

In this example, the final expression, the **end of loop action**, uses another C++ operator, ++ (called **increment**), which causes the object referred to by the following variable name to be increased by one (i.e. `count` goes from 0 to 1, then from 1 to 2, etc.). Having done that, the program backs up to the test expression and checks to see if it has reached the end. It hasn't yet so the controlled statement repeats but this time with `count`=1. The program keeps going until `count` reaches 20, and then stops (climbing steps).

Here is another snippet of code using a `for`-statement:

```
for(int i(0); i != 5; ++i){
   plot(0, 2-i, black);
}
```

This time we have a complete piece of C++ code. I have used `i` as my **control variable** (so called because it is the one whose value controls when the loop stops). The program will continue to loop round executing the controlled statement (or block of statements) increasing the value referred to by `i` by one each time then checking to see if it has reached 5. If it hasn't it will go round the loop again. This time the controlled statement uses the current value of `i` so each repeat is slightly different. Let me spell it out for you:

```
Start an int called i at 0
Check that it isn't 5
Plot the point (0, 2) in black on paper
Increase i by 1 to make it 1
Go back and check that i is not equal to 5
Plot the point (0, 1) in black on paper
Increase i by 1 to make it 2
Go back and check that i is not equal to 5
Plot the point (0, 0) in black on paper
Increase i by 1 to make it 3
Go back and check that i is not equal to 5
Plot the point (0, -1) in black on paper
Increase i by 1 to make it 4
Go back and check that i is not equal to 5
Plot the point (0, -2) in black on paper
Increase i by 1 to make it 5
Go back and check that i is not equal to 5
It is equal to 5 so stop repeating
```

Please take the time to follow that through. Make sure you understand how the `for`-loop that is provided by a `for`-statement works.

Now you have got the idea, check the following:

```
for(int i(0); i != 5; ++i){
   paper.plot(2-i, 0, black);
}
```

Yes, it plots five points but this time horizontally from (2, 0) to (−2, 0). Suppose that you wanted to go the other way (the result will be the same) from (−2, 0) to (2, 0). A simple change accomplishes that – replace the contents of the controlled block with:

```
paper.plot(i-2, 0, black);
```

TECHNICAL NOTE

Counting from zero

Many people have difficulty getting accustomed to counting from zero. Even programmers coming from some other programming languages can have difficulty because the language they first learnt happened to work differently.

In C++, counts always start at zero. Unfortunately English does not make it particularly easy to talk about this. And we even have this problem with different English-speaking cultures. Which is the first floor of a hotel? In US hotels and international hotels that belong to US-based companies the first floor is the one at street level. The one below that is the basement, and if there are several they might be numbered B1, B2, B3, etc. There is no floor between B1 and the first floor.

In the UK (and much of Europe) the street level floor is called the "ground floor" and the first floor is the one above that. So in this case there is a floor between the first basement and the first floor. In effect there is a floor zero.

C++ is among the computer languages that count more like the British way of numbering the floors of a building; it starts at zero. We follow a pattern that can be best illustrated as:

```
      Set target count
      Set current count to zero
loop: is current count equal to target count, if yes STOP
      do action
      increase current count
      repeat from loop
```

As compared with the pattern:

```
      Set target count
      Set current count to zero
      do action
loop: increase current count
      is current count greater than target count, if yes STOP
      do action
      repeat from loop
```

Both these patterns make sense but only the first one caters for the possibility that the action might not be carried out at all. There are other looping patterns and you will learn later about programming mechanisms that model them, including the second one above.

Time to go back to drawing a cross on the screen. Here is a new version that is simpler (has fewer statements) than the one we started with.

```
#include "playpen.h"
#include <iostream>

using namespace std;
using namespace fgw;

int main(){
  playpen paper;
  paper.scale(3);
  for(int i(0); i != 5; ++i){
     paper.plot(2-i, 0, black);
  }
  for(int i(0); i != 5; ++i){
     paper.plot(0, 2-i, black);
  }
```

```
  paper.display();
  cout << "Press return to end";
  cin.get();
}
```

Note that I have indented some statements. This **pretty-printing** is a convention to allow programmers to see the structure of a piece of source code. The compiler does not care, but most humans do. Eventually, laying out your source code to show its structure will become second nature. Indeed you will become uncomfortable with code that is not pretty-printed and your fingers will itch to change it.

The above program is not much shorter than the one you wrote and in fact you might argue that it was less efficient because the point (0, 0) gets plotted twice. But the convenience and ease of modification is well worth it. Suppose that I told you I wanted a cross with a long tail and longer arms than the one we have. A quick change with the editor and it is done. Here are the bits that need to be changed:

```
for(int i(0); i != 9; ++i){
   paper.plot(4-i, 0, black);
}
for(int i(0); i != 8; ++i){
   paper.plot(0, 2-i, black);
}
```

You will notice that I have only had to change three numbers (I have highlighted them in bold typeface). That must be good news.

Time for some more practical work.

Drawing a Cross Revisited

Open up Quincy and start a new project (call it draw_cross but this time save it in the sub-directory titled Chapter 2). Look at the options in the tools menu of Quincy. Make sure that the Include item has the right entry (the sub-directory called fgw_headers in the same directory as Quincy2002). Also make sure that all the options, such as ''debugging'', have been selected. Make a habit of doing these things every time. That will save you a lot of puzzlement and frustration – always make sure the choices are those you want.

Now include the same files that you did before (fgwlib.a and libgdi32.a). Be careful that you include them in the right order. Open a new C++ source file and type in the following:

```
#include "playpen.h"
#include <iostream>

using namespace std;
using namespace fgw;

int main(){
  playpen paper;
  paper.scale(3);
  for(int i(-4); i != 5; ++i){
     paper.plot(0, i, black);
  }
  for(int i(-4); i != 5; ++i){
     paper.plot(i, 0, black);
  }
```

```
  paper.display();
  cout << "Press RETURN to end";
  cin.get();
}
```

I have taken this as an opportunity to demonstrate that we can vary aspects of a for-loop. We do not have to start at 0, though it is almost always a good idea to do so when we want to count up to a specific value. In other words when we want to repeat something a known number of times we usually start at zero.

Save your work, giving it a name (I will leave you to choose names for files from now on, but remember that names should be helpful in guiding your expectations as to what the file contains) and compile it (F5). When you have corrected any errors and get a "build successful" report, include this file in your project and press F9 to create and run the program.

Play around with this program until you are happy with the way it works. By playing around, I mean add things like color and scale; change the position and the size of the cross. Even when I do not explicitly ask you to play with a program, I expect you to do so. You will not do any permanent damage by experimenting with the programs I give you, though you just might (although it is very unlikely) lock your computer up so that you have to switch it off to regain control.

Practicing Looping

The following are some suggestions for programs you can write that will help you become more confident in using for-statements in your programming. I hope you will spend some time trying them. At the end of the chapter I give my solutions with a commentary where relevant.

Before you start the exercises there are a few things that will help you. You will need to be able to display the value of an int variable (such as those we have been using to control our for-loops). You can do this in much the same way that you output a message. The following short program should display the numbers from 0 to 9 in your console window:

```
#include <iostream>

using namespace std;

int main(){
  for(int i(0); i != 10; ++i){
     cout << i;
  }
}
```

If you try that program you will discover that its output is probably not what you wanted because there are no spaces between the numbers. We can insert a space (or any other text, such as a comma and space) between the numbers by changing the output line to:

```
  cout << i << " ";
```

or, if we want a comma and a space:

```
  cout << i << ", ";
```

A special case is where we want to start a new output line. C++ provides a special code for a newline character. Whenever we want a newline character in our output we use '\n'. We will go into more detail about this in a later chapter, but to see it in action, try the following program:

```
#include <iostream>

using namespace std;

int main(){
  for(int i(0); i != 10; ++i){
     cout << i << '\n';
  }
}
```

The result should be the numbers from 0 to 9 displayed in a vertical column.

Simple Arithmetic Operators

We have already used + (add) and − (subtract) operators in our source code. As they are identical to the symbols used in mathematics I used them without making a comment. In the following exercises you will also need to multiply.

Multiplication operator

Because of the potential for confusing the traditional multiplication symbol (×) with the twenty-fourth letter of the English alphabet (x) most computing languages use the asterisk symbol (*) as a multiplication sign. So instead of writing 2 × 3 when writing source code, we write 2 * 3.

Division operator

The conventional division sign in mathematics (÷) was easily confused on older display devices with the plus symbol (+) and is replaced in computer programming with the less common mathematical alternative of "/" (called a solidus). So instead of writing 4 ÷ 2, in source code we would write 4 / 2.

Negative and subtraction operator

The same symbol is used in mathematics as an instruction to subtract and as a qualification of a number. When the symbol we call "a minus sign" is placed between two numbers it is an instruction to subtract the second number from the first. When a minus sign comes before a number without a preceding number it describes the number as being a negative number.

For example 8 - 3 reads as "eight subtract three" or "subtract three from eight". Notice that even in English we do not always read strictly left to right.

However -8 reads as "negative eight".

In everyday speech we often read both uses of the symbol as "minus" so we get "eight minus three" and "minus eight".

We have the same two uses of the minus sign in computing as well. It generally does not matter but it sometimes helps to remember that minus may be either an instruction or a description.

Write a program that displays the three times table in the form: 3, 6, 9, . . . (finish with 36) as a single row of output. Your program should be a simple modification of the program above that outputs the numbers from 0 to 9.

Repeat Exercise 1 but display the answers in a vertical column in the form:

$$1 \times 3 = 3$$

$$2 \times 3 = 6$$

...

Finish at $12 \times 3 = 36$. This is an exercise in combining output of numerical values with symbols and newline characters (the `'\n'` mentioned above).

EXERCISE 3

Write a program that outputs a number, its square and its cube for all numbers from 1 to 20. Place the results for each number on a line; i.e. your output should start:

```
1  1  1
2  4  8
3  9  27
```

You will not be able to keep the output in neat columns with what you currently know about output in C++ so do not spend time trying to do so. The solution to this exercise is a program that is similar to that for Exercise 2.

EXERCISE 4

Write a program that outputs the values for multiplication tables from 1 to 12. The results for each table should be on a single line (i.e. the way the results were displayed in Exercise 1). There are many ways to achieve the required result but you should be looking for one that only uses two `for`-statements.

Note: With your current knowledge you will not be able to display the results in twelve neat columns so please do not spend time trying to do so.

CHALLENGING

EXERCISE 5

Write a program that displays all 256 colors provided for your `playpen` objects. The result should exactly fill the Playpen. That window is 512 pixels by 512 pixels. If you display 16 colors on each of 16 rows using a scale of 32 the results fit exactly. You will need to experiment to get the right starting points.

There is quite a lot of similarity between this program and the one for Exercise 4. One good solution uses two `for`-statements. However, remember that at this stage in your programming any program that produces the required output is satisfactory.

Write a program that produces a square box with 9 pixels per side (this time you may need four `for`-loops). Please note that where I label something as a task I consider it very important that you do it before you read on.

Try some other shapes if you want, but not too many because in the next chapter we will be covering another way to avoid repetition.

ROBERTA'S COMMENTS

Following an earlier version of this chapter I had great difficulty in getting my head around *for*-loops. The original exercise was to produce nine vertical lines evenly spaced across the Playpen.

In desperation and not wanting to appear too stupid to Francis so early in the book, I asked another programmer friend to help. However, I asked how to solve the question without giving him enough information and the C++ code he sent me was completely unintelligible to me at that time (although I do understand it now). So I struggled on trying to do it myself. This resulted in what I thought were major problems. I thought I had broken Quincy because the program didn't finish properly. It turned out that during my experiments I had a continuous *for*-loop operating.

FRANCIS

Getting into an unending loop is going to happen to everyone at some time. Indeed it is part of the "rite of passage" that you do so. It is also useful to know how to get out when you have got yourself into this position.

The first thing is not to panic; nothing really bad will happen, your computer is more robust than that. Calmly close the various files you have open in Quincy by clicking the close button at the top right corner of each window.

Next close down Quincy itself. Finally press CTRL C (i.e. hold down the CTRL key and tap the C key) and the program will stop and close down.

Here is a tiny program you can use to practice getting out. This one does not run for ever but it will run for quite a long time even on a fast machine.

```
// long loop demo written by FG 10/06/03
#include <iostream>
int main(){
  for(int i(0); i != 1000000; ++i){
     std::cout << i << '\n';
  }
}
```

Once I had a copy of the much-improved second draft of Chapter 2, I didn't have any problems. However, the exercises in Chapter 2 were added at a later date and I didn't actually try them until much later. The solution to Exercise 5 is useful for a later chapter but I know I would have struggled to do it at this stage in the book – so don't despair if you have to look at the answer.

Naming Files: Although Francis has mentioned the importance of giving descriptive names to files I feel that it is important to stress this because I didn't pay enough attention to it. When I first started doing the exercises I simply named the projects and files *task1.PRJ* or *exercise1.cpp*, etc., but in retrospect I wish I had used more descriptive titles. As you get further into the book you will want to refer back to earlier programs and a descriptive name will be far more useful than knowing which exercise it refers to. Now I would probably name Exercise 1 *three_times_table_row* and Exercise 5 *display_all_the_colors*, for example.

Thinking up descriptive names is a very important part of programming because lots of other things will need names too and even if the name seems long and cumbersome at the time it really is a worthwhile habit to develop.

SOLUTIONS TO EXERCISES

Remember that these are not the only solutions. They are not even the only good ones. They are just the ones I chose to write within the restrictions of what you know from reading this book.

I am only providing the source code for `main()` in each case. To provide a working program you need to include some header files and add `using` directives. Don't forget the comments identifying the writer and the date of creation.

Exercise 1

```
int main(){
  for(int i(1); i != 13; ++i){
     cout << i * 3 << ", ";
  }
  cout << '\n';
}
```

Exercise 2

```
int main(){
  for(int i(1); i != 13; ++i){
     cout << i << " x 3 = " << i * 3 << '\n';
  }
}
```

Exercise 3

```
int main(){
  for(int i(1); i != 21; ++i){
     cout << i << " " << i * i << " " << i * i * i << '\n';
  }
}
```

Exercise 4

```
int main(){
  for(int table(1); table != 13; ++table){
     for(int value(1); value != 13; ++value){
        cout << table * value << " ";
     }
     cout << '\n';
  }
}
```

SOLUTIONS TO EXERCISES

Exercise 5

```
int main(){
  playpen paper;
  paper.scale(32);
  for(int row(0); row != 16; ++row){
     for(int column(0); column != 16; ++column){
        paper.plot(column-8, row-8, (row * 16 + column));
        paper.display();
     }
  }
  cout << "Press RETURN to end display.";
  cin.get();
}
```

This one merits a few comments. The nested `for`-loops provide coverage of the visible Playpen when the scale has been set to 32 as long as we remember that the origin is in the middle of the screen, hence the `column-8` and `row-8` in `paper.plot()`.

What I had to do next was to work out which color to display at each point. Basically I wanted colors 0 to 15 on the bottom row, 16 to 31 on the next row, etc. In other words each row must start with the color that is sixteen times the row it is on. As we move across a row we want to move to the next color. Go back and look at `(row * 16 + column)` and I think you will find it does just that. The parentheses are only there to help the human eye identify the calculation being used as a single value: the compiler would still do the right thing without them.

Summary

Key programming concepts

- Programmers avoid repeating source code.
- A common mechanism for providing repetition in many programming languages is a `for`-loop.

C++ checklist

- C++ provides the `for`-statement as a method for repeating actions. A `for`-statement has four parts: the initialization expression, the continuation condition, the end of loop action and the action (compound) statement.
- The initialization is done once before the first check of the continuation condition. The continuation condition is checked before the action statement is undertaken. If it fails, the `for`-loop is finished. The end of loop expression is done after each action statement has been completed.
- C++ has many operators. Most of them are straightforward with obvious meanings. You can find a summary of all the operators in Appendix B on the CD. Those we have used (and others we might

have) for making decisions in this chapter are:

<	less than
>	greater than
!=	not equals
<=	less than or equal to
>=	greater than or equal to
==	"compares equal to" and must not be confused with =, meaning assignment
++	increase the stored value by one
--	decrease the stored value by one

- C++ supports the traditional arithmetic operations but uses * for multiplication and / for division.
- C++ has a number of built-in arithmetic types. The simplest of these is called `int` and it provides sufficient storage for simple whole number values. The language guarantees that an `int` can store any value from −32767 to 32767.
- To display the value of an `int` variable, stream it to `cout` with the << operator.

```
cout << i;
```

displays the current value of `i` in your console window.
- `'\n'` represents a newline. When it is streamed to `cout` with the << operator, subsequent output is placed on a new line.
- When we create a variable we can (and usually should) provide its initial value.

CHAPTER 3

You Can Write a Function

A function is another tool for avoiding writing things twice. In this chapter I will introduce you to the design, implementation and use of functions in your programming. A second benefit of using functions is that they provide a mechanism for naming what you are doing.

Drawing a Square

When you did Task 2 at the end of the last chapter you probably found yourself cutting and pasting source code and then making a couple of small changes. Here is a typical solution to the problem of drawing a box (I have left out the `#include` statements and `using` directives):

```
int main(){
  playpen paper;
  paper.scale(3);
  for(int i(0); i != 9; ++i){
     paper.plot(i, 0, black);
  }
  for(int i(0); i != 9; ++i){
     paper.plot(0, i, black);
  }
  for(int i(0); i != 9; ++i){
     paper.plot(i, 8, black);
  }
  for(int i(0); i != 9; ++i){
     paper.plot(8, i, black);
  }
  paper.display();
  cout << "Press RETURN to end";
  cin.get();
}
```

You may even have condensed the four for-loops into a single for-loop:

```
for(int i(0); i != 9; ++i){
   paper.plot(i, 0, black);
   paper.plot(0, i, black);
   paper.plot(i, 8, black);
   paper.plot(8, i, black);
}
```

However, you surely must have felt an echo of your feelings at the end of Chapter 1. Once again we are repeating ourselves. Once again there is a better way. The loop concept addresses the problem of doing the same general thing several times in succession but has little to offer when we want to do the same basic thing in several different places (in this case plotting a line of pixels to put a line on the screen as one arm of a cross, the side of a square, etc.).

For this problem we need another basic building block of programming: the function.

The Function Concept

A function is another fundamental element of programming. Functions in computer programming have their equivalents in all those other kinds of program that I mentioned earlier. You do not tell your blind guest how to open and close a door. You assume they know and give the instruction *open the door*. You might tell them which side the door handle is and you might tell them what kind of handle – that is just data fed into the ''door opening function'' that they already know.

Think about the process of using an ATM. The process requires several things and has an expected consequence. You need a suitable card that must be inserted in the slot in the machine and you need to key in your PIN. If everything is successful you get your card back as well as anything else you asked for.

The basic function here is that of using an ATM, which requires a card and a PIN and returns your card to you. There are many possible side effects to your use of an ATM, one of which is that the machine will hand out some money to you.

A programmer might represent this process in pseudo-code:

```
card & use_ATM(atm & machine, card & users_card, int pin){
      if(not valid(users_card, pin)) do_invalid();
      else {
               do{
                      display_menu()
                      select_option();
                      do_option();
               } while(not finished);
      }
      return users_card;
}
```

Even if you had never seen a computer program before, the above would give you a fair idea about using an ATM. The one curious feature that you might want to ask about is those three uses of ''&''. When we place an ampersand directly after a type's name we are specifying that we will need the original object as opposed to a copy. We call this a reference because it will refer to an existing object rather than creating a new one. Confused? Well do not be. Think how the ATM machine works: it needs your card and it will return that card to you. However it only needs a copy of your PIN, which you supply by keying it in. It cannot destroy or change your PIN but it can do both to your card because it has the card, not just a copy.

If you wanted to know how to use an ATM, only the first line matters to you. It tells you that you will need an ATM, a card, and you will need to supply a copy of a PIN. It also tells you that you will get a card back (it does not actually tell you that you get the same card back, but that is a minor detail that we will sweep under the carpet for now).

For a second example let me return to climbing the stairs. The general process might be described in pseudo-code by:

```
nothing climb_stairs(staircase const & stairs, person & me){
	for{int i(0); i != stairs.number_of_steps(); ++i){
			me.step_up_one_step();
	}
}
```

We need an actual staircase and an actual person to climb stairs. Climbing a staircase should not change it, which is the significance of the `const` (a C++ keyword which I will have more to say about later).

There are many other things that can be represented as functions. A function is a process that starts with some ingredients, does something with them and produces a result. A cookery recipe is a function that gives instructions for processing its ingredients into some form of food. Starting a car is a function that uses a key, a car and a driver and results in a car with its engine running. Setting your VCR is a function that results in a recording of the TV program you want to watch.

Some functions have no end result as such; they do something to one of the initial ingredients. Climbing a staircase is like that; it changes the person involved in several ways, the most important one being that they have changed their location.

However, many functions hand a result back to the user. We call the thing handed back a return value, and we specify the type of this before writing the name of the function. In the case of the `use_ATM()` function, the type of the return is a `card &`, and what we get back is a card, hopefully the card we put in. Reference types are commonly provided to a function and we will use them a lot. They are far less common for return types (the values or objects that are returned when the function finishes).

Functions in C++

We have two major kinds of function in C++. The first are often called "free functions". The second are called "member functions" and provide the behavior for non-fundamental types (ones that are not built directly into the language). You have already used member functions when you wrote such things as `std::cin.get()` and `paper.plot(0, 0, black)`. Whenever you follow an object name (`std::cin` and `paper` in the examples) by a dot and then a name that ends with a pair of parentheses, the item after the dot is a member function. We will look further at member functions in Chapter 5. For the rest of this chapter we are going to focus on free functions, i.e. ones that are not tied to providing behavior for objects of a specific type.

Functions allow us to name an activity. Many activities require specific data and so we need a mechanism for handling that as well. In our ATM example, a function to validate the user requires that you provide your card and key in your PIN. A simple ATM program in C++ pseudo-code might look like this:

```
int main(){
	validate_user(atm, card, pin);
	get_money(atm, amount);
	return_card(atm);
}
```

In order to make sense of that code we need to know that `validate_user()`, `get_money()` and `return_card()` are the names of functions and we need to know what kind of data each one requires. We will also eventually need to know how to actually carry out the action for each. Notice that I do not need to know how the machine handles these functions in order to describe how to use an ATM.

Let us move our focus back to computer programming. We have to look at three fundamental aspects of functions: declarations, definitions and uses.

A **function declaration** tells the compiler that the name provided is the name of a function. It also tells the compiler what types of data the function will require when it is used in your source code and what type of data it will return (hand back) when it finishes.

A **function definition** is a set of instructions to tell a compiler how a function works (often called an implementation).

A **function use** (often referred to as **calling a function**) is exactly what it sounds like (an instance of using the function).

Going back to our `use_ATM` example, the essential declaration is the line:

```
card & use_ATM(atm & machine, card & users_card, int pin){
```

That says that there is a function called `use_ATM` that requires an actual ATM and a card and that will need to know what your PIN is. At the end the ATM will return a card.

In programming terms we use the ATM with a statement such as:

```
use_ATM(this_machine, my_card, my_PIN);
```

We do not need to know how the ATM works in order to use one. Put your card into a machine and type in your PIN then follow the instructions on the screen. However the manufacturer of the ATM does need to know because it has to provide all the mechanisms that make it work the way the user expects. It is the latter information that is provided by a definition.

Writing a Function

There are two common ways of developing a function. We can start by writing code that calls (uses) it (equivalent to my using an ATM to get some money) or we can start by writing a declaration (equivalent to describing what is needed). Whichever way we start, experienced programmers leave writing the definition (providing the mechanism that will make a declaration do what the documentation says it will do) till last. They will take time out to write and compile a program to test their work. The definition will not be needed till we come to run the test. In addition, the definition is the thing that we will sometimes change as we spot better ways to achieve our objectives or correct faults (called bugs) in our code. We should have test programs that check that such changes are purely internal and do not change programs that use the function.

In the following, I walk you through developing two functions, one by starting with code that calls it and one by writing the declaration first.

Let us look at the idea of a function by taking the problem of drawing a line across a Playpen and considering the three aspects of a function.

Using a function

It may seem a little odd to start at the end as it were. However that is almost always where programmers start the design of a function. We think about how we want to use it. In other words, "What should it do?" and "What will it need?" When we call a function to draw a cross in a Playpen we will wish to provide:

- Information about who "owns" the Playpen.
- Details of the cross such as where to start the crosspiece and how many pixels make it up, where to start the upright and how many pixels that is made of.
- What color to use.

We will also need to think of a good name for the function, preferably one that does not need comments to explain it. Less obviously we will have to decide what the program gets back from the function. All normal functions in programming return something even if we promptly ignore it. However in the case of this task I am going to ignore that requirement for now (but not for long, because I will have to deal with that when I come to the declaration).

Typically I might want to write something like:

```
int main(){
  playpen paper;
  int const left_x(-5);
  int const left_y(0);
  int const width(11);
  int const bottom_x(0);
  int const bottom_y(-6);
  int const height(11);
  draw_a_cross(paper, left_x, left_y,
     width, bottom_x, bottom_y, height, black);
  cout << "Press RETURN to end";
  cin.get();
}
```

Before we look at the last statement (the call of the `draw_a_cross` function) a word about the previous seven statements. The first of those declares `paper` to be the name of a `playpen` object. It also has the effect of creating a `playpen` object of that name (i.e. it is also a definition; that is normal for objects: declarations are also definitions). The remaining six statements declare (and define) the names of six integers with fixed values; that is the significance of the `const` in each declaration (and definition – in future I will assume that define subsumes declare and definition subsumes declaration). The result is that `left_x` becomes a name for −5, `left_y` a name for 0 and so on. Remember the "magic numbers" mentioned in Chapter 1? We always try to give descriptive names to the numbers we use. The technique I have used in the above code is common among competent programmers.

We want to draw a cross in the window belonging to the `playpen` (remember that is the general type) object called `paper` (and that is a name referring to a specific object of that type; think of the difference between dog – a class of animals – and Fido, a specific dog). The upright is to start at `(bottom_x, bottom_y)` and have `height` pixels (screen points), the crosspiece to start at `(left_x, left_y)` and have `width` pixels. And we want the drawing done in black.

Or, if I am happy with a few magic numbers:

```
draw_a_cross(paper, -5, 0, 11, 0, -6, 11, 0);
```

That should give you a good idea as to why we prefer to use named values even if it does make our source code lengthier and so take longer to type in. Even if you do not agree now, try to read your code written in this way a month from now and see if you still feel that way.

Now we have a typical use, let us see how we can tell a compiler that there will be a function called `draw_a_cross` that can use the information we provide.

Declaring a function

Here we have to think about what our function will hand back to the program. `draw_a_cross` is a function that has no obviously useful data to give back – we are only interested in what it does. Because the rules of C++ (along with many other programming languages) require that a function has some form of return, the designers of C++ invented a very special type called `void` (as it is a C++ keyword, Quincy will display it in blue). This type can be used anytime we want to specify that a function will *not* have a useable return value. In other words a `void` return type says that the function does not hand back anything when it ends. So we can start our declaration:

```
void draw_a_cross
```

We must next list the types of data that will be used by the function (the ingredients of the recipe). This list is called a parameter list. It is a list of types in the order in which the caller will provide the data. The parameters are separated by commas and placed inside parentheses. We could write it like this:

```
void draw_a_cross(fgw::playpen &, int, int, int, int, int, int, fgw::hue)
```

However if we do so, we have magic again. We would have to add a bundle of comments to explain those six `int` parameters. Once you know that `fgw::hue` is the type used for palette codes and `fgw::playpen` is a type for handling a Playpen object, we probably do not need comments to explain those two parameters. (I will remind you about the `&` in a moment.) Note that both `hue` and `playpen` have been qualified with the library to which they belong. You should always use the full names in declarations because we normally place declarations in header files (more about these shortly). Never (until you are an expert) write a `using` directive in the header file.

Rather than litter our code with comments we take advantage of the grammar (language rules) of C++ that allows us to provide a name for each parameter. These parameter names in a function declaration just document what the parameters are; in a declaration they have no other significance. We should make a special effort to choose names that document the parameters. Here is my second version of a declaration for the `draw_a_cross` function:

```
void draw_a_cross(fgw::playpen &,
  int left_of_cross_piece_x, int left_of_cross_piece_y,
  int width_cross_piece_bar,
  int bottom_of_upright_x, int bottom_of_upright_y,
  int height_of_upright,
  fgw::hue);
```

Some authorities would advocate naming all the parameters; that is not my style. I focus on the parameters that need to be documented because the type's name is not enough.

Note the semicolon at the end; that tells the compiler that this is just a function declaration and *not* a definition as well (we will get to the definition in the next section).

Now here is a further explanation of the `&`. From the perspective of the user of the function, it stands as a warning that the function will access the original data and so may be able to change it. In this case that is exactly what we want. We want the function, `draw_a_cross`, to change the `playpen` object so that it displays a cross in the Playpen. There is sometimes an additional benefit because data provided to an `&` parameter (called a reference parameter) will not be copied. This "do not copy" behavior matters for large objects (for example a `playpen` object uses over a quarter of a megabyte of RAM) where copying can use valuable space and also take time. It is also important because some objects cannot be copied (for example, you cannot copy `std::cout`).

Notice that it is the function designer's job to decide whether a reference parameter is desirable or not. The user of the function is only concerned if they have something that must not be changed. The use of a plain reference parameter in a declaration warns the caller that the object passed to the function may be changed by it. It also means that the compiler can provide some protection by refusing code that tries to hand over a `const` qualified object (i.e. one that the programmer has specified as immutable) to a function declared with a plain reference.

Defining a function

In order to write a function definition we must provide all the information required for a declaration (that means that every function definition is also a declaration) but we have to add source code that tells the compiler how the function does its job. This is like the difference between telling someone to open a door and giving them exact instructions as to how doors are opened. The former is a use of a function (door opening) and the latter is a definition (how to open a door).

In general, the function definition will use the data provided by the user via the parameter list (i.e. each piece of data – called an argument – is matched to the corresponding parameter). This means that all parameters that are used (there are rare occasions where a parameter is not used) must be named in a definition. There is no requirement that the names used in a definition are the same ones used in a declaration. I often use different parameter names in a definition because in the context of a definition I want good names for use in my source code rather than names that document what the parameters are for. The documentary names that are suitable in declarations are often too long for convenient use inside the source code that defines a function.

The second aspect of a definition is that instead of ending with a semicolon it ends with a block of statements enclosed in braces. It is the opening brace of the block that tells the compiler it is dealing with a definition rather than just a declaration. This is how I might define my `draw_a_cross()` function:

```
void draw_a_cross(playpen & paper,
  int left_x, int left_y, int width,
  int bottom_x, int bottom_y, int height, hue shade){
  for(int i(0); i != width; ++i){
     paper.plot(left_x + i, left_y, shade);
  }
  for(int i(0); i != height; ++i){
     paper.plot(bottom_x, bottom_y + i, shade);
  }
}
```

Notice that as I have used the simple names `playpen` and `hue` from my library that the above definition will have to be preceded by a `using namespace fgw;` directive and a `#include "playpen.h"` statement.

Now we can replace the program that drew a cross with:

```
#include "playpen.h"
#include <iostream>

using namespace std;
using namespace fgw;

int main(){
  playpen paper;
  paper.scale(3);
  draw_a_cross(paper, -4, 0, 9, 0, -4, 9, black);
  paper.display();
  cout << "Press RETURN to end";
  cin.get();
}
```

Yes I know that I have all those magic numbers, but I want to focus on the way that the call to `draw_a_cross()` works with the declaration and definition. In order that the compiler can compile the above it must be able to see the declaration of `draw_a_cross()`.

Where declarations and definitions go

There is a rule in C++ that says that things must only be defined once. However declarations must be visible wherever we want to use the function, type or other entity. C++ programmers manage this by putting things that are shared (at this stage mainly function declarations) into special files called header files. The parts of source code that must be unique such as the definitions of functions are placed in implementation files. These two kinds of file are conventionally distinguished: header files have a .h extension; implementation files have a .cpp extension.

IDEs – Quincy, in our case – recognize the different extensions and treat the files differently. You have to include all the required implementation material in your project. Implementation material is either in a user-written implementation file or in a provided library file.

Any header (.h) files used by your implementation (.cpp) files must be in places where Quincy can find them. It knows where the headers are for the C++ Standard Library. It knows where the header files are for my library because you tell Quincy that as part of the setup for a project (when you tell it that `includes` are in fgw_headers). It can also find header files if you place them in the same directory as the project.

The following practical session will take you through the process of creating header and implementation files for functions.

Header and Implementation Files

Creating a header file

Open Quincy and create a new project. Make the target name drawing and select Chapter 3 as the target path. Save it. Now insert the fgwlib.a and libgdi32.a library files into the project. (Refer back to Chapter 1 if you need help with getting the project started so that you set such things as the include path correctly.)

Now create a new header file called drawing_functions.h (Quincy will add the .h for you as long as you select the header file type from the New dialog in the File menu).

Because the declarations that you are going to put in this file use names from my graphics library, such as `fgw::playpen` and `fgw::hue`, we need to tell the compiler about those, so type in:

```
#include "playpen.h"
```

Type in the declaration of `draw_a_cross()` that I gave you earlier. Now there should be four items in your header file, including the two comment lines with your name and date.

I want you to acquire the best habits right from the start so I am going to ask you to add three more lines that provide extra safety that is sometimes needed by header files. We need to ensure that the same header file is not included more than once in an implementation file (things can go wrong if you include a header file twice in an implementation file, perhaps once directly and once as an include in another header file).

Right at the start of the header file add these two lines:

```
#ifndef DRAWING_FUNCTIONS_H
#define DRAWING_FUNCTIONS_H
```

Now add as the very last line in the file:

```
#endif
```

(make sure you complete the line by pressing the Return key).

ROBERTA

Why is it important to press Return?

FRANCIS

When the compiler comes across a #include instruction it finds the header file and pastes the contents in as a substitution for the #include instruction. If the header file does not end with a newline, whatever comes next is added directly onto that unfinished line.

If you are lucky the result is nonsensical and the compiler will give an immediate error. However there is a real chance that the result of adding the first line of the next file directly on to the end of the last one will not cause an immediate error. The resulting error is not diagnosed till many lines later in an entirely different file from the cause.

Any time you get an error in a header file that has been used successfully before, suspect that the cause may be an earlier included file missing a final newline character.

Note that the above protection against multiple inclusion is *only* for header files (the ones in which we put declarations and include other files of source code). Whenever you create a header file you should play safe with something like those first two lines and the last line. For other header files replace `DRAWING_FUNCTIONS_H` with the actual file's name written in all uppercase with the dot before the ''`h`'' replaced by an underscore. One day you will forget to do this in a case where it matters. The result will be that you will see a whole bundle of error messages complaining about redefinitions and other faults. For now, get in the habit of writing those lines (consider them as a magic invocation to ward off evil – in Chapter 5 we will come to code where it matters).

Now save the file (in the Chapter 3 sub-directory).

Testing the function

Create another C++ source code file and call it test_drawing_functions.cpp. Type in the source code that I provided above for `main()`. You will need to add in a `#include "drawing_functions.h"` so that the compiler can see the declaration of `draw_a_cross()` – that is the principal purpose of header files, to provide the compiler with declarations when they are needed. This is another form of ''write once, use many times'' because putting declarations in header files means that they can be used wherever they are needed with only the cost of including the header file.

Now use F5 to compile test_drawing_functions.cpp. When you have made any corrections and it compiles successfully, add the file to the project. If you try linking and running it by pressing F9 you will get errors from the linker that complain about missing definitions. That is hardly surprising because we have yet to define `draw_a_cross`. Time to do so.

Creating an implementation file

Open a C++ source code file and type in the definition of `draw_a_cross` (as above). You will need to include the following two lines before the definition of `draw_a_cross`:

```
#include "drawing_functions.h"
using namespace fgw;
```

Save it as drawing_functions.cpp. Use F5 to compile this file. Correct errors and when you get a successful build add it to your project. Press F9 and everything should now link and the program should run.

Note that I went from writing some code that used `draw_a_cross` to writing a declaration of that function. At that stage I started testing. Then I added the definition (i.e., the implementation of `draw_a_cross`). Finally I successfully ran my test code.

Now put that to one side while we back up again and focus on functions that draw horizontal and vertical lines on your screen.

Drawing Lines

Let us now have a look at designing a function in the alternative sequence; work out the declaration, write a test and then write the definition. For this I am going to develop a function that draws a line across the screen.

Designing a function

The property of lines that go straight across the Playpen is that all the pixels that make them up have the same y-coordinate. However for most monitors it will also be a horizontal line so I am going to call the function draw_horizontal_line. Here is the declaration (add this declaration to your drawing_functions.h header file):

```
void draw_horizontal_line(fgw::playpen &,
          int vertical_position, int begin, int end, fgw::hue);
```

The first parameter, fgw::playpen & (the full name because this goes in a header file) declares that an actual playpen object is provided by the call (use). That is all the & means. We read it as "playpen reference" or "reference to playpen." We need the actual playpen object because we are going to draw a line on it.

The next three parameters are all of the same type (int), so what do they represent? I have added names to provide the answers so that anyone using draw_horizontal_line() will know which parameter is which. That will tell them the order in which they must provide the arguments (data for the parameters). These are value parameters because all I need is the number or value of each. The function can discard these values when it finishes (like the ATM and the PIN).

The last parameter is another value parameter. I have chosen not to provide a name in the declaration because the parameter type – fgw::hue – says all that I think is needed.

So we could read the declaration as: draw_horizontal_line() is a function that returns nothing (its return type is void) and that takes a playpen object by reference, an int value that represents the vertical position of all the points on the line, two int values that represent the values of the beginning and the end of the line and a hue value that specifies the color of the line.

Testing the function

Once we have a declaration of a function we can use it – usually referred to as "calling" it. Calling a function requires that you write the function name (without the return type) and follow it with data (often called arguments) in parentheses. The arguments will be matched up with the parameters listed in the declaration. In other words the names of types will not normally be found in a function call.

As soon as the compiler can see a declaration, it will accept uses of that declaration. It does not need a definition; only the linker, which puts all the pieces together to make a program, needs a (compiled) definition. For example, if I want to draw a line from (−5, 10) to (12, 10) with red2 on the Playpen via an object called paper I would write:

```
draw_horizontal_line(paper, 10, -5, 12, red2);
```

Do not take my word for that, add that statement into the main() function in test_drawing_functions.cpp and try to compile it by pressing F5. It should build successfully. However when you press F9 you should get complaints about a missing definition. The header file included a promise that I would provide the definition of a draw_horizontal_line() function that could handle the data I used in the call, but the linker was unable to find any such code in any of the files in the project.

Calls can sometimes look deceptively like declarations. The most obvious difference to an experienced programmer is that a call does not start with the name of a type. The next feature of a call of a function is that the parentheses contain a list made up of values and variable names. Make sure you now have a clear understanding of the difference between a call (use) and a declaration.

Defining the function

At the top of a recipe is a list of ingredients. When you come to make your cake you will need actual ingredients or close substitutes (yes we have an analogue of that in programming). The rest of the recipe tells you how to produce your cake from the ingredients (and return a cake). When you go shopping you only need the list of ingredients. Indeed you might be a hopeless cook and simply be getting the ingredients for someone else to use. However we eventually need the instructions that make use of the ingredients. In programming terms, we need a definition or implementation.

ROBERTA

I find the terms definition and implementation a bit confusing. It seems that they are used interchangeably. Is there any difference and why are there two terms in use when one would do?

FRANCIS

This is a hard question because much of the time they can be used interchangeably and yet they are not synonyms. We would never talk about implementing a variable or object. When we talk about defining a type we normally mean saying what it will do (i.e. what its behavior will be). Providing the code that will provide that behavior is called "implementing a type". However when it comes to functions the terms implement and define are just about interchangeable.

The following is a definition of `draw_horizontal_line()`:

```
void draw_horizontal_line(playpen & pp, int y,
          int x1, int x2, hue c){
  for(int x(x1); x != x2; ++x) pp.plot(x, y, c);
}
```

Well almost. It has a nasty bug (that is the term programmers use for code that compiles but will sometimes not execute correctly) in it. Before you read on, see if you can spot it. You will have to be honest and stop here for a moment. The kind of bug in this source code is nasty because when you simply test the code you might entirely miss the problem and never use any tests that show it up.

By the way, did you notice that all the parameters now have names, and that they are not the same ones that I used in the declaration? You already knew that we would have to add names for the `playpen &` (reference) and for the `hue` (value). I changed the other names because I prefer short names in a definition context – not least because it prevents overly long statements. I use relatively long names in parameter lists in declarations as documentation and so avoid cluttering my source code with comments. On the other hand, long names often get in the way when you are trying to write implementations (the definition part). As you already know what the parameters are for, you do not need those long descriptive names in otherwise very short functions.

Back to that bug: the problem is that the above implementation of `draw_horizontal_line()` assumes that `x1` is smaller (to the left) of `x2`. What happens in the `for`-loop if `x1` is already bigger than `x2`? It will keep adding to `x` (which starts as the value of `x1`). Mathematically it will never get back to `x2`. In computer arithmetic, because `int` has a limited range of values, it may eventually loop round and get to `x2`, but with the range of values usually provided for `int` (much, much more than the minimum required range) that will probably take a long time (many seconds) even on a fast modern machine. If you want to try testing the bugged version with:

```
draw_horizontal_line(paper, 10, 1, 0, red4);
```

You will probably need to start the program and then go and have lunch, because it takes a long time even on a fast machine.

To remove this bug we need to learn about the `if` keyword. This allows us to choose what happens next depending on a test that gives a true/false response. We only execute the (compound) statement following an `if(test)` if the `test` comes out as true. We can add an `else` (another keyword) to state what must be done if it is not true. The ability to make decisions is extremely important and so `if`-statements are among the most powerful tools in C++ programming. All computer languages have something that serves the same purpose and most call it "if".

Here is a corrected implementation of `draw_horizontal_line()`:

```
void draw_horizontal_line(playpen & pp, int y, int x1, int x2, hue c){
  if(x1 < x2){
     for(int x(x1); x != x2; ++x) pp.plot(x, y, c);
  }
  else{
     for(int x(x1); x != x2; --x) pp.plot(x, y, c);
  }
}
```

There are several equally sensible ways of achieving the objective, but they all share the same test applied to `x1` and `x2`. I hope you guessed that `x1 < x2` reads as "x1 less than x2"? That < is another C++ operator which is also used in mathematics. -- is the decrement operator (count down by one or reduce the value stored in x by one) and behaves very like the ++, increment, operator.

If you are being very observant you may have noticed that the start point (x1, y) is plotted but the end point (x2, y) is not. This is not an oversight. I meant it to be that way. If you look even more carefully you may realize that if you try to draw a line from a point to itself, the result will be to do nothing, i.e. have a line of zero length. It is too early in your programming career to have a long discussion of this issue. However it is the kind of issue that those designing functions for use by others have to take very seriously. Often there is no single right answer, only a best choice in context.

Please get into the habit of asking yourself what assumptions you are making when you write a piece of code. It is easy to assume things when you write code and having sharp eyes and a quick mind to spot the assumptions are among the qualities that make a good programmer. None of us are immune from making assumptions. I will tell you about a couple I made when preparing code for this book, but not now.

TASK 3

Most tasks in this book require you to produce something new for yourself. This one doesn't, it is more a piece of practical work to consolidate what you have learnt so far. It is also a task with much more text than most.

Use the header and source code files that you created earlier (for `draw_a_cross`) for the following work. Provide an implementation (i.e. a definition) of `draw_horizontal_line()`. Type the definition given above into drawing_lines_functions.cpp (after `#include "drawing_functions.h"` and the `using` directive).

Use F5 to compile it. Correct any typos and continue until it compiles successfully. One common cause of compilation errors is using commas instead of semicolons. I was tired

when testing the above code and made exactly that mistake. The result was a couple of dozen error messages for just a single typo. Whenever I ask you to type something in, it has been directly cut and pasted from my copy of the file, so as long as the publishers do not "correct" it you should be OK.

When you can compile this file, save it and close it. It should already be in the project from when you were implementing `draw_a_cross()`. If you now press F9, your program should build successfully and run to produce a Playpen window with a black cross and a red line in it.

Please add this statement to `main` so that we test drawing a line from right to left:

```
draw_horizontal_line(paper, 15, 20, -12, blue4);
```

Always write your test programs to try all variations, that way you will catch most errors early when they are easy to correct.

There is nothing special about this test program so feel free to make up your own. But make sure it tests lines that go right to left and ones that go left to right. You might find it helpful to use a bigger scale for that test so that you are certain that you can see the result.

When Roberta tried this task, I received an anguished email that said that although the source file compiled, she was getting error messages when she tried to build and run it. I could guess what she had missed. Can you?

She had missed my instruction to add drawing_functions.cpp to the project.

Try missing it out yourself (remove it from the project) so you can see the kind of error messages that it produces. Hopefully that will help you identify similar mistakes when you make them later.

We all make mistakes, lots of them. In fact, I think the better you are the more little mistakes you make. The difference is that as you gain expertise you will correct such mistakes with increasing ease. Part, but not all, of that is the result of becoming familiar with the kind of mistakes you personally make. For many people the more mistakes they make initially the more they learn to avoid them in the future.

One quick question: did you remember to add comments to all the files to identify author and date? If not, go back and add them now and try to remember to develop good habits right from the start. I won't keep nagging you, but that does not mean I have forgotten, just that I trust you to do the right thing.

TASK 4

Now rework all the above but with the changes needed to draw lines vertically up and down the screen. Add the declaration to the existing draw_functions.h. You can add the definition to draw_functions.cpp. Consistency in naming is important so choose an obvious name for this second function.

Always test code early. That is why I tell you to get your files to compile successfully before adding them to a project. Testing early and often will make life much easier because when things do not work, you look first at what you have just added or changed.

Drawing Sets of Lines

Now you have got those two functions working and checked out, I will let you into a secret; they both already exist as part of fgwlib.a and are declared in line_drawing.h. Well almost, but in order to avoid name collisions I called mine `horizontal_line()` and `vertical_line()`.

The reason that these functions are part of my graphics library is that they have some added features that I will reveal in a later chapter. However do not throw away your draw_functions.h and draw_functions.cpp files, just remove the declarations of `draw_horizontal_line()` and `draw_vertical_line()` (or whatever you called it) from the header file and their definitions from the implementation file. You are about to replace them with something else.

You need some exercises to help you consolidate a little further on both `for`-loops and functions. The following are not labeled as tasks because you can if you feel really happy with what you have done, skip them. However I hope you won't because I think they will add to your programming skills.

EXERCISE 1

Go back to the draw_functions.cpp file and look at the definition of `draw_a_cross` that should still be there. Now remove those two `for`-loops and replace them with suitable calls to `horizontal_line()` and `vertical_line()`. You should now press F9 and get the same result that you did before. What we have done is demonstrate one of the major advantages of using functions: you can change an implementation of a function and link it with already existing code. That means that if you discover a better way of doing something, you only have to make the change in one place, the implementation of the function.

EXERCISE 2

There is another way that we could define a cross; we could give the point of intersection of the horizontal and the vertical together with the lengths of each of the four "arms". The declaration of such a function would be:

```
void draw_another_cross(fgw::playpen &,
        int intersection_x, int intersection_y,
        int left_arm, int right_arm,
        int lower_arm, int upper_arm, fgw::hue);
```

Here is a test program for this function:

```
int main(){
  playpen paper;
  paper.scale(3);
  draw_another_cross(paper, 5, 5, 10, 10, 20, 5, blue4 + red4);
  paper.display();
  cout << "Press return to end";
  cin.get();
}
```

Implement `draw_another_cross` and compile and execute this program so that you test your implementation. (You should get a khaki cross with a long tail.)

EXERCISE 3

I want you to implement the following function declaration (put the declaration in drawing_functions.h and the definition in drawing_functions.cpp) and then test it. If you haven't realized, when I ask you to test something I mean write a program that uses it and tests that it works even when used in ways that you did not think about initially (like drawing lines from right to left as well as from left to right).

```
void verticals(fgw::playpen &, int begin_x, int begin_y,
        int end_y, int interval, int count, fgw::hue);
```

Let me make certain that you understand the problem. I want a function that will produce a number (given by `count`) of vertical lines separated by the given interval. The first line must start at `(begin_x, begin_y)` and end at `(begin_x, end_y)`. Each subsequent line should be an `interval` to the right of the previous one. For now you can assume that you will not be given a negative `count` (we are not quite ready to deal with impossible requests), but your solution should be able to handle a negative `interval` (which should draw successive lines to the left instead of right).

If you think carefully you will find that you can recycle the mechanisms you used in drawing a line and the functions that draw lines (or at least one of them). Good programming builds on what has gone before both by reusing code and reusing ideas.

This one should be easy. Repeat Exercise 3 but develop a function called `horizontals`, which draws a column of horizontal lines from similar data.

CHALLENGING

EXERCISE 5

Use the functions you have developed for Exercises 3 and 4 to write (and test) a function called `square_grid` that draws a grid of n-by-n squares on the screen.

This exercise has a little kicker in the tail. Unless you are abnormally insightful your first almost successful attempt will, on close inspection, be missing a single pixel. Remember how our line drawing `for`-loops stop when they reach the end without actually plotting that end pixel? Now look at your solution to this exercise and add that final tiny piece that completes it.

This is also a common programming experience where we have to deal with a boundary case. As you gain experience you will get increasingly used to checking these tiny details that make the difference between "almost right" and "perfect".

Aren't you getting a bit irritated by having to add the source code that halts your program until you press the return key? Remember that programmers do not like doing the same thing again and again. That is what functions are for.

Create header and implementation files called utilities.h and utilities.cpp. Remember to add the sentinel to the header file (UTILITIES_H in this case). Now put the following declaration in the header file:

```
void pause();
```

Add the appropriate implementation to the implementation file.

Because you will want ready access to your utilities in future projects, put these files in the fgw_headers directory. By doing that the compiler will be able to find your utilities.h in the same place that it finds my playpen.h. You will need to include utilities.cpp into any project where you use functions that are in it.

Creating Your Own Utility Functions

In future whenever you have a convenience function that avoids continually rewriting the same code, add it to your utilities files. I may sometimes make suggestions as to things worth putting in your utilities files, but do not wait for me; if you want a function you have written to be generally available put it in these files. Eventually you will want to provide specialized files with descriptive names for functions that are more than utilities.

Let me finish with a little added motivation for doing this kind of thing. Imagine that you wanted to give your prize program to a French friend. You can convert that message to French just by writing a French implementation of your utilities. Now all the places where your programs use that mechanism to wait before going on can, almost cost free, do it in French.

This raises an issue that often confuses newcomers, programming in foreign languages. The keywords of C++ are based on English. The names of the hundreds of things in the C++ Standard Library are all derived from English. This effectively means that source code is written in an English-like form. If you are not a native English speaker that may seem unfair, but the alternatives are just too much for the computer industry. Professional source code is almost always written using words and names based on English. However this is not an excuse for making the users of programs use English. You should think of ways to make it easy for your programs to work in other languages: not now but eventually if you have an ambition to become a professional programmer.

For fun

What about going back to your modern art program and adding some more features now that you know how to draw lines? You can also write some more functions to draw other simple shapes composed of vertical and horizontal lines. If you want to extend a bit further you could write a function to draw a line at 45°. Other slopes will be more challenging but try some as a way to improve your programming fluency.

The more you experiment the better you will come to understand what you are doing and the more fluent your programming will become. Watch young children learning to move about, they do not imitate adults but work out ways to achieve their goals, even if their resources are limited. They do not wait to be taught, they learn by experiment.

ROBERTA'S COMMENTS

In the early chapters of the book I was struggling to learn and remember all the new terminology as well as how things work. As you will discover I didn't quite grasp everything about functions to begin with. I was happy about the difference between declaration and definition and which files they went in but I now realize I hadn't fully understood how to use or call a function and I wasn't too certain about return types either if I am honest. I did things but didn't understand them till later. Even if I thought I understood I sometimes didn't and it is only in retrospect I can see this. I seem to be about three chapters behind in comprehension most of the time. Why am I saying this? Because I can promise you that if you are finding this difficult you will understand it eventually.

At first I didn't think Task 5 was worth doing because it is only two lines of code which only seemed to be used at the end of `main()` when using `playpen`. However, I later discovered that this tiny bit of code can be used to pause a program at any point and is useful when testing more complicated code.

Incidentally, I thought you might like to know that `cout` and `cin` are pronounced cee out and cee in and not coot and sin as I originally thought.

SOLUTIONS TO EXERCISES

These are just my answers. If yours are different but produce the same output just study mine and consider whether they show you anything you missed. Of course my code may just give you a warm fuzzy feeling that you have done well.

Exercise 1

```
void draw_a_cross(playpen & paper,
  int left_x, int left_y, int width,
  int bottom_x, int bottom_y, int height, hue shade){
  horizontal_line(paper, left_y, left_x, left_x+width, shade);
  vertical_line(paper, bottom_x, bottom_y,
     bottom_y+height, shade);
  }
```

Exercise 2

```
void draw_another_cross(playpen & paper, int x, int y,
     int left, int right, int down, int up, hue shade){
  draw_a_cross(paper, x-left, y, left+right+1,
          x, y-down, down+up+1, shade);
}
```

I have recycled the earlier `draw_a_cross` function to do the actual work. This process is called **delegation**, which is yet another way to avoid repetition. If you are curious about the +1s remember that we have to allow for the ''size'' of the intersection ''point''.

Exercise 3

```
void verticals(playpen & paper, int begin_x, int from,
        int to, int interval, int count, hue shade){
```

SOLUTIONS TO EXERCISES

```
    for(int line(0); line != count; ++line){
      vertical_line(paper, begin_x + line * interval, from, to,
  shade);
  }
}
```

Exercise 4

```
void horizontals(playpen & paper, int begin_y, int from,
        int to, int interval, int count, hue shade){
  for(int line(0); line != count; ++line){
    horizontal_line(paper, begin_y + line * interval, from, to,
  shade);
  }
}
```

Exercise 5

```
void square_grid(playpen & paper, int begin_x, int begin_y,
                               int interval, int count, hue
                                       shade){
  verticals(paper, begin_x, begin_y,
           begin_y + interval*count, interval, count+1, shade);
  horizontals(paper, begin_y, begin_x,
           begin_x + interval*count, interval, count+1, shade);
  paper.plot(begin_x + interval*count, begin_y + interval*count,
   shade);
}
```

Notice the `count+1` in the calls to `verticals` and `horizontals`. That is because `count` is the number of squares across and up, not the number of lines.

Remember when you test these functions that you will need to use the `display()` function of `fgw::playpen` if you are to see the result.

Summary

Key programming concepts

- Programming languages provide a way of encapsulating an action that may be used more than once. This is often provided by something called a function.

- Functions are provided with specific data when they are used, via arguments passed to a matching parameter list.
- Functions return a value of some specified type.
- There is a mechanism for making decisions in a program. Commonly this is provided by some variation of `if` and `else`.

C++ checklist

- C++ has a mechanism for making decisions using two keywords: `if` and `else`.
- `if` and `else` are followed by either a simple or a compound statement. `else` is optional, if you leave it out nothing is done if the test fails.
- C++ functions return values and if there is nothing to return we use a special return type called `void`.
- A function will have a (possibly empty) list of data types that it expects to be provided when the function is called (used).
- Functions are declared in header files and defined in implementation files.
- Function declarations specify what is needed to use a function. This information is valuable to programmers as well as being essential for compilers.
- Function definitions provide the information that can be compiled to produce object code that can be linked in to provide a complete program.
- Definitions are provided by library files (.a files with this compiler) or by source code files – usually identified by a .cpp extension. You need to tell the linker about them by including them in the project. The C++ Standard Library is an exception to this rule; the linker already knows where to find that.
- When you call a function you must provide a list of data (called arguments) to satisfy the parameter list specified in the function's declaration.
- There are two major kinds of parameter. Value parameters, which use copies of the data, and reference parameters, which have access to the original object.
- If the parameter type ends with &, it is a reference parameter.
- A variable or parameter that is declared as `const` is one whose value is fixed by the definition or call and cannot subsequently be changed.

Extensions checklist

- There are two functions provided in the graphics library that allow you to draw lines straight across and straight up the screen. Their declarations are:

```
void horizontal_line(playpen &, int y_value, int from_x, int
    to_x, hue);
void vertical_line(playpen &, int x_value, int from_y, int
    to_y, hue);
```

- The line_drawing.h header file provides the declarations of the various line drawing functions provided by my library.

CHAPTER 4

You Can Communicate

In this chapter I will be covering various aspects of programming that can be loosely placed under the heading of communication. Good use of names and the C++ namespace facility makes source code more readable. Getting information into and out of a program is important and you need to learn more about the C++ streams mechanism for doing those things effectively. Finally you need to know a little about how a program can communicate internally when it meets unexpected problems such as a disk being full, or being given unuseable data. On the way I will introduce you to a couple more of the types provided by C++.

Names and Namespaces

In *Alice Through the Looking Glass* (chapter 8) there is a dialog between Alice and the White Knight about how important it is to distinguish between something and its name and what a name is called and so on. Of course Charles Dodgson (Lewis Carroll's real name) was a Victorian mathematician who was very familiar with the importance of names. If you haven't ever read the Alice books http://www.alice-in-wonderland.net/ is an excellent place to start.

Our ancestors believed (at least some of them did) that knowing something's name gave you power over it. They were right. In a purely practical sense knowing a person's name gives you the ability to attract their attention, ask about them or tell other people about them. Knowing what something is called makes it much easier to find out more about it on the Internet or ask a shopkeeper if they have it in stock. If I had not known the name of the book in which Charles Dodgson had written an amusing and informative dialog about names it would have been hard for me to have found the reference I wanted and even harder for me to have told you about it.

Giving names to things is an important human ability. We use many kinds of names but for now the most important are names for groups of things (e.g. "dog") with shared properties and names for individual objects (e.g. "Fido"). We classify things in various ways but in programming we tend to be more rigid. We attach names to individual objects though one object can have several names; we reuse names in different contexts; and we apply names to groups with shared characteristics. A name like "dog" in most contexts refers to a kind of animal, not an individual animal but to all animals that share certain biological properties.

On the other hand, "Francis", "Roberta" and "Fido" would normally be individuals. However many individuals share my first name so context becomes important. In the context of this book, Francis is me, the lead author, Roberta is the student author and Fido is my sister's dog.

C++ uses names to refer to individual objects and names for groups of objects that share general behavior. The latter use of a name is called a type name. C++ also provides named contexts called namespaces. Throughout this book I use two particular named contexts (namespaces): `std` and `fgw`. `std` is the context in which the C++ Standard Library provides names; `fgw` is the context of my library.

There is also the widest context of all: global. The global context is for names that are declared neither in a namespace nor in a local context, such as a compound statement (a collection of statements contained in braces). An understanding of context (called scope in programming) for a declaration of a name is important; names in different scopes may look the same but have different meanings, just as ''Francis'' will refer to different people depending on where you are and who you are talking to.

There are various other contexts available in C++ and you will learn about some of them in the later chapters of this book.

A **variable** is an important kind of name. A variable is a name that is used to refer to an object. An object is a region of storage (RAM) with associated behavior. For example a `playpen` object is a large region of storage (over a quarter of a megabyte) that has such associated behavior as being able to display itself in the Playpen window. A type is the combination of storage and behavior; and an object is a specific region of storage used as an instance of a type. Think about the difference between the dog idea (a type) and Fido (an object).

The definition of a variable associates a name with an object. Normally the definition causes the object to be created in some way. However it is possible to associate a name with an already existing object; that is what a reference is (a new name for an existing object). Defining a non-reference variable, parameter or return type means that a new object will be created for the variable, the argument or the return value. Defining a reference variable (we won't be using those much, if at all, in this book), a reference parameter or a reference return means that we are attaching that name to an existing object.

In Chapter 5 we will use objects in contexts where it matters a great deal whether we use an existing object through a reference parameter or a new object through a value (non-reference) parameter. At that point I will give you an example to try.

We use names for types: fundamental types (which are an inherent part of the C++ language) and user-defined types (either from the C++ Standard Library or from my library); we use names for variables and parameters that refer to objects, either newly created ones or existing ones; and we use names for functions. We also use names to refer to namespaces (i.e. named contexts for other names). From this you should appreciate how important names are to programming.

Choosing good names will make your code easier to understand. Bad ones may be easier to type but will make your code harder to understand when you return to it.

Return values are examples of unnamed objects, whether specially created to return information from the function or existing objects that can return the information.

Interaction

So far our programs have used little interaction with the user. We have used `cout` (or, to give it its full name, `std::cout`) to display simple messages (e.g. ''Press RETURN'') and values in the console window of a program. We have used `cin.get()` to obtain the response. The time has come for our programs to have greater interaction with the outside world, including the program user (i.e. the person who interacts with an executable as opposed to the programmer using someone else's source code).

There is a lot of new information in this chapter (it is also a very long chapter, but do not let that put you off, just take it steadily). You do not need to completely understand it in order to use it. One of the advantages of having a book is that you can always return to earlier material and read it again. As you gain experience, each successive reading will deepen your understanding. At each stage, all that is essential is enough understanding to write successful programs.

If you feel that you are getting in too deep, ask for help. These days there is no need to try to learn in complete isolation. Even if you do not have a learning partner or a mentor, the ACCU mentoring scheme (though you do have to be a member, membership is less than the cost of a book) and mailing lists will willingly help you. Remember that you should try to supplement a book such as this one with other resources. You can learn to program from this book alone but you can make it easier for yourself without cheating.

The char and int Types

It is time to add a bit more detail about the `int` type that we have used to control loops and for a little arithmetic. You will also need to learn about the fundamental type used for handling symbols in C++. It is called `char` (variously pronounced as ''car'', ''care'' or the first syllable of charcoal).

Dealing with characters

C++ has four types that handle characters but we only need the one called `char` for now. Like `int`, `char` is a fundamental type and its name is a C++ keyword. The language guarantees that the range of values that can be stored in a `char` variable can represent the characters in the system's execution character set. That is mostly the symbols that you can type on your keyboard (though not all of them). A few have to have special names when used in source code because typing them has a direct effect. For example typing `\n` provides the `char` value that represents the effect of the Return or Enter key.

Because the backslash character is used to identify these special characters, we need a way to use the backslash as a character in its own right. If you want an actual backslash (for example as part of a directory path) in text that is within quotation marks you have to double it up. For example, if you write the following in your source code:

```
std::cout << "to go to a new line type \n in your code."
```

the output would be:

To go to a new line type
in your code.

To get the result you probably wanted, you need to write:

```
std::cout << "to go to a new line type \\n in your code."
```

When we want to specify a character literal we place the symbol inside single quotes. So `'a'` provides the value that represents the lowercase letter a on your computer. Likewise `'9'` provides the value that represents the symbol 9 as opposed to the numerical value 9 and `'\n'` provides the value that represents the effect of pressing the Enter or Return key.

Be careful of quotes when programming. `'a'` and `"a"` are not the same thing. The first is a character literal (i.e. an explicit `char` value), the second represents a string literal that happens to be composed of a single character. The compiler can tell the difference and will often handle them differently.

Look at the following code fragment:

```
cout << "press a key and then press RETURN";
if(cin.get() == 'a')
  cout << "that was an a.";
else
  cout << "that was not an a,";
```

The first statement prompts for input. Next we check by comparing (note the double equals sign which reads as ''compares equal to'') the input with `'a'` and printing one of two messages in accordance with the result.

Write and test a program that checks the various claims I made above. As this program does not use graphics you will not need to include playpen.h in it but you will need to include <iostream>. Again, as there are no graphics, the project will not need to include the two library files – fgwlib.a and libgdi32.a.

Using the int type

In Chapters 1 and 2 we used the `int` type without knowing very much about it. It is now time that I filled in a bit more because you will need to start using it on your own initiative when tackling some of the exercises in this chapter.

When I create a variable of type `int` the compiler will allocate a small amount of memory (the storage part of a type), sufficient to store a single whole number from a range. C++ guarantees that that range for an `int` will be at least from −32767 to +32767 inclusive. Most systems provide for a much greater range, but the important thing is that you can be certain that you will not get strange results as long as your program keeps within the guaranteed range.

All the common programming languages have the concept of an `int` type and most call it by that name. C++ provides a wide range of operators that can be applied to `int` values (whether given explicitly, such as `17`, or stored in an `int` object). As we saw in Chapter 3, these include the common arithmetic operators +, −, * (multiply) and / (divide).

Assuming that `i` and `j` have been defined as `int` variables (and so refer to `int` storage or objects), here are a few examples of arithmetic expressions using `int` values and variables:

```
i + j              i + 3
i * (3 + j)        i * 3 + j
(i + j) / 7        i + j / 7
8 / 4 / 2          8 / (4 / 2)
10 - 6 - 3         10 - (6 - 3)
```

Computer arithmetic follows the same rules that you learnt at school; work out the value of expressions in parentheses first, do multiplications and divisions (working from left to right) before additions and subtractions (working from left to right). Notice how these rules affect the results you get for the last four examples. 8 / 4 / 2 (divide eight by four and then divide the result by two) gives 1 but 8 / (4 / 2) comes to 4 (i.e. eight divided by the result of dividing four by two). Ten subtract six subtract three is one; ten subtract the result of six subtract three is seven.

There are also a number of operators that can only be applied to `int` variables (such as `i` above) and not to `int` values (such as 7 or 10). The most obvious of these is assignment (=). In computer programming, assignment means that we must first work out the value of the expression on the right of the "=" sign and then store it in the memory provided for the variable on the left. That storage process will over-write what was previously being stored in that memory. One consequence of that rule is that the left side of an assignment must provide memory to store the result. So when I write:

```
i = 7;
```

the memory for `i` will now contain the computer representation for 7. If I now follow that with:

```
j = i + 5;
```

the value stored in the memory belonging to `i` will be obtained (the 7 we just put there) and 5 added to it; the result will be placed in (the memory provided for) `j`. I put that phrase in parentheses because we normally do not spell out that level of detail and would simply say that "five is added to the value of `i` and stored in `j`". Indeed programmers usually abbreviate that further and say "five is added to `i` and stored in `j`" or even "`j` equals `i` + five". They take it for granted that you will know from the context that it is the value found in `i` that is used and the memory provided for `j` that is changed.

The process of assignment is quite different from the process of initializing an object when a variable is defined. Some types provide default initialization (e.g. a `playpen` object starts with a white screen unless you explicitly specify otherwise). The fundamental types such as `int` and `char` are left in some random state (called "uninitialized") if no starting value is provided by the definition. In this book the initial values for objects are always provided by placing them in parentheses after the variable name being defined. If you are not providing initial data for an object there must be no parentheses after the variable name. For example:

```
fgw::playpen paper;             // defines a white playpen object
fgw::playpen canvas(black);     // defines a black playpen object
fgw::playpen foo();             // declares foo as a function
```

Note that in the last case, empty parentheses after a name in a declaration means that you are declaring a function that has no parameters.

In C++ there are other ways of changing the value being stored. In the previous chapter we used the increment and decrement operators while managing our `for`-loops. Both of those operators change the value stored (and so can only be applied to a variable). There is nothing special about the way we used an `int` variable to control a `for`-loop. We were just using part of the normal behavior of an `int`.

The compiler will pick you up if you try to use an operator that will not work with a pure value. For example, if you write `7 = i` or `++10` the compiler will issue an error message because you cannot change `7` to something else, nor can you increment `10`. We call such pure values (ones that are not stored in memory belonging to a variable) literals. As I hope you would expect, literals are immutable (cannot be changed by the program).

An `int` variable coupled with either an increment (`++`) or a decrement (`--`) operator is useful when we want to count up or down. Typically we will see code like this:

```
int count(0);
// do something
if(test) ++count;
```

Where *`test`* is replaced by some expression that evaluates to true or false. I would usually choose a more descriptive name for `count`, one that would tell the reader of the code what was being counted.

Streams

The concept of input and output to a program is encapsulated in C++ (as well as in many other languages) by the idea of a stream of data. We can export information from our program through any available output stream and we can input data from any available input stream. C++ separates the process into two parts (the structuring/formatting of data and the process of transferring it) for the benefit of experienced programmers, but C++ I/O has been carefully designed so that we do not need to learn about the hairy details when all we want to do is to stream ordinary data into and out of our program.

Some kinds of stream are essentially one-directional. For example a keyboard can only supply data (technically, it is a **source**) and an ordinary monitor can only display data (it is a **sink**). Some kinds of stream are naturally two-way. A file is the most common example of a stream that can be connected to input, output or both. A parallel port on a standard PC is normally bi-directional: the printer can talk to your computer to pass back information such as being out of ink or paper.

I/O in C++ has been carefully designed to make the actual data source or data destination largely irrelevant to the source code. Of course it is very relevant to the way in which a program can be used. In the following I will introduce you to three common types of stream: console streams, file streams and, briefly, string streams.

Console streams

Whenever you include the header `<iostream>` in a program, you will automatically be supplied with the some standard console stream objects. The four most frequently used ones break into two pairs and deal with `char` representations of values (see above).

The first pair, cout and cin, provides normal communication between your program, a standard output device (usually a monitor) and a standard input device (usually a keyboard). The second pair, cerr and clog, provides error and logging facilities. Initially both the latter use the same device as cout. I will ignore the difference between these output objects until we have a need to know more about them. It is enough for now that you know they exist and can be used in exactly the same way that cout can be used.

cout is relatively easy to use because you have complete control over what you send to it. In addition to the << operator that we have already used, it has access to the many member functions (functions that are specific to a type and are called with the object-dot-function syntax) of output streams. cout is an object (strictly speaking it is a variable referencing an object; we tend to elide some of the words when talking about objects and variables – a variable is a name and an object is the thing the name refers to), so it is fair to ask what type it is. The answer is that it is an ostream object and so shares all the behavior of the ostream type. We will mainly use the << operator to send data out to the screen.

cin is more problematic because it is collecting data from outside the program. We have no control over the supplier of that information. Worse, the supplier is usually a fallible human being who, even when not taking a perverse delight in trying to break our programs, will make mistakes.

There is an >> operator for istream objects (I hope that you are not surprised to learn that that is the type of cin) that shifts data from the input source to your program, but it is very fragile and easily stops working. I could hide this fragility from you but, as you will have to deal with it sometime, I think honesty is a better policy.

Here is a small code snippet (i.e. it is not even a whole function, just three lines that might be written as part of your source code) that illustrates the problem:

```
cout << "Please type in a number between 0 and 10: ";
int i(0);
cin >> i;
```

There are several weaknesses in that source code. The instruction lacks precision because it does not specify if 0 and 10 are considered valid responses. It also does not specify whether only whole numbers will do. That lack of precision makes it harder for the program user to give a correct response.

However there is a much more serious problem with this code: it assumes that the user of the program in which it occurs will respond with a valid whole number to store in our int variable. C++ has very rigid ideas as to what constitutes a valid whole number. It may optionally start with a + or − sign, but the rest must use only the digits 0 to 9. Nothing else will do. For example it is no use typing in "five"; any human being will understand that means 5 but the program will not.

As soon as cin has found the start of the input (it skips over spaces, tabs, newlines, etc. when searching for the start of the input for a number) it extracts characters from the input until it finds an invalid character (anything other than the ten digits or an initial + or −). If it has not read any digits at that stage (i.e. the first character that is not some kind of space is not a digit or + or − followed by a digit) it puts itself into a fail state and refuses to process any further input until the program deals with the failure. Subsequent attempts to use cin in your program will do nothing until it is restored to its normal state.

Your first instinct is likely to be to consider such behavior to be a mistake by the designers of the C++ Standard Library. I think that experience will show that any other behavior would have been worse. However we must understand the behavior and learn to cope with it.

Now I am going to give you a piece of advice that will put you ahead of a very substantial part of the C++ programming community: do not use the >> operator on cin unless you immediately check for failure and handle it.

File streams

There are three types of stream used to handle files: ifstream, ofstream and fstream. The first two are similar to istream and ostream types except that they are designed to work with files as the source or destination for data. The third type, fstream, takes advantage of the fact that a file, in general, can be both read from and written to. You will not be making much, if any, use of that bi-directional type because there are too many complications that arise when we try to mix reading and writing to the same file.

You will find, once you learn how to create your own file stream objects, that using them is simple. They have all the functions and operators that apply to the `istream` and `ostream` objects plus a few extras to support specific file behavior (such as opening and closing the files they are using). In programming terms, the file stream types are special types of the I/O stream types (`istream` and `ostream`) and can be used wherever those types can be used. Be careful! If I need, for example, an `istream` object, an `ifstream` one will do but not vice versa. In other words, all input file streams are input streams but not all input streams come from files.

String streams

These suffer from a redesign problem. Through much of the 90s, C++ programmers used `strstream` objects. For now, just note that such things exist and they are not the same as the modern `stringstream` objects.

`stringstreams` use `string` objects (`string` is a type that can store a sequence of characters; more about it shortly) as the source and destination for data. Just like files, they come in three flavors, `istringstream`, `ostringstream` and `stringstream`. The three versions are exactly analogous to the three types of file stream.

We will be using string stream objects (of all three types) quite extensively in later chapters.

The string Type

Just as C++ has types to manage numerical data (`int` is the only one we have used so far), it has types that manage text data or sequences of symbols. The only one we need in this book is `string` (or, `std::string` to give it its full name).

`string` provides the resources and behavior to store and manipulate text (sequences of `char` objects). Like many other things we will learn about, it has many member functions that provide useful behavior. It even has some operators, e.g. + is used to join two `string` objects together to create a new one.

I think it is time that you had some practical work to help you digest all this new information.

Creating a Simple Dialog

Let us look at preparing a program to hold a simple dialog with the user. This will allow us to use several of the items above and improve your understanding of how I/O works.

```
#include <iostream>
#include <string>

using namespace std;

int main(){
  cout << "Please type in your full name: ";
  string fullname;
  getline(cin, fullname);
  cout << "Hello " << fullname << ", I am pleased to meet you.\n";
  cout << "\nPress RETURN to end.";
  cin.get();
  }
```

First get the program working and then I will go through it with you.

You will need to create a project in Quincy. By now you should be getting familiar with this process so I will not mention it again. This time you need to create a blank project in the Chapter 4 sub-directory. You do not need to insert either of the special library files (libgdi32.a and fgwlib.a) because we are not using any graphical resources. The linker will be using some of the Standard Library, but it knows where to find that.

Now create a new C++ source file and type in the above program. As always, be careful about typos; the code above works as is, if yours does not you have missed some small detail. You can use the `pause()` function from your own utilities files if you wish. If you do, you will have to include your utilities.h in this program and add your utilities.cpp to the project.

When the source code compiles successfully, add it to the project and press F9 to link and run it. You should get a console window and a simple dialog with which you can interact. Now let us look at what you have done so far.

The `#include` statements make two parts of the C++ Standard Library available for use. The header names are placed between angle brackets (⟨ and ⟩) to tell the compiler that we are using standard headers rather than ones that have been written as extras.

The third statement (the `using` directive) is one that leads to interminable arguments between programmers. The reason for the argument is that it makes all the names in the Standard Library useable without prefixing them with `std::`. You should *never* place a `using` directive in a header file; doing so would cause problems to programmers who include that header file into files of their own. As .cpp files are only included into projects and not directly into other files we have more freedom of choice for those. Within .cpp files (which Quincy provides when we create a new C++ source file) it is up to us to choose whether we use elaborated names (those that specify the context in which they are declared) or simple names. The `using` directive in this program allows us to use simple names (i.e. without the namespace qualifier) for things from the C++ Standard Library (`cout` instead of `std::cout`, `string` instead of `std::string`, etc.) that are declared in the header files we have included.

```
int main(){
```

We already know about that statement: it defines the starting point for a program and is followed by a block of statements whose execution makes our program.

```
cout << "Please type in your full name: ";
```

This statement prompts the user for some input.

```
string fullname;
```

This statement defines `fullname` as a variable referring to an object of type `(std::)string`. It is a declaration because the statement starts with the name of a type. It is also a definition because the default behavior of C++ is to create objects when variables are declared within a function.

```
getline(cin, fullname);
```

`getline()` is a free (non-member) function that has two reference parameters (i.e. it uses existing objects). In this case we are telling `std::getline()` to use `std::cin` to get data into `fullname`.

```
cout << "Hello " << fullname << ", I am pleased to meet you.\n";
```

Notice that we can use << to chain together data that we want to send to an output stream. In this case we sent two pieces of literal text and the contents of the `string` object referred to by `fullname`. The final `\n` is the `char` code that tells the compiler that we will want to go to the start of a new line after the rest has been done.

```
cout << "\nPress RETURN to end.";
cin.get();
```

You do not actually need those statements in programs that do not use a `playpen` object because they were only there to prevent the Playpen being closed before you were ready. This program uses the console window and Quincy will keep that open until you have finished.

ROBERTA

If you do not need them why did you put them in?

FRANCIS

It is a bit difficult to highlight that something is not needed unless it is there to start with. We have always needed them previously so I followed previous practice and then commented that this was a place where it was not needed.

So now we can send data to the screen and we can read a whole line (up to the next Return key) of input from the keyboard and store it in a `string` object. We can use the resources provided by the console I/O to decide when we have finished with the program.

Next we are going to see how we can get some names, sort them and then write them out to the screen in alphabetical order. To do that, we need something to contain the names.

Sequence Containers

The idea of a container is fairly straightforward. In everyday life we have tins of plums, packets of sugar lumps, shopping lists, dictionaries and so on. In computing terms there are two distinct types of container: sequence containers and associative containers. We will leave the latter until another time and focus on the former.

C++ containers are always restricted to a single type of content. We cannot have tins of mixed fruit, only tins of plums, of cherries, of peas, etc. Eventually we will come to understand both what that restriction means and how we can get round it. For now we will focus on a sequence container called `std::string` and a mechanism to create specialized containers, `std::vector`.

The defining property of a sequence in programming is that its members are in some, possibly arbitrary, order that can be rearranged. A shopping list is a sequence container because there is no single correct order for the items in it. A dictionary is not; one of the properties of a dictionary is the order of the words (it isn't a dictionary if the words are in an arbitrary order).

Because a `std::string` is a sequence container of `char` objects (the special type used for characters – symbols – in C++) we can rearrange the contents if we want to, there is no special correct order for the `char`s that make up a `std::string`. Of course if you jumble up the letters of a word or message the result is likely to be meaningless text, but it is fine as a sequence of `char`s. For now it will be enough to remember that a `std::string` is a sequence of `char`s.

Next let us turn to `std::vector`. This is a much more interesting kind of sequence container because of its versatility. `std::vector` has a lot of built-in behavior provided by operators and member functions. The C++ Standard Library also supplies a lot of behavior for sequences by way of various free functions that are declared in the `<algorithm>` header.

An important characteristic of `std::vector` is that it is only half of a type: we need to say what we are going to store in it to make it a full type. We can have a `std::vector<std::string>` (to collect `std::string` values) or `std::vector<int>` (to collect `int` values). There is one requirement for the type that completes a `std::vector`: its objects must be copyable. That means that we must be able to create new objects as copies of existing objects. Some types inherently cannot be copied (in real life, people cannot be copied and copying a credit card is almost certainly fraud, but there is no problem with giving someone your phone number). I will fill in details of `std::vector` as we need them.

Creating an alphabetical list of names

The problem we are going to tackle is to write a program that will collect some names, sort them into alphabetical order and then display the result on the screen. We will finally save the result in a file.

If we are going to collect some names we need an object (a suitable container) to keep them in until we are ready to use them. A `std::vector<std::string>` is a suitable type of object. That `<std::string>` bit tells the compiler what type of `std::vector` container we want: one for storing `std::string` objects. Notice that the combination of `std::vector` and `<std::string>` creates a type, no different in essence to `playpen`, `istream`, `int` or any other type. We will need an actual object of that type, so we will need to declare one:

```
std::vector<std::string> names;
```

The next thing we need to know is how to get data into the container. We will focus on a single mechanism for now, a member function (i.e. one that uses the object-dot-function syntax) called `push_back` which is used to copy an item into a `std::vector` object. Please note my use of the word "copy"; C++ containers work with copies. If you need to use originals, you would need to add another layer of complexity (called "indirection").

Time, I think, for a program. Create a new project in the Chapter 4 sub-directory. Now create a new C++ source file and type in the following:

```
#include <algorithm>
#include <iostream>
#include <string>
#include <vector>

using namespace std;

int main(){
  string const endinput("END");
  cout << "type '" << endinput << "' when there are no more names.\n\n";
  vector<string> names;
  for(int finished(0); finished != 1; ){
     cout << "type in the next name: ";
     string name;
     getline(cin, name);
     if(endinput == name)
           finished = 1;
     else
           names.push_back(name);
  }
  sort(names.begin(), names.end());
  for(int i(0); i != names.size(); ++i){
     cout << names[i] << '\n';
  }
}
```

Get this code working and then we will have a look at it.

Walkthrough

I think that most of the included headers are self-evident; the one that might not be is `<algorithm>`. That one declares some free functions from the C++ Standard Library that work with containers. In this case we want to be able to use the `sort()` function so we need to include the `algorithm` header so that the compiler will recognize `sort` when we use it.

The next feature of the code is that `string const endinput`. When we add `const` to a type we are telling the compiler that the variable we are declaring cannot be used to change its corresponding object. That allows the compiler to take some short cuts. It also makes the compiler check that we do not try to change the object. I need a fixed `string` object that we can compare with each input to `name` to see if we have finished with input.

In this particular instance I am simply creating a name for a string literal so that my code will be more intelligible. This is similar to using names for numbers to identify their meaning (e.g. such things as `red4`, `turquoise`, etc., used with `playpen`). I am avoiding magic values.

Now look at the `for`-loop. Remember that I mentioned that one or more of the parts of a `for`-loop could be blank? This is an example. I do not want to change `finished` from zero until I detect that I have finished inputting names. The second part of the mechanism is found in the `if-else` inside the controlled block of statements. If the program determines that the user has just typed END, it changes the value of `finished` to 1 which will be detected the next time that the condition part of the `for`-loop is executed.

It is usually considered poor programming to change a loop control variable inside the controlled statement/block of a `for`-loop. However, if the third expression of the `for`-statement is empty – as it is here – you know that you must check the controlled statement/block to see how the loop will end. In a later chapter you will learn about an alternative looping construct in C++ that is generally better for loops that end for reasons other than finishing a count. You will also learn of a better type (`bool`) that can be used where we simply want a choice between true and false.

Until the user types in END, the `push_back` behavior of `std::vector` is used to copy the current text in `name` to the back of the sequence called `names`. Eventually the user finishes typing in names and types in END. (We are trusting our user to get that right, if we were writing a serious program to be used unsupervised we would have to add a lot more polish.)

ROBERTA

Are you going to tell us how to add that polish later on?

FRANCIS

Not really. It is hard tedious work trying to anticipate all the stupid things naïve users do. Even highly experienced professional programmers miss things with the result that programs fail in surprising ways. We just have to recognize there is a problem and reduce it as far as possible as we go along.

Next we want to sort the collection of names. This is a place where the raw power of C++ shows through. All we need to do to sort a `std::vector<string>` into alphabetical order is to call the `std::sort` function with the data that states where to begin and where to end. What makes this simple is that every C++ Standard Library container type includes two member functions: `begin()` and `end()`. Later we will find that these return things are called "iterators", but we do not have to know about iterators or understand them in order to use them. If we want to sort an entire container we just call `std::sort()` and give it `begin()` and `end()` for the container; C++ will do all the rest.

We use two other features of std::vector. Every container knows how many items it contains and returns that value via its size() member function. std::vector supports subscripting (sometimes called indexing), as does std::string. The index starts from 0 so the first item in names is names[0], the next is names[1] and when we get to names.size() we have finished (think about the way we drew lines, which are basically containers of pixels). The last entry in names is names[names.size() - 1].

Does that program make sense now? I hope so, even if it took you a while to piece it all together. I also hope you were not waiting for me to tell you to experiment with the program. I hope you were impatient to try it out. I hope you also tried it to see what happened if you did not type in any names but straightaway typed in END. Yes, std::sort works for empty containers, just as our line drawing function worked for zero length lines.

Now for a quick demonstration that a string is a sequence container (of char) and behaves very like a std::vector. Try this program:

```
#include <algorithm>
#include <iostream>
#include <string>

using namespace std;

int main(){
  cout << "type in a sentence: ";
  string sentence;
  getline(cin, sentence);
  sort(sentence.begin(), sentence.end());
  for(int i(0); i != sentence.size(); ++i){
     cout << sentence[i];
  }
  cout << "\n\n";
}
```

It might not do exactly what you want because it places uppercase letters before lowercase ones. But this should demonstrate how C++ is designed for consistency of concept. There are places where that breaks down, but there are a surprising number of places where we can apply something we have learnt in one context to a different one.

Using files

I said when I outlined the problem at the beginning of this section that we would write the sorted names to a file. Perhaps others have suggested that this will be difficult; some people try to make easy things seem hard.

In order to write the names to a file we need to do several simple things. First we need to warn the compiler we will be streaming data to or from a file by including the <fstream> header. Next we need to create an ofstream object and connect it to the file we want to write to. Then we stream the data to the ofstream object (no different to streaming the data to cout).

Here is the amended earlier program with the additions in bold type face:

```
#include <algorithm>
#include <fstream>
#include <iostream>
```

```
#include <string>
#include <vector>

using namespace std;

int main(){
  vector<string> names;
  string const endinput("END");
  cout << "type " << endinput << " when there are no more names. \n\n";
  for(int finished(0); finished != 1; ){
     cout << "type in the next name: ";
     string fullname;
     getline(cin, fullname);
     if(endinput == fullname) finished = 1;
     else names.push_back(fullname);
  }
  sort(names.begin(), names.end());
  ofstream outfile("names.txt");
  for(int i(0); i != names.size(); ++i){
     cout << names[i] << '\n';
     outfile << names[i] << '\n';
  }
}
```

Three extra lines, though we might add a fourth – `outfile.close();` – if we want to close the file explicitly, however C++ provides automatic closure of files when a program ends. (Did you notice that I included the standard header files in alphabetical order? That is a good habit which I hope you will follow.)

After you have compiled and run this program you can look at the result by opening names.txt in Quincy (you will need to make Quincy list all the files in the Chapter 4 directory to see it – my thanks to Al Stevens, the author of Quincy, for modifying Quincy to make this work).

Those of you who have been thinking carefully about what I wrote earlier about making assumptions will have noticed that the above program assumes that `outfile` will manage to open a file called names.txt. What would happen if it fails (for example because such a file already exists but is marked by the operating system as read only)? The answer is that `outfile` will go into a fail state. That means that attempts to use it will do nothing. In the context of this program, that is safe: the worst that can happen is that I lose my data if it fails. In other circumstances, it could be serious and I will show you how to handle that problem later.

That is enough theory for now. It is time that you did some more practical work so here are a few program exercises for you to try.

Use your text editor to write a file of names, one per line. (Use Quincy to do this by creating a new ASCII text file – it is at the bottom of the list of new file types.) Make the last entry END and do not forget to complete that last line by pressing Return. Please do not use a word processor for this because they add all kinds of formatting information that will confuse your programs.

Now write a program that will read in that file, sort it and write the result out to another file. If you have understood how streams work in C++, this a fairly straightforward task.

[Hint available, see end of chapter]

EXERCISE 2

Write a program that will get a line of text from `std::cin` and count the number of times the letter "a" is used. Bonus credit if your program correctly handles "A" as well as "a".

[Hint available]

EXERCISE 3

There is a very simple free function that takes a `char` argument and returns the uppercase equivalent if the argument represents a lowercase letter. If the `char` argument represents anything else the argument is simple returned unchanged. The declaration of this function, provided in the `<cctype>` header is:

```
char toupper(char);
```

If you have understood the subscripting of a `std::string` object, you should be able to write a simple program that gets a line of text from the keyboard and then displays that text with all lowercase letters converted to uppercase.

[Hint available]

EXERCISE 4

In the early days of computing when the main output device was only capable of printing letters, creative programmers used to write programs that produced pictures entirely composed of letters and punctuation marks. Produce a simple picture on the screen in the same way.

[Hint available]

EXERCISE 5

Modify the program you wrote for Exercise 4 so that the user is prompted for the name of the file with the data in it. Use a `std::string` object called `filename` to capture the response.

You will need to use one of my utility functions to open the `std::ifstream` object with a file name that is stored in a `std::string` variable because the C++ Standard Library does not provide such a function (that is no great problem to experienced C++ programmers, just a minor irritant).

In my header `fgw_text.h` there are declarations for functions to open files for `ifstream` and `ofstream` objects given the filename in a `std::string` variable. The declarations are:

```
void open_ifstream(std::ifstream & input_file,
                   std::string const & filename);
```

```
void open_ofstream(std::ofstream & output_file,
             std::string const & filename);
```

These declarations are in namespace `fgw`; so you will need to add `fgw::` to the function name when you use it. (Or put a `using namespace fgw` directive after you have included the header file fgw_text.h.) A typical call would be:

```
fgw::open_ifstream(input, filename);
```

where `input` and `filename` have been suitably defined. You do not need to include fgwlib.a into the project because the definition is directly available in the header file. (I used a little trick called inline delegation which allows me to get away with putting a definition in a header file.)

Note

None of the above five exercises is as visually exciting as the things that you can do with our `playpen` graphics facilities. However, each one requires programming skill so I hope you will take up the challenge and not elect to skip them.

Getting ints from the Keyboard

As I wrote the above five exercises for you I found myself increasingly frustrated by the fact that there was no good way for you to get a number from an input stream. The problem is simply that we have to put too much trust on the source supplying an `int` value when we ask for one. The classic way of getting an `int` value from the keyboard is demonstrated by this very short program:

```
#include <iostream>

int main(){
  int i(0);
  cout << "type in a whole number: ";
  cin >> i;
  cout << "the square of " << i << " is " << i*i << '\n';
}
```

ROBERTA

I thought you told us not to use the >> operator without immediately checking that it had worked.

FRANCIS

Yes I did, but I have to show you why and to do that I need to break the rule. Actually the program still works safely it is just that `i` will remain 0 if the user gives bad input.

I hope by now that your first instinct has been to create a project, compile and run that program and then test it to see how it behaves when you type in invalid data. If you have not already done that, please do so and get used to always testing code. That way you build up experience with both success and failure.

Now let us create a little function that will handle the problem. Note that this is just one of numerous alternatives, but we do not need to worry much about efficiency or speed because input from the keyboard is unbelievably slow in computer terms.

```
#include <iostream>
#include <string>
using namespace std;

int getint() {
  for(;;) {
     int value;
     cin >> value;
     if(cin.fail()) {            // if cin >> failed?
        cin.clear();             // reset cin...
        string garbage;
        getline(cin, garbage); // ...and ignore whole line
        cout << "\nThat was not a whole number, try again.\n";
     }
     else {
        return value;
     }
  }
}
```

It reminds me of using a fuse. `cin.fail()` inspects the state of the input stream and if it has failed (i.e. the fuse has tripped) it tells us and we reset it (that is what `cin.clear()` does). Having done that, `cin` will work but it still has garbage blocking it (whatever the user typed that was not a number) and so we just read it in and throw it away. Now we ask the user to try again.

If `cin` is still working then the user has given us what we asked for and we can carry on. Notice that we have a "for ever" loop because the first three elements of the `for`-statement are empty. We get out by returning from the function.

The `getint()` function enables us to rewrite the program more safely. Put the `getint()` function in your utilities files then try the following source code:

```
int main(){
  int i;
  cout << "type in a whole number: ";
  i = getint();
  cout << "the square of " << i << " is " << i*i << '\n';
  cout << "Press RETURN";
  cin.get();
}
```

Handling the Unexpected

`getint()` works fine if we are getting input from the keyboard because we know we have a user who can be badgered into providing what we need. In practice we might count the failures and only allow so many before we assume that the keyboard is not being managed by an intelligent being – perhaps your cat is experimenting with programming. Limiting tries is an extra refinement that we can leave for now.

Note that there is nothing special about incorrect input from a keyboard because we know that even the most careful human being will make mistakes from time to time. But what about erroneous data from a file? There is no point in trying to handle that with retries: something is wrong and we do not expect files to contain wrong information. Well even if we do, there is no general solution to correct it. All we can do is detect the error and shout for help. C++ provides a mechanism for that, **exceptions**. There is a lot of detailed refinement to the system but we are going to deal with the bare bones for now.

The first step is to wrap up source code from which an exception (a shout for help) may come. We call that wrapper a `try`-block. The idea being that your program tries the code in the expectation it will work as planned but prepares to catch problems.

Much later we will see that specific kinds of problem can be caught and handled in whatever way the programmer chooses. For now we are going to deal with the catch everything mechanism which is written as `catch(...){}`. The action on catching a problem is placed in the braces.

The third part of the mechanism is called "throwing an exception" and happens where a problem is detected. An exception can be any object that can be copied but is usually an object of a type designed for signalling a problem or exception.

The following code uses a very simple exception mechanism to prevent a program continuing when a file has been corrupted (does not contain the expected data):

```
int getint(istream & source) {
  int temp;
  source >> temp;
  if(source.fail()){            // test source worked
     source.clear();  // reset the source stream
     cerr << "Corrupted data stream accessed in getint.\n";
     throw fgw::problem("Corrupted data stream.");
  }
  else return temp;
}
```

If `temp` successfully obtains a value from the input stream it will be copied back as the return value from the function. However, if it fails the message `"Corrupted data stream accessed in getint."` is sent to the error output stream (remember that that defaults to the screen). A similar message is wrapped up into a nameless `fgw::problem` object (a simple type provided in my fgw_text.h header file to report problems via the exception mechanism) that is thrown to warn the part of the program that was expecting `getint` to return a number that it couldn't.

Before I go on, I should clarify how it is that I can use the same function name for this form of getting an `int` as I did for the case where I just wanted to get one from `cin` and was willing to wait until the user satisfied my need. C++ allows us to reuse function names as long as either the context is different (for example, in a different `namespace`) or the types of the parameters are different. That is a little like reusing the name "Francis" as long as it is in a different family or there is some other way of distinguishing (such as senior and junior).

However `int getint(istream & input)` is *not* the same function as `int getint()` which means that it needs its own declaration in the relevant header file (your utilities file). It is only when the compiler can see these different declarations of functions that share a name (but have different parameter lists) that it knows that it will have to choose between them when the name is used. It chooses on the basis of which one best matches the provided data.

In this case, the first version of `getint` has an empty parameter list and the second form has a single `istream &` parameter. That means that the compiler can tell which I want when I call `getint` by whether I provide any data. If I do, it will try to call the second form and, if I do not, it will use the first one. This mechanism is called overloading and is used a lot in C++. Experienced programmers largely confine the use of overloading to cases where there are different ways to achieve the same objective. Our use of `getint` is an example of sound use of overloading. In both cases we want to get an `int` value. In one case we can check the data and ask for it again if it is inappropriate. In the other cases we know we cannot ask again so we need to report the problem for the program to deal with it elsewhere.

Now let us look at that simple program, but with the data coming from a file stream rather than the keyboard.

```
#include "fgw_text.h"
#include <fstream>
#include <iostream>

using namespace fgw;
using namespace std;

int main(){
  try{
     ifstream source("data.txt");
     if(source.fail()) {
        cerr << "Failed to open data.txt.\n";
        throw problem("data.txt failed to open.");
     }
     int i(getint(source));
     cout << "the square of " << i << " is " << i*i << '\n';
  }
  catch(...){
     cerr << "***Something went wrong.***\n";
  }
}
```

The `try` followed by an open brace tells the compiler that the source code up to the corresponding close brace may fail with an exception. In this case there are two points of failure: the file called data.txt may fail to open (perhaps it does not exist) or it may open and become the source of data for `input` but it might not contain the data we need (an `int` value).

Because I want to keep things simple, if there is a failure I just want to tidy up and end the program. I am not interested in what went wrong. Of course in serious programs I will probably want to distinguish the different kinds of failure and take different actions.

For now I want you to develop good habits. You need to get in the habit of checking for problems that could stop your programs from working as intended and take some form of action. The nice thing about C++ (not shared by all programming languages) is that we can report a problem when it is detected and *throw* it to the place where we can handle it. We separate detection of problems from solving them. This is an important concept when we build programs out of functions (that call functions, that themselves call functions, etc.). The writer of a function often does not know what the caller will want to do when things go wrong. Throwing and catching exceptions allows the responsibility to be handed over from the place where it can be detected to the place where it will be dealt with.

We will see more about exceptions as we progress but for now I want you to get into the habit of wrapping the source code of `main` into a `try`-block. After that block I just want you to `catch(...)` and issue a message like the one in my example. Later on we will do more. Even if you are not convinced you fully understand this, trust me and do it anyway. Develop good programming habits now and you will not have to unlearn bad habits later.

Try the above program. When it compiles and executes it should give you an error message and then end, unless you have provided a file called data.txt and put a number at the beginning of it. Try the program with and without an available data.txt file. Finally try it with a data.txt file that does not start with a number.

EXERCISE 6

Use your text editor (Quincy will do fine) to create a file of whole numbers. Do not use any punctuation; just separate the numbers with spaces or with newlines (either will work). Make 0 the last number in the file.

Now write a program that will open the file, read in the numbers one by one and display each number with its square (number multiplied by itself) and cube (the square of the number multiplied by the number, so the cube of 2 is four times two, which is eight) on the screen, one line of output for each number in the file. Stop when the number read in from the file is zero.

CHALLENGING

EXERCISE 7

Use a suitable sequence container to store all the numbers from the file in Exercise 6. Find the arithmetic mean of the numbers (the total divided by the number of items, frequently called the average) and display the answer on the screen. Now calculate and display the median of the collection of numbers. The median is the middle number when they are arranged in order of size. Strictly speaking if there is no single middle item (because you have an even number of items) it is the average of the middle two.

CHALLENGING

EXERCISE 8

Use the numbers in the file you created for Exercise 6 as data for a bar chart. What I want is for you to create a display with bars that represent the numbers in the file. For example if the first three numbers in the file are 13, 5, 9, I want three horizontal bars of 13 units, 5 units and 9 units in length.

You can write a program that creates the bars from repeated symbols ("*" is often used for this) or you can use the graphics resources of `playpen`.

If you feel up for a challenge, ensure your program can deal with negative numbers with bars going to the left.

Finally attempt the same task using asterisks but in vertical columns. See if you can arrange that the positive values are represented by upward columns and negative ones with downward columns.

Note that I do not expect readers to complete all parts of Exercise 8. It isn't that you need fancy programming, but you need to see how to use the tools you have to achieve the objective. That is what programming is about and it takes a lot of practice to achieve simple programs for tasks such as the above. Sometimes I will give you a tough exercise as a challenge to the very brightest of my readers.

ROBERTA'S COMMENTS

I didn't have any problems with the alphabetical names program other than my usual typing of commas instead of arrows (angle brackets). But when I followed the instructions to send the names to a file I was initially disappointed that it didn't seem to do anything. What I didn't realize is that the program actually creates a file called names.txt in the same directory in Quincy. I have added some more comments about the exercises but asked Francis to put them with the solutions.

Exercise 1

You will need to use an `ifstream` object to get data in. That object will need to open the file of names you created and so will need to know what that file is called.

Exercise 2

Roberta came up with a very unconventional solution to this problem (see Solutions) but I expect your answer to set up an `int` that is initialized to zero. Then it can be incremented each time you identify the required letter.

Exercise 3

If name is a `std::string`, then `name[0] = "H";` will replace the first symbol of `name` with an H. For example, if `name` had contained "cowl" it will now contain "Howl".

Exercise 4

You could use your text editor to create a picture from letters and symbols and then write a program that reads the file, line by line, into a string and displays the result on the screen. There are other ways of achieving an answer. Try to come up with alternative solutions.

SOLUTIONS TO EXERCISES

Exercise 1

```
int main(){
  string const endinput("END");
  vector<string> names;
  ifstream source("namefile.txt");
  for(int i(0); i != 1; ){
     string fullname;
     getline(source, fullname);
     if(endinput == fullname) i = 1;
     else names.push_back(fullname);
  }
```

SOLUTIONS TO EXERCISES

```
    sort(names.begin(), names.end());
    ofstream outfile("names.txt");
    for(int i(0); i != names.size(); ++i){
        cout << names[i] << '\n';
        outfile << names[i] << '\n';
    }
}
```

ROBERTA

I first decided to make sure I had successfully got the file by sending the output to the screen before continuing. Perhaps I should have more faith in myself but I am beginning to learn that it is better to test early and often.

Exercise 2

Roberta's solution

```
int main (){
    cout << "type in a sentence. \n";
    string sentence;
    vector<string> letter_a;
    getline(cin, sentence);
    for(int i(0); i != sentence.size(); ++i){
        if(sentence[i] == 'a'){
            letter_a.push_back("a");
        }
        else if(sentence[i] == 'A'){
            letter_a.push_back("A");
        }
    }
    cout << "there are " << letter_a.size() << " 'a's in '"
            << sentence << "'\n";
}
```

This program exhibits a programmer's turn of mind. She took what she knew and created a correct program that would solve the problem. It does not matter that it is not the way that an experienced programmer would have done it.

One of my main reasons for sharing her solution with you is that it shows how much variety there can be in coming up with successful programs.

SOLUTIONS TO EXERCISES

My solution

```
int main (){
  cout << "type in a sentence. \n";
  string sentence;
  int count_of_a;
  getline(cin, sentence);
  for(int i(0); i != sentence.size(); ++i){
     if(sentence[i] == 'a'){
        ++count_of_a;
     }
     else if(sentence[i] == 'A'){
        ++count_of_a;
     }
  }
  cout << "there are " << count_of_a << " 'a's in '"
          << sentence << "'\n";
}
```

Actually that is not exactly what I wrote first time round but Roberta's basic program was so good that I just edited it to demonstrate the solution I was expecting.

ROBERTA

As you can see Francis was rather amused at my solution to Exercise 2. He had assumed that I would use an `int` to count but in the earlier draft of this chapter, he had not included any information about `char`s and `int`s so my solution was, as far as I was concerned, the only possible solution.

Perhaps because he made such a big thing of my solution I have become very fond of vectors. I seem to use them rather a lot – my current philosophy of programming is "when in doubt use a vector."

Exercise 3

```
int main (){
  cout << "type in a sentence. \n";
  string sentence;
  getline(cin, sentence);
  for(int i(0); i != sentence.size(); ++i){
     sentence[i] = toupper(sentence[i]);
     }
  }
  cout << sentence << '\n';
}
```

SOLUTIONS TO EXERCISES

ROBERTA

I couldn't do this at first because I misread the instructions and didn't really understand much about functions at the time. Once I realized that I had to call the function whose name was toupper, it worked. (I didn't have the benefit of solutions to help me at that time.)

Exercises 4 and 5

I am not giving solutions to these. However you do have to be careful if you want to use a "\" in your picture because of its special significance as an escape character in C++. Which means that for every backslash you want displayed you will have to use two in your source code.

ROBERTA

I couldn't see the point of Exercise 4 at the time but when I came to write a program for my own use later I found that it was useful after all.

Exercise 6

```
int main(){
  try{
     ifstream source("numbers.txt");
     if(source.fail()) {
        cerr << "Failed to open numbers.txt.\n";
        throw problem("numbers.txt failed to open.");
     }
     for (int finished(0); finished != 1;){
        int i(getint(source));
        if(i == 0){
           finished = 1;
        ]
        else {
           cout << i << " " << i*i << " " << i*i*i << '\n';
        }
     }
  }
  catch(...){
     cerr << "***Something went wrong.***\n";
  }
}
```

SOLUTIONS TO EXERCISES

ROBERTA

For various reasons I couldn't get *getint(istream & source)* to work so I continued with the exercises using *getint()*. I didn't seem to have any problem with the exercise but when I added the code for Exercises 7 and 8 to the file the resulting answers were out by 1 each time. The problem was in this piece of code:

```
for(int stop( 0); i != 1; ){
   int i(getint());
   if(stop == i) stop = 1;
   else cout << "the square of  " << i << " is "
      << i*i << ", and the cube is  "<< i*i*i << '\n';
   numbers.push_back(i);
}
```

Actually this is not my original code. When I came to add my comments to the book I was rather embarrassed by my earlier attempts.

*When Francis checked my answers, he spotted the problem straight away. In Exercise 6 I should have enclosed the two expressions after **else** in curly braces.*

```
else {
   cout ... ;
   numbers.push_back[i];
}
```

ROBERTA

I learnt quite a lot from this mistake not least the fact that an error early in the code that does not show up immediately can affect the program later. Because the first exercise worked, I assumed it was correct.

Exercise 7

```
int main(){
  try{
     ifstream source("numbers.txt");
     if(source.fail()) {
        cerr << "Failed to open numbers.txt.\n";
        throw problem("numbers.txt failed to open.");
     }
     vector<int> numbers;
```

SOLUTIONS TO EXERCISES

```
    for(int finished(0); finished != 1;){
      int number(getint(source));
      if(number == 0){
        finished = 1;
      }
      else {
        numbers.push_back(number);
      }
    }
    int total(0);
    for(int i(0); i != numbers.size(); ++i){
      total = total + numbers[i];
    }
    cout << "the mean is " << total/numbers.size() << '\n';
    int middle(numbers.size()/2);
    cout << "the median is ";
    if(middle*2 == numbers.size()){
      cout << (numbers[middle-1] + numbers[middle])/2
           << '\n';
    }
    else {
      cout << numbers[middle] << '\n';
    }
  }
  catch(...){
    cerr << "***Something went wrong.***\n";
  }
}
```

There are several issues with this program (which is by far the hardest that I have asked you to do so far). The first is that you do not yet know how to use decimal fractions so all your arithmetic is integer arithmetic. The main significance is that divisions will always round down to a whole number.

I made use of this when working out the median because I needed a way to discover if I was dealing with an odd or even number of numbers. If `numbers.size()` is even then twice half of it will get me back where I started. If it is an odd number twice half of it will be one less than what I started with because of the rounding loss.

The rest of the program is just careful attention to detail such as remembering to sort the numbers before calculating the median.

Exercise 8

```
int main(){
  try{
    ifstream source("numbers.txt");
    if(source.fail()) {
      cerr << "Failed to open numbers.txt.\n";
      throw problem("numbers.txt failed to open.");
```

SOLUTIONS TO EXERCISES

```
      }
      int const max_neg(-40);
      for(int finished(0); finished != 1;){
         int const number(getint(source));
         if(number == 0){
            finished = 1;
         }
         else {
            int spaces(40);
            int stars(0);
// calculate case where input is negative
            if(number < 0){
               if(number < max_neg)
                     throw fgw::problem("number out of range.");
               spaces = spaces + number;
               stars = -number;
            }
            else {
               stars = number;
            }
            for(int i(0); i != spaces; ++i){
               cout << " ";
            }
            for(int i(0); i != stars; ++i){
               cout << "*";
            }
            cout << '\n';
         }
      }
   }
   catch(...){
      cerr << "***Something went wrong.***\n";
   }
}
```

Look at the definition of `max_neg` and its use later on. Try to decide why it is there. What assumption am I avoiding with it?

The above program is far from complete because it makes assumptions about the range of input values. I am giving you this much code as a starter if you have found the exercise difficult. Work through my code and then start adding some polish. For example you could write a function to output `n` repeats of a `char` and use it instead of some of those inner `for`-loops. Indeed you should start to suspect nested loops and wonder if the inner ones should be converted into functions, not least because the function names should help make the code more readable. It isn't just magic values that we should be avoiding; we should take the opportunities provided by C++ to attach names to processes.

Summary

Key programming concepts

- Programming uses the concept of data streams: flows of data from one place to another. A stream that provides data is a source and one that stores data is a sink.
- The commonest streams in elementary programming are the keyboard as a source and the monitor screen as a destination.
- Files are common sources and sinks for data. Because files can both provide and store data they can be connected to a program through bi-directional streams (ones that allow data to flow both ways).
- Streams provide the ability to handle data flows largely independently of the nature of the source or sink.
- Stream types may support special facilities determined by their specific nature. For example a file stream will include facilities to connect it to a specific file by opening the file.
- Programs handle the concept of text by a low-level concept of a single character (symbol) and a higher level concept of a string of characters. The character concept has to include non-printing characters such as a carriage return and a tab.
- Programming has the concept of a container that can hold zero (an empty container) or more objects. A string is a container of characters. There are two main groups of containers: in an associative container the order of the contained objects is a property of the container; in a sequence container the order of the objects is not a property.
- Sequence containers can be sorted. Associative containers cannot be sorted because their internal order is determined by the container.
- Programs need to handle unexpected events such as incorrect data or missing peripherals.

C++ checklist

- In this book the concept of a character is provided by the C++ `char` type.
- C++ has a type called `std::string` that matches the string programming concept and is a sequence container of `char`.
- `std::vector` is a C++ sequence container. The type of the object contained in a `std::vector` must be supplied to make a complete data type. For example we can define a variable as a vector<int> (a container of `int`), a vector<string> (a container of `string`) or even vector< playpen> (a container of `playpen`).
- All C++ sequence containers have some identically named member functions. In this chapter we used `begin()`, `end()` and `size()`.
- The `begin()` and `end()` member functions are used to locate the first object and just beyond the last object. If `begin() == end()`, the container is empty.
- The `size()` member function reports the number of objects in a container.
- Objects in `string` and `vector` can be located with the subscript (index) operator, `[]`. E.g. if `message` is a `string`, then `message[0]` is the first `char`.
- The C++ sequence containers have a member function, `push_back()`, which places a copy of its parameter at the end of the container.
- `sort()` is one of more than fifty free functions provided by the C++ Standard Library for use with containers. The <algorithm> header provides the declarations of all the available free functions that can be applied to C++ containers.
- C++ provides a mechanism to handle problems detected at the execution time of a program. This mechanism is called exception handling and is provided by a throw/catch mechanism. Code that detects a problem can use `throw` to communicate the problem to somewhere else in the program that specifies that it is willing to `catch` and deal with the problem.

- Regions of code that may result in a throw of an exception are encapsulated into a block (compound statement) preceded by the keyword `try`.
- C++ allows two or more functions in the same scope to have the same name as long as there is a difference in the parameter types. Such sets of functions sharing a name are called ''overloaded functions''.
- C++ provides the concept of named contexts for declarations, called ''namespaces''.
- The `fail()` member function of both `istream` and `ostream` (input and output streams) tests whether the named stream object has failed to provide useable data. For example `if(cin.fail())` deals with the case that you did not get any data the last time you used `cin`.

Extensions checklist

- The fgw_text.h header includes declarations of a number of elements of my library that are unrelated to Playpen.
- fgw_text.h provides declarations of two functions to deal with opening and connecting a file to an `ifstream` or `ofstream` variable which allows you to use a `std::string` to contain the name of the file to be opened (connected to) the stream object.

```
void open_ifstream(std::ifstream & input_file,
                   std::string const & filename);
void open_ofstream(std::ofstream & output_file,
                   std::string const & filename);
```

CHAPTER 5

You Can Create a Type

This chapter and the next were originally one but it grew to be an unreasonable size. This chapter now focuses on creating **user-defined types**. The major objective is to help you understand more about what a type is by following through the process of creating one. I will also introduce the basic floating-point type (`double`) used in C++.

The type I have chosen (one that represents a point on a two-dimensional plane) requires some mathematical expertise. This may make it harder for some readers to follow the fine detail but it makes it a good example of encapsulating specialist knowledge. That encapsulation of knowledge empowers people who lack it because they can use the type without having to know how it works; they only have to know what it does.

On Not Being Underrated

Many years ago I met and became a friend of Colin Mortlock who was an outstanding Warden of Oxford's outdoor pursuits center in Wales. He was considered ''mad'' by most other wardens of outdoor centers because he allowed, for example, inexperienced young people to canoe on white water in midwinter. He believes that young people have tremendous abilities that they should be encouraged to exercise. He also recognizes that young people often lack wisdom and a sense of judgment. He once told me of an episode where he was in charge of a group of 16-year-olds who had elected to specialize in white water canoeing for the second week of a two-week visit. Their first experience of canoeing had been a single day the previous week.

On the third day of the ''specialist'' course Colin wanted this group of eight youths to come down a fairly severe rapid on the river Wye. Because they lacked the experience to read the water, he needed to show them the route. Because he was worried about the discipline of the group he went down backwards so that he could keep an eye on them.

He was amazed that they promptly started to canoe the rapid backwards; that illustrates their lack of judgment. Seven of the eight completed the task successfully (the eighth capsized but safely recovered); that illustrates the ability of the young to achieve having been given guidance. That left Colin with the task of ensuring they all understood how important the guidance was to their success.

While programming is not (normally) physically dangerous there is an element of judgment that runs alongside pure skill. It is the choice of route that is hard even when you have the basic techniques. A way to achieve the wisdom to choose a good solution is seeing someone with more expertise tackle a programming task.

In this chapter I want you walk with me on the wild side of programming. I will show you the way. At the end I will not expect you to be able to go and do likewise, but I do expect you to have deepened your understanding of what programming is about and why it can give us so much pleasure.

Designing a Type

We spent time in Chapter 3 looking at designing a function. We had to think about how the function would be used, what we would need to provide and how we should make it work. Designing a type is a similar process.

Type design depends on the language that you are using. Some languages are extraordinarily restrictive; others allow complete freedom to the programmer. C++ sits squarely in the middle; the amount of restriction is left to the type designer to decide.

For example, C++ allows us to use an existing type by another name. That places the burden for correct use entirely on the shoulders of the user. If I recycle the `int` type as a `year` type, nothing other than personal discipline prevents the user from multiplying two years together. The result is meaningless but the language will allow it.

The tool for this crude mechanism of creating new names for existing types is a `typedef`. We will find that, used sensibly, it allows us to focus on the critical aspects of our programming without cluttering our code with extraneous verbiage. However we should generally limit ourselves to using `typedef` when the new type we want has all the behavior of the type being used. We will see a use for `typedef` in the next chapter. When we come to use it I will go into the details of how to do so.

There are two major points of concern when we start designing a type: what we can do with the type and how we store the information that objects of that type will contain. We call that information **the state of an object**.

To try to understand the issues of type design let us consider some of the things that would arise if we were designing a type to represent dates.

The date concept

The fundamental idea of a data type in programming is the combination of data and appropriate behavior. For example think about the concept of a date. We know that dates provide a way of locating events in time. We also know that a particular day can be identified in many different ways. For example Christmas Day 2002 describes a date that most Europeans might represent by 25/12/2002, whilst those across the Atlantic would write 12/25/2002. Perhaps you also know that the Japanese write dates in ISO Standard format and so would write 2002/12/25. You are less likely to know that that same date would be written as 20 Shawwal 1423 by a Moslem or 22/11 Rén-Wü in the Chinese calendar. The Julian Day 2452634 starts at noon on that day.

Even more confusing is that some terms such as New Year's Day identify different days according to which calendar you are using (there are at least eight calendars in common use round the World and most of them have fewer than 365 days in a normal year). What I am trying to highlight here is that the raw data has to be represented in some way. There can be many reasonable representations for the same date; the one we choose depends on what we want to achieve.

Dates also have behavior. We can subtract one date from another and get an answer as a number of days (note that it is not a date and it can reasonably be represented by an `int`). That answer should not depend on the representation we are using to identify a day. We also expect to be able to add or subtract a whole number (`int`) to/from a date and get another date as the answer. However we do not expect to be able to add two dates together, multiply dates by anything or divide a date by a number. In other words we have a clear understanding of the behavior of dates: what we can do with them and to them; what we can ask of them and what we can tell them. Largely that behavior is independent of the way we choose to represent a date.

There is also a body of optional behavior whose inclusion would depend on our reason for designing a date type. Whether we support asking for a date in, for example, the Persian Astronomical Calendar (used in Afghanistan) would depend on our objectives.

The concept of a date is independent of its representation but is strongly bound to its behavior. Modern computing languages often provide facilities whereby the programmer can provide kinds of data that have strictly limited behavior that is de-coupled from the internal representation. This combination of data and behavior is what we generally mean by a type (often called an "abstract data type"). In other words, to use a type we need to know what it can do but, generally, do not need to know how it is done. Only the type designer needs to worry about the latter.

Abstract data types and C++

C++ provides a mechanism whereby we can separate the internal representation and management of data from its behavior and external representation. We can store the information internally in any way we find useful (a common internal representation for dates is using a Julian Day where day 1 is Monday January 1, 4714 BC in the Julian Calendar). We can then make that data available in any form we choose to supply.

Because of the large number of representations and fiddly details such as when a new day starts (midnight, dawn, noon, sunset, etc.), I am not going to take you through implementing a date type. Instead we are going to tackle a type that will be useful for extending our graphics capabilities. We will then explore some of the ways it can be used and the extensions that we can add with free functions to help our graphics programming.

The double Type

In order to implement our two-dimensional point type we will need the type that C++ provides for floating point data. It is a fundamental type called a `double` (a name derived from "double precision floating point number"). `double` is a keyword so Quincy will display it in blue. An immense range of decimal numbers to a limited (but very high) accuracy can be used as `double` values. I am not going to worry about exactly what that range is unless and until I use it in a context where it matters.

The `double` type supports all the normal arithmetic operators that we might expect (+, -, * and /) as well as a number of C++ extended operators (see Appendix B on the CD). Note that the way the arithmetic operators behave depends on the types of the values they are being applied to. For example, 3/2 is 1 (`int` values use whole number arithmetic) but 3.0/2, 3/2.0 and 3.0/2.0 are all 1.5 because as soon as a decimal point is involved the compiler switches to floating-point (decimal) arithmetic.

The limited accuracy of a `double` has implications. Some simple fractions, for example, one-fifth, cannot be exactly represented in the binary code used by computers (just as one-third cannot be exactly represented in decimal notation). That means that a `double` value will often be an approximation (a very good one) of an exact value but it might not be exactly that value.

An exact floating-point value can have more than one close approximation in terms of a `double`. Which approximation we get can depend on the calculations that led to the result. This is important because it impacts on the concept of equality. If we want to compare two `double` values we must decide how nearly equal will do for our purposes or else be prepared for surprises. In general, do not compare `double` values for equality; compare them in some other way such as being almost equal (e.g. take one from the other and check that the result is relatively very small).

I/O for double objects

Now you have been introduced to `double` we need to consider streaming a `double` value to and from an appropriate stream object.

Sending a `double` to an output stream (`ostream` object) is straightforward. Treat it exactly as you did an `int`. Later you will find there are some refinements available to determine whether output is in common format (e.g. 212.345) or in the exponential format (2.12345e2) that is often used by mathematicians, scientists and engineers. There are also mechanisms to determine how many figures are displayed after the decimal point. At this stage those are of no importance to us, just note that there is more than I write here. We will go into further detail if and when you need it. Here is a simple example:

```
double value(12.34);
cout << value << '\n';
```

This code results in 12.34 being displayed in your console window. If you use a file stream, that data will be stored in the file attached to the stream:

```
ofstream decimaldata(ddata.txt);
if(decimaldata.fail()){
  throw problem("problem with file");
}
decimaldata << value << '\n'
```

This code saves the value of `value` (12.34, unless we changed it) at the start of the file ddata.txt. In other words, apart from using a different type, everything behaves the way it did for `int`. The same will largely be true of other fundamental types. I will try to remember to draw your attention to any exceptions as and when they turn up.

We will have exactly the same problem for input that we had with `int`. If we have a human being in the circuit they may make mistakes and if we have a file (or other input stream that does not allow retries) it may be corrupted. That means we cannot safely use the >> operator that C++ provides without wrapping it up. We need to do what we did for `int` with `getint` (both forms), but this time for a `double` by carefully replacing all the references to `int` with `double`.

Try writing a `getdouble()` function for yourself to increase your understanding of the problem of getting input. Remember to test that your new code works.

Avoiding repetition

Remember how much programmers hate repeating themselves? Surely as you wrote the `getdouble()` function for Task 7 you had an uncomfortable feeling of repeating yourself. The only difference between `getdouble()` and `getint()` is that one extracts and returns a `double` and the other extracts and returns an `int`.

There are many other types, both fundamental and user-defined, and most of them are going to face the problem of extracting data from an input stream. Most of them will support a version of the >> operator and will have almost the same problem as we have tackled for `int` and `double`; fallible human beings and corrupted files.

It is far too early in your programming life to teach you how to use the C++ mechanism (called templates) to solve this problem. However it is very like the mechanism we used for dealing with vector containers of different types, but this time we are going to do it for functions. Well strictly speaking, I have done it and you get to use it.

In fgw_text.h there is a set of overloaded function templates for extracting data from an input stream. They are all variations of `read<>()`. You have to complete the function name by saying what type you want to get in the angle brackets. The parameter list determines where and how the data will be extracted. The three versions are:

`fgw::read<>(std::string)` in which the caller (i.e. the calling function) provides a prompt and the data is extracted from `std::cin`.
`fgw::read<>()` which uses a default prompt of `":"` and gets the data from `std::cin`.
`fgw::read<>(std::istream)` which extracts the data from the specified stream.

The first two versions allow three tries before throwing an `fgw::bad_input` exception. The third version throws an `fgw::bad_input` exception immediately it fails on the basis that it is too dangerous to continue processing a general input stream if it is delivering bad data.

When you use one of the `read` functions you have to put the required type in the angle brackets. So, for example:

```
int i(0);
i = fgw::read<int>("Please type in a whole number");
```

results in the display of the message ''Please type in a whole number'', followed by an attempt to get an `int` value from `cin`. If the attempt fails you will get a message telling you that the data was wrong followed by a repeat of the prompt. If it fails three times an exception is thrown.

One advantage of using the `read<>` functions is that you can initialize a variable directly with the required value. That is, instead of writing:

```
double d;
// do something to get the value for d
```

we can write something such as:

```
double d(read<double>("What is your weight in kilograms? : "));
```

Even better is that we can use the `read<>` functions to initialize immutable data, i.e. data that is fixed and must not be changed after it has been initialized. For example:

```
int const yob(read<int>("What year were you born? : "));
```

The rules of C++ require that `const` qualified variables must be initialized (given a value) in the process of defining them. The more traditional methods for obtaining data from input fall foul of that requirement and make it difficult to declare `const` variables (yes I know that is a weird combination, giving us a variable that must not change). The `read<>` mechanism quietly solves that problem.

Creating a Two-Dimensional Point Type

I want to be able to work with lines and shapes. Mathematically lines are made up of points. The mathematical concept of a point is not very practical in the context of computer graphics because it has no size. On the other hand, our graphics representation in a Playpen has a problem because it is made of pixels and we can only have an exact number of pixels, they are the ''atoms'' of our graphics system. We deal with pixels as discrete, indivisible elements. Discrete elements are not very good tools for representing something that is continuous such as a mathematical plane. We need a compromise that will allow us to do accurate mathematical calculations whose results can be used to determine the details of what we draw.

First I need to bring you up to strength on some domain knowledge. Even if you feel confident of your understanding of coordinate systems you will probably benefit from a quick reminder. If these are strange to you, or caused you sleepless nights when you were learning about them at school, do not worry, read the following and then relax and let me do the work.

Coordinate systems

Mathematicians have a concept of a plane that extends forever in all directions. They locate positions on that plane by choosing some special point that they call the "origin" and a primary direction, which is normally called the "x-axis". You can identify all other points on the plane by imagining a line drawn from the origin to the point and recording two pieces of information; the length and direction of that line. Conventionally the direction is measured as a rotation anticlockwise from the primary direction. This way of identifying points on a plane is called "polar coordinates".

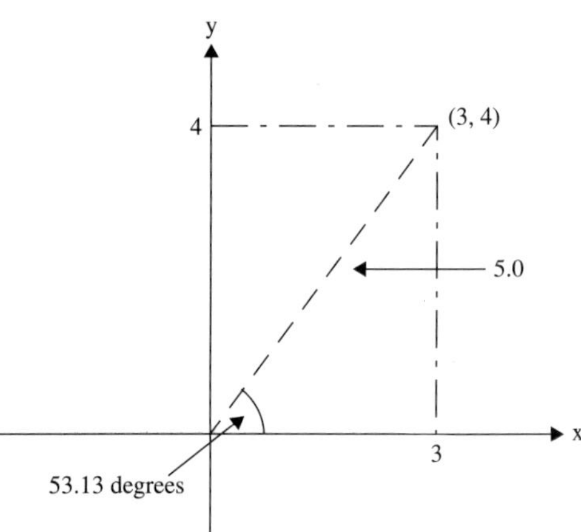

The distance from the origin is called the "modulus" and the direction is referred to as the "argument". Each pair of numbers – a modulus and an argument – defines a unique location on a plane. By convention we give the modulus first and the argument second.

There is a second way of locating a point that is attributed to Descartes and so is called "Cartesian coordinates". This is the system you probably learnt in school. We add a secondary direction through the origin, called the "y-axis". The y-axis is at right angles to the x-axis. A point is located by giving its distance from the y-axis (to the right is positive, to the left is negative) followed by its distance from the x-axis (up is positive, down is negative). This diagram illustrates the two methods for locating a point on the plane.

The point (3, 4) in Cartesian coordinates is the same as the point (5, 53.13 . . .°). The dots represent the fact that the angle is not exactly 53.13°.

Measuring angles

This is another issue where domain knowledge rears its head. Most of us expect to measure angles in degrees. However mathematicians use an entirely different mechanism called radian measure. It happens that radian measure works well with fundamental mathematical formulae for computing various mathematical values. Perhaps that was a major motive for making radian measure the standard way of representing angles in computing. For example a right angle is 90° in our common terms, but in radians it comes to approximately 1.5708 (or $\pi/2$, for the mathematicians among my readers).

For the convenience of those who prefer to stick with the measurement with which they are familiar I have provided two small utility functions to do the conversions between radian measure and degrees. You will find them in fgw_text.h.

The full names of the two functions are `fgw::degrees` and `fgw::radians`. Their use should be pretty straightforward. For example, if you write `fgw::radians(90)` it should return the value of 90° in radian measure, i.e. roughly 1.5708. If you write `fgw::degrees(1.5)` you should get a number slightly less than 90 which is the number of degrees that is equivalent to 1.5 in radian measure.

Their declarations in `namespace fgw` are:

```
double degrees(double radians); // convert radians to degrees
double radians(double degrees); // convert degrees to radians
```

Note that inside a namespace block the qualification is unnecessary. When we are outside the `fgw` namespace we have to identify the `degrees()` and `radians()` functions as belonging to `namespace fgw` (either by explicit qualification with `fgw::`, or by the directive `using namespace fgw;` which dumps all the names into the current `namespace`). Remember that we never use the second form in a header file. I use explicit qualification in header files and, generally, a `using` directive in an implementation file.

Write a program that will prompt you for an angle in degrees and output the equivalent radian measure to the screen. The program should repeat the prompt and response until you input a number greater than 10000.

Designing the point2d type

Before continuing I need to specify what the `point2d` type will be used for. Until I have done that it is impossible to decide how we should design it.

What I want is a type that will allow me to accurately specify points on a general mathematical plane. I want to be able to use these points to specify the vertices of polygons, the ends of lines, the centers of circles, etc.

I will use the simplest of all polygons, the triangle, to demonstrate some of what I want to be able to do with my `point2d` values. A triangle has three vertices. To put that another way, if I know the location of three points they will define a triangle.

Once I have a triangle there will be various things that I may want to do to it. Mathematically these are called transformations. The common transformations are:

Translation Moving an object (the triangle) without distorting it. If I can move each of the three vertices the same amount then I will have moved the whole triangle by that amount. Given the Cartesian coordinates, translation is easy, just add the same amount to the three x coordinates of the vertices and then add another amount to each of the y coordinates. Notice that there is nothing about whole numbers in that. Movement to the right is positive and movement upwards is positive.

Moving the triangle defined by [(3.7, 2.9), (7.2, 1.5), (5.1, 7.2)] 3.3 to the left and 2.2 up will give a triangle defined by [(0.4, 5.1), (3.9, 3.7), (1.8, 9.4)]. I subtracted (moved left) 3.3 from each of the three x coordinates and added (moved up) 2.2 to each of the y coordinates.

Rotation Rotating the triangle about some point without distorting it. For the moment, let me confine myself to rotation about the origin. Rotation requires that we turn the line joining each point to the point of rotation (origin for now) through the same angle. It is not easy to work out the new locations of the vertices in Cartesian coordinates, but it is very simple when using polar coordinates; we just add (or subtract) the same amount from the argument value of each point. Given a triangle defined by [(12.5, 45°), (6.3, 85°), (8.2, 115°)] the triangle we get by rotating 30° anticlockwise (remember that that is positive in polar coordinates) about the origin will be given by: [(12.5, 75°), (6.3, 115°), (8.2, 145°)].

So translation is easy in Cartesian coordinates and rotation is easy in polar coordinates.

Magnification Changing the size of a triangle (both increasing and reducing) is equally easy to do in both systems. We multiply lengths by the magnification factor. That is we multiply both the coordinates in the Cartesian representation, or just the distance one in the polar representation.

However stretching (shrinking) our triangle in only one direction changes its shape and is another case that is easier to do with Cartesian coordinates.

Reflection Reflecting in either the x-axis or y-axis is easy using Cartesian coordinates, as it is for reflecting in lines parallel to those. "Reflecting" through a point is also easy with Cartesian coordinates. Reflecting in other lines is more complicated.

My conclusion is a slight preference for using Cartesian coordinates but I would want to use polar coordinates sometimes. Following through I want the following behavior for my `point2d` type:

- Report its x coordinate (Cartesian coordinates)
- Report its y coordinate (Cartesian coordinates)
- Report its modulus (polar coordinates)
- Report its argument (polar coordinates)
- Change its x coordinate (Cartesian coordinates)
- Change its y coordinate (Cartesian coordinates)
- Change its modulus (polar coordinates)
- Change its argument (polar coordinates)

There is a less obvious requirement in that I need to be able to create `point2d` objects. For that I need something that C++ calls a constructor. More about that in a moment.

Please notice that we are not yet concerned with drawings, only the way that we might store and recover information about the location of a single point.

To summarize, I want to be able to handle an approximation to mathematical points in both the Cartesian and the polar coordinate systems, picking whichever best suits the task in hand.

Some readers may wonder whether I should be including managing points through both the polar and Cartesian coordinate systems. Certainly, I could limit myself to the more widely-known Cartesian system and temporarily make it easier for the non-mathematical reader. I hope that once you see how polar coordinate representations add power to the `point2d` type you will agree with my decision to support both from the start. Incidentally this is another way to avoid repetition: if we are going to convert between the two representations do it once. In this case, the "once" is in the design of the type.

The above list of eight behaviors and the constructor describe what programmers call the requirements for a **public interface**. Each of those nine things will be provided by a member function (well, the constructor is strange because it does not conform to the normal requirements for a function, as we shall see when we get to declaring one).

Declaring the behaviors

The first four behaviors are concerned with getting data out of a `point2d` object. In other words what can we ask a `point2d` object about the location it represents. The declarations are simple once we decide to use the fundamental C++ type called `double`. This is a good type for our purpose because it provides a good deal of numerical accuracy with a range of values that is much larger than we need. A `double` represents values that we would normally write as decimal numbers such as 2.71, 8407.56, −0.0023 and so on. (If you are interested, a `double` guarantees 10 significant figures of accuracy in decimal numbers.)

So here are the four function declarations that correspond to the four requirements for getting data:

```
double x() const;
double y() const;
double modulus() const;
double argument() const;
```

The data each one asks for is provided by the return value; that is, the return value is the answer to the question the function represents. When we call the function we will get back a `double` value as an answer. The call can be used exactly as if we had used the number directly (had we known what it was) or used a variable containing the value we want. Because these will be member functions we will be able to use them via the object name and dot syntax used in this code fragment:

```
point2d pt(3, 4);
cout << pt.x(); // sends the x-coordinate value of pt to cout
cout << pt.y(); // sends the y-coordinate value of pt to cout
```

Before I go on to the four functions that will allow us to change the state of a `point2d` object, I need to explain the use of the `const` keyword when it is added after the closing parenthesis of a member function declaration or definition. It has a very special meaning. It tells the compiler that the member function concerned will **not** change the object. In other words it states that the member function will report on some property of the object without changing anything. You might like to think of it as a read-only function. It is very important to add that `const` qualification to all member functions that do not change an object's state (i.e. its data). If you forget (and you surely will sometimes) you will eventually get error messages when you try to use those functions on a `const` qualified object. `const` objects can only use `const` member functions.

The declarations of the four member functions for changing the location a `point2d` object represents are:

```
point2d & x(double new_x);
point2d & y(double new_y);
point2d & modulus(double new_modulus);
point2d & argument(double new_argument);
```

Note that these are not qualified as `const`. The reason is that these four functions are designed to change the information stored inside a `point2d` object. I have given these four functions the same names as the four corresponding functions for getting information. The compiler will not be confused because the ones asking for information have empty parameter lists (they have nothing to tell the `point2d` object) while the four functions that change the state of a `point2d` object have parameters to pass in the new data used by the function to change the stored information.

The return type of each of the four functions that change a `point2d` object is surely strange. Do not worry about it now. Functions have to have return types (even if only `void`). I am using one of the popular idioms for member functions that change an object and return a reference (remember that references provide the original object, not a copy) to the object being changed. That means that the return type must be a reference to a `point2d`.

Now we have declarations of pairs of member functions that will read or write each of the four properties of a point that we might wish to use or change.

Creating new objects

How do we create (or declare or define) a fresh `point2d` object? C++ has a special mechanism for this. We call it a constructor. Constructors look very like functions except that they do **not** have return types and they use the name of the type being created as their name. It is customary to refer to C++ constructors as functions. Strictly speaking they are not functions because they lack a return type (not even `void`) but everyone calls them functions. In the case of `point2d` the constructor will be:

```
point2d(???);
```

with those question marks replaced by a suitable parameter list. We will choose the parameters in a moment.

The job of a constructor is to create a new object of a type when we want one. It is an important tool in programming because it allows us to set up new objects in a safe fashion. Not all languages provide such a mechanism. Those that do not rely on the programmer to be careful not to use an object until it has been given suitable data. Fortunately you have chosen to learn to program with C++ and so will not be called on to be that careful.

There are three sensible ways of constructing a new `point2d` object. We could do so by knowing the x and y coordinates of the new `point2d` object, we could do so from the modulus and argument of the new object or we could do so by copying an existing `point2d` object.

The last of those is called copy construction and we will leave that for now because as long as we do not interfere, the compiler will make up a copy constructor for us when it needs one. It will do the right thing for objects of simple types such as `point2d`.

We have to choose which of the first two ways we will use to construct a `point2d` object. We cannot use overloading here because both Cartesian and polar coordinates use two `double`s to represent them. I am going to opt for a constructor that uses data that represents the location in Cartesian coordinates. For most of us that will be the simpler choice. Now we can fill in the parameter list for our constructor:

```
point2d(double x, double y);
```

Defining the type

It is about time I put this together in the way that the compiler expects to see it. New types created by programmers are called classes (think of classes or categories of objects). The (incomplete) definition of `point2d` looks like this:

```
class point2d {
public:
     // constructor:
  point2d(double x, double y);
     // read access functions
  double x() const;
  double y() const;
  double modulus() const;
  double argument() const;
     // write access functions
  point2d & x(double new_x);
  point2d & y(double new_y);
  point2d & modulus(double new_modulus);
  point2d & argument(double new_argument);
private:
     // data declarations to be decided
};
```

We start with the keyword `class` to tell the compiler that we are providing a new type. We follow with the name of the new type. Then we have an open brace that tells the compiler that we are about to declare all the bits that make up our new type. We call this list of declarations a "class definition" (and this is one of those cases where definitions go in header files). We close the list of declarations with a closing brace and a semicolon.

There are two new keywords in the above source code: `public` and `private`. They are called "access specifiers" and tell the compiler what source code is allowed to use (access) the functions and variables that are declared. Declarations in a `public` block can be used anywhere that the class definition is visible. Names declared in a `private` block can only be used in the definitions of the members of this class.

Access is a very important concept for modern object-oriented programming. It is important to the class designer because he keeps control and has the freedom to make internal changes to the way that a type works. It is also important to the users because it stops them from accidentally using objects of the class in unintended ways. The commonest items to place in a `private` block are the declarations of the data that will store the information that this type of object will use. In this case I have not yet provided such declarations because I have not committed myself as to how to represent the location of a `point2d` object as internal data.

Starting coding

The declarations Please follow in my footsteps and experience the development of the `point2d` type. Start a new project. Create a header file called point2d.h. Put in the inclusion guard:

```
#ifndef POINT2D_H
#define POINT2D_H
#endif
```

I will not always spell this out for you because you should be getting used to it, however this is one of the times where it may matter and leaving it out could result in surprising error messages about redefinitions. Type in the definition of `point2d` that I gave above (remember that the `#endif` should be the last entry in the file and the other two lines should be the first two). Did you remember to add your name and date as comments? Save this file.

Testing Start a C++ source code file to test `point2d`. Call it point2dtest. A test should cover every member function. Something like this will do:

```
#include "point2d.h"
#include <iostream>
using namespace std;

void showstate(point2d const & pt){
// note that the 'const &' above means that we can read
// the original but not change it
  cout << pt.x() << '\n';
  cout << pt.y() << '\n';
  cout << "modulus: " << pt.modulus() << '\n';
  cout << "argument: "<< pt.argument() << "\n\n";
}

int main(){
  try{
     point2d apt(3, 4);
     showstate(apt);
     apt.x(4);
     apt.y(-3);
     showstate(apt);
     apt.modulus(10);
     showstate(apt);
     apt.argument(90);
     showstate(apt);
  }
```

```
    catch(...){
        cout << "\n***There was a problem***\n";
    }
}
```

ROBERTA

Can you explain that *showstate()* function? I thought you put function declarations in header files and then implemented them somewhere else. Here you have provided a complete definition in the same file as *main()*.

FRANCIS

Sometimes we want a purely local function. We place its definition in the file that uses it. (Much later I will show you how to make a function strictly local and completely invisible outside the file where it is defined.) As the declaration must be seen by the compiler before your code calls the function, it is easiest to put the definition (remember that definitions are always declarations) before the function that is going to call it.

If you later decide that you want to use the function elsewhere, you cut out its definition, paste it into a new C++ source code file and then create a header file with its declaration that can be included everywhere that you want to use the function.

In other words we do not go to all the trouble to provide for general reuse of a function until we decide that we are going to reuse it.

Try to compile this file. (When you create a project, do not include fgwlib.a. If you do include it, do not put in a `using namespace fgw;` directive; if you do, you will get name clashes from names in my library.)

I do not know if you find it surprising that the code compiles (assuming you have not made any typing mistakes). If you try to link it (build the project or press F9 to build it and run it) you will get several errors because we have only declared but not defined the member functions of `point2d`. We have not provided anywhere to store the data for a particular `point2d` object. The compiler does not care, the public interface of our definition of `point2d` acts as a contract between the compiler and us. We have undertaken to provide the necessary definitions when they are needed. It is the linker that can spot if they are missing and starts giving us messages to tell us about our breach of contract.

That is one of my major motives for walking you through this design. The `public` interface of a class is what is needed in order to create and use objects of the type we are designing. The `private` interface is only significant when we come to implement the type (make it work). Please get this concept fixed in your mind; it is the `public` part of a class that matters to users. You may be curious about the `private` part but it should not influence your use of the type. If knowledge of the `private` part influences your use then there is something very wrong.

Now it is time to fulfill our contract and define all those member functions that we have used and add the `private` declarations of data that `point2d` objects will need for storing information.

Implementing the point2d type

We call the combination of member function definitions and declarations of `private` data the "implementation of a class type." The compiler needs to know how much storage our type needs, so those declarations of data storage need to be visible to the compiler. Some languages have ways of hiding that information from programmers so that they are not even tempted to misuse those `private` declarations. C++ makes life easier for the compiler and just puts you on your honor to ignore everything marked as `private` (a bit like notices about keeping off the grass, which you might ignore when there are no park wardens around). If the compiler spots you using `private` material it will stop you. Most of the time it will manage to spot such uses and call an access violation.

Choosing the data representation

First we must reach a decision on how we will store the position information in `point2d` objects. We have two sensible choices, either we can store the Cartesian coordinates or we can store the polar ones. The great thing about making the data `private` is that we are free to change our minds later, so this decision is not final. I am going to opt for using Cartesian coordinates internally. That means I need to add two data items of type `double` to represent the x and y coordinates. Here are the two necessary declarations:

```
double x_;
double y_;
```

Go to the definition of `point2d` and add those two lines to the `private` block.

The use of an underscore at the end of the name of an item of member data is a personal convention of mine. If you want to choose other names for the two coordinate values you are free to do so – those names have no significance outside the class implementation. However choose a name that makes it clear what it refers to and that does not clash with the name of a member function – we can overload function names but we are not allowed to use the same name for data and a function. The class definition should look like this:

```
class point2d {
public:
     // constructor:
  point2d(double x, double y);
     // read access functions
  double x() const;
  double y() const;
  double modulus() const;
  double argument() const;
     // write access functions
  point2d & x(double new_x);
  point2d & y(double new_y);
  point2d & modulus(double new_modulus);
  point2d & argument(double new_argument);
private:
  double x_;
  double y_;
};
```

Make sure you actually save this header file and check that the test program still compiles. Frequent testing catches typos early and saves a great deal of time and anguish.

Implementing the constructors

Create a new C++ source file called point2d.cpp and start with the following statement:

```
#include "point2d.h"
```

The header file is needed because the compiler must see the complete definition of a class in order to accept definitions of the member functions that have been declared there. In other words it needs to know what we contracted to do so that it can verify that we define the same functions that we declared. The compiler can catch a lot of typos this way.

Standard constructor This one is easy but strangely different from normal function definitions. Let me show it to you first and then explain it.

```
point2d::point2d(double x, double y): x_(x), y_(y) {}
```

The two colons (`::`) between the repeated `point2d` is called the scope operator and is exactly the same operator and syntax that we use for namespaces. A class scope is a bit like a namespace. It tells the compiler that you are about to define a constructor for `point2d`, i.e. the special ''function'' that tells the compiler how to create a new object of this type.

The next part, in parentheses, is just a parameter list that tells the compiler what data to expect when it is asked to create a `point2d` object.

The single colon is special punctuation for constructors; it tells the compiler that you are going to provide a list of instructions to initialize the data members of the object. The above syntax tells the compiler that you want the `point2d` object that it is constructing to start with `x_` containing the value provided by the parameter called `x` and `y_` to contain the value provided by `y`.

If I had failed to provide a constructor the compiler would have made one up for me. Allowing the compiler that much freedom is a poor idea (there are many cases where it will get it badly wrong). Do not do that unless you know it will get it right (as I do in the case of constructing a new `point2d` object as a copy of an existing `point2d` object).

The final open and close braces just enclose the body of the constructor. As we have already done everything there is to do, there is nothing to put between them. However the compiler needs the braces even though there is nothing between them just to reassure it that you have done all you intended to do.

Add the source code for the constructor to your point2d.cpp file and check that this file compiles. If it does not, correct the typos and try again.

Default constructor We may sometimes want to create `point2d` objects without supplying data. The constructor that does this is called a default constructor. In other words we need a constructor with an empty parameter list. I almost forgot it, but it is not a problem because we can go back and add what is needed. We are always allowed to add features to a class that we are responsible for.

Add the following line just after the other constructor in the class definition (in the header file):

```
point2d();
```

And then add this line to the implementation file:

```
point2d::point2d():x_(0), y_(0) {}
```

Effectively that says that any new `point2d` object created without explicit data will be placed at the origin, (0, 0), until we change it by providing some other data by using one or more of the write access functions of `point2d`. Initializing the object's data with some fixed values is good practice as it ensures that the new object is in a useable state (one that will not cause any damage) even when we do not provide any explicit data. If you do not initialize variables you will get random garbage. Sometimes that garbage will result in damage if you accidentally try to use it. That kind of thing is called undefined behavior. This could result in damage to your program or, in theory, other possibly more serious damage. There is a joke among programmers that undefined behavior can result in the compiler emailing your boss telling him you are incompetent.

Implementing the Cartesian coordinate functions

I am going to deal with these next because they are very simple functions and will allow us to focus on the syntax for defining member functions. First the two functions for reading the state of a `point2d` object:

```
double point2d::x() const {return x_;}
double point2d::y() const {return y_;}
```

We start with the return type, which must agree with the type declared for the member function in the definition of the `class`. Then `point2d::` tells the compiler that this is a member function of `point2d`.

Then we write the function name as supplied in the class definition followed by the parameter list in parentheses. Finally we provide the body of the function in braces. In these two cases it is very simple, the body just copies the internally stored values of the x and y coordinates to the user. Note that it copies and does not let the outsider near the original. If you want to change the object's data you must use the correct procedures. As the user's code cannot depend on assumptions about how data is stored we (as the class owner/designer) are free to change the internal mechanisms for storing the point's data at some later date. For example, if after some experience of using `point2d` we decide that it would have been better to use polar coordinates internally, we could make the change, though the above functions would no longer be easy ones to write. We would have to provide definitions that converted the internal polar coordinate representation to Cartesian coordinates for external use.

Copy those function definitions into point2d.cpp and compile it. If you accidentally leave out the `const` qualifier (the thing that makes it a read-only function), it will not compile. Try it and see the kind of error messages you get.

Let us now tackle the two functions that change the x and y values. These are also simple apart from the syntax that allows an object to return a reference to itself. For now, just learn the idiom – whenever you want to return a reference to an object from a member function write: `return *this;` as I have done below.

```
point2d & point2d::x(double new_x){
  x_ = new_x;
  return *this;
}
point2d & point2d::y(double new_y){
  y_ = new_y;
  return *this;
}
```

When you typed this code in you may have noticed that `this` changed to blue showing that it is a keyword of the language. `*this` is a special expression that always refers to the object calling a member function; i.e. the object whose name comes before the dot in a call of a member function. Think of it like the pronoun "me" in English that always refers to the speaker; `*this` always refers to the object using a member function.

Yes, the asterisk has more than one meaning in C++; between two values it is a multiplication sign but when it precedes a single value, it has a special meaning which we will be looking at in more detail in a later chapter.

Implementing the polar coordinate functions

These are harder because they call on domain knowledge. Our functions must do real work because they have to convert from the Cartesian to the polar coordinate system. This is one of those cases where you may have to trust the "expert". That puts a burden on experts because they have to be worthy of that trust.

Getting the modulus Do you remember Pythagoras' Theorem? That is what we use to work out a modulus from the x and y coordinates of a point. We will need to calculate a square root, which means we need to use the mathematical functions that are in the C++ Standard Library. To make those available, we will have to include the `<cmath>` header with the other headers in point2d.cpp by writing:

```
#include <cmath>
```

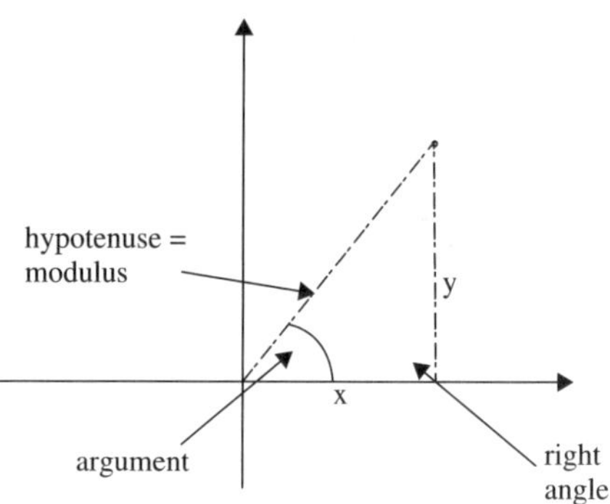

Remember that the standard headers go in angle brackets not quotes. The function that calculates a square root is `std::sqrt`.

This is the definition of the `modulus()` function:

```
double point2d::modulus() const {
  return std::sqrt(x_*x_ + y_*y_);
}
```

Remember that an asterisk between any combination of variables and values is a multiplication sign in computer programming. So the calculation tells us to multiply `x_` by itself (i.e. square it) then add on the result of multiplying `y_` by itself and then return the square root of the result. That is just Pythagoras' Theorem applied to Cartesian coordinates to get the modulus. The diagram may help you see the relationship between the modulus and the Cartesian coordinates.

Changing the modulus This is harder but please read my commentary even if you ignore the math part because there is some programming in there as well. Changing the modulus requires that we rescale our point. For example, if we treble the modulus we will have to treble the values of `x_` and `y_`. We need to calculate the ratio of the new modulus to the old one so that we will know what scale factor to use. How can we get the old modulus? Well we just did it above; we can use that function as part of our solution for this one.

Here is the source code:

```
point2d & point2d::modulus(double new_modulus) {
  double const old_modulus(modulus());
  double const scale(new_modulus/old_modulus);
  x_ *= scale;
  y_ *= scale;
  return *this;
}
```

The definition of `old_modulus` tells the compiler to create a `double` that is not going to be changed from its initial value (that is the effect of the `const`) and make the initial value the one it gets by calling the version of the `modulus` function that has no parameters. Note the way that `modulus()` is itself inside parentheses. Those outer parentheses are a way of telling the compiler that the program must use the data inside the parentheses to initialize the variable being defined. In this case that means that a new variable will be created for local use (inside the block of source code contained in braces) called `old_modulus` and set to remember the result of calling `modulus()`.

ROBERTA

But *modulus()* is a member function and you do not have an object and dot before it.

FRANCIS

True, this is a special case. The definition of a member function can call other member functions without the object-dot syntax because the compiler deduces that you are using the object that called the member function you are defining. It is equivalent to writing ***(*this).modulus()*** *and that is what the compiler will treat it as.*

The second definition also provides a `double` that is not going to change during its lifetime. This one is the ratio of the new modulus to the old one. That will give us the scale by which lengths are being changed. If a variable should not be changed while being used, protect yourself against accidents by declaring it as `const`.

The next two lines use one of C++'s special operators for changing the value stored in a variable. *= means replace the value of the variable on the left side by the result of multiplying its value by the value on the right (see Appendix B on the CD for similar operators). So if the value of `scale` is 3, the result would be to treble the values of `x_` and `y_`. There are a lot of these special assignment operators in C++. They are useful in that they highlight the places where we are using an old value to calculate a new one.

We already know about the last line. It is the same idiom as I used in the earlier definitions of member functions that modify an object's data.

Implementing the argument functions Implementing these two functions relies heavily on domain knowledge and expertise. If the idea of recalling your knowledge of trigonometry turns you into a pale shuddering wreck, just accept this code as it is. Programmers need to understand what is reasonable for them to do and what they should ask someone else to do. This is another part of my motive for using `point2d` as an example of defining a new type. It covers a wealth of programming but, at the same time, it emphasizes that good programming includes asking for help and trusting other specialists.

As I mentioned earlier, C++ does its trigonometric calculations in radian measure. You will almost certainly want to work in degrees. At least I do. If you need to convert between degrees and radian measure use the two functions I described earlier. They are declared in fgw_text.h and reside in `namespace fgw`. Here is the function to calculate the argument (in degrees) of a `point2d` object from the internal representation in Cartesian coordinates:

```
double point2d::argument() const {
  return fgw::degrees(atan2(y_, x_));
}
```

TECHNICAL NOTE

Note that `std::atan2` is the C++ Standard Library function that computes an arc tangent – sometimes called an inverse tangent. This function is very useful because it copes with all possible pairs of coordinates, including the case where the x coordinate is zero. Those who remember their school mathematics may recognize that calculating a tangent involves a division, which would be impossible (without the use of infinity) if `x_` were zero. The `atan2()` function sidesteps that problem.

Finally we have the function to change the argument, i.e. rotate the point to a new position. We want to keep the modulus the same and use trigonometry to calculate the new values of `x_` and `y_`.

```
point2d & point2d::argument(double new_argument){
  double const mod(modulus());
  x_ = mod * cos(fgw::radians(new_argument));
  y_ = mod * sin(fgw::radians(new_argument));
  return *this;
}
```

You will need to include the fgw_text.h header file for the declaration of `radians()`. However use the fully elaborated name because a `using` directive (`using namespace fgw;`) may cause ambiguity problems. Of course you can solve those with fully elaborated names but the cost of that solution (writing `using namespace fgw;` and then prefixing the relevant calls with `fgw::`) seems excessive here.

Check that all this works by compiling and linking the project. You should get four blocks of four lines of output if you use the test program I provided.

Wrap-up

In this chapter we have designed and implemented a class. That is not something you should expect to do any time soon. Even if you just followed the discussion, I hope you got some feel for the kind of work that goes on deep down in developing libraries for use by others.

Designing a class takes several types of expertise. You need to understand what it is for (far too many classes are designed with grandiose ideas that are unrelated to the needs of the user). You need to understand the domain (in this case, mathematics in general and trigonometry in particular). And you need to be reasonably competent as a programmer. There is no reason that all programmers should be math whizzes, nor is there any reason to expect a math expert to be a competent programmer, so sometimes you may need to get two experts to work together with each contributing their own expertise.

Now we have a `point2d` type let us get on and use it. The complete and tested implementation is in our graphics library in `namespace fgw`. That means its full name is `fgw::point2d`, which is why you had to be careful about possible name clashes that could happen if you included my library and wrote a `using` directive for my namespace.

It is important that you realize that all the above development of `point2d` is done in the global namespace – where things are not in a `namespace` block. I did it that way so that as you worked through the code you would not confuse the compiler when it could already see the version in fgwlib.a. If the compiler gives an ambiguity error, you can use full qualification to make your choice. Simply `::` for the global case and `fgw::` for my library's version.

ROBERTA'S COMMENTS

I found this chapter intimidating and scary, not least because I have forgotten absolutely everything I had ever learnt about mathematics (which wasn't much in the first place). So I didn't really approach this chapter with much confidence. Rather than just get on with it I moaned and groaned to Francis that I couldn't see the point of doing something that he had already done for us nor could I see the relevance to a beginner. In retrospect I wish I had tried it. Because I didn't pay enough attention to the first part of this chapter, I struggled with a later chapter.

SOLUTIONS TO EXERCISES

Exercise 1

```
int main (){
  try {
     cout << "Please type in a number of degrees. Any value\n"
        << "larger than ten thousand will end the program: \n";
  for(int finished(0); finished != 1; ){
        double angle(read<double>("Next number: "));
        if(angle > 10000.0){
           finished = 1;
        }
        else{
           cout << "that is " << radians(angle)
              << " radians. \n";
        }
     }
   }
   catch(...){
      cout << "***There was a problem.***\n";
   }
}
```

Summary

Key programming concepts

- Some programming languages, such as C++, provide tools for the programmer to create new (data) types.
- An abstract data type (ADT) is a type with public behavior that can be used anywhere, but with the representation of the data available only to the mechanisms that provide that behavior.
- Types should be designed with a clear understanding of their intended use.
- There is no need to provide behavior for an ADT until there is a use for that behavior.

- Behavior once provided is almost impossible to remove (there will be other code relying on that behavior) even if the design is faulty.
- Adding behavior that does not damage or change existing code is acceptable.
- The rules for mathematical programming do not always match those found in mathematics.
- Programming sometimes uses mathematical concepts and measures that are different from those in common use.

C++ checklist

- C++ supports the ADT concept with a mechanism for creating a new type called a class. The public behavior of a class is introduced by the `public` keyword.
- The behavior of a class is provided by member functions that are declared in the public section of a class. This collection of public declarations is called the public interface.
- A C++ class type usually has a private section in which are declared the data members that will be used to store the details of individual objects of the class type.
- Every object has its own data but shares the behavior provided by the member functions of its class.
- A class may have `private` member functions that are used to help with providing the public behavior but are not themselves useable outside the class.
- A class definition is composed of the declarations of the `public` and `private` members. The definition of a class is closed by a brace followed by a semicolon.
- The definitions of member functions are provided in an implementation file and are distinguished from free functions by prefixing member function names by the class name and the scope operator.
- A constructor is a special function that creates an object of the type that is being defined.
- Constructors can be overloaded; there can be more than one way to create a new object of a particular type.
- The compiler will generate the code to create a new object as a copy of an existing one. It will also generate the code to assign the state of one object to another of the same type. In advanced programming (but not in this book) it is sometimes necessary to replace the compiler generated code.
- `double` is a fundamental C++ type. It provides storage for numbers that include a decimal point.
- The compiler has built-in rules for converting between `double` and `int`. Programmers sometimes need to know of these conversion rules because they do not exactly match those used in mathematics. Mathematics rounds to the nearest whole number, C++ (along with most programming languages) rounds by discarding the fractional part (the part after the decimal point).
- The C++ Standard Library provides a number of math functions that are declared in `<cmath>`.
- `typedef` is a keyword that is used to give an alternative name to an existing type.

Extensions checklist

- The following functions are declared in fgw_text.h and are used to convert between degrees and radian measure:

```
double degrees(double radians);
double radians(double degrees);
```

- The definition of `point2d` is provided by including point2d.h.
- My library provides three special types of functions for reading data from input. It is important to use these because they serve three purposes: they handle input failure when using `std::cin`; they allow you to initialize variables directly from input; and they ensure that blank spaces at the end of input

lines do not cause difficulty when you subsequently use `std::getline()`. The three forms are:

```
// from std::cin with prompt:
    read<required type>("message prompt")
// from std::cin with a default prompt of ": "
    read<required type>()
// from an istream without using a prompt
    read<required type>(stream object)
```

CHAPTER 6

You Can Use point2d

In the last chapter you accompanied me as I designed a new type to represent the concept of a point on a plane. In this chapter I will show you how that simple type greatly extends what you can do. The main focus of this chapter is developing and using geometric shapes. We will discover that coupling the concept of a container (for our purposes, `std::vector`) with our newly defined `point2d` provides a great deal of power. At the end of this chapter I add some detail about handling the origin used by Playpen objects.

Adding Functionality with Free Functions

There are many features that we can add to `point2d`. However they are not fundamental to the type, they are just things we can do with it. Experienced programmers avoid cluttering their types with non-essential member functions. If possible, we use free functions to add functionality.

The ability to display itself in a Playpen is not an inherent property of the `point2d` type. If we provided a `point2d` member function to display the point in a Playpen we would force all users of `point2d` to include the baggage of the `playpen` type into their project even if they were not going to use it (perhaps they wanted to use some other graphics library). `point2d` and `playpen` are entirely independent types and yet it is quite natural to provide functionality that displays one in the other.

The only function that needs to know about both the `playpen` and the `point2d` types is the one that causes a point to be displayed as a Playpen pixel.

Think of the typical way that you might call a display function. What data will it need? Where should you provide the functionality? Where should the declaration go? And what about the implementation? What should we call the function? What data should it have? Will the function need to change the state of one of its parameters? If so it will have to be a reference parameter? Have we got anything that is close to what we want?

Displaying a `point2d` object in a Playpen reminds me of plotting a pixel. One of the few member functions of a `playpen` is the one that plots a pixel. Does that help? Let me help your thoughts by suggesting that we keep things simple. When asked to display a `point2d` object in a Playpen we will plot the nearest pixel. In other words if a `point2d` object is holding (2.7, −3.9) we want to plot the pixel at (3, −4). Go back and check what `playpen::plot()` needs. See what is missing? Yes, we need a palette code. I think we are just about ready to write the function declaration. As we are going to plot a pixel to represent a `point2d` object, I think the function should be called `plot`. That gives me:

```
void plot(fgw::playpen &, fgw::point2d, fgw::hue);
```

Not all authorities would agree with me, but I think that this is a case where adding parameter names in the declaration (remember they are optional) would make the declaration less clear. To me that declaration shouts loudly that I am going to plot a `point2d` value on a `playpen` in a color of my choice.

A typical use will be something like:

```
plot(paper, apoint, green2+red3);
```

assuming that `paper` and `apoint` are variables for a `playpen` object and a `point2d` object, respectively.

How about the definition? This looks about right to me:

```
void plot(playpen & pp, point2d pt, hue shade){
  pp.plot(pt.x(), pt.y(), shade);
}
```

Basically that code redirects the data of `plot` to a member function of `playpen` to do the actual work. This is a very common programming process; it is called delegation. A function that delegates to another is often called a forwarding function.

Create a header file for the free functions that add behavior to `point2d`. Call it point2d_extensions.h. Remember to put in the inclusion guard. You will need to include playpen.h for the declarations of `playpen` and `hue` and point2d.h for my library's `point2d`. We need those things because all those types are used in the declaration of our `plot()` function.

Create an implementation file point2d_extensions.cpp and include the corresponding header file (for now that is the only header file you will need there). Copy the definition of the `plot` function.

Now try to compile. Barring typos it will compile as long as you have included the necessary header files. (I think you should now be working those out for yourself.)

TASK 8

Write and test a function that calculates the distance between two `point2d` objects. The declaration will be as follows:

```
double length(point2d from, point2d to);
```

(Do not use the more intuitive `distance` as the function name because the result will be an unpleasant name clash with a function in namespace `std`. If you want to experiment try using `distance` and see the kind of error messages you get.)

[Hint available for non-mathematicians]

Write and test a function that calculates the direction of one `point2d` object from another one. Use the declaration:

```
double direction(point2d from, point2d to);
```

[Hint available for non-mathematicians]

Supporting I/O for point2d

We are going to confine ourselves to input and output in the Cartesian coordinate format in this section. Later we might add versions for the polar coordinate format. If you want you can always add them yourself. The method would be very similar to that for Cartesian coordinates.

We write Cartesian coordinates for a two-dimensional point by placing the "x" and "y" values in parentheses and separating them with a comma, e.g. (3.7, −4.5). It would be good if we could manage to make our I/O format conform to that convention.

Writing out a point2d object

Let us consider the output first. I have my own convention of calling functions that are designed to write to an output stream `send_to`.

A typical use of `send_to` for outputting a `point2d` to a stream would look like this:

```
send_to(apoint, cout);
```

The function needs two parameters, what to send and where to send it. The `ostream` parameter needs to have access rights to the output because it needs to "change" it by writing out data. That tells me that it will have to be a reference parameter. A `void` return type will be fine. I think that gives me the declaration:

```
void send_to(point2d, ostream &);
```

Try writing and testing that function for yourself. If you get lost, or want to compare your solution with mine, you can find it at the end of this chapter. However please try to do it for yourself before looking. A small hint, you will need to output five things: two of those will be the coordinates, the rest will make it look right.

Reading in a point2d object

Now let us tackle the hard one, input. You might object on the basis that we have those nice read<> functions. Unfortunately they only work if the type we are interested in has a >> operator to extract data from an input stream. Unless we write such a function first, we cannot use the read<> functions. I would be selling you short if I did not draw your attention to the need to supply input functionality before you can use it.

As before, we need two versions, one for console input (where we only need two values and can dispense with the parentheses and comma) and one for the general input that will include files, etc. and will need to handle opening and closing parentheses as well as a comma (we need to be able to read in exactly what we write out). This is tougher because we have to extract and discard the formatting characters. If we had a function that would search the input stream for the next time a specific character turned up we would have a good starting point. What I would like to write is:

```
point2d Getpoint2d(istream & inp) {
  Match(inp, '(');
  double const x(read<double>(inp));
  Match(inp, ',');
  double const y(read<double>(inp));
  Match(inp, ')');
```

```
  return point2d(x, y);
}
```

In this function you collect the data from the input stream and when all five items have been processed you create a `point2d` object that can be copied back via the return value. We need a `Match(istream &, char)` function which should use `istream`'s `get()` member function to munch through the input data till it comes to a `char` in the input that matches the one we provide.

Write and test a `Match(istream &, char)` that does what we want (i.e. skips characters till it finds one that matches). Use an uppercase "M" to avoid getting tangled in name clashes (there is already a `match()` function in my library). When you implement `Match()` note that even `get()` can fail (if you go off the end of the file, for example) so you should still test the input stream for failure after each use and deal with failure by throwing an exception.

Once you have all the bits, write the above `Getpoint2d(istream &)` function and test it. Also write a `Getpoint2d()` version that uses `std::cin`. Notice that in this case we can simply ask for two numbers; we do not have to worry about eating up formatting characters. The average user will not thank us for requiring parentheses and commas.

Using the library versions

Now you have written these functions for yourself you should understand the process well enough to use the versions provided in my library. The necessary declarations are in point2d.h. `match()` is not declared there because it is a more general-purpose function and so is declared in fgw_text.h.

I have also provided a >> operator for `point2d` (which uses the `getpoint2d()` functions to make it work) so you can use the `read<>` functions to extract data from an input stream.

Drawing Lines and Polygons

Now you know about `point2d`, it is time to introduce you to a function I have written that draws a straight line from one point to another. It is in the graphics library and its declaration in line_drawing.h is:

```
void drawline(playpen & pp, point2d begin, point2d end, hue);
```

The details of the implementation of this function are much more complicated than the cases of drawing vertical and horizontal lines that we had in Chapter 3. Even though I knew how to do it, it still took me four attempts before I got the last (I hope) bug out of it. You do not need to know the details of my implementation of `drawline`. It behaves like the other line drawing functions in that the actual end point is not plotted. Remember that that means that switching the start and end points will result in a slightly different line. I have designed it that way because that works best for the way I wish to use it.

TASK 13

Write a program that will prompt you for data for point2d objects. After you have given it the first two point2d values it will draw the line between them in the Playpen and then prompt you for more data and draw a line from the end of the previous line to this new point. It continues this process until you input a value that signifies that you want to finish. Use any point whose x-coordinate is greater than 999 as the stop signal. Note that you will still have to give a y-coordinate.

Modify the program you wrote for Task 13 so that it stores the input in a vector<point2d>. When you have finished the drawing, open a file called myshape.txt as an output stream (ofstream object) and first write how many point2d values there are in the container (you will need that number to safely recover the data) and then write out the point2d values stored in the vector<point2d>. [Hint available]

Write a new program that opens the myshape.txt file as an input stream (ifstream object) and then reads the contents into a vector<point2d> container. Remember that you have to first read in the number of entries as an int so that you can count in the entries and push them into the vector. Finally push_back a copy of the first vertex (if s is the shape, then s[0] will be the first vertex) so the shape will close. Use the data stored in the vector<point2d> object to draw the shape in the Playpen.

Referring to a shape type

If you have completed the last three tasks you will have the basis for representing shapes that are made from straight lines. When you are ready to start designing your own classes (not until you are ready to read a book explicitly on C++) you could encapsulate the data in a Shape class and then provide suitable behavior for such a class. For now we will keep things simple and deal with various features on a piecemeal basis.

Create a pair of header and implementation files called shape.h and shape.cpp. And while you are doing it, it would be good practice to create a file called testshape.cpp where you can create a main that will test our functions as we add them.

It would be nice to refer to a collection of point2d values as a shape even if we are not yet ready to create our own type. C++ provides a mechanism for providing alternative names for a type. That is what the keyword typedef is for. It is important that you recognize that this mechanism only provides another name and not a new type.

typedef is used to declare a new name for an existing type. The following is an example of such a declaration which you should add to your shape.h file. (You did remember your header guard didn't you?)

```
typedef std::vector<fgw::point2d> shape;
```

The above declaration makes shape a synonym for std::vector<fgw::point2d>. I am using the declaration to provide something akin to the way we named numbers in Chapter 1 to reduce the use of magic numbers. In this instance, I am avoiding magic types, i.e. the use of a type with a name that does not help the reader of our code to understand what it is being used for. Wherever we write shape the compiler will treat it as if we had written vector<point2d>. Once again the compiler does not care, but programmers will.

Using typedef is usually a bit of a cheat because it is rare that something we provide via a typedef will have all the characteristics of the underlying type. For example, we had better not sort the vertices of a shape: that would almost certainly give us an entirely different shape. But at this stage in your programming it is better to stick with the simple solution rather than get involved with designing a completely new type.

Drawing a shape

Let us start with a simple function to draw a shape whose vertices are stored in a shape (i.e. vector<point2d>) object. Here is a function that you can add to your shape files. I am leaving it to you to separate out the declaration for the header file and the definition for the implementation file. And do not forget that you will need full qualification of playpen and hue in the header file.

```
void drawshape(playpen & pp, shape const & s, hue shade){
  for(int vertex(0); vertex != (s.size()-1); ++vertex){
     drawline(pp, s[vertex], s[vertex+1], shade);
  }
}
```

Try to follow that code through and understand why it is right. Note that as we start at 0, we will reach the end of the elements of the container when we get to s.size(). However, because the last line will join the last two points in the collection of vertices stored in the vector<point2d> object we must end the loop when we reach the last entry.

In case you were wondering, the shape parameter has been qualified with const because the process of drawing a shape should not change the data that defines it. By adding the const qualification we allow the compiler to check that we do not accidentally write code that would change the data. It is also needed if we are to draw shape objects that are themselves marked as const and so not modifiable. The compiler will not allow us to hand over read-only objects to functions that do not promise not to change them.

You will want some shape data to test that function with. What about that myshape.txt file you created earlier? A little cut and pasting from the program that reads in that file and you have a good starting point for developing the test program for shape. This is yet another example of avoiding repetition; reusing what you already have.

Moving a shape

One of the transformations that can be applied to a shape is translation (or moving the shape). Basically we want to adjust all the vertices of our shape by adjusting each x and y value in the same way. Though mathematical experts might want to argue, I am going to represent the amount of that movement with a point2d variable. The function declaration will look like this:

```
void moveshape(shape & s, point2d offset);
```

This time we want to modify the original shape object so we pass it as a reference (the & in the parameter declaration) but it is not const qualified because we are going to change it.

TECHNICAL NOTE

Reference and non-reference parameters

I promised earlier that I would give you an example of why it can matter whether a parameter is a reference one or not. The various functions that transform a shape are excellent examples of the importance of a reference parameter. The purpose of these functions is to modify a `shape` object. In order to make the modification you need the original so that you can change it.

For example, if you leave out the `&` in the declaration of `moveshape()` all your code will still compile and run. However the shape passed into `moveshape()` will not have moved. The copy will be in a different place, but the copy is binned when the function ends. Try writing a program that takes a shape, displays it with `drawshape()`, calls `moveshape()` to move it and then calls `drawshape()` again. You should see both the original and the moved version in the Playpen. Now edit out the `&` from both the declaration and the definition of `drawshape()` and recompile and run the program. You should now see just one shape (or none if you are in `disjoint` plotting mode).

If you use an `& const` parameter, the object will not be changed (that is why you added the `const` qualification). There is generally no difference in *behavior* between a non-reference and a `const` reference parameter. The difference in this case is purely one of efficiency. We do not want to copy large objects just to make their data available elsewhere. A `const` reference makes the object available but not changeable.

Implement and test the `moveshape()` function.
[Hint available]

TASK 16

Other transformations

As well as moving a shape, we might want to change its size (magnification). For example if we want to double its size, we need to double the coordinates of each of the vertices.

Rotating might seem a little harder. However I did all the hard work when I ensured that the `public` interface of a `point2d` object could handle polar as well as Cartesian coordinates. Rotating points about the origin is hard in Cartesian coordinates but very simple in polar ones. For example if we want to rotate a `point2d` object 15° anti-clockwise about the origin we add 15 to its argument. To rotate a shape 15° about the origin rotate each vertex 15° about the origin (i.e. add 15 to the argument of each vertex).

Finally you might wish to distort a shape by stretching (or shrinking) it in only one direction. More generally you might want to stretch/shrink an object differently in the x and y directions. Actually scaling a shape is a special case of this where the amount of stretch/shrinkage is the same in both directions.

Declare and define functions to:

- Distort a `shape` object by a factor of `m` in the x-direction and `n` in the y-direction.
- Apply a scale factor of `sf` to a `shape` object.
- Rotate a `shape` object by `n` degrees anti-clockwise.

TASK 17

Make sure you have tested all your functions. Mathematical readers will realize that they now have all the tools they need to move, rotate about any point, and stretch a shape in any direction. We have not yet provided a shear function. If you understand shearing, try to write a function to apply a shear to a shape. If you are not fully familiar with the concept, skip it; this is a book on programming not on mathematics. I provide a solution at the end of this chapter.

EXERCISE 1

A triangle is a shape with exactly three vertices. There are several formulae for calculating the area of a triangle. One of them is based on the lengths of the three sides. Conventionally the lengths of the sides of a triangle are represented by a, b and c. Using s to represent (a + b + c)/2, the area of a triangle is given by the square root of s*(s − a)*(s − b)*(s − c). (I have used the computing symbols for multiplication and division to help non-mathematical readers.)

Use the above information to write a function to calculate the area of a triangle.

CHALLENGING

EXERCISE 2

Any polygon can be decomposed into (n − 2) triangles where n is the number of vertices. The simplest way to do this is to choose a vertex and join it to each of the other vertices that are not adjacent to it. The following diagram illustrates that process for a pentagon and a hexagon:

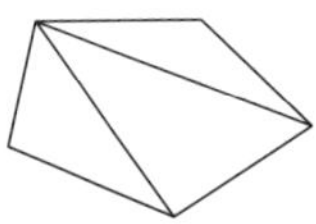

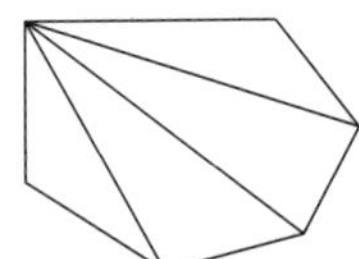

In the above cases the area of the whole polygon is the result of adding together the triangles of which they are composed. Unfortunately this is not always the case, as you will see if you use the following shape and the point indicated: For the purposes of this exercise you can assume that you do not have such a case.

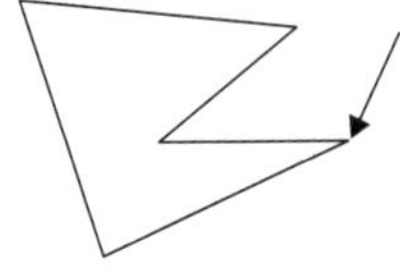

Write a function that calculates the area of a polygon by summing the areas of the triangles that are obtained by joining the first vertex of a shape object to each of the others.

I am not providing a model answer to this one because I do not want to place temptation in your way. If you cannot manage it now, come back to it later.

FOR MATHEMATICIANS ONLY

EXERCISE 3

Those with a fair knowledge of transformation geometry may be familiar with transformation matrices. If you are, try to write a function that applies the concept of a transformation matrix to a `shape` object. At the moment you are limited in the ways that you can package the `double`s that make up the matrix and so you may want to revisit this problem when you have learnt more about C++.

I am not providing a solution to this exercise because I consider it too specialized to be of general interest.

FOR MATHEMATICIANS ONLY

Given the three vertices of a triangle you can compute a pair of mathematical (3-dimensional) vectors that together with a single vertex represent the triangle. As we are working in two dimensions, the vector cross product will give a value in the third (unused) dimension whose absolute value is twice the area of the triangle.

Write a function that will determine the area of a triangle using a vector cross product. Do not discard the sign of the result.

Now use this function to calculate the area of a `shape` object assuming that the vertices define a shape whose sides do not intersect.

My solution is provided at the end of the chapter.

FOR MATHEMATICIANS ONLY

The problem with our `shape` objects is that some orderings of the vertices will give polygons (without intersecting sides) and some will not. Your task is to write a function that will determine whether a specific `shape` object is a polygon with non-intersecting sides.

Please note that, in general, there is more than one ordering of vertices that produces a polygon so it is not possible to write a function that re-orders the vertices in a way that provides a unique polygon.

This problem has largely been included to highlight the difference between domain knowledge, programming knowledge and programming skill. At this stage you have all the programming knowledge required to complete this exercise. If you also have adequate domain knowledge, the only thing holding you back is programming skill. Without the domain knowledge you cannot complete this exercise.

Drawing Regular Polygons

A regular polygon is a polygon with all its sides of equal length and whose angles (between adjacent sides) are equal. A square is a regular polygon; a general rectangle is not (because the sides are not all equal unless it is also a square). A general rhombus is not a regular polygon (because the angles are not all equal unless it is also a square).

A more useful (for our purposes) property of a regular polygon is that its vertices are equally spaced round a circle. Given the radius of the (circumscribing) circle and the number of vertices (three for an equilateral triangle, four for a square, five for a regular pentagon, etc.) we can create a `shape` object that represents a polygon of the desired type and size.

Add in the assumptions that the center is the origin and that a first vertex is on the positive extension of the x-axis and we are just about done. Here is an answer for you:

```
shape make_regular_polygon(double radius, int n){
  shape polygon;
  if(n > 0) {
     double const angle(360.0/n);
     point2d vertex(radius, 0);
     for(int i(0); i != n; ++i){
        polygon.push_back(vertex.argument(i * angle));
     }
// add a copy of the first vertex so that the shape will close
     polygon.push_back(polygon[0]);
  }
  return polygon;
}
```

This function first creates `polygon` as an empty `shape` object (i.e. one with no vertices stored in it). It next checks that there is at least one vertex (a bit extreme, but mathematicians would be happy with it). If there is, it proceeds to calculate all `n` vertices and copy the answers directly to the `shape` container.

You might wonder why I wrote `360.0/n` instead of `360/n`. Surely the two should give the same answer. Well, actually no. If you divide an `int` by an `int` you get the result for whole number arithmetic. That is the answer to questions such as "How many?" Consider a box that contains 22 chocolates. I share them out between my five children. How many will each get, and how many will be left over?

What I want is to divide the 360 degrees exactly between n vertices. What I need is the answer to the question "How much?" or "How big?" To get that answer I must let the compiler know that fractions are OK. The easiest way is for me to use at least one `double` in the calculation. By writing 360.0 for the number of degrees in a complete rotation I fulfill that requirement.

Whether there were any vertices or not, it returns a copy of the result to the function that called it.

This function demonstrates another way to deal with unexpected requests. The careless programmer who asks for a polygon with a negative number of sides might be surprised by the consequence (an empty `shape`, representing "nothing to do") but the program will continue with a result that it can handle. Note that we have also handled the potential problem of dividing by zero because when we divide 360.0 by `n` we already know that `n` is greater than zero.

CHALLENGING

Write a function that will create the data for an n-sided regular polygon given its center and one of its vertices as `point2d` objects.

[Hint available]

Drawing circles

There are several ways of drawing circles. The one we are going to use here uses a lot of storage but has the merit of being simple. The three-way pull between saving storage, saving time and reducing complexity is a common theme of programming. I believe that the greatest importance should be laid on simplicity of source code. We consider the other two aspects only when we need to do so. At this stage of your programming I think focusing on simplicity is most important.

As we increase the number of sides of a polygon it becomes ever closer to a circle. What we need is to produce a polygon that is as close to a circle as the resolution of our screen will allow. A little consideration will show that the number of pixels that are used to draw the circumference of a circle cannot be more than the length of that circumference (because we are using pixels as the unit of measurement). You may recall from your school math that the circumference of a circle is twice pi times the radius.

A little experimentation shows that a polygon with a vertex for every 3 pixels will be good enough for our purposes. As we are working to limited accuracy, multiplying the radius by 2 and rounding down to the nearest whole number will do fine.

Here is my declaration for a function to return a `shape` object that is a good approximation to a circle:

```
shape makecircle(double radius, point2d center);
```

Try to implement and test the `makecircle()` function. I provide my solution at the end of the chapter.

Drawing ellipses

An ellipse can be considered a circle that you have stretched in one direction. So once you can make a circle you can turn it into an ellipse by applying our function to transform a `shape` object by stretching it in the direction of the x-axis. We can then apply a rotation if we want an ellipse with some other orientation.

A Type and an Origin

I promised that I would tell you how to move the origin of your Playpen windows. By default each new `playpen` starts with the origin at its center. The origin is only used by two member functions (`playpen::plot` and `playpen::get_hue`). However that means that it affects every single function that uses one or other of those.

There are two member functions of `playpen` that handle the origin. `playpen::origin(int across, int down)` sets a new origin. An origin is always given relative to the window coordinate system. The origin of a window is fixed as the top left pixel of the window. Unlike conventional Cartesian coordinates, down is positive. The only place you currently need to know about the native structure of a window provided by the operating system is here. The conversions are otherwise handled by `playpen` functions.

There is also a version of `playpen::origin` that takes no parameters and returns the current origin. This presents a design problem because an origin is provided by two `int` values. A function can only return a single thing in C++. That means we have to provide a type whose only purpose is to pack and unpack a pair of `int` values that represent the position of a `playpen` origin so that they can be returned as a single thing. As this type is only needed by a `playpen` function I have made it a local type to `playpen` and called it `origin_data`. The declaration of the member function that returns the current origin of a `playpen` object is:

```
playpen::origin_data origin();
```

To use it you need a `playpen::origin_data` variable to store the returned result. Here is a snippet of code to demonstrate how it might be used:

```
playpen paper;
playpen::origin_data org(paper.origin());
std::cout << "the origin is: (" << org.x() <<"," << org.y() << ")\n";
```

The above demonstrates the complete behavior of a `playpen::origin_data` object. `point2d` is an example of a user-defined type that is a powerful tool hiding behind a simple interface. `playpen::origin_data` is an example of a user-defined type that does only one thing. Both types have their place in C++ programming. Such facilities are one of the reasons that I think C++ is a good language to use for learning to program.

ROBERTA'S COMMENTS

While I found Chapter 5 intimidating and scary, once I started using the **`point2d`** *functions in this chapter and creating shapes I really began to enjoy myself and even had the grandiose idea of writing my very own program.*

My ambitious idea was to design a flag program and I realized that to do this I would need to color in the shapes. So I asked Francis whether I should be able to write a function to fill a shape with color. He replied, "Probably not for a general shape. That is an exceptionally tough problem which I might just cover towards the end of the book."

FRANCIS

The solution is actually in the next chapter because a colleague remembered that he had done something like it based on an academic paper published in 1989.

But he also said, "Stars can be done by nesting ever smaller stars (just as you can do filled circles that way)."

Well I didn't know how to draw a star at that point but I did work out how to fill a polygon by nesting. Knowing that it was also possible to draw a star I worked out how to do this and felt very proud of myself.

I realized at that stage that writing a flag program might be a bit too ambitious but I did manage to create the US flag with stars and stripes.

Now I was beginning to build up a reasonable collection of functions and realized that I needed to organize myself a bit. I couldn't remember which functions were in which files and realized the benefits of very clear filenames.

Task 8

We have already done this for a special case because a modulus is the distance between a `point2d` object and the origin, which itself can be represented as a `point2d` object.

Task 9

Think about how you solved the last task.

Task 14

Remember that you can index a `std::vector` so if your `vector<point2d>` was called shape, then you can get the individual points with `shape[0]`, `shape[1]`, etc.

Task 16

The following statement will make the correct adjustment to the x-value of the first vertex of your shape:

```
s[0].x(s[0].x() + offset.x());
```

In words, that says that we should set the x value of `s[0]` to the result of adding the current x value of `s[0]` to the x value of `offset`. You may have to read that several times while looking at the source code.

Exercise 6

Break the problem into several steps. Using the center and the known vertex you can calculate the radius of the circumscribing circle. Now you can generate a correctly-sized polygon that is centered at the origin. Now translate (move) it and then rotate it to the desired position and orientation. Note that I do not provide a solution.

SOLUTIONS TO TASKS

Task 8

```
double length(point2d from, point2d to){
  double const x(to.x() - from.x());
  double const y(to.y() - from.y());
  return std::sqrt(x*x + y*y);
}
```

ROBERTA

I didn't have too much trouble writing the function but, my now familiar problem rears its head again, I did have a problem testing it.

I kept getting a strange warning that "address of double length will always return true." In spite of the warning, it did compile OK but gave a result of 1 which was obviously wrong. So I had to ask for help again.

I didn't want to show Francis my code so I told him about the warning and asked him to tell me what was wrong. He said "You have used a function but forgotten the parentheses."

I had forgotten to put the brackets after the length function when using it in my test code. When I added the brackets, I got the error message "too few arguments to function." When it eventually clicked, I added `(pt_from, pt_to)` and it worked.

Sometimes I feel very silly. What kind of programmer (even a beginner) can write a function but not know how to use it?

Task 9

The cleanest solution is to realize that we already have a function that gives us the answer if we are standing at the origin. So we imagine that we can move the location to the origin and apply the same move to the remote point. This is a nice example of a programming problem that becomes almost trivial once we see how to adjust it to one we have already solved. Spotting such solutions takes practice, lots of it.

```
double direction(point2d from, point2d to){
   point2d const temp(to.x()-from.x(), to.y()-from.y());
   return temp.argument();
}
```

In other words find the direction of `temp` from the origin. If this puzzles you, try drawing yourself a diagram on transparent paper. Now move (without rotation) the first point to the origin. Where is the second point? Because we have not rotated the diagram we have not changed any directions, only positions.

Task 10

```
void send_to(point2d pt, ostream & out){
  out << '(' << pt.x() << ", " << pt.y() << ')';
}
```

It would be a mistake to add a newline to that output because that decision should be left to the caller of the function. Do not make unnecessary decisions for other programmers.

SOLUTIONS TO TASKS

ROBERTA

Francis had written "if you get lost etc." and this made me think it was going to be difficult but I'm happy to say I found it quite easy. `cout << point2d(x, y)` simply shows the numbers 3.7 – 4.5. To display it in the standard format as (3.7, −4.5), a bit more work is necessary.

Task 11

```
void Match(istream & in, char c){
  for(;;){
     if(in.get() == c) return;
     if(in.fail()){
        cerr << "*** input failure in match ***\n";
        throw problem("input failed.");
     }
  }
}
```

Note that we have an example of what is nicknamed a ''forever'' loop. The first three clauses of the for-statement are empty. Of course it does not go on forever because either a matching character turns up in the input and the function returns to the caller, or something comes unstuck (such as running out of data) and the function reports a problem and exits by throwing an exception.

There is an assumption in the above solution; it skips everything till the right character turns up. My library version works differently in that it only skips whitespace, if the first non-whitespace character is not what we want it returns false, else it returns true.

ROBERTA

I only had one problem with this task and this time it wasn't my fault. I had the wrong version of one of the header files and the compiler complained

> ***"playpen.h redefinition of class::tools problem***
> ***fgw_text.h previous definition of class etc.***
> ***graphics confused by earlier errors, bailing out."***

But I am glad I got this error message because it came up at a later time (when I had written a function in a test file and then added it to a header and implementation file without removing the original test function from the test file) and I knew what was wrong immediately.

FRANCIS

Yes that was definitely embarrassing for me, though part of the problem is writing a book, refining a library and teaching a student all at the same time.

Task 12

```
point2d Getpoint2d(istream & inp) {
  Match(inp, '(');
```

SOLUTIONS TO TASKS

```
  double const x(read<double>(inp));
  Match(inp, ',');
  double const y(read<double>(inp));
  Match(inp, ')');
  return point2d(x, y);
}

point2d Getpoint2d() {
  double const x(read<double>("x: "));
  double const y(read<double>("y: "));
  return point2d(x, y);
}
```

Tasks 13 and 14

I am only providing a solution to Task 14 (as that includes a solution to Task 13). This code is a little large for a single function and I would give serious consideration to splitting it into separate functions before going further with it. Note the fix-up to deal with cases where the user does not give any information. Again, if this was for real use I would spend time providing a more elegant solution to that problem.

```
int main(){
  try{
     vector<point2d> vertices;
     playpen paper;
     double const endvalue(999.0);
     for(int finished(0); finished != 1; ){
        cout << "type in a point, any x-value greater than "
           << endvalue << " will end input.\n";
        point2d const point(read<point2d>());
        if(point.x() > endvalue){
        finished = 1;
        // ensure that there is a point
           if(vertices.size() == 0){
             vertices.push_back(point2d(0.0, 0.0));
           }
        // handle making first and last point the same
           vertices.push_back(vertices[0]);
        }
        else {
           vertices.push_back(point);
        // now draw the line between the most recent two points
           if(vertices.size() > 1){
                        // second and subsequent points
              int const last_vertex(vertices.size() - 1);
```

SOLUTIONS TO TASKS

```
            drawline(paper, vertices[last_vertex-1],
                    vertices[last_vertex], black);
            paper.display();
         }
      }
    }
    ofstream storage("myshape.txt");
    if(storage.fail()){
      throw problem("File did not open");
    }
    storage << vertices.size() << '\n';
    for(int i(0); i != vertices.size(); ++i){
      send_to(vertices[i], storage);
      storage << '\n';
    }
    cout << "Press RETURN to close Playpen window.";
    cin.get();
  }
  catch(...){
    cout << "***There was a problem***\n\n";
  }
}
```

ROBERTA

My solution was quite different from Francis' solution:

```
int main(){
  vector<point2d> points;
  playpen paper;
  paper.scale(2);
  point2d first_point(read<point2d>("type in numbers at x y "
       "prompt. To finish enter 9999 and any other number.\n"));
  points.push_back(first_point);
  for(int i(0); i != 1;){
    point2d point(read<point2d>("type in next point: \n"));
    if(point.x() > 9998) i = 1;
    else{
      drawline(paper,first_point,point,black);
      paper.display();
      points.push_back(point);
      first_point =point;
```

SOLUTIONS TO TASKS

```
      }
   }
// Test vector
// cout<<points.size();
   drawline(paper, points[0], points[points.size() -1], black);
   paper.display();
   cout << "Press Return";
   cin.get();
}
```

This program didn't work perfectly first time but at least it produced an interesting result: instead of a shape I got a sort of umbrella with all the lines coming from the second point. I had written *`point = first_point`* instead of *`first_point = point`*.

I think that I am beginning to understand things a bit better now and can guess some of the things that might be wrong. When I think a bit of code might be iffy I put a comment in at that point as a reminder.

Task 15

This solution is largely a rewrite of the first part of the solution to Task 14 to take input from a file rather than from the keyboard.

```
int main(){
   try{
      vector<point2d> vertices;
      playpen paper;
      ifstream storage("myshape.txt");
      if(storage.fail()){
         throw problem("File did not open");
      }
      int const count(read<int>(storage));
      for(int i(0); i != count; ++i){
         point2d const point(read<point2d>(storage));
         vertices.push_back(point);
// now draw the line between the most recent two points
// as long as there are at least two points
         if(vertices.size() > 1){
            int const last_vertex(vertices.size() - 1);
            drawline(paper, vertices[last_vertex-1],
                     vertices[last_vertex], black);
            paper.display();
         }
      }
      cout << "Press RETURN to close Playpen window.";
```

SOLUTIONS TO TASKS

```
      cin.get();
   }
   catch(...){
      cout << "***There was a problem***\n\n";
   }
}
```

Task 16

```
void moveshape(shape & s, point2d offset){
   for(int vertex(0); vertex != s.size(); ++vertex){
      s[vertex].x(s[vertex].x() + offset.x());
      s[vertex].y(s[vertex].y() + offset.y());
   }
}
```

Task 17

Note that if you only want to stretch the shape in one direction you just make the other stretch factor 1. If you are concerned that that does unnecessary work, the answer is that you should not worry about efficiency at this stage. Only add extra functions for efficiency when you have determined that it is necessary for the task in hand.

```
void growshape(shape & s, double xfactor, double yfactor){
   for(int vertex(0); vertex != s.size(); ++vertex){
      s[vertex].x(s[vertex].x() * xfactor);
      s[vertex].y(s[vertex].y() * yfactor);
   }
}

void scaleshape(shape & s, double scalefactor){
   growshape(s, scalefactor, scalefactor);
}
```

See how easy that was, just a simple delegation to the function we have already written.

```
void rotateshape(shape & s, double rotation){
   for(int vertex(0); vertex != s.size(); ++vertex){
      s[vertex].argument(s[vertex].argument() + rotation);
   }
}
```

I hope by now you appreciate the usefulness of those member functions providing data in polar coordinates. If we invest time correctly designing a type we often get a big payback later on.

SOLUTIONS TO TASKS

Task 18

```
shape makecircle(double radius, point2d center){
  shape circle(make_regular_polygon(radius, int(radius * 2.0)));
// that creates a circle centered at the origin
// now move it where we want it
  moveshape(circle, center);
  return circle;
}
```

The use of `int` in the declaration of a shape in the above code, as in `int(radius * 2.0)`, is the way we authorize the conversion of a `double` to an `int`. As the second parameter of `make_regular_polygon` is an `int`, the compiler will make that conversion for us even if we do not authorize it. Good compilers will issue a warning. I like to silence warnings by authorizing the conversion after I have checked that it is correct.

SOLUTIONS TO EXERCISES

Exercise 1

I am using conventional mathematical lettering for this solution even though it is unusual to use single capital letters as parameter names.

```
double area_of_triangle(point2d A, point2d B, point2d C){
  double const a(length(B, C));
  double const b(length(C, A));
  double const c(length(A, B));
  double const s((a+b+c)/2);
  return sqrt(s*(s-a)*(s-b)*(s-c));
}
```

Notice how the source code directly represents the paper and pencil solution. First calculate the length of the side opposite each vertex (that is why I chose the variable names the way I did). Then calculate the semi-perimeter and finally plug the results into the formula you were given. Using domain style names can ensure that the code is correct because domain experts will be able to write it the way they think.

ROBERTA

I completed the exercise to calculate areas – but can't see the use of these functions at the moment. As far as I can see they aren't used.

I stayed well clear of the exercises for mathematicians.

SOLUTIONS TO EXERCISES

Exercise 2

Non-mathematicians will probably not understand why it produces the desired answer. However anyone can use it, even though you need domain knowledge to write it in the first place.

```
  double area_of_triangle(shape & s){
// if too few points for a triangle make the area 0
    if(s.size() < 3) return 0.0;
// if too many vertices for a triangle, just use the first three
    point2d side1;
    point2d side2;
    side1.x(s[1].x()-s[0].x());
    side1.y(s[1].y()-s[0].y());
    side2.x(s[2].x()-s[0].x());
    side2.y(s[2].y()-s[0].y());
    return (side1.x() * side2.y() - side1.y() * side2.x())/2;
}
```

Note that the sign of the returned value represents whether the angle between `side1` and `side2` is measured anticlockwise (positive) or clockwise (negative). This feature is useful when you are trying to calculate the area of a polygon. Just add the (signed) areas of the triangles that you can decompose the polygon into. It will take care of the cases where some of the triangles produced by the decomposition lie partly or entirely outside the polygon itself.

Other exercises

Solutions are not provided for the other exercises in this chapter because there is too wide a variety of satisfactory solutions to single out just one.

ROBERTA

I got a spectacular result when I tried to execute the project I had produced to solve Exercise 4. The .cpp file and the project built fine but the operating system (Windows XP) didn't like it. It gave the message that the program had encountered a problem and would be shut down. I was rather amused by this and that means I'm not quite so scared of computers as I was. I sent my code to Francis.

The problem was caused by the following bit of code in `main()`:

```
shape polygon;
polyshape(center, pt, n);
```

Francis explained that `shape polygon;` creates an empty shape called `polygon`. The line below calls a function that creates a shape whose internal name is `polygon`, it then returns a copy of the data that is promptly ignored. He told me to replace the two lines with:

```
shape polygon(polyshape(center, pt, n));
```

This copies the shape created by *polyshape* into *polygon*.

When I did this it worked. I was obviously still suffering from the problem of being able to write functions but not use them properly. But I'm still not sure why Windows objected.

FRANCIS

The problem was that `polygon` never acquired any vertices and the program then tried to use an empty shape. As the code did not detect this, the program tried to use non-existent data. Not surprisingly the operating system decided that was not on and, suspecting the program was about to do something nasty, it closed the program down.

Sometimes we are lucky like that, sometimes we are not and we finish up having to switch a computer off to get control back again.

A shear function

This function applies a shear in the direction of the x-axis, using the x-axis as the zero shear line (i.e. the movement is proportional to the distance from the x-axis):

```
void shearshape(shape & s, double shear){
  for(int vertex(0); vertex != s.size(); ++vertex){
     s[vertex].x(s[vertex].x() + s[vertex].y()*shear);
  }
}
```

Summary

C++ checklist

- `typedef` is a keyword that is used to give an alternative name to an existing type.

Extensions checklist

- `playpen` has an overloaded pair of member functions, `origin()`, to handle the graphical origin. The one that has no parameters returns a special nested type, `playpen::origin_data`, to package the x and y coordinates of the current origin with respect to the top left of the `playpen` window.
- The second `origin()` member function has two `int` parameters which are used as the window coordinates (i.e. measured from the top left of the Playpen in raw pixels) for a new location for the origin used by Playpen functions. It returns a reference to the `playpen` object using it.

CHAPTER 7

You Can Have Fun

Programming isn't all about learning new things; a big part is using what you know. The first six chapters have been packed with new ideas and facts. The purpose of this chapter is to give you a break from learning new things and a chance to use what you have learned. I also hope you will take some time to plan for the future.

Valuing Your Skills

Programming is a serious subject but it is also one that should give you some reward. Despite the common myth, most programmers do not earn large amounts of money. However, almost invariably, the good ones take pleasure from their achievements. Financial rewards, though necessary for living, also give value and respect to the individual's talents.

Many years ago an artist friend of mine had a one-person exhibition of her work. In that exhibition there was one of the most beautiful pieces I have ever seen, entitled "The Bud Opens". There was a substantial price tag on it, far out of the reach of a young teacher and father. I looked longingly but had to give it a miss. Years later when I was rather better off I asked the artist if she could paint me a version. She explained that she could not because she was no longer the person who had produced the original and so any copy would be just that and lack the spark of the original. She then asked me why I had said nothing about the original when it was on sale. I told her why. She told me something that I had never thought of: the price tag was simply to ensure that whoever bought it really wanted it. Had I asked, I could have had it for whatever I could have afforded because she knew that I would have treasured it. The reward would have been the appreciation not the money.

While I am sure that people such as Bjarne Stroustrup (the creator of C++) would not work for nothing, I am also confident that the lifelong reward lies in the appreciation of those who see a job well done. The downside of that is that negative criticism hurts.

Just for Fun

Almost 25 years ago I bought my first computer – a Research Machines 380Z. By today's standards it was a slow clumsy device but by the standards of the time it was a good machine with exceptional graphics facilities and was probably the most expensive machine I have ever bought even though it did not even have a floppy disk drive.

My seven-year-old daughter wanted to try to design a logo for software produced by the family. She needed a little help in navigating the screen so I wrote a simple five-line program in a language called BASIC that would put a reference grid on the screen for her. That way each time she wanted to restart she could run the program.

A couple of hours later, her mother insisted that she went to bed. I looked at the screen and wondered what would happen if I superimposed grids of different sizes and colors. It did not take me long to write a few additions to the original program with the result that it would keep generating new grids that were either slightly different in size or in position on the screen. The program randomly selected a color for each grid from those that were available (a palette of just 16 colors at any one time selected from a possible 256). The grids were normally plotted using the equivalent of the `disjoint` mode you have in `playpen`, but a small percentage used one of the other plotting modes.

The above description may not sound very interesting but the result amazed many who saw it. At one time a professional programmer who specialized in educational programs offered to swap any program he had written for a copy of *Tartan* – which is what I had named it. I pointed out that the program was just a computer doodle with mostly lines of BASIC handling the choice of parameters for a run of the program. He did not care; he was just fascinated by the result.

The program was a doodle, thrown together in an idle moment. The result was little more than computer wallpaper, though there was a little educational merit in that the general form of the results did depend on the data provided by the user.

Time moved on and my 380Z was sidelined, gathered dust and was eventually broken up in 1995. I discarded all the once expensive electronics and put the fan, connectors, etc. in the spares box. Newer computers came along which were not so easy to program. Their color resources were differently organized and writing Tartan for them would have been a major undertaking.

Then, some time in the mid 1990s, a friend of mine put forward an idea for providing a very limited graphics resource to be used for teaching programming. That led to the creation of the first version of Playpen. I implemented Tartan using Playpen as a basis for the graphics but other things demanded my attention and Playpen languished and so did my programming.

Finally I was persuaded that I really should write this book and Roberta ''volunteered'' to be my test student. I got out Playpen and found a colleague who would clean it up and turn it into a robust tool for the current generation of machines. And, of course, I wrote Tartan again to test the line drawing functions you have seen in earlier chapters.

Tartan relies on only one feature of C++ that you have not yet learned – a pseudo-random number generator. I am not going explain what one of those is here (I will cover that topic in detail in a later chapter). For now, all you need to know is that there are a couple of functions `srand()` and `rand()` that work together to provide a sequence of wildly varying whole numbers. There is also a special C++ operator % that has nothing to do with percentages but calculates a remainder. So 23%4 is 3 (four goes into 23 five times remainder three), 37%9 is 1 (nine goes into 37 four times remainder one), etc.

Here is the source code for Tartan using the grid function you wrote in Chapter 3. There is an executable version on the CD.

```
#include "fgw_text.h"
#include "line_drawing.h"
#include "playpen.h"
#include <cmath>
#include <string>

using namespace fgw;
using namespace std;

void verticals(playpen & pp, int begin_x, int begin_y, int end_y,
        int interval, int count, hue shade){
```

```
  for(int line(0); line != count; ++line){
     vertical_line(pp, begin_x + line * interval, begin_y, end_y, shade);
  }
}

void horizontals(playpen & pp, int begin_y, int begin_x, int end_x,
        int   interval, int count, hue shade){
  for(int line(0); line != count; ++line){
     horizontal_line(pp, begin_y + line * interval,
                        begin_x, end_x, shade);
  }
}

void square_grid(playpen & pp,int begin_x,int begin_y,
            int interval, int count, hue shade){
  verticals(pp, begin_x, begin_y,
       begin_y + interval * (count - 1),
       interval, count, shade);
  horizontals(pp, begin_y, begin_x, begin_x + interval * (count - 1),
       interval, count, shade);
  pp.plot(begin_x + interval * (count - 1),
       begin_y + interval * (count - 1), shade);
}

// small wrapper function to produce a full window grid offset from
// the bottom left. It assumes that the playpen is using a scale of 2; if
// that is not true, it will continue to work but less efficiently

void tartan_grid(playpen & pp, int offset, int interval, hue h){
  square_grid(pp, offset-127, offset-127, interval, 2+256/interval, h);
}

int main(){
  try{
     playpen paper;
     paper.scale(2);
     paper.setplotmode(disjoint);
     srand(read<int>("Enter a whole number."));
     cout << "I need the minimum and maximum mesh for the grid.\n";
     int const minmesh(read<int>("the smallest mesh size is: "));
     int const maxmesh(read<int>("the largest mesh size is:  "));
     int const maxoffset(read<int>
          ("the variation in the location of the grids is: "));
     int const mesh_range(abs(maxmesh-minmesh)+1);
     for(int i(0); i != 1;){
     int const repetitions(read<int>("How many superimposed grids? "));
        string garbage;
        getline(cin, garbage); // clear out the last Return key
```

```
        if(repetitions == 0) i = 1;
        else{
          for(int j(0); j != repetitions; ++j){
            tartan_grid(paper,
              rand()%maxoffset,
              minmesh + rand()%mesh_range,
              rand()%256);
            paper.display();
          }
        }
      }
      cout << "Press Return to end program";
      cin.get();
    }
    catch(...){
      cout << "Something unexpected happened.\n";
    }
  }
```

Perhaps it is worth my drawing your attention to the purely local functions that I have declared and defined before `main`. If you want to pull some bits of a program out into functions to make the overall program easier to follow you can simply define them before the first function that uses them. If you hope to reuse the functions for other programs, make the extra effort to put declarations in a header file and definitions in a separate implementation file. But if you just want to use the functions in a single program, you can do it the way I have above. If you change your mind you can always cut and paste the bits to their own files and create suitable header files to go with them.

If you look at the above source code you will see that a large proportion of it is input and output. The guts of the program is in the `for`-loop in `main`. It is surprising how much can be done with so little.

If you want to add features and embellishments please do so. For example you may want to slow it down a bit. *Tartan* is for fun.

Fun Programming Ideas

Here are some ideas for you. If you think of better ones or do something you feel particularly pleased with remember to send it in for use on the book's website. You should feel proud of what you achieve. You will also make me feel happier for a job well done if you have something to show for all your work.

- Write a program to display a set of Olympic rings.
- Draw a picture of some common object.
- Do some more abstract art.
- Draw a sad face that changes into a happy face when you press the return key.
- For the ambitious: write a program that will draw a picture selected from a menu. Yes, you do know enough to put all that together. The rest of you will be able to do that after reading the next couple of chapters.

Looking Forward

By now you should be getting the feel for what programming is about. It isn't just learning a bunch of rules but about working with those rules to achieve your objectives. Probably the most important single talent needed by a programmer is the ability to keep things simple.

Writing music requires that you learn the rules of musical composition and how to express your intentions in standard musical symbols. But that does not turn you into a composer, it just provides you with the tools to express your musical ideas. Some composers can instinctively compose music, but they still need a way to express it. Some people can instinctively program, but they still need to learn how to express those programs in terms that a computer can translate into an executable program.

You need to distinguish between problems with programming and what we call domain knowledge. If you do not know what an *arithmetic mean* is then no matter how skilful a programmer you are you will not be able to write a program to work one out. In other words, to write a program to deal with a calculation you have to know how to do that calculation as well as how to write a program. There was an example of domain knowledge in Chapter 1. If you did not know the rules for mixing light then you would not be able to work out what palette code will give you orange, or light gray or magenta.

Domain knowledge is not enough to write a program and programming skill is not enough either. You need to combine the two. As you move through the rest of this book keep that in mind. This is a book about programming but you cannot practice programming without having something to write programs about. When you are attempting a programming exercise never feel embarrassed about asking someone else to help you with domain knowledge, but do try to write the programs yourself.

This also means that you should not feel that you should only write programs for the exercises and tasks that I set. I think trying those exercises will help you understand the theoretical material, but doing them should just be a central spine. Branch out; write your own exercises. Yes, I am serious about that. You would not think much of an English teacher who rejects a story, a poem or a letter that you have written because they did not ask you to do so, nor should you think much of a programming instructor who never encourages you to write programs to do things you have thought of.

If you think of an exercise that you find challenging or enjoyable share it with the rest of us by sending it in so that it can be put on this book's website to inspire others.

Some programming problems will be completely beyond you and possibly beyond even the most talented programmers; it helps to be able to spot them. One of the classic works on programming is called "The Art of Computer Programming". It is being written by Donald Knuth, one of the most talented programmers the world has seen. He planned to write seven volumes 30 years ago. The world is still waiting for Volume 4 (which is planned to be published in three parts and is currently listed as to be published in 2007). The exercises in that book are graded from 00 to 50. Grade 00 questions are ones that the reader should be able to answer immediately. Grade 50 problems are ones for which there was no known solution at the time of writing. I am not going to give you any of those, but be aware that they exist because you might accidentally set yourself one.

What next?

In the first six chapters I had to introduce a high proportion of C++ so that you would have the basic tools you need in order to program. I have also given you a fairly high proportion of example code. You now have sufficient fundamentals to continue with relatively little new C++. Note that this is not because we have covered a great deal of C++; we haven't. C++ is a very large language and the C++ Standard Library is substantial. Even when you finish this book there will be a large amount of C++ to learn if you intend to become a skilled C++ practitioner. But remember that this is not the purpose of this book. My purpose is to help you discover that you can program. If you want to master a high proportion of C++ you will eventually need to study another book (possibly the next volume in this series).

The remaining chapters of this book will focus on a variety of different programming skills. Each chapter will have some specific objective and be built round a suitable problem. Most chapters will introduce small additions to your C++ knowledge (but often large concepts). While I cannot promise that you can change the order in which you study the chapters, I expect that will usually be possible. Roberta and other test readers will have tackled the book in the order in which it is presented. That means that they will not spot places where later chapters assume you have mastered earlier ones.

Boring exercises

When I first learnt to program, almost 35 years ago, I attended an evening course on a programming language called FORTRAN IV. The course presenter was an enthusiastic campanologist (bell ringer). He thought that the most exciting program anyone could write would be one that printed out the correct changes to ring on a set of bells. He spent some time instructing us about the different changes that were used and how they were worked out so we could write such a program.

I do not know about you, perhaps you are a campanologist and would find programs to work out the correct sequence for ringing the changes on a clarion of 38 bells interesting and useful. However unless that is the case, you, like me and the other students on that course, would be bored to tears doing something that was completely useless and uninteresting.

In my days as a school teacher I often had pupils ask me what they should choose for a programming project. I always started by asking them what they were interested in. Once they had shared that information with me I was in a better position to suggest something that they could tackle. Writing programs, even novice ones, requires a substantial investment of time and mental energy. You have, I think, a right to expect that the end product will interest you and possibly be useful to you.

Another reason for writing programs is to understand how the products you buy actually work. You are unlikely to write your own competitor for Adobe's Photoshop, but writing a simple program to edit photo images may help you to understand how to use that product and what some of the technical terms mean.

I once wrote a full screen text editor – like the one you use in Quincy – in Forth (a somewhat unconventional programming language which is markedly different to mainstream languages such as C++). That task left me with both a product my pupils could use and a much deeper understanding of the complexity of line wrapping and screen scrolling. Both have subtle problems that are hard to appreciate until you have "been there and done that."

In the following chapters I will set exercises but these are by way of suggestions. Try to extract the main programming concepts from the chapter (I will try to make that easy for you) and then think how they could be used to solve a problem that you find interesting. Of course that will not always be possible and you will still need the practice. That is where you fall back on the specific exercises and suggestions that I make.

A task from the past

In days gone by it was customary for young ladies learning needlecraft to produce a sampler that would exhibit their skills. In many cases, samplers followed a fairly standard format but it was still up to the individual to inject their own creativity into the task.

In my days as a teacher I got my pupils to practice their programming with something that was creative and useful. For example, one year I set my class of fifteen year-olds the following task: work in pairs or threes (no singletons or groups larger than three allowed) to produce an application for educational use by a child in the age range 5 to 9. The end product must include all relevant elements including suitable documentation.

Now you probably think that was a pretty hard task, not least because the specifications were so open. You might be even more surprised to learn that this was the first actual program that any of them would have written and they had only had six weeks of a two-year course. They were given six weeks to complete the task.

With guidance they went out and researched what would be suitable by asking parents, relations, friends, etc. They understood that a simple project well executed would be much better than an ambitious one that required skills they lacked. They knew that they could consult me on programming issues but the choice of project, the documentation and the presentation was entirely theirs.

Every one of the dozen teams presented work that they could feel genuinely proud of. However there is one that I still remember today, more than 20 years later. A pair of lads decided that they would write a program to help young children learn simple number bonds. Just adding and subtracting single figure numbers with single figure answers. They researched the problem and applied their limited programming knowledge to design and implement an appropriate program.

The end result presented the questions in large symbols (and these were the days when computers used fixed size fonts). All that the child had to do was press the numerical key that matched the answer.

They had discovered that repetitive tasks need motivation to keep the interest of the child. They designed an animated steam engine complete with puffs of smoke and moving rods on the wheels that moved forward one stop every time the child gave a right answer and chugged back one stop every time the child gave a wrong answer. Ten stops along the line was a small engine shed. When the child finally managed to get the engine into the shed, a little man came out and waved.

Now you may think that the two lads had access to programming resources that far exceed what you currently have. Well they did have a direct keyboard read available to them (i.e. their program did not have to wait for the user to press the RETURN key) and they did have a small graphic feature that allowed them to place a simple pattern of 8 by 8 pixels anywhere on the screen. On the other hand the screen was less than half the linear size of the one Playpen provides.

I am telling you this to emphasize that programming isn't about what you know about a programming language but about what you do with what you know.

A challenge

I would like you to think about writing a program that will meet some real need or interest of yours or of some person or group that you know. This program is to be your sampler that will demonstrate your programming expertise. If you can work with someone else I think you should. Programming is not a solo activity but one where teamwork is important.

I would love to have thousands of sampler programs for this book's website. Yours might not be the kind of dramatic product that sticks in the mind for more than two decades but it will be something to which you can point with pride. Others may not see it as something special, but you will know that it is a real program that met a real need (and I include entertainment in that heading).

The challenge, which I hope you will accept, is to write your own sampler program and send it in. There is no time limit but you should think of finishing within a couple of months after you finish this book.

Some words of advice: choose something simple and do it well and choose something you know about. Try to set a standard that you can live up to, so by all means get help but make sure the end product is your own work. Do not hurry to choose your task now but as you study the rest of this book keep thinking about it.

Remember that this book will be widely known in the C++ community. If you claim to have read it, people are going to ask you what your sampler program was. You should have a good answer when the question is asked.

CHAPTER 8

You Can Write a Menu

In this chapter I will show you the basics of writing a menu-driven task. Modern operating systems and applications make extensive use of menus of all kinds. They both show the user (of the program) what can be done at this point and provide a mechanism for choosing which of those things to do. At this stage in your programming we will be writing simple text and keyboard driven menus. However the principles are the same as those used for graphical and mouse driven (sometimes called "graphical user interface", or GUI – pronounced gooey to rhyme with gluey – for short) programs.

In addition to the specific objective (menus) you will also see how a program develops by dealing with one problem at a time rather than trying to do everything at once.

On the way you will learn about another form of user-defined type and I will introduce you to two functions from my library that fill areas of the Playpen with a single color.

ROBERTA

I can't remember a previous "user-defined type." Are you referring to `typedef` or have I missed something?

FRANCIS

User-defined types are those that are provided by a library (such as the C++ Standard Library or my library) together with any types provided directly by an implementation file (`.cpp`). In other words, all types other than the fundamental types of the language (`int`, `char`, `double`, etc.).

Be careful not to confuse them with user supplied type names, that is the task of a `typedef`. This can be used to provide an extra name for any type.

A variable is a name for an object and a type name is a name for a type. An object can have more than one name (think of the way we pass around our Playpen object, one object whose name depends on the local context); a type can have more than one name.

Offering a Set of Choices

There are many situations in programming where you want the user of a program to choose from a set of actions. For example, we might write a program for producing "modern art" based on the ideas and mechanisms we had in Chapter 1. Fundamentally our choices would be:

- Change the scale
- Change the mode for plotting

- Plot a pixel
- Clear the `playpen`

This is not a complete list but it will do as a starter. We will need to tell the user what actions are available and give them a way to make their choice. Our program will then complete the selected action. I want to be able to write a program that is like this:

```
int main(){
  playpen picture;
  for( ; ; ){
     display_choices();
     get_choice();
     do_choice();
  }
}
```

From now on I will assume that you will know that you have to include suitable header files and `using` directives (or use fully qualified names). I have left out the `try...catch` that should wrap the source code in `main()` because I want to focus on the working code and not the things that should always exist in a properly designed program. Let us develop this code into a working program.

Another way to loop: do...while

Perhaps you are unhappy with writing a `for`-loop that has an empty initialization, an empty control condition and no action at the end of each pass (iteration). C++ has a couple of other loop constructs. In this case we know that we want to carry out the controlled block at least once and we have not decided how to stop. This fits a programming idiom that C++ expresses by using two keywords: `do` and `while`. We introduce the controlled statement with `do` and make the decision about repetition at the end with `while` followed by the controlling expression in parentheses. Our program can be rewritten as:

```
int main(){
  playpen picture;
  do{
     display_choices();
     get_choice();
     do_choice();
  } while(????);
}
```

This highlights the need to decide how to stop the loop by replacing the question marks with a suitable expression.

A new type: bool

The fundamental C++ type `bool` provides a good answer to that question. It is about the simplest type you can imagine. It has exactly two values: `true` and `false`.

We need to know very little about this type in order to use it correctly. In simple terms you can create a variable of type `bool` and store either `true` or `false` in it. If you try to store a number in it, a zero value will be converted into `false`, all other numerical values are converted into `true`. If you (unwisely) use a `bool` in some arithmetic, `false` is treated as zero and `true` is treated as one.

Eventually you may need to learn a bit more about `bool` to avoid misusing it because C++ had to make some design compromises for historical reasons that do not concern us here.

Note that several programs in earlier chapters could have used `do...while` and a `bool` variable had you known about those things then. For example those `for`-loops that were written as:

```
for(int finished(0); finished != 1; ){
  // do something
}
```

Could be written as:

```
bool more(true);
do {
  // do something
} while(more);
```

The initialization of a control variable has been moved to directly before the `do...while`-loop and when we want to end the loop we reset it to `false` somewhere in the loop.

Why use this mechanism? Simply because it expresses our intentions more clearly in the code. Generally we use a `for`-loop when we want to repeat some action a fixed number of times and we use a `do...while` when we want to do it at least once and repeat it until some property changes.

Knowing when to stop

Let us use this new type in our program:

```
int main(){
  playpen picture;
  bool more(true);
  do{
     display_choices();
     get_choice();
     do_choice();
  } while(more);
}
```

Unless something changes the value stored in `more` to `false` the program is never going to stop. In general that is not a good idea. Some thought suggests that one of the choices in our menu should be "Finish". When we come to do that choice we will need to change the value of `more` to `false`. How should we do that?

Unless you have seen it before, the solution to this problem is not obvious. The answer is to make our `do_choice` function return a `bool` that can be used to update the value stored in `more`. Now our program is:

```
int main(){
  playpen picture;
  bool more(true);
  do{
     display_choices();
     get_choice();
     more = do_choice();
  } while(more);
}
```

This is beginning to shape up, but how will do_choice() "know" what choice was made by get_choice()? We need a way to relay the choice between the functions. For now I am going to use a char for that purpose and identify the choices with letters. Later I will show you a more general way to achieve our objective.

Now our program becomes:

```
int main(){
  playpen picture;
  bool more(true);
  do{
     display_choices();
     char const choice (get_choice());
     more = do_choice(choice);
  } while(more);
}
```

Why did I define more outside the do...while-loop, but define choice inside? I need more to still be around when I get to the while that completes the do...while pair. The rules of C++ specify that variables are only available within the block (including any blocks nested in that block) where they are declared. That means that I must define more before I start the do...while-loop. However I only use choice inside the loop, it has no use outside. It is generally good programming style to keep variables as local as possible. If we do not need something outside a block, do not declare/define it outside. That tells me that choice should be defined inside the block where it is used.

Function declarations and definitions

Back in Chapter 3 I wrote that one sequence for designing a function was: *use → declare → define*. I now have some tentative code that uses three functions so I am ready to take the next step and declare them before I go on to define them. Here is the first attempt at suitable declarations that will work with the uses we have in our code:

```
void display_choices();
char get_choice();
bool do_choice(char choice);
```

Time to create a new project. Call it Menu and save it in the Chapter 8 directory. Type the code for our program into a C++ source file called menu_test.cpp. The only header files you will need to include are playpen.h and the one you are about to write called art_menu.h.

Create a new header file called art_menu.h and type in the three declarations above. (Please remember those standard lines that start and finish a header file; I won't remind you again.)

Now let us work to provide a definition for each of those declarations. Start a new C++ source file called art_menu.cpp. Now we are ready to get down to work.

```
#include <iostream>

using namespace std;

void display_choices(){
  cout << "Select one of the following by pressing the\n"
     << "key indicated and then pressing the Return key.\n\n";
```

```
  cout << "\tC   Clear the Playpen Window.\n"
         << "\tM   Change the plotting mode.\n"
         << "\tS   Change the scale.\n"
         << "\tP   Plot a pixel.\n"
         << "\tF   Finish. \n\n";
}
```

The "\t" inside the quotes is the special char value that represents a tab (very similar to "\n" used to represent a newline). The menu will be displayed offset from the left margin of your console window by the width of one tab.

At a later date you might want to return to this definition and rewrite it so that it reads the text from a file. One reason for doing that is that you could then provide the menu in other human languages without having to rewrite the source code, just change the file that your program uses. Do not worry about that now but realize that making your program communicate in other languages adds polish.

Next let us deal with get_choice(). This function should validate its input to make sure that the user makes a legitimate choice. However there is no reason to insist that the choice is made with an uppercase letter so it should be case neutral.

```
char get_choice(){
  string const choices("CFMPS");
  cout << "Action: (Press letter followed by Return): ";
  do{
     string input;
     getline(cin, input); // get whole line
// and use the first character
     char const letter(toupper(input[0]));
     int const choice(choices.find(letter));
// Check that choice is valid
     if(choice < choices.size()){
        return choice;
     }
// Note you can only get here if the choice was not valid.
     cout << '"' << letter << '"'<< "is not an option.\n";
     cout << "Please try again: ";
  } while(true);
}
```

As I am using std::string, I will need to include the <string> header in the project. I will also need to include <cctype> for the declaration of toupper(). std::toupper returns the uppercase equivalent of the argument passed in. If the argument is not a lowercase letter the function returns the value passed in.

While I only want the first character typed in by the program user, I grab the whole line so that I will not have to worry about junk (including the Return key) being left to get in the way of later processes. I then convert the first letter to uppercase (if it isn't already) and save the answer as letter. The above code assumes that the user types in at least one character. I will live with that assumption for now, but I will have to deal with it eventually because input[0] can do bad things if input is empty. Can you think of a simple way to fix this problem?

The std::find() member function of std::string that I have used here searches the string (choices) for the character (choice) provided as an argument and returns its position in the string (starting from 0, so choices[0] would be "C", choices[1] would be "M", etc.). If it does not find the character find() returns a value greater than the highest valid index (as there are currently five choices, the highest valid index will be 4). string::find provides a tidy way to convert the possible choices to int values.

Multi-way choices with switch

In order to define the third function I need another C++ structure, switch. Several decades of programming experience has convinced expert programmers that having lots of conditional expressions (such as those provided by if) often leads to contorted code that is difficult to follow. Such code is easily written incorrectly and is a cause of bugs in programs. C++ has a special way to handle the case where we want to choose one of several options. It only applies to cases where the control variable is a whole number. In this context the numerical codes that represent char values are treated as whole numbers.

We need four new keywords. To make it easier to follow I am going to write a short C++ program and then explain what each of the keywords does. I have highlighted the new keywords.

```
#include "fgw_text.h"
#include <iostream>

using namespace std;
using namespace fgw;

int main(){
  int const value(read<int>("type a number between 0 & 4 exclusive: "));
  switch(value){
     case 0:
        cout << "0 is outside the range.";
        break;
     case 1:
     case 2:
     case 3:
        cout << "the square of "<< value << " is " << value*value;
        break;
     case 4:
        cout << "4 is not included in the range.";
        break;
     default:
        cout << value << " is not acceptable.";
  }
}
```

switch(value) starts the process. It tells the compiler what number will be used to select an action. You can put expressions inside the parentheses as long as they will result in a whole number when the program runs.

The case keyword must be followed by an integer constant. By that I mean a whole number that is visible to the compiler. We cannot use variables after a case because the compiler would not know the value they stored but we can use named numbers such as those defined as having type int const and initialized with a literal. The mechanism I use to initialize an int const from read<int> will not do because while that gives an immutable number it is one provided at the time the program runs which is after the compiler has finished its work.

When the program runs it will look for a case-value that matches the value in the switch() and then execute the code that follows the colon. It will continue until something stops it. That is the job of the break keyword in the above code. break causes the program to jump to the end of the switch-block (the closing brace that corresponds to the opening brace after switch(value)).

Notice that we do not have to have a break for every case. If, as in the above, there are several values that we want to treat the same way, we can provide a list of cases and provide the shared action at the end of the list.

The fourth keyword, default, is to allow us to provide a blanket option for all the other possible values of the control variable that we do not deal with on an individual basis.

If you need to make a multi-way choice based on a whole number value then the switch-statement is almost certainly the way to go. However always think about whether there is a simpler way to develop the code. Some people get lazy and use decision statements such as switch when there are better options. One of the problems with switch is that you must know all the choices at the time you write the source code. That is not always possible.

ROBERTA

You say that you must know all the choices when you write the code but in the next chapter you demonstrate that you can add more later. So can you elaborate please?

FRANCIS

You can add more later on but only by editing your source code. In other words you have to recompile the code. There are more advanced mechanisms than switch that allow retro-fitting choices without recompiling code. Those are beyond the level of this book.

We now have all that we need to provide a reasonable definition of our third function, the one that acts on the choice that the user has provided via get_choice(). Here is my code:

```
bool do_choice(int choice){
  bool more(true);
  switch(choice){
     case 0:
        clear_playpen(???);
        break;
     case 1:
        more = false;
        break;
     case 2:
        change_plotmode(???);
        break;
     case 3:
        plot_pixel(???);
        break;
     case 4:
        change_scale(???);
        break;
```

```
      default:
         throw problem("Not a valid option");
   }
   return more;
}
```

The values used in the switch statement are provided by the order of the letters in the choices string, which happens to be in alphabetical order rather than the order of the menu entries. This is another example of magic values. We will eventually remove the magic values with the result that the code will be easier to follow.

Notice that in most cases I delay the action by delegating to a function that I have yet to write. That is generally good programming practice. The only case that I can deal with immediately is the one that handles finishing. By the way, do those magic uses of 0, 1, 2, 3 and 4 worry you? I think they should but we will deal with that shortly.

What about those question marks? I had completely forgotten that the various actions would need to know what playpen object was being used. Careless, but because I have kept each step simple, it will be easy to go back and correct the problem. do_choice needs an extra parameter to track the playpen object so that it can pass it on to the functions that need to use the Playpen to do their work.

I need to go back to the declaration of do_choice and change it to:

```
do_choice(fgw::playpen &, int action);
```

I will also need to go back to the test program and correct that to:

```
int main(){
   playpen picture;
   bool more(true);
   do{
      display_choices();
      int const choice(get_choice());
      more = do_choice(picture, choice);
   } while(more)
}
```

And finally correct and complete the definition of do_choice():

```
bool do_choice(playpen & pp, int choice){
   bool more(true);
   switch(choice){
      case 0:
         clear_playpen(pp);
         break;
      case 1:
         more = false;
         break;
      case 2:
         change_plotmode(pp);
         break;
```

```
      case 3:
         plot_pixel(pp);
         break;
      case 4:
         change_scale(pp);
         break;
      default: throw problem("Not a valid option");
   }
   pp.display();
   return more;
}
```

We still have work to do because we have to provide the four functions that carry out the actions. I am going to work on a need to know basis. The only part of my program that needs to know about these four functions is the definition of do_choice. That suggests to me that I should hide these functions away in the same file that contains the definition of do_choice. If I later decide that the functions are of more general use I can publish their existence by placing suitable declarations in a header file. In the meantime, I want to restrict the functions to the file where they are defined.

C++ provides a mechanism to do that. You place the declarations and definitions (usually just an early definition which will also be a declaration) in an **unnamed namespace** (that is simply a namespace without a name). Anything declared in an unnamed namespace can be used freely within the file but cannot be used anywhere else. This is a useful technique where you want functions, types, etc. that are strictly local to a file. This is another form of information hiding. Good programming tries to restrict information on a need to know basis. The less outsiders know, the less room they have for making mistakes.

Here are (incomplete in some cases) definitions of the four functions:

```
namespace { // open an unnamed namespace
   void clear_playpen(playpen & pp){
      hue const new_hue(read<int>("What background color? "));
      pp.clear(new_hue);
   }

   void change_scale(playpen & pp){
      int const new_scale(read<int>("What is the new scale? "));
// for you to finish
   }

   void change_plotmode(playpen & pp){
// write an implementation that gives the user a
// menu of the four options and asks them to choose
// then use a switch to apply the choice
// if you are not ready to do this just leave in the following
// line:
      cout << "***not implemented yet.***\n";
   }

   void plot_pixel(playpen & pp){
      int const x(read<int>("What x value? "));
      int const y(read<int>("What y value? "));
```

```
      hue const shade(read<hue>("What color? "));
      pp.plot(x, y, shade);
   }
}
```

Note that the unnamed namespace must be closed (have the terminating right brace) before you define anything that is to be available elsewhere. You can reopen the unnamed namespace later on if you wish. Do not worry that you cannot qualify names declared in the unnamed namespace, the compiler treats all those names as if they had been declared in the enclosing namespace but only in the file where you placed the unnamed namespace. An unnamed namespace in a different file will be a different namespace and not an extension of an existing one.

If you later decide you want to use a function in another file, you just add its declaration to a suitable header file then cut the definition and paste it outside the unnamed namespace. Some programmers advocate that all functions and global variables (those outside any functions, classes, etc.) should be placed in an unnamed namespace until you know you want to use them elsewhere. As soon as you place declarations in a header file you implicitly use them elsewhere and so the definitions of those functions must not be placed in an unnamed namespace.

Complete the definitions for `change_scale()` and `plot_pixel()`.

When you complete the above and add them to the `art_menu.cpp` file you should be able to build the Menu project and test it. You will need to make sure you add those functions before the place they are first used. Otherwise you will have to provide declarations for them before they are used. A compiler must have seen a declaration (or a definition doubling up as a declaration) before it will accept a use of a name.

Look carefully at the output when you use your test program. Unless you have done much better than average, you should notice two things. The first is that the Playpen does not respond to your choices. Two of the choices should make visible changes. We have to call `display()` for the `playpen` object to make the changes visible.

There are two solutions to this; we can arrange that a function that changes the Playpen always updates the display by calling `display()` or we can make updating the display a menu option. In the context, I think the former choice is better. Unless you already did this, go back and add a `pp.display()` to the `clear_playpen()` and `plot_pixel()` functions.

Now let us look at the second problem. When the request to enter a choice is repeated you are getting a message that says "*is not an option, please try again*". This is almost certainly baffling you. The problem is that some of the choices require extra information. After they acquire it they are not clearing out such things as the Return that ended the input. The `getline()` function is treating this residual data as if it were new input.

There are several ways to fix this but rather than leave you struggling I have provided another function like `std::getline()` except that it skips lines that do not contain at least one character that is not whitespace (spaces, tabs and newlines). This function is `fgw::getdata()` and is a drop-in replacement for `std::getline()` wherever blank lines should be ignored. It is declared in fgw_text.h. A side effect of using `getdata()` is that it also fixes the problem of assuming the user inputs some data. `getdata()` will wait for input that is not whitespace.

Please amend the code for `get_choice()` and test again. You should find that the program now works as expected.

Notice the fallback position that I have provided for `change_plotmode()`. This is a common programming idiom called a "stub function". It allows the rest of the code to work

and allows you to take your time with elements that you are not ready to complete. There are various ways that `change_plotmode()` could be written. As we are currently focusing on menus, a menu solution will give you a chance to consolidate your understanding of the menu idiom.

Implement and test the `change_plotmode()` function by selecting from a menu of the plot mode options.

Dealing with Dependencies

Before I give you a few things to do, let me address the issue of ensuring that the function that gets the user's choice and the one that acts upon that choice can be kept consistent. Let me put that another way, `do_choice()` has got some nasty magic numbers in it. We have `case 0:`, `case 1:`, etc., in the `switch` statement relying on the programmer of `get_choice()` keeping the menu items in the same order as the implementer of `do_choice()`.

Another user-defined type: enum

There are several ways of tackling this. I am going to show you one that relies on a simple kind of user-defined type called an `enum` (like `class`, `enum` is a keyword of C++). An `enum` lets you declare a list of names and the integer values they will represent.

```
enum art_menu_choices{
  clear_am = 0,
  finish_am = 1,
  plotmode_am = 2,
  scale_am = 3,
  plot_am = 4
};
```

The above code results in `clear_am` representing 0, `finish_am` representing 1, `plotmode_am` representing 2, `scale_am` representing 3, and `plot_am` representing 4. I have added the `_am` to each name to avoid clashes with other uses of "clear", "finish", etc.

ROBERTA

I would be interested to know what your other options were and why you decided as you did. It would help to understand the mind of an expert.

FRANCIS

When I look at it there aren't any other reasonable alternatives in the context of this book. When you learn much more about C++ and the special resources provided by graphical user interfaces (i.e. programs that work with a window and a mouse) you will come across other (more idiomatic) solutions.

You may be wondering why I need to worry about name clashes. The problem is that the braces enclosing the list of enumeration constants (that is what we call names provided by an enum) do not form a scope. This is the only case I know of in C++ where a pair of braces does not provide a scope for declaring names. The result is that the enumeration constants escape into the enclosing scope, i.e. wherever art_menu is defined.

If I put that definition of (enum art_menu_choices) in the art_menu.cpp file, I can use it to make my code more readable and make it easier to add new items to the menu. Notice that I am placing the enum in the unnamed namespace in a .cpp file. That is because nothing outside this file needs to know about it. It is purely for improving the implementation of the functions get_choice() and do_choice(). Let me demonstrate that

Using an enum to improve readability

First I need to tackle the problem of keeping the enumerated values in line with the keys that select a choice. I thought about several options before I decided that the enumeration constants should be the values of the letters that select the choices.

We will still be able to use a string of possible letters to check if the user has pressed a valid key, but we will no longer use the result of find() to convert the key to an int. First let me redo the enum:

```
enum art_menu_choices {
  clear_am = 'C',
  finish_am = 'F',
  plotmode_am = 'M',
  scale_am = 'S',
  plot_am = 'P'
};
```

The layout is purely cosmetic, and will make it easier to add extra choices. I have replaced the numerical values of the enumerated constants (the named values) by char literals. I have made use of the fact that C++ attaches an integral value to each char literal. I do not care what the actual values are, only that they are the ones for the letters being used.

Having done that, I am going to rewrite the display_choices() function so that the letter it displays for each choice will necessarily match the one used in the enum.

```
void display_choices(){
  cout << "Select one of the following by pressing the\n"
       << "key indicated and then pressing the Return key.\n\n"
       << '\t' << char(clear_am) << "\tClear the Playpen Window.\n"
       << '\t' << char(plotmode_am) << "\tChange the plotting mode.\n"
       << '\t' << char(scale_am) << "\tChange the scale.\n"
       << '\t' << char(plot_am) << "\tPlot a pixel.\n"
       << '\t' << char(finish_am) << "\tFinish. \n\n";
}
```

Placing the enumeration constants such as clear_am in parentheses preceded by char forces the compiler to treat the enumeration constant as a char value. Without that mechanism the compiler would convert clear_am, etc., into int for the purpose of streaming them to cout. We want to see those values as letters. This mechanism of overruling a type and insisting the compiler uses the one we choose is called casting.

This may seem a tricky bit of code but it ensures that if you change the letter that selects an option, the menu will automatically match that change. This follows a programming principle that you should design code so that changes are easy and localized. A change in one place should not require changing code somewhere else.

Now I have to make some small changes to the get_choice() function to give this:

```
char get_choice(){
// string const choices("CFMPS"); has been removed from here
// and moved adjacent to the definition of enum art_menu_choices.
  cout << "Action: (Press letter followed by Return): ";
  do{
     string input;
     getdata(cin, input);
     char const letter(toupper(input[0]));
     int const choice(choices.find(letter));
// Check that choice is valid
      if(choice < choices.size()){
        return letter;
      }
// Note you can only get here if the choice was not valid.
     cout << '"' << letter << '"'<< "is not an option.\n";
     cout << "Please try again: ";
  } while(true);
}
```

I have highlighted that altered line and where I have removed the definition of choices. I have moved that from this function and placed it immediately after the definition of enum art_menu_choices. I have done that because when you add new choices you will also have to add letters to the choices string so I want the two close together (in the same locality). I have placed both enum art_menu_choices and choices in the unnamed namespace so that their details cannot leak out into the rest of the program.

And finally I need to make some changes to the do_choice() function. The switch-statement must be modified to read:

```
switch(choice){
  case clear_am:
     clear_playpen(pp);
     break;
  case finish_am:
     more = false;
     break;
  case plotmode_am:
     change_plotmode(pp);
     break;
  case plot_am:
     plot_pixel(pp);
     break;
  case scale_am:
     change_scale(pp);
     break;
  default: throw problem("Not a valid option");
}
```

Voilà, the magic numbers have gone. If we now decide to change the end choice from ''F to Finish'' to ''Q to Quit'' or ''X to exit'', we just need to change the ''F'' to ''Q'' or ''X'' in the `enum` and in the `choices` string. Change the text of the message from ''Finish'' to ''Quit'' if you wish. You have probably noticed the way that professional programmers handle letters used for selecting menu choices. The good ones try to make the prompt have a mnemonic value. If ''F'' is an obvious letter for some other choice, they would use something like ''X exit'' or ''Q quit'' for the end choice.

You have probably noticed that menus rarely have more than a dozen options. Where more options are needed the professional introduces sub-menus.

I think the only slightly opaque part of the above code is where I convert the `enum` values back to letters for the purposes of display. Once you get used to that you should find the code very easy to maintain. I hope so because that is your next task.

Because I want you to focus on writing new code I have provided the source code files for what I have done above. You will find them in your Chapter 8 directory. Create a project and use them to create a simple menu driven ''art'' program. That should not take you long.

Now enhance the program by adding features. At a minimum you should provide options to draw a variety of shapes. I think that should be provided via a sub-menu from the main menu (an example of a sub-menu is the ''Change plotmode'' option we already have). This time you need a full menu system because most of the choices need further input.

Do not worry too much if you find some of this task hard. You are experiencing real programming in that you have to come up with solutions to problems built on your understanding of your tools. The only way to gain skill is practice.

There are many other tasks that you could set yourself. For example, when you feel confident enough of your programming to write functions that draw dotted or dashed lines you could add them as options. When you have studied the next section you could come back to this task and add filled shapes to the options.

How much you stretch yourself is very much up to you. Try to avoid overreaching and breaking your confidence. You should succeed in your tasks often enough to find it fun and nourishing your sense of intellectual adventure. Sometimes your mentor (assuming you are fortunate enough to have one) might suggest putting a task aside for a time until you have acquired more skill. Do listen to the advice and avoid letting your pride drive you beyond your current limits. Success at a price of promising never to do it again is no real success.

Functions that Fill a Polygon

When Roberta worked through the first draft of this book she wanted a mechanism for drawing a filled polygon. I suggested a couple of possibilities, which worked for the limited cases that she was interested in. I also pointed out that a general solution for any polygon was far from easy.

I then came up with some tentative solutions that more or less tackled the problem. I was unhappy with them and used my regular column in an ACCU journal (C Vu) to ask if any of the readers knew a reasonably good answer. One of the readers, James Holland recalled having found an algorithm for filling an area described by David Rogers in the book ''Procedural Elements for Computer Graphics''. He also remembered that he had had quite a struggle implementing the algorithm from the author's description. James was kind enough to write an article for publication along with an implementation for filling an area in a black & white image. The article and code gave me enough to produce a fully working implementation to fill an area defined by a border in a specified color.

I then reworked the algorithm to provide a function that will change a contiguous area in one color to some other color.

These two functions required quite a lot of time to get working satisfactorily and, like the general line-drawing function provided by drawline(), their implementation is outside the scope of this book. So I have provided them in my library and their declarations are in the flood_fill.h header file.

The declarations of the functions are:

```
void seed_fill(fgw::playpen & canvas, int x, int y,
               fgw::hue new_hue, fgw::hue boundary);
void replace_hue(fgw::playpen & canvas, int x, int y,
               fgw::hue new_hue);
```

Each of these functions needs a reference to a playpen and the coordinates of a pixel. Both of them also need to know what the new color will be. In the case of the seed_fill() you must also provide the color of the boundary. In case you are wondering, the edges of the Playpen always count as a boundary so the functions will not try to change the color of pixels that are off the screen.

The replace_hue() function uses the color of the seed pixel to identify which color has to be changed to the new_hue.

Though (x, y) determines a "pixel" in the terms of the public representation (i.e. takes account of the current scale and origin) the actual functions work down at screen pixel level. The values given for x and y must be inside the region that you want to flood with a color. If you choose a point that is actually on a boundary the results will not always be what you expect.

The only way to understand what these functions can do for you is to use them, so the remainder of this chapter will focus on ways to use these functions.

In Chapter 6 you learnt how to produce polygons in various different ways. Now we are going to revisit that but make the polygons solid blocks of color. You need not frantically sort out your code from Chapter 6 because my library provides most of the functions for handling shapes. There are declarations in shape.h for:

```
shape make_regular_polygon(double radius, int n);
shape makecircle(double radius, point2d centre);
shape read_shape(std::istream &);
```

The last of those three reads data from a stream. The first item of data must be the number of point2d values that define the shape; these values are in the format (x, y). For a closed shape the last input must match the first.

```
  // function to store a shape to an ostream
void write_shape(shape const & s, std::ostream &);
  // the basic function to draw a shape
void drawshape(playpen & pp, shape const & s, hue shade);
  // the following functions transform a shape
void moveshape(shape & s, point2d offset);
void growshape(shape & s, double xfactor, double yfactor);
void scaleshape(shape & s, double scalefactor);
void rotateshape(shape & s, double rotation, point2d centre);
void rotateshape(shape & s, double rotation);
void shearshape(shape & s, double shear);
```

There are some other declarations in shape.h but the above are the ones that might be useful to you in the rest of this chapter. The pair of overloaded functions `rotateshape()` provide for rotation about a specified point and rotation about the origin.

EXERCISE 1

Use the above function declarations (from flood_fill.h and shape.h) to write an implementation (definition) of:

```
void filled_polygon(fgw::playpen & pp, shape const & s,
        fgw::point2d centre, fgw::hue);
```

Then write a program to test your function. You can use the myshape.txt file you created in Chapter 6 as the source of a shape for this program.

EXERCISE 2

Write and test a function that will display a solid (filled in) regular polygon given the number of sides, the center, the distance of the center to a vertex and the color. You might start by writing a function that will do this with the center at the origin.

For bonus points enhance your function so that you can specify a rotation.

EXERCISE 3

Write a function that will display a solid disk on the screen given its center, radius and color.

EXERCISE 4

Enhance the art menu program to utilize the functions you wrote for Exercises 1, 2 and 3.

EXERCISE 5

Go back to the art menu code and add in menu choices to load a shape from a file. Note that this will entail capturing the file name and using `fgw::open_ifstream()`, declared in fgw_text.h.

ROBERTA'S COMMENTS

I got far too carried away by the idea in Chapter 7 of writing my own program. So rather than use the art program as suggested I decided to adapt the code in this chapter to produce a menu program to change the colors of the various parts of my US flag. I was quite delighted with the result and it will always have a special place in my heart because it was my very first independent program.

When it was time to revise the book I realized that I hadn't actually tried the `flood_fill()` functions (they did not exist when I read the first draft of this chapter). I dug up my American flag program from the archives, updated it a bit to reflect revisions in the book and then tried to improve the stars which weren't very good.

The major problem was that I couldn't understand the function I had written to produce 50 stars. I knew it worked but how it did so was by now a complete mystery. It was so badly written that I couldn't use the `flood_fill()` in it because I couldn't even locate a point within the stars let alone identify the center.

I played around with `flood_fill()` and realized that if I had had these functions at the time I would have written most of the program quite differently and given the knowledge gained over the next few chapters even more so. The same applies to the next "real" program I embarked on immediately I had finished the flag one.

So, while I do think I gained much from these early attempts, not least confidence, I realize now that not only was I trying to run before I could walk but that waiting a while would have given me far more tools to work with. I think it would have been far better to write down ideas for my programs and wait even if only a short while before attempting them. I'm not trying to put you off having a go, however, I'm just relating my own experience which in my own way was an attempt to canoe a rapid backwards.

I found using namespaces to store function definitions very useful. It seems far easier than having to create separate header and implementation files. Perhaps it made me lazy though because after discovering namespaces I used them most of the time and when I eventually had to use a header file again I had almost forgotten their existence.

The elements of the menu program in this chapter and the next can be easily adapted for any program you might want to write. It might be worth creating a template file of the basics to use whenever you want to use a menu.

Finally, I know this will make me look silly again but I can't resist sharing it. When I completed my flag program Francis asked me to send it to him. I didn't know how to. I hadn't realized that the .exe file was a stand-alone program in its own right and could be run on any suitable PC.

SOLUTIONS TO TASKS

Task 19

I will start with the two easy ones before dealing with the harder one. The first one is almost exactly the same as the `clear_playpen()` function.

```
void change_scale(playpen & pp){
  int const new_scale(read<int>("What is the new scale? "));
  pp.scale(new_scale);
}
```

The next one is not actually harder; it is just that there is more data to collect from the user. Unfortunately they will have to provide the hue as a number from 0 to 255. That is unless you feel up to writing a `get_shade()` function that can manage textual input such as `red4` or `green2`. You could write such a function (and there is quite a good menu-based solution) but it is not trivial.

```
void plot_pixel(playpen & pp){
  int const x(read<int>("What x value? "));
```

SOLUTIONS TO TASKS

```
  int const y(read<int>("What y value? "));
  hue const shade(read<hue>("What color number, 0 - 255? "));
  pp.plot(x, y, shade);
  pp.display();
}
```

Task 20

In this one we want to restrict the user's choice. If he tries to give me a choice that has not been covered, I am going to default to doing nothing rather than nag for a correct answer.

```
void change_plotmode(playpen & pp){
  cout << "\t\tWhich Plotmode do you want?\n";
  cout << "\tD for direct mode.\n";
  cout << "\tF for filter mode.\n";
  cout << "\tA for additive mode.\n";
  cout << "\tJ for disjoint mode.\n";
  char const new_mode(cin.get());
  switch(toupper(new_mode)){
     case 'D':
        pp.setplotmode(direct);
        break;
     case 'F':
        pp.setplotmode(filter);
        break;
     case 'A':
        pp.setplotmode(additive);
        break;
     case 'J':
        pp.setplotmode(disjoint);
        break;
     default:
        cout << "***Invalid response ignored.***\n";
  }
}
```

I placed the code for displaying the menu, getting the response, and processing it in the same function because this seems a simple case where there is nothing to be gained by dividing the action into three files. It is not the kind of case where I will want to add new menu items; there are only four plotting modes.

I have taken the opportunity to illustrate that a `switch` will work with `char` literals (note that it will not work with string literals because those do not have numerical values representing them).

SOLUTIONS TO EXERCISES

I am not providing solutions for these exercises. There is considerable room for variation and the only real test is whether your code worked. Ask your mentor, if you have one, to check your solution and comment on the coding quality.

Summary

Key programming concepts

- The conventional way of asking a user to make a choice is with a menu.
- There are three stages to a menu: listing the choices (with indications as to how to make your choice), getting the choice (checking that it is a valid choice) and acting on the choice.
- Where a user can make repeated choices the menu should include a quit or exit choice.
- Most programming languages have a mechanism for supporting the Boolean concept – the idea that a statement can be either true or false. This is used for making decisions that are essentially two-way.
- Multi-way decisions are prone to programming errors if handled by successive `if...else` statements. Languages often provide an alternative mechanism that makes it clear that one of several is being chosen.
- Limit the availability of names and information. The more widely information is visible in a program the easier it is to misuse it.
- When writing code, use a stub function (a dummy function that is just enough to keep a test program happy) until you are ready to complete the definition.
- Test early and test often.

C++ checklist

- The C++ `bool` type has two values, `true` and `false`, which are C++ keywords.
- There are conversions between numerical types (such as `int`, `double` and `char`) and `bool`. Zero values convert to `false`; all other values convert to `true`. `true` converts to one and `false` converts to zero.
- The C++ keyword `enum` provides for user-defined integer types with a set of named values called enumeration constants.
- `Do...while` provides an alternative form of loop. do introduces the body of the loop and `while(expression)` determines if the loop will be repeated. As long as the `expression` evaluates as `true` the body is repeated.
- `switch` is the basis for multi-way choices in C++. `switch(`*control expression*`){` initiates the set of choices. The control expression must evaluate to a whole number. `case` followed by a compile time constant followed by colon identifies a choice. The code after the colon is run until the keyword `break` is encountered. `default:` identifies code that will be run if there is no matching `case`.
- Declarations and definitions placed in an unnamed namespace are local to the file they are in and will not clash with identical names in other files.
- `find()` is a member function of `std::string` that returns the position (starting from zero) of the first occurrence of a specified `char` in a given `string`. It returns a special value named `npos` if no match is found.

Extensions checklist

- `fgw::getdata()` is a function that skips whitespace in an input stream and then extracts all data up to and including the first "`\n`" after the first non-whitespace character. It should be used as a replacement for `std::getline()` when an empty line should be ignored.
- Two functions that fill areas with a selected color are declared in flood_fill.h. `seed_fill()` changes all pixels within a boundary provided by a `boundary` hue to a new shade. The edges of Playpen will be used as part of the boundary if necessary. `replace_hue()` changes a contiguous area (orthogonally connected) with the same color as the seed pixel to the new one.
- Several functions that handle shapes (defined as `vector<point2d>` containers) are declared in shape.h.

CHAPTER 9

You Can Keep Data

Persistence has a special meaning in programming; it refers to the property of data that survives from one execution of a program to another. In this chapter you will learn how to develop the sample menu program of the last chapter so that you can save and restore the images you create.

You will learn about a mechanism for saving actions that a program user takes during an execution of the program rather than just the end result. A consequence of that will be the ability to provide editing and undoing of actions. To do this you will learn how to use `std::stringstream` objects as temporary data stores.

You will also learn about the important programming concept of an **iterator** and how that concept is supported by C++.

Saving and Restoring Images

Saving a Playpen image to a file provides the basis for a simple form of persistence. Once we have saved the image we can restore it whenever we wish.

When we choose to save a graphical image we need to decide how we store it. Graphical data is often very large. In its raw state a Playpen image takes over 250 kilobytes of storage even if it is a blank image. That is inefficient but, even worse, the images can only be used by Playpen-based programs. Compressed data can often be saved and restored quickly because, in computer terms, hard drives are exceptionally slow devices in contrast to RAM. The time saved by storing compressed data often exceeds the time used in compressing and uncompressing it. Modern disk drives are about four times faster than those of ten years ago, but computational speed is more than a hundred times faster so the balance continues to swing in favor of compression.

Lossless and lossy compression

There are two main kinds of data compression. Lossless compression mechanisms are ones that ensure that the exact original can be restored from the compressed data. This kind of compression is important for text and programs.

In lossy compressions, we opt to allow the possible loss of quality of data in order to provide better compression ratios. We frequently apply lossy compression to storing pictures and music. For example, JPEG for graphics and MP3 for music are lossy compressions. JPEG even allows us to select how much degradation of data we can tolerate in exchange for a smaller file.

Portable Network Graphics is an interesting compression system designed to allow people to swap graphical images over a network. In the strict sense it is a lossy compression because we can reduce the number of colors in an image in exchange for a smaller file. Interestingly from our perspective it does this by means of a palette of 256 (or fewer) entries that are mapped to mixtures of red, green, blue and transparency (how much an existing image is allowed to show through). Playpen does not use transparency but it does use a palette of 256 colors mapped to the hardware's ability to display the primary colors of light (red, green and blue). That means that we can use the PNG format as a lossless compression for Playpen images.

We get another advantage by using a standard format for saving our graphics images; we will be able to load them into other programs that can use files in PNG format. With care we will be able to reverse the procedure and load PNG files from elsewhere. However these must have been created in a 256-color palette format and be 512 by 512 pixels.

TECHNICAL NOTE

Creating PNG images

I have found that Jasc's Paint Shop Pro 7 works well with Playpen PNG images. The following technique produces a suitable image for loading into a Playpen:

1. Load an image into Paint Shop that contains the material you want to import to the Playpen.
2. Cut out the required part of the image (select the area and press Ctrl-C). To avoid distortion, the part you cut out should be approximately square.
3. Create a new image (press Ctrl-V).
4. Resize the image (press Shift-S) by making appropriate selections in the dialog box – only the data in the white areas matters. You will need to deselect ''Maintain aspect ratio'' if you are to be able to specify exactly 512 by 512 pixels.
5. Save the result (press Ctrl-S). Select the PNG format and then select options.
6. Choose *Noninterlaced* with *Optimized Palette* and select Run optimizer.
7. The important choices are: Palette based, 256 colors, 100% dithering.
8. Click OK and wait for the save menu to return. Choose whatever name you want for the file and save it in your current working directory (Chapter 9 for now).

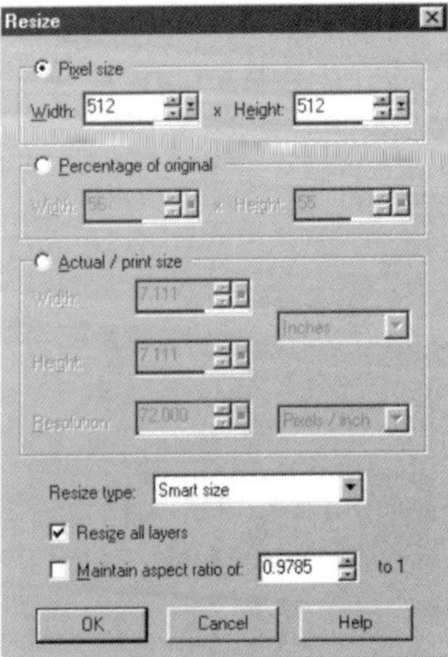

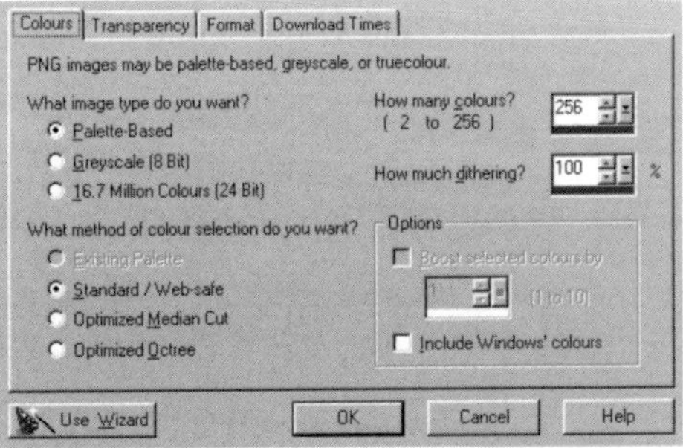

PNG files for Playpen

The declarations needed for PNG support for Playpen images are in playpen.h. The two functions you will need are:

```
void LoadPlaypen(fgw::playpen &, std::string filename);
void SavePlaypen(fgw::playpen const &, std::string filename);
```

If they fail for any reason they throw a `MiniPNG::error` exception. Currently we are not processing exceptions other than catching them in `main` with `catch(...)` so you do not yet need to know more about that exception type.

A typical piece of code (not a complete function) to save a Playpen image would be:

```
cout << "What file do you want to store the image in? ";
string savefile;
getdata(cin, savefile);
SavePlaypen(paper, savefile);
```

where `paper` is the name of the active `playpen` object. Very similar code can be used to load an image from a file where you have previously saved it.

When you save a .png image you also save the palette it is using. When you restore an image you also restore the palette. The actual palette coding when you load an image created elsewhere will be whatever that graphics tool created for the image.

TASK 22

I have provided an image called rose.png in the Chapter 9 directory. Write a program that loads that image into the Playpen.

Add the line `paper.rgbpalette()` (assuming that `paper` is your `playpen` object) after the load of rose.png. That resets the palette for the Playpen to the default one you have been using throughout this book. This allows you to see how palettes change the display.

Much later we will be taking a more detailed look at the subject of palettes, saving them and restoring them. For now I just wanted to take an opportunity to demonstrate that what a Playpen image looks like is influenced by the palette being used.

TASK 23

Add Save and Load options to the menu you created in Chapter 8 and add any necessary support functions as well as modifying the menu functions.

If you do not have a graphics application (such as Paint Shop Pro) that allows you to create your own PNG images in a suitable format for Playpen, you can use rose.png as well as any that you create and save.

Please check my solution because there are some important comments attached to it.

Using Captured Data

Rather than saving the result as a Playpen image we can look at ways of recording the actions that produced the result. You might think about saving actions in a vector of actions. That is a fine idea, but it presents us with a problem because C++ sequence containers such as `vector<>` require a single homogeneous type. That means we will have to find a way to make all the actions have the same type, even though some require very different data to the others.

The first part of the solution to this problem is to recognize that all the data that leads to a specific action in the program from Chapter 8 is provided from the keyboard. If we could save that data in some form of output stream we could read it back again from that source instead of from the keyboard.

You may wonder about storing the data in a `string` object because all the data is created from keyboard input. That would be an excellent idea because we could use a `vector<string>` to store the actions. However `string` is not a stream object and so is not a sink for data.

Cast your eyes back to Chapter 4 where I mentioned `stringstream` types. That is the key to our problem. We can use a `stringstream` object to create a string with the data packaged in a readable form. Here is a little program to demonstrate that:

```
#include <iostream>
#include <sstream>
#include <string>

using namespace std;

int main(){
  stringstream datastore;
  datastore << "This is a demonstration ";
  datastore << 123;
  datastore << " ";
  datastore << 23.45;
  datastore << '\n';
  cout << "And here is the result: \n";
  cout << datastore.str();
}
```

First of all notice how we can use the `stringstream` object called `datastore` exactly as we have used the console output stream `cout and fstream` objects elsewhere. That is one of the great things about the C++ stream types; they have the same basic behavior, learn it once and use it everywhere. The header that gives us access to the `stringstream` types is `<sstream>`.

The last line of the above program uses a special `stringstream` member function `str()` that returns a copy of the `string` object that `stringstream` is using as a buffer to store the data. There is a second version of `str()` that takes a `string` argument which it copies to use as a source of data.

Here is an example program showing how that second version of `str()` can be used:

```
#include "fgw_text.h"
#include <iostream>
#include <sstream>
#include <string>

using namespace fgw;
using namespace std;

int main(){
  stringstream datastore;
```

```
  datastore.str("Here is an example \n 345 \n2.34\n");
  string message;
  getline(datastore, message);
  cout << '\n' << message;
  int const i(read<int>(datastore));
  double const d(read<double>(datastore));
  cout << i << " " << d << '\n';
}
```

We can use the standard operators for streams, member functions and free functions (including those we write ourselves) with `stringstream` objects in exactly the way that we use them for any other stream.

Also notice that the string literal I used to provide data for `datastore` includes `\n` after each item of data. That allows me to use `std::getline()` or `fgw::getdata()` to extract the message text by taking everything up to the `\n`. It discards the `\n`.

Storing keyboard data

Here is a program to demonstrate capturing data from the keyboard, storing it in a `vector<string>`, sorting it and then sending it to a file.

```
// Demo program by F. Glassborow
// Written 3rd January 2003
// includes and using directives omitted

int main(){
  try{
     string const terminator("END");
     bool more = true;
     vector<string> details;
     do{
        cout << "Next name ("<< terminator << " to finish): ";
        string name;
        getdata(cin, name);
        stringstream data;
        data << name << '\n';
        if(name == terminator){
           more = false;
        }
        else {
           cout << "How old are you? ";
           data << read<int>() << '\n';
           cout << "What is your height in meters? ";
           data << read<double>() << '\n';
        }
        details.push_back(data.str());
     } while(more);
// sort all but the last item which is the terminator string
     sort(details.begin(), details.end()-1);
// show the results on the screen
```

```
      for(int i = 0; i != details.size(); ++i){
         cout << details[i];
      }
// get a file and store the data in it
      cout << "What file do you want to store the results in. ";
      string filename;
      getdata(cin, filename);
      ofstream outfile;
      open_ofstream(outfile, filename);
      for(int i = 0; i != details.size(); ++i){
         outfile << details[i];
      }
   }
   catch(...){
      cout << "There was a problem.\n";
   }
}
```

I hope you are able to follow that program through. We have seen all the functions before but you may have forgotten a couple of them. Check through the end of chapter summaries, particularly for Chapter 3, to refresh your memory.

The first use of `getdata()` in this program avoids any risk of getting a file name that starts with blanks. You could add code to clear it out but `fgw::getdata()` does that for you. Learn to use the tools you have rather than spend time doing things from scratch. If you open the file you specified, in your editor, you should see all the test data you entered in a readable form.

Recovering stored data

Now I am going to demonstrate that we can read that data back into another program. The data is now *persistent* because it survives from one program to another.

```
// includes and using directives omitted
int main(){
   try{
      string const terminator("END");
      cout << "What file contains the data? ";
      string filename;
      getline(cin, filename);
      ifstream input;
      open_ifstream(input, filename);
      vector<string> details;
      bool more = true;
      do{
      stringstream datastore;
      string name;
         getdata(input, name);
         if(name == terminator){
```

```
            more = false;
         }
         else {
            datastore << name << '\n';
            datastore << read<int>(input) << '\n';
            datastore << read<double>(input) << '\n';
            details.push_back(datastore.str());
         }
      } while(more);
      for(int i = 0; i != details.size(); ++i){
         cout << details[i];
      }
   }
   catch(...){
      cout << "There was a problem.\n";
   }
}
```

Does that program look vaguely familiar? It should do because it is the previous program modified. We prompt for a file to use as a data source, throw away the input prompts, change the functions to versions that get input from any stream rather than just the console. There is no need to sort or save the data because we have already done that.

I hope you are beginning to appreciate how well the different types of data stream work together. Furthermore `stringstream` types are a marvelous tool for storing data as a `string`. That allows us to store all the data for a specific action in a single package. Because we can do that, we can collect data into a container.

Before you go on, make sure you understand how the above programs work.

Modify my program that prompts for names, ages and heights, so that after it has sorted the data it redisplays it in the form:

Name: Francis Glassborow
Age: 61
Height: 1.70 meters
[Hint available]

A Menu-Driven Program with Persistence

Let us start with the program we had in the last chapter and consider what changes we will need to make and propagate those changes through the levels of function call. Here is the top-level program:

```
int main(){
  playpen picture;
  bool more(true);
  do{
    display_choices();
```

```
    int const choice(get_choice());
    more = do_choice(picture, choice);
  } while(more);
}
```

First let me clean that up a little. If you look at the way that `more` is used you might, correctly, conclude that we do not need it and can write this instead:

```
int main(){
  try{
     playpen picture;
     int choice;
     do{
       display_choices();
       choice = get_choice();
     } while(do_choice(picture, choice));
  }
  catch(...) { cout << "An exception was thrown.\n";}
}
```

An experienced programmer would be likely to choose that form, not just because it is shorter, but because it is clearer to those who understand how `do...while` works.

First I will need somewhere to store the actions. I am going to use a `vector<string>` object to save the data in the program and add an option in the menu to write it out. I am also going to take the precaution of writing it out in the event that an exception gets thrown. Here is the start of a modified version:

```
int main(){
  vector<string> actions;
  try{
     playpen picture;
     do{
       display_choices();
       int const choice(get_choice());
     } while(do_choice(picture, choice));
  }
  catch(...){
     cout << "A problem has occurred. Attempt to save data"
          << " to a file follows.\n";
  }
     cout << "Do you want to save your work? y/n ";
     if(yn_answer()){
        save_actions(actions);
     }
  }
```

Note that this program will not work because we have not yet added any mechanism for storing actions. We will be tackling that shortly.

The `actions` object has to be declared outside the `try`-block because we need it to be available even if something goes wrong and `throws` an exception. I am assuming that nothing goes wrong in either the yn_answer() function or the save_actions() function. I have written the yn_answer() function in such a way that it cannot fail (well your computer might stop working, but there is little we can do as programmers to handle that situation). If something goes wrong in writing to file, there will generally be no recovery available in this context so letting the program give up seems reasonable. If nothing can be done, do not waste time trying to do anything.

The declaration of yn_answer() is in fgw_text.h and the definition in namespace fgw is:

```
bool yn_answer(){
  do {
     char const answer(toupper(cin.get()));
     if(answer == 'Y') return true;
     if(answer == 'N') return false;
  } while(true);
}
```

This function continues to extract characters from cin until it gets one that either converts to an uppercase Y or an uppercase N.

save_actions() and the matching append_actions() are in the updated menu files in the Chapter 9 directory. These files are named art_menu2.h and art_menu2.cpp. Note that save_actions() has a vector<string> const & parameter but append_actions() has a vector<string> & parameter (no const). Both functions need access to the original actions object, but the save version will not change the original, just write it to a file. On the other hand the append version will change the actions object by appending data from a file. Here are the declarations:

```
void save_actions(std::vector<std::string> const & actions);
void append_actions(std::vector<std::string> & actions);
```

Write your own definitions for the above functions. Then edit your menu functions so that these two functions can be called through the menu. Add a third choice to load an actions file to an empty vector<string> actions variable. My art_menu2.cpp file contains an implementation of the menu functions I have been developing in the last chapter and in this one. Please look and see how it goes together.

Capturing actions

Being able to save the vector<string> data and recover it is fine, but we need to record the data in the first place. To do that we need to convert the input data into a string and then add it as an item of the vector<string> we are calling actions in the above code. If we look at the three functions we wrote for our menu-driven program we should notice that one of those functions will have all the required information about an action. That is the only function that needs to know where to record the information.

Spotted which function we need to enhance? Yes, that is right; the do_choice() function will need an extra parameter which can receive the name of the vector<string> used to record the actions. The following declaration will allow us to pass that information in:

```
bool do_choice(fgw::playpen, int selected_action,
          std::vector<std::string> & actions);
```

Perhaps it is worth noting that, because of C++ function overloading, the new version of `do_choice()` can co-exist with the old one – the compiler will be able to choose which to use in any given case by the number of arguments we supply. In other words if we do not provide a third argument – the `vector<string>` object – the version that does not record the action data will be chosen.

Once we understand the value of overloading, we add the above declaration to our header file instead of changing the one that already exists. Doing it this way avoids breaking any existing programs that use the simpler version.

We will also need to provide new (overloaded) versions of the functions that implement the actions that we want to record. Enough preamble, let us look at some code:

```
bool do_choice(playpen & pp, int choice,  vector<string> & actions){
  bool more(true);
  switch(choice){
     case clear_am:
        clear_playpen(pp,  actions);
        break;
     case finish_am:
        more = false;
        break;
     case plotmode_am:
        change_plotmode(pp,  actions);
        break;
     case plot_am:
        plot_pixel(pp,  actions);
        break;
     case scale_am:
        change_scale(pp,  actions);
        break;
     default: cerr << "Not a valid option \n";
  }
  return more;
}
```

That was easy and follows a standard programmers' trick of putting off doing work until it cannot be avoided. All that you need to do is to decide which action functions need to know where to save their data. Actions like "Finish" need not be recorded.

Implementing action recording

Every time you write a new function you must decide who/what needs to know about it. If a function needs to be generally available it needs to be declared in the appropriate header file. If it only needs to be known to the implementation of another function, it belongs in the unnamed namespace of the file where it is used. If you later decide that a function needs wider access you can always add a declaration to a relevant header file and move its definition out of the unnamed namespace. Please get in the habit of limiting knowledge on a need to know basis. Using unnamed namespaces is a great C++ tool for doing that.

I am going to work through the code modifications for just one of the actions that we might wish to record. When I have done that, I would like you to tackle the other ones, including all those you have added. So let me look at `plot_pixel(playpen &, vector<string> actions)`. I think this code meets our needs:

```
void plot_pixel(playpen & pp, vector<string> & actions){
  stringstream storage;
```

```
    // and initialize it with the code for the plot_pixel choice
    storage << char(plot_am) << " ";
    int const x(read<int>("What x value? "));
    storage << x << " ";
    int const y(read<int>("What y value? "));
    storage << y << " ";
    hue const shade(read<hue>("What color? "));
    storage << shade;
    actions.push_back(storage.str());
    pp.plot(x, y, shade);
    pp.display();
}
```

Note that it is basically the original function with extra statements added to create a `string` object that can store the data. This string (extracted from the `stringstream` with the `str()` member function) is copied to the end of our container of actions. Providing the other function overloads should be straightforward. The only place you need to be careful is with any action that itself uses a `string` object. Currently we are using a space character as a data separator within each action string. When we come to store action strings in a file, the newline character will be used to separate the action strings.

TASK 25

Write and compile the overloads for the other functions that implement the menu choices for your art menu so that the choices and data are stored as a `string` in a `vector<string>`.

That is it from the recording side, though we could add a menu item to save the data stored in the `vector<string>` in a file. We have several options for ensuring that we do not try to read in more strings than we have saved. However why redo something we already have code for? Look back to where we wrote `save_actions()` and `append_actions()`. Those already do what we want.

Note that written this way we have a choice as to whether we append the actions from a file to those entries we already have in `actions` or remove the current entries and replace them with those from the file. It all depends on whether we empty the `actions` container before we load the file or not.

If we want to replace the actions from a file rather than add them to those we have recorded so far we can simply reuse the `append_actions()` like this:

```
void reload_actions(vector<string> & actions){
  vector<string> temp_actions;
  append_actions(temp_actions);
  actions.swap(temp_actions);
}
```

The purpose of the `swap()` in the last line is to exchange the data in `actions` with that in `temp_actions`. That is the tidiest way to replace the data of a container.

Repeating actions

Now we can store actions in a `vector<string>`, save the results in a file and restore those results to a `vector<string>` it is time to turn our minds to the problem of using those stored actions to redo them.

When we come to redo we will not use a menu; instead of responding to a user's choice we will need to extract the choice from the action string and use it to select and execute the correct action. Let us consider a single action string. We want to be able to write something like:

```
do_action(paper, actions[n]);
```

in order to get the nth entry in our `actions` vector carried out on the `playpen` called `paper`. That leads to the declaration:

```
do_action(fgw::playpen &, std::string const & action);
```

This is going to be very similar to `do_choice()` except that all the data is already packaged in the `action` string. Here is my implementation for the original set of actions:

```
void do_action(playpen & pp,
       vector<string> actions string const & action){
  stringstream data_source(action);
  char const choice(read<char>(data_source));
  switch(choice){
    case clear_am:
      clear_playpen(pp, data_source);
      break;
    case plotmode_am:
      change_plotmode(pp, data_source);
      break;
    case plot_am:
      plot_pixel(pp, data_source);
      break;
    case scale_am:
      change_scale(pp, data_source);
      break;
    default:
      cerr << "Action code " << char(choice) << " ignored.\n";
  }
  pp.display();
}
```

Remember that `std::cerr` is for using the console to report errors. It behaves exactly like `std::cout`. The `vector<string>` parameter isn't strictly needed at this stage but when you add save and restore functionality for actions you will need it.

The above version of `do_action()` is a simpler function than the one where we have to get the data from the keyboard. We do not have to deal with the special case of "Finish" so we do not need a `bool` return value. In addition we do not have to deal with the results of menu choices that we have not stored (such as save actions to file, redo actions, edit action list, etc.). All we have to do is to create a `stringstream` object, initializing it with the `action` string and then extract the first character to determine which function uses the rest of the data.

Now we pass the `playpen` object and the `stringstream` object to the selected function. These functions will be based on the ones we already have, but overloaded with a data source. As these functions are a pure implementation detail they will be hidden away in the unnamed namespace of the implementation file (only `do_action()` needs to know that these functions exist).

TECHNICAL NOTE

A lot of people have a problem with the idea of an unnamed namespace. Think that each implementation file has a special unlabeled box where it can keep things that no other file needs to know about. It is a special and very useful facility provided by C++. It limits the degree to which our code can mess up the work of others with things like accidental name clashes.

I would, however, make `do_action()` publicly available by placing its declaration in the header file and keeping its definition outside the unnamed namespace.

Here is my implementation of `plot_pixel(playpen &, stringstream & source)`:

```
void plot_pixel(playpen & pp, stringstream & source){
  int const x(read<int>(source));
  int const y(read<int>(source));
  int const shade(read<int>(source));
  pp.plot(x, y, shade);
}
```

Again this is simpler than the version using the keyboard because we no longer have to provide prompts for data input. However we should notice that this function can fail by throwing an `fgw::bad_input` exception if the data in the string we used to create the `stringstream` is corrupted.

TASK 26

Provide the declarations and definitions for some other functions to deal with other possible actions provided as a string of data (just as you did for recording actions). In general you should now have three overloads for each menu function apart from the menu functions that provide facilities for saving and restoring the action data. For the latter you will need two overloaded functions.

Note that there is no solution to this because it depends what you choose to add.

Implementing a redo function

We are now ready to write our redo function:

```
void redo(playpen & pp, vector<string> & actions){
  pp.scale(1);
  pp.setplotmode(direct);
  pp.origin(256, 256);
  pp.rgbpalette();
  pp.clear();
  for(int i(0); i != actions.size(); ++i){
     do_action(pp, actions, actions[i]);
  }
}
```

Note that we have to reset the Playpen because actions might have changed such things as the scale, the plotting mode and the palette.

Displaying actions

If we are going to edit or remove actions from a stored list, we will almost certainly want to see a list of what has been stored. Initially we might think of just writing a function that shows the whole list. However I think that you might guess that this would cause problems when we have a lot of actions – the list isn't going to fit in the console window. Perhaps we should start with a function that shows a block of actions. A suitable declaration would be:

```
void show_actions(std::vector<std::string> const & actions,
                  int from, int to);
```

TASK 27

Try writing that function for yourself before you look at my code (at the end of the chapter). Be careful to check that the range requested (`from`, `to`) exists. In other words be careful that `from` is not negative (i.e. attempts to refer to items before the start) and that `to` does not take us off the end.

TASK 28

Use that function to write a simpler function to display the most recent actions. Here is a suitable declaration:

```
void show_recent_actions(std::vector<std::string> const & actions);
```

The difference with this function is that it will calculate a suitable range and then call `show_actions()` to do the work. Implementing it should be straightforward.

TASK 29

Write a menu function that will prompt the user if there are more than 12 actions as to whether they want the most recent ones or some other block. Then use this function to implement a menu option to display a block of actions. Just displaying the stored strings will be satisfactory, you do not have to expand them into text. That is, 'C' is OK you do not have to output Clear Playpen to color, etc.

Where do you think these functions should be provided? Until we have reason to make a different choice, we only need those functions to support the implementation of our menu. Following the principle of restricting knowledge on a need to know basis, such functions should be out of sight, in the implementation file that is using them, so hide the function names in the unnamed namespace.

Implementing an undo function

The vector container supplies a special member function, `pop_back()`, that removes the last element. There is a catch in using it; it makes a mess (the correct term is "Has undefined behavior") if you apply it to an empty container. The C++ vector container has a member function, `empty()`, that answers the question "Are you empty?"

As long as we remember to check for an empty container first, the `pop_back()` function is exactly what we want for removing the last recorded action from our stored actions. Once we have done that, we only need to call our `redo()` function to update the Playpen.

Putting all that together we come up with:

```
void undo(playpen & pp, vector<string> & actions) {
  if(not actions.empty()){
     actions.pop_back();
     redo(pp, actions);
  }
}
```

This function does nothing if the `actions` container is empty, otherwise the last action is removed and the Playpen window is updated.

Further Practice

I am not giving you an explicit set of tasks or exercises because what you do for practice depends on what you have done in the previous chapter. However I think you would benefit a great deal from developing a menu type program to include both persistence (i.e. storing data to a file and later recovering that data in another program, or another run of the same program) and a simple undo option.

When you have a completed program it will be time for you to read the next section.

Iterators

The time has come when we need to tackle one of the areas of computer programming that has a reputation for being difficult and confusing. We need a mechanism for locating objects by where they are rather than by what they are called.

The concept of something whose responsibility is to deal with the question "Where are you?" is called an "iterator" in computer programming. When I tell you that something is an iterator I will mean that it provides information that identifies an object by providing some form of location information. We will even deal with special iterators whose purpose is to identify the lack of an object.

When I describe something as an iterator type, I will mean one of the special types provided in C++ to store location information. Unfortunately the experts get very sloppy in their use of terminology and use the term iterator to mean any one of:

- an **iterator value** which is the actual information to locate a specific object;
- an **iterator variable** which is storage for an iterator value;
- an **iterator type** which is the type of an iterator variable.

What makes it worse is that iterator variables are objects in their own right and so we can talk of an iterator to an iterator. It is little wonder that many competent programmers find themselves getting confused when the conversation turns to iterators. Let me see if I can keep the ideas clear enough so that you do not join them in their confusion.

For the time being we are going to focus on a group of iterator types that are collectively called **random iterators** (using the term in the third meaning above). Remember that the concept of a type is data combined with behavior, so what kind of behavior can an iterator have? Given an iterator value I can ask/command any of the following:

- What is the object for which you are a locator (usually called dereferencing)?
- Do this to the object for which you are a locator.
- What is the iterator (value) of the previous object?
- What is the iterator (value) of the next object?
- What is the iterator value of the nth object before/after you?
- How many objects are there between two iterators?

Each of those six items is handled by a specific mechanism provided for iterators in C++. Given that `iter` is the name of an iterator kind of object we can use the following mechanisms:

- `*iter` is the object that `iter` locates.
- `iter->action()` applies the `action` member function to the object `iter` locates.
- `--iter` changes `iter` to locate the preceding object.
- `++iter` changes `iter` to locate the following object.
- `(iter - n)` is the iterator value for the nth item before `*iter`.
- `(iter + n)` is the iterator value for the nth item after `*iter`.
- `(jter - iter)` returns an integer value such that `(iter + n)` is the same location as `jter`.

Locating data with an iterator

Let me try to give you a non-computing example. Here is my current street address:

64 Southfield Road

Let us suppose that is stored in an object called `address`.

Once you know that that is an address in Oxford (England), you can ask ''What is at that address?'' (`*address`) and get the answer ''A house owned by Francis Glassborow''.

You can deal with relevant behavior such as ''transfer of ownership'', ''painting'', etc., with:

```
address->sell(new_owner);
address->paint(white);
```

We can ask ''What is the next address?'' (`address + 1`) and get ''65 Southfield Road'' or ''What is the address of the house before it?'' (`address - 1`) and get ''63 Southfield Road''. You could ask ''What is at the address five more than 64 Southfield Road?'' `*(address + 5)` – note the asterisk – and get the answer ''a block of flats''. We can change `address` to the next address with `++address` or to the previous address with `--address`.

All that `address` does is to locate a specific plot of land. The rules for determining the address of other plots in the same street vary from place to place. I was surprised to discover that in many parts of the USA addresses don't increase by one as they usually do in the UK. They increase by their distance from some fixed point. Nonetheless an `address` iterator should work correctly by doing the right thing when incremented, decremented, etc. In most UK streets all the even numbers are on one side of the street and the odd ones are on the other. The addresses of the building plots either side of me are 62 and 66 Southfield Road. So a correctly working address iterator should supply the correct answer to "What is the address of the next building plot?"

What I am trying to show you is that we use iterator-like ideas in everyday language and that we need to know things about them before we can use them correctly. Even the simple concept of a street address turns up with different flavors in different places.

Fortunately when programming we do not need to know the computational rules for iterators, all we need to know is how to ask the questions and the programming language will do the rest for us.

Iterators in C++

For the work we want to do in the remainder of this chapter you only need to know about an iterator type provided for `vector` containers. It is a nested type of `vector` and is called `iterator` (that should make it easy to remember). That means its fully elaborated name is `std::vector<item type>::iterator`. Using this type and standard iterator behavior allows me to do some useful things.

Let me first rewrite my earlier `redo()` function but using an iterator instead of an `int`:

```
void redo(playpen & pp, vector<string> & const actions){
  pp.clear();
  for(vector<string>::iterator iter(actions.begin());
           iter != actions.end(); ++iter){
     do_action(*iter, pp);
  }
}
```

`++iter` increments `iter` to locate the next item. `*iter` obtains the actual item that `iter` is locating and passes it to `do_action()`. If you keep your mind on using iterators correctly you will find that the underlying concepts will slowly become a part of your thinking. The thing that generally causes confusion to start with is trying too hard to understand *how they work* when what we really need to do is to learn *how to use them*.

Most types of C++ container provide their own iterator type and member functions `begin()` and `end()`. The `begin()` function supplies the iterator value for the first element of the container. The `end()` function supplies a special iterator value to mark the end of a container (not the last item, that would be given by `(end() – 1)` for a non-empty container). An empty container can be identified because `begin()` and `end()` are equal.

Iterators are a far more general way of locating objects in a container than the `int` values we have been using until now. When we come to use C++'s non-sequence containers we will find that they have iterators even though they do not have numerical indices. Many of the more useful functions in `<algorithms>` work with iterators. The `sort()` function we have already used relies on being given iterators to mark out the range of items that need to be sorted (which were provided by `begin()` and `end()`). In addition some of the member functions of containers such as vectors use iterators. It is one of those member functions that makes it necessary for you to know about iterators and how to use them.

Removing an action from a list

The `pop_back()` function was fine for removing the last action but what should we do if we want to remove the last but two, or the third from the beginning? To do this we are going to use one of two versions of `erase()` provided as member functions of `vector`. This version needs the iterator of the item that we wish to discard (in other words it needs to know where the item is rather than what it is). Typical uses would be:

```
actions.erase(actions.begin() + 3);
// discards the third action from the beginning
```

```
actions.erase(actions.end() - 4);
// discards the fourth from the end
```

Remember that we count from 0 and the `end()` value does not locate an element, it is a special value that marks the end. The iterator to the last item is `(actions.end() – 1)`. It is our responsibility to check that we do not go outside the limits. For example we are on our own if we start referring to `(actions.begin() – 1)`.

That said we are ready to write a function to remove an action. Here is my version:

```
void delete_action(playpen & pp, vector<string> & actions){
  int const choice(read<int>(
     "What is the number of the action you want to cancel? "));
  if(choice < 0 or choice >= actions.size()){
     cerr << "No such action. Request ignored.\n";
  }
  else{
     actions.erase(actions.begin() + choice);
     redo(pp, actions);
  }
}
```

I have used another of C++'s logical operators – the `or` operator. The result of using `or` between two expressions is `true` if either of the expressions is `true`. If the first expression is `true` it does not calculate the value of the second one. This rule is an example of lazy evaluation which refers to doing no more work than is necessary to get an answer.

Editing an action

This is really a programming problem rather than a coding one. By that I mean the secret is in discovering that you already have all the tools, you just need to put them together slightly differently. What we want is to find out what action string we are going to use to replace the one we want to edit. There really is no value in actually editing the action string; just replace it.

Consider the following strategy:

```
Ask which action is to be replaced.
Validate that such an item exists.
Show the item to be replaced.
Check the user wants to proceed.
Get the replacement item.
Make the replacement.
Update display.
```

```
void replace_action(playpen & pp, vector<string> & actions){
  int const replace(read<int>(
     "What is the number of the action to be altered? "));
  if(replace < 0 or replace >= actions.size()){
     cout << "No such action. Request ignored.\n";
```

```
        return;
    }
    try {
        cout << actions[replace] << "\n Replace this? (y/n) ";
        if(yn_answer()){
            vector<string> replacement;
            display_choices();
            int choice = get_choice();
            do_choice(pp, choice, replacement);
            if(replacement.size() == 1){
                actions[replace] = replacement[0];
            }
        }
    }
    catch(...){
        cout << "A problem has occurred. Original data restored\n";
        return;
    }
    redo(pp, actions);
}
```

If you feel uncomfortable with being offered the general menu even though some items are not sensible choices, you could write new functions that will only offer and process choices that can be recorded: `display_recordable_choices()`, `get_recordable_choice()` and `do_recordable_choice()`. You need the new function names because they will have the same parameters as the original ones and so cannot be selected by overloading, only by having different names. There are other options for achieving the same end but I think we have gone far enough for now.

Before the Next Chapter

If you have worked all the way through this chapter you have a lot to digest. The framework provided by my art_menu2.cpp can easily be modified to do other things. If you look at what we have done you should see that some functions are specific to drawing on a Playpen using the fundamental tools you were given in Chapter 1. Other functions are about managing a sequence of choices and two forms of persistence; saving and loading the Playpen image; and saving and restoring a sequence of commands.

In Chapters 2 to 6, you learnt several other things that could be done such as drawing lines and changing the origin. It would be nice to add some of those but our menu is getting rather large. If you want to spend some time consolidating on what you have learnt (and I hope you will, but maybe you want to postpone it for now and come back to it later) think about how you can break the menu into parts (sub-menus). We have already had a small example of a sub-menu in the function that handles changing the plot mode. It would make sense to pull out the editing and file handling functions to their own menu, with their own `enum` (perhaps with an extension such as `_dm` for data management). That way you can free up some letters for the main menu and use rather more sensible letters for selections.

Because I want you to feel comfortable working with some reasonably good code, I have provided my final code for an art menu program in a sub-directory of Chapter 9. I hope you understand that this is to give you a good foundation to go forward rather than giving you an excuse for skipping coding for now.

Good luck and have some fun. I hope that I will be seeing lots of interesting programs derived from my art menu that can be placed on the honor roll at this book's website.

Exercise 1

You can install a `string` object for use as an input source simply by using the `str(data)` member function that is called with a suitable `string` as data. Once you have installed a copy of a data string you can extract the data from the `stringstream` object as you need it in exactly the same way as you would if you were using a file as a source for data. Iterate through the strings stored in the vector processing each one to give the required data format on the screen. Stop when you read in the name of "END".

SOLUTIONS TO TASKS

Task 22

This one should not have caused you much difficulty. Here is the code:

```
int main(){
  try {
     playpen canvas;
     LoadPlaypen(canvas, "rose.png");
     canvas.display();
     cout << "Press RETURN to restore default palette.\n";
     cin.get();
     canvas.rgbpalette();
     cout << "Press RETURN to end program.\n";
  }
  catch(...){
     cout << "An exception occurred.\n";
  }
}
```

Task 23

If you followed me in the last chapter you should have finished with some source code that is easy to edit to complete this task. The only file that needs editing is art_menu.cpp. Neither the header file nor the program that tests the code needs alteration.

I am only going to show the code that needs changing. First two functions to do the work:

```
void save_pp(playpen const & pp){
  string filename;
  cout << "What is the file name? ";
  getdata(cin, filename);
  try{
     SavePlaypen(pp, filename);
  }
```

SOLUTIONS TO TASKS

```
  catch(...){cerr << "Save failed.\n"; }
}
void load_pp(playpen & pp){
  string filename;
  cout << "What is the file name? ";
  getdata(cin, filename);
  try{
     LoadPlaypen(pp, filename);
  }
  catch(...){cerr << "Load failed.\n";}
}
```

I hated having that much repetition but as one needs to change the `playpen` object and the other does not I decided to live with it. They look very similar but combining them would be artificial. Do not take coding guidelines as immutable law.

Now to the `enum art_menu_choices` and `choices`, the string of key letters:

```
string const choices("CFMPSVL");
  enum art_menu_choices {
     clear_am = 'C',
     finish_am = 'F',
     plotmode_am = 'M',
     scale_am = 'S',
     plot_am = 'P',
     save_am = 'V',
     restore_am = 'L',
};
```

"S" has already been used for "scale" so I have used "V" to select the "Save Playpen" option.

The following two lines have to be added to the `display_choices()` function:

```
 << "\tV   save Playpen to disk.\n"
 << "\tL   load Playpen from disk.\n"
```

And finally the changed `do_choice()` function:

```
bool do_choice(playpen & pp, char choice){
  bool more(true);
  switch(choice){
     case clear_am:
        clear_playpen(pp);
        break;
     case finish_am:
        more = false;
```

SOLUTIONS TO TASKS

```
      break;
    case plotmode_am:
      change_plotmode(pp);
      break;
    case plot_am:
      plot_pixel(pp);
      break;
    case scale_am:
      change_scale(pp);
      break;
    case save_am:
      save_pp(pp);
      break;
    case restore_am:
      load_pp(pp);
      break;
    default: cerr << Not a valid option.\n";
  }
  return more;
}
```

I hope that demonstrates how much we profit from getting the original menu design right.

Task 24

```
void save_actions(vector<string> const & action_data){
  string const terminator("END");
  cout << "What file for storage (note that if you use an "
      << "existing file \n it will be replaced)? ";
  string filename;
  getdata(cin, filename);
  ofstream destination;
  open_ofstream(destination, filename);
  for(int i(0); i != action_data.size(); ++i){
    destination << action_data[i] << '\n';
  }
  destination << terminator << '\n';
}

void append_actions(vector<string> & action_data){
  string const terminator("END");
  cout << "What file contains the stored actions? ";
  string filename;
  getdata(cin, filename);
```

SOLUTIONS TO TASKS

```
  ifstream source;
  open_ifstream(source, filename);
  bool more = true;
  do {
     string action;
     getdata(source, action);
     if(action == terminator){
        more = false;
     }
     else{
        action_data.push_back(action);
     }
  } while(more);
}

void reload_actions(vector<string> & actions){
  vector<string> temp_actions;
  append_actions(temp_actions);
  actions.swap(temp_actions);
}
```

Task 25

Here are my solutions to the original menu functions, modified to record the actions as they happen. I have emphasized the code additions. I think you will see that they are actually almost mechanistic. Unfortunately despite the amount of repetition, this is one of the places where we have to bite the bullet and just add the code. The cut and paste facility provided by the editor does reduce the amount of typing.

There are a couple of ways to reorganize the code so that some of the common code is moved to a single place. For example, instead of creating the `stringstream` instance locally we might have done it in the `do_choice()` function and pushed the menu letter into it there. We could then have passed the `stringstream` (by reference) to alternatives to these functions that take a `stringstream` rather than a `vector<string>`. The `push_back()` would then be done by `do_choice()`. Doing that sort of extraction of common code is called refactoring.

Why didn't I refactor this code? For two basic reasons: I wanted to emphasize the consistent changes to the functions to make them record their behavior and I wanted to mention the concept of refactoring just so you would have some idea what it is if someone mentions it.

```
void clear_playpen(playpen & pp,  vector<string> & actions){
  stringstream storage;
// and initialize it with the code for the clear_playpen choice
  storage << char(clear_am) << " ";
  hue const new_color(read<int>("What background color? "));
  storage << int(new_color) << " ";
  actions.push_back(storage.str());
```

SOLUTIONS TO TASKS

```
  pp.clear(new_color);
}

void change_scale(playpen & pp, vector<string> & actions){
  stringstream storage;
// and initialize it with the code for the change_scale choice
  storage << char(scale_am) << " ";
  int const new_scale(read<int>("What is the new scale? "));
  storage << new_scale << " ";
  actions.push_back(storage.str());
  pp.scale(new_scale);
}

void change_plotmode(playpen & pp, vector<string> & actions){
  stringstream storage;
// and initialize it with the code for the change_plotmode choice
  storage << char(plotmode_am) << " ";
  cout << "\t\tWhich Plotmode do you want?\n";
  cout << "\tD for direct mode.\n";
  cout << "\tF for filter mode.\n";
  cout << "\tA for additive mode.\n";
  cout << "\tJ for disjoint mode.\n";
  char const new_mode(cin.get());
  storage << new_mode << " ";
  actions.push_back(storage.str());
  switch(toupper(new_mode)){
     case 'D':
        pp.setplotmode(direct);
        break;
     case 'F':
        pp.setplotmode(filter);
        break;
     case 'A':
        pp.setplotmode(additive);
        break;
     case 'J':
        pp.setplotmode(disjoint);
        break;
     default:
        cerr << "***Invalid response ignored.***\n";
  }
}
```

SOLUTIONS TO TASKS

```
void plot_pixel(playpen & pp, vector<string> & actions){
  stringstream storage;
// and initialize it with the code for the plot_pixel choice
  storage << char(plot_am) << " ";
  int const x(read<int>("What x value? "));
  storage << x << " ";
  int const y(read<int>("What y value? "));
  storage << y << " ";
  hue const shade(read<int>("What color? "));
  storage << int(shade);
  actions.push_back(storage.str());
  pp.plot(x, y, shade);
}

void save_pp(playpen const & pp, vector<string> & actions){
  stringstream storage;
// and initialize it with the code for the change_plotmode choice
  storage << char(save_am) << " ";
  string filename;
  cout << "What is the file name? ";
  getdata(cin, filename);
  storage << filename;
  try{
     SavePlaypen(pp, filename);
     actions.push_back(storage.str());
  }
  catch(...){cerr << "Save failed.\n"; }
}

void load_pp(playpen & pp, vector<string> & actions){
  stringstream storage;
// and initialize it with the code for the change_plotmode choice
  storage << char(load_am) << " ";
  string filename;
  cout << "What is the file name? ";
  getdata(cin, filename);
  storage << filename;
  try{
     LoadPlaypen(pp, filename);
     actions.push_back(storage.str());
  }
  catch(...){cerr << "Load failed.\n";}
}
```

SOLUTIONS TO TASKS

Note that art_menu2.cpp includes overloads for other menu functions in addition to the original ones from Chapter 8.

Task 26

These are just simple modifications to the original menu functions to use a `stringstream` instead of `cin` as a source of data. In some cases one or more statements can be removed making these functions simpler than the originals.

```
void clear_playpen(playpen & pp,  stringstream & data){
  hue const new_color(read<int>(data));
  pp.clear(new_color);
}

void change_scale(playpen & pp,  stringstream & data){
  int const new_scale(read<int>(data));
  pp.scale(new_scale);
}

void change_plotmode(playpen & pp,  stringstream & data){
  char const new_mode(data.get());
  switch(toupper(new_mode)){
     case 'D':
        pp.setplotmode(direct);
        break;
     case 'F':
        pp.setplotmode(filter);
        break;
     case 'A':
        pp.setplotmode(additive);
        break;
     case 'J':
        pp.setplotmode(disjoint);
        break;
     default:
        cout << "***Invalid response ignored.***\n";
  }
}
void plot_pixel(playpen & pp,  stringstream & data){
  int const x(read<int>(data));
  int const y(read<int>(data));
  hue const shade(read<int>(data));
  pp.plot(x, y, shade);
}
```

SOLUTIONS TO TASKS

```
void load_pp(playpen & pp,  stringstream & data){
  string filename;
  getdata(data, filename);
  try{
     LoadPlaypen(pp, filename);
  }
  catch(...){cerr << "Load failed.\n";}
}
```

Note that the save_pp() function is not overloaded. We do not want to overwrite files without at least giving the user a chance to choose a new file name. I will just use the original save_pp() function and prompt the user for a file name. You could overload the function so that it prompts with the original file name and asks the user if they want to skip the save or perhaps save it by a different name.

Note that art_menu2.cpp includes overloads for other menu functions in addition to the original ones from Chapter 8.

Task 27

```
void show_actions(vector<string> const & actions, int from, int to){
  if(from < 0) from = 0;
  if(to > actions.size()) to = actions.size();
  if(to <= from){
        cout << "That is an empty set of actions.\n";
        return;
  }
  for(int i(from); i != to; ++i){
     cout << i << '\t' << actions[i] << '\n';
  }
}
```

This function has to validate its parameters carefully. Of course users should get it right, but sometimes they will not and the consequences of attempting to display a non-existent string can be catastrophic.

Task 28

```
void show_recent_actions(vector<string> const & actions){
  int const maximum_to_display(12);
  int const start_at(actions.size() - maximum_to_display);
  show_actions(actions, start_at, actions.size());
}
```

By providing a name for the maximum number of actions I am going to display I can easily change my decision at a later date. As I know that validation of the range is provided by show_actions() I can skip it here. Some programmers like to check every step of the way. My preference is to put validation at the critical points. If show_actions() does not validate the range of

SOLUTIONS TO TASKS

actions, it is broken (i.e. contains a bug). If you cannot trust other code to do its job correctly you should not be using it. Note that that places a burden on us: we must write code that can be trusted.

Task 29

The following function uses your solutions to Tasks 26 and 27 to support a new entry to the menu for your art program. Actually these are solutions to general menu-driven programs as these functions do not care what is being recorded.

```
void display_actions(vector<string> & actions){
  if(actions.size() < 13){
     show_actions(actions, 0, actions.size());
  }
  else {
     cout << "There are " << actions.size() << " recorded.\n";
     cout << "Do you just want the recent ones? ";
     if(yn_answer()) {
        show_recent_actions(actions);
     }
     else {
        int const first(read<int>(
              "Which is the first one you want listed? "));
        int const last(read<int>(
              "Which is the last one you want listed? "));
        show_actions(actions, first, last+1);
     }
  }
}
```

The actual version in art_menu2.cpp is more polished because it displays the output in two columns.

Summary

Key programming concepts

- Persistence is the property that makes data survive after the end of a program. Persistent data can be recovered for later use.
- Compression techniques reduce the amount of storage necessary for data.
- Compression is particularly important where data may need to be transported elsewhere. For example, a one megabyte file will typically take about five minutes to send over a dial-up connection to the Internet. If that file can be reduced by 70% (typical of the text compression provided by tools such as Zip) it will only take a minute and a half.

- Compressed files can often load and be decompressed faster than an uncompressed file can load.
- Lossless compression allows decompression to restore the exact original.
- Lossy compression (usually used for things like pictures and sound) trades a loss of data quality for size.
- An iterator is a general mechanism for locating an object.

C++ checklist

- The C++ Standard Library provides types to stream data to and from a `string`. They are declared in the `<sstream>` header. In this book we will be using the bi-directional version called `stringstream`.
- There is an important pair of overloaded member functions of `stringstream`:

```
void str(string s);
```

  makes a copy of `s` the source/sink for data for a `stringstream` object.

```
string str() const;
```

  returns a copy of the internal data of a `stringstream` object as a `string`.
- The `vector` container includes the following member functions:

```
bool empty();
```

  allows us to enquire if a `vector` container is empty.

```
void pop_back();
```

  discards the last element from a `vector` container. This function must never be applied to an empty container.
- `vector` has a local (nested) iterator type called `iterator`, which provides the functionality to handle items by tracking their locations. This type is important because it provides an essential tool for many of the functions in `<algorithm>` and some of `vector`'s own member functions.
- C++ provides a number of logical operators. In this book we will be using `not`, `or` and `and`.

Extensions checklist

- My graphics library provides functions to save and load a Playpen image:

```
void SavePlaypen(playpen const &, std::string filename);
void LoadPlaypen(playpen &, std::string filename);
```

- Those functions can throw a `MiniPNG::error` exception if something goes wrong.

CHAPTER 10

Lotteries, Ciphers and Random Choices

The main focus of this chapter is on the concept of random numbers. In computing this takes two forms: genuinely random values determined by some unpredictable external event and pseudo-random values generated by carefully designed functions.

In this chapter we will provide genuinely random values by using a feature of my library that allows a program direct access to a computer's keyboard. Pseudo-random numbers will be provided by two functions from the C++ Standard Library.

Both kinds of random value are useful in programming as I will demonstrate by developing programs that use one or other in an appropriate fashion.

Random and Pseudo-Random Sequences

Most of us have an intuitive sense of what "random" means though sometimes our intuition is a poor guide. In general when we say that something is random we mean that all the possible results are equally likely and we have no way to predict them. Here are a few examples of events we expect to be random:

- Whether a coin lands heads or tails.
- The top face of a six-sided die when it has been rolled.
- The top card of a shuffled pack of cards.

If, over a series of twenty throws heads and tails alternate or we get all heads or we get two heads followed by two tails, etc., we may feel confident that we can correctly predict the result of the twenty-first toss. If our confidence is justified, then we no longer have random results. Any sequence can happen by pure chance but there are times when our practical experience leads us to suspect that there is a better explanation than chance.

Another example of non-randomness is, as most of us know, that dice can be weighted so that one face will turn up more often than the others. (I believe that the oldest existing pair of dice, from Roman times, is a weighted set.) How soon we become suspicious that the rolls of a pair of dice are not producing random results depends on our experience and our opinion of the person providing the dice and how predictable the results seem.

Some of us are less fluent in our understanding of compound events. For example, the totals of throwing a pair of dice are random but not equally likely. For example there is only one way to throw a total of two (both dice must land with 1 upper-most) but there are two ways to get a total of three (a 1 followed by a 2 or a 2 followed by a 1).

Now which do you think is more likely: that the top three cards of a randomly shuffled pack of cards are ♥A, ♥K, ♥Q in that order or ♣3, ♦7, ♥2 in that order? Both are equally likely, however the first stands out as suggesting that the pack has not actually been shuffled. In other words there is a good alternative explanation for getting the top three hearts in order. Indeed, if the fourth card was ♥J, I am pretty sure I would not believe that the pack had been shuffled properly.

Getting three cards in a known sequence suggests a prediction for the fourth but getting three cards that do not conform to a known pattern makes us more likely to accept that the choices are random. That is just a best guess: it may just be that we do not recognize the sequence and so cannot use it for prediction. In fact the second set of three cards was not random; I selected them according to a rule that predicts that the next card is ♠5 and the one after that is ♣J. (Rotate the suits in alphabetical order and increase the face value by twice as much each time – 4, 8, 16 (or 3), 32 (or 6), etc. – looping through the values one (ace) to 13 (king).)

Lotteries are based on elaborate mechanisms to ensure genuinely random selections. The chance that the winning numbers are 1, 2, 3, 4, 5, 6 is exactly the same as that they are 5, 9, 11, 27, 39, 41. However persuading the average person that there is nothing suspicious if the first selection happens is a different matter. Oddly there are many people who choose to back a sequence such as 1, 2, 3, 4, 5, 6.

What, you may ask, has this got to do with computer programming? Well many programs need to include an element of randomness. When I write a program to generate a UK lottery entry I need a way to select six numbers from the possible forty-nine. Initially I want that selection to be random, though there are more sophisticated mechanisms to avoid making popular choices. For example, 1, 2, 3, 4, 5, 6 is a very poor choice because of its popularity among part of the population. (If that selection ever came up, the pot would be shared by more than 100 winners.)

In the case of lottery entries, I probably want the choices to be really random. By that I mean that I do not want the program to produce predictable output.

However there are programs where I want a repeatable "random" selection. I have placed the random in quotes because a repeatable selection is hardly random in the normal sense: after running the program once, I can predict the results for future runs.

Algorithms for Random Numbers

There are special algorithms (recipes for computation) that produce sequences of numbers that look random and that meet the mathematical requirements of various programs that need "unpredictable" sequences of numbers. A surprising number of engineering programs rely on statistical methods that require a repeatable random-like sequence of numbers. The algorithms that produce such sequences of numbers are called "pseudo random number generators" (PRNGs for short).

C++ has a pair of functions that work together to provide a pseudo-random number generator. `srand()` takes an `unsigned int` (a variation of the `int` type that has only positive values including zero) argument that is used to select a starting point in an immensely long sequence of apparently random whole numbers that are usually limited to values in the range 0 to 32 767 (the upper limit, named `RAND_MAX`, can be larger). After `srand()` has been used to select a starting point each call of `rand()` returns the next number from the sequence. I do not need to know how this sequence is calculated; only that it meets the mathematical criteria for simple pseudo-random number generation.

The number of values for an `unsigned int` is important because that limits the number of distinct starting points that `srand()` can use. On some older computers, there are only 65 536 values for an `unsigned int` and so that is the maximum number of different sequences that `rand()` can then produce. Most modern systems support `unsigned int` with a range of at least 0 to 4 294 967 295. For most practical purposes this is large enough to avoid serious problems, but the former (65 336) is too small for some purposes. For example, there are 13 983 816 possible results for the UK lottery and a program that could only choose one of 65 536 would clearly not meet our reasonable expectations.

Understanding a Lottery Program

Among the reasons for learning to program is that of knowing enough to understand the work of others. Many of us happily use the products of other people's programming without wondering what might go wrong. Experience teaches us that most programs have flaws and some have downright errors in them. Subtle flaws that are not easily spotted are possibly the worst. In this chapter we are going to develop a program to select a lottery entry. This will highlight a number of issues concerning the quality of such a program.

I am going to start with a simple program to work out an entry to the UK lottery. In this lottery you choose any six numbers from one to 49. The main prize of several million pounds is shared equally between all those who exactly match the six numbers. These are selected by drawing balls that are kept thoroughly mixed. As far as is humanly possible every one of the 13 983 816 combinations is equally likely. When you make an entry you do not want hundreds of other people to make the same choice because that would mean that when your choice comes up you would win a disappointing amount of money.

A very bad lottery selection program

Before you read the following program you need to know about the C++ remainder operator. We discovered earlier that when doing integer arithmetic the C++ division operator (/) produces the answer to "How many x are in y." So, for example, 29/5 is 5. C++ provides a special operator to discover what the remainder is when you carry out a whole number division. It uses the % symbol. You may be used to verbalizing that symbol as "percent" but in C++ it is read as "modulus" which is the mathematical term for computing a remainder. 29%5 (read as "twenty-nine modulus five") is 4.

Examine the following program. Even better type it in, compile it and try out the resulting executable.

```
// Bad lottery pick program by Francis Glassborow
// 21/02/2003

#include "fgw_text.h"
#include <iostream>

using namespace fgw;
using namespace std;

int main (){
  int const selector(read<int>("Enter a number below 100: "));
  cout << "Your lottery entry is: ";
  int const first(selector % 49);
  int const second((first + 7) % 49);
  int const third((first + 11) % 49);
  int const fourth((first + 13) % 49);
  int const fifth((first + 29) % 49);
  int const sixth((first + 41) % 49);
  cout << first << ", ";
  cout << second << ", ";
  cout << third << ", ";
  cout << fourth << ", ";
  cout << fifth << ", ";
  cout << sixth << '\n';
}
```

You will find that looking at other people's code will help you to develop your own coding skills, but only if you take the time to look for the bad as well as the good. Spend a few minutes identifying why this is a bad program.

Quite apart from the poor quality of the design, there is also a serious fault, which will show up if you run the program and enter 49 as your choice. That will result in one of your lottery numbers being 0. Quite a few other choices will give you 0 as one of the numbers picked. In addition, however hard you try, you will never get 49. We can patch up that mistake by changing the last six output statements to:

```
cout << first  + 1 << ", ";
cout << second  + 1 << ", ";
cout << third  + 1 << ", ";
cout << fourth  + 1 << ", ";
cout << fifth  + 1 << ", ";
cout << sixth  + 1 << '\n';
```

That makes the output seem reasonable. But if you carefully check you will find that this program only has 49 possible results. Because you have the source code in front of you, you can see that and see that among all the other faults with the program there is a fundamental one; it only chooses one of forty-nine possible entries rather than one of almost fourteen million actual possibilities.

However much we clean up the quality of the source code, the fundamental flaw remains. Think what would happen if you put a glossy front end on this program and then put it on the market. To keep the figures simple, suppose you sold forty-nine thousand copies. That means that on average a thousand people would use each of the forty-nine possible picks. Guess how popular you would be if any of those came up. 1000 people and their friends, relatives and colleagues would be furious at winning so little because the program does not pick a random lottery entry from all those possible.

So let us see what we can do to improve it.

A bad lottery selection program

For this one we are going to use a couple of special purpose functions from the C++ Standard Library that I mentioned a little earlier; `srand()` and `rand()`.

Choosing a starting point is the task of `srand()`. Once that choice has been made everything else is fixed. Even technically better implementations of `rand()` that provide long, complicated sequences are still limited by the restriction that `srand()` can only provide a limited, if large, number of arguments which it will use to set the starting point. Once the starting point has been selected the subsequent sequence is fixed; use the same start and you get the same sequence of numbers. In other words it is not that different to the behavior of the program above.

Using this information, look at the following program and see if you can discover what is wrong with it.

```
// Bad lottery pick program 2 by Francis Glassborow
// 21/02/2003

#include "fgw_text.h"
#include <algorithm>
#include <cstdlib> // for rand() and srand()
#include <iostream>
#include <vector>

using namespace fgw;
using namespace std;
```

```
int choice(){
  int const c(rand() % 49);
  return c + 1;
}

int main (){
  int const selector(read<int>("Enter a number below 100: "));
  srand(selector); // select start of pseudo random sequence
  vector<int> lottery_pick;
  for(int i(0); i != 6; ++i){
     lottery_pick.push_back(choice());
  }
  sort(lottery_pick.begin(), lottery_pick.end());
  cout << "Your lottery entry is: ";
  for(int i(0); i != 6; ++i){
     cout << lottery_pick[i] << " ";
  }
  cout << '\n';
}
```

The code looks a lot better though it is still plagued with magic numbers. However it has another deep flaw in it (as well as only inviting the user to choose from a hundred starting points). Try building the program and entering 23 as your number. You will see that the number six is chosen twice. Even naïve customers are going to spot that as a problem.

The problem is that once you have picked a number to be one of your six, it should not be chosen again, but this program ignores previous choices and so can, and often will, repeat a choice. We need to handle this in our program.

A better lottery selection program

One way would be to check each pick to see if we have already got that number. If we have, we try again. Another way would be to emulate the way the lottery works. Put pieces of paper with each of the forty-nine numbers in a bag. Once we have, take one out at random. Now we only have forty-eight left. Take one of those at random and so on.

Let's write a function that selects a number from a collection (e.g. `std::vector<int>`) and removes it from the collection before returning the value to the caller (i.e. the calling function).

```
int select(vector<int> & choices){
  int const choice(rand() % choices.size());
  int const value(choices[choice]);
// now erase the choice so that it cannot be used again
  choices.erase(choices.begin() + choice);
  return value;
}
```

We have to be careful with the `std::erase()` function because it needs an iterator (if you skipped part of the last chapter you might benefit from going back to read the section on iterators). `choices.begin()` gives us the iterator for the first element of `choices`, by adding `choice` we get the iterator for the one we have used. `std::erase()` will remove that element from our `choices`.

That is all very well, but we cannot even test the function until we have a `std::vector<int>` with some values in it (and if you are a perfectionist, you will already have noted that my `select()` function assumes that the `std::vector<int>` has at least one entry). So we need a function that will push some numbers into our `std::vector<int>`. It is worth making this a function because we might want to use it again in another program. I wish I was better at naming functions but at least the following does what we need:

```
void load_numbers(vector<int> & choices, int first, int last){
  for(int i(first); i != last + 1; ++i){
     choices.push_back(i);
  }
}
```

Now finally let me write a test program to use those two functions:

```
// Lottery test program, March 3rd 2003
// by Francis Glassborow
#include <algorithm>
#include <iostream>
#include <vector>
using namespace std;

int main(){
  try {
     int const numbers(49);
     int const choose(6);
     vector<int> choices;
     load_numbers(choices, 1, numbers);
     vector<int> chosen;
     for(int i(0); i != choose; ++i){
        chosen.push_back(select(choices));
     }
     sort(chosen.begin(), chosen.end());
     cout << "Here is your lottery entry: \n";
     for(int i(0); i != choose; ++i){
        cout << chosen[i] << " ";
     }
     cout << '\n';
  }
  catch(...){
     cout << "***There was a problem.***\n";
  }
}
```

Take the above code and create the necessary structure so that you can compile and run it. When you have got it to run, go back to the `select()` function and improve it so that it traps the possibility that it is misused by calling it with an empty `choices` container. Notice that

until we do this our code is vulnerable to a divide by zero error because the % operator has to do a division in order to get a remainder.

Finally take some time considering the pros and cons of the different ways you might have organized your code. There is no single right way for all circumstances so you need to start making your own decisions based on your plans for using code you have written.

Generating numbers that are really random

The program we have just produced is pretty good apart from two things. The first is that it always produces the same answers because we didn't call `srand()` to seed the random number generator. The second is that the program relies on a pseudo-random number generator and so is vulnerable to the problem of some systems having relatively few (just the minimum 65 536 required by C++) values for `unsigned int`.

Now we could fix the first problem by asking the user to type in a number that we can use as a seed. However, you might think about why this is not such a good idea. What do you do when asked to type in a number between 0 and 65 536 inclusive? I bet you tend to type in small numbers and ones whose digits are consecutive. In other words you share a common human characteristic of being a poor random number generator. We need something better.

Imagine that you have a spinning wheel with the numbers from 1 to 99 round its circumference and a pointer. You also have a button that allows you to stop it. If the wheel is spinning slowly you will be able to select the number you want. If it is spinning faster you can still get a number close to the one you want. But if it is spinning very fast (say ten thousand revolutions per second) your experience will tell you that the number you get when the wheel stops will be pure chance; you simply cannot time your press of the button to narrow the choice down.

In the early days of home computers, programs ran slowly enough so that emulating our spinning wheel resulted in it being comparatively slow. However, modern desk top machines can count through numbers so fast that even a "wheel" with 65 536 numbers on it will spin many thousands of times a second. Code like:

```
while(true) {
  for(int i(0); i != 65535; ++i);
}
```

loops forever through the numbers from 0 to 65 536. It would do so many times a second. That will give us the basis for our fast spinning wheel. Now we need a way to stop it. We cannot do that by using something such as `std::cin` in the following:

```
while(true){
  for(int i(0); i != 65535; ++i);
  cin.get();
}
```

because the program will stop and wait for input. We want a way for our program to watch the keyboard but continue to count until we press a key. C++ does not provide a standard function to do this (because C++ can be used for programs that run on machines that do not even have keyboards). However my library provides you with such a mechanism.

Just as `fgw::playpen` provides you with a special graphics window type `fgw::keyboard` provides a special keyboard type. That type has a single useful member function called `key_pressed()`. If you have not pressed a key, the function returns 0. Otherwise it returns a value depending on what key or combination of keys you press. For now we do not need details of that behavior, only that "no key pressed" results in 0. Actually there is a second requirement in that your program must have what is called the focus. In other words it must currently "own" the keyboard, which it does when the console or, if you are using it, the Playpen is the active window. Note that as this code relies on Playpen to function correctly, there must be a Playpen even though we are not actually using it for graphics.

With that information, look at this code:

```
int spinner(int lower, int upper){
  keyboard kbrd;
  while(true){
     for(int chosen(lower); chosen != upper; ++chosen){
        if(kbrd.key_pressed()) return chosen;
     }
  }
}
```

This function repeatedly counts from `lower` to `upper` with the normal convention that `upper` is the first invalid value (i.e. the count stops at `upper`). After each increment the keyboard is checked. If any key is pressed the current value of chosen is returned from the function. It will run until a key is pressed.

`spinner()` relies on the counting process from `lower` to `upper` running so fast that the actual value of `chosen` will effectively be random. On slow computers the range from `lower` to `upper` will need to be comparatively small.

Here is a test program to see how fast the values are being processed. It uses a modified version of `spinner()` to keep count of the number of times the `for`-loop is executed for a given pair of values.

```
#include "fgw_text.h"
#include "keyboard.h"
#include "playpen.h"
#include <iostream>

using namespace fgw;
using namespace std;

int test_spinner_speed(int lower, int upper){
  keyboard kbrd;
  int passes(0);
  while(true){
     for(int chosen(lower); chosen != upper; ++chosen){
        if(kbrd.key_pressed()){
           cout << passes << '\n';
           return chosen;
        }
     }
     ++passes;
  }
}

int main(){
  try {
```

```
    playpen p; // needed for the keyboard routine
    int const first(read<int>("What is the smallest value? "));
    int const last(read<int>("What is the largest value? "));
    cout << "Press a key twice as quickly as you can.\n";
    test_spinner_speed(first, last+1);
    test_spinner_speed(first, last+1);
  }
  catch(...){
    cout << "***There was a problem.***\n";
  }
}
```

As I am not interested in keeping the Playpen open I do not need a mechanism to pause the program before the end of the `try`-block.

If the second number from this program is one or more the program is looping through the range of numbers faster than you can press keys. Actually if the second number is more than two you are pretty secure in using this routine to generate random values in the specified range. On my 850 MHz AMD Duron machine I can just about press keys fast enough so that the second key press is late in the first pass when the range is 0 to 65 536. I think that is almost good enough and that is a larger range of values than I would normally want.

One warning, however, is that the `key_pressed()` function of the `keyboard` type is pushing the technology and exactly what happens can depend on which version of MS Windows you are using. The program will work but whether you see the keys you press displayed in the console window will depend on factors outside my control.

So how can you deal with ranges of numbers that are too big for the speed of your machine? The answer is that you can get them in stages, though there are some traps. Suppose I want a random number in the range 1 to 65 536 and decide that my machine is only fast enough for `spinner()` to produce a random result in the range 0 to 999. I could start by getting the left-hand two digits (I imagine that I write 1 as 00001, 2 as 00002, etc. so that my answer will always have five digits). The left-hand two digits will be in the range 00 to 65. The right-hand three digits will be in the range 000 to 999 except when the left two are exactly 65 when the right three will be 000 to 535.

Put that together and we get:

```
int main(){
  try {
    playpen p;
    cout << "Press Return twice.\n";
    int const left(spinner(0, 65));
    int random_value(left * 1000);
    if(left == 65) random_value += spinner(0, 536);
    else random_value += spinner(0, 1000);
    cout << "Your random value was " << random_value << '\n';
    cin.get();
  }
  catch(...){
    cout << "***There was a problem.***\n";
  }
}
```

ROBERTA

What is that +=?

FRANCIS

*C++ has a nifty way of dealing with cases when you want to apply an operation directly to a variable. += means adjust the thing on the left by adding the thing on the right to it. In general if you see op= (e.g. -=, *=, /=, etc.) it means adjust the thing on the left by applying op to it using the value on the right.* `x op= y` *is equivalent to writing* `x = x op y;`

A problem with reading the keyboard directly is that it is system dependent. Using MinGW on Windows ME, the last key seen by `key_pressed()` hangs around, whereas other combinations of compiler and operating system swallow it (as was intended). Despite months of trying ways to fix this I have failed to do so and we will have to work round it. The `cin.get()` in the above code is designed to remove the surplus input. I suppose you could write:

```
cout << "Press RETURN repeatedly to end program\n";
cin.get();
```

It isn't elegant but sometimes we have to choose the least ugly solution.

Try the above program for yourself. Study the way it works. If you understand how I determined the values to be fed to each call of `spinner()` you should be able to write your own general purpose function to generate random values for any range starting at 0 and ending with a number less than one million. You could generalize that further. The idea is useful, because on really slow machines you could get the numbers two digits at a time, or even one digit at a time.

Now you are ahead of most programmers who needlessly rely on pseudo-random number generators even when they want real random choices.

TASK 31

Go back to the lottery program and rewrite it so that it uses the spinner function to choose one value at a time until you have the six numbers you need for your entry (i.e. pick one from 49, and then pick one from the remaining 48 and so on).

There are no solutions provided for the following five exercises. It is time you started to get a little independence. I will still give you some solutions but usually because there is a programming point that I want to make.

The UK Lottery has a game called "Thunderball". In that game, an entry consists of five numbers chosen from 34 (1 to 34) plus one number, the Thunderball, chosen from 14 (1 to 14). The Thunderball can be a duplicate of one of the five ordinary choices. Write a program that will select your entry to this game.

CHALLENGING

EXERCISE 2

Write a program that will ask you for your choice of six numbers for a lottery entry and then simulate the UK Lottery's Lotto game. In that game six main numbers are chosen from 49 and then the bonus ball is chosen from what is left.

You win the Jackpot if your choice matches the first six. You win a bonus if your pick includes five matches with the six main numbers and your remaining choice matches the bonus ball. You also win lesser amounts if you get five matches, but not the bonus ball, four matches or three matches with the main six. Note that the bonus ball only counts in the special case of five matches with the main numbers.

Your program should report the computer's choice of numbers and how well the player did.

EXERCISE 3

Write a program where the computer chooses a number from 1 to 100 inclusive at random (your choice as to how). It then invites you to guess the number. If your guess is wrong it will tell you whether your guess was too high or too low. You are allowed six guesses. Note that this is a reasonable game of chance because even with an optimum strategy you cannot be certain of identifying the number in less than seven guesses.

Now write a program where you choose a number between 1 and 100 inclusive and the computer has six guesses. The challenge is to build in enough randomness so that you cannot defeat the computer by knowing how it is guessing. However if you build in too much randomness the computer's chance of winning will be reduced.

CHALLENGING

EXERCISE 4

This is an extension of Exercise 2 with some added rules to determine profits.

An entry costs one monetary unit. Matching three balls wins you 20 units, matching four balls wins you 100 units, matching five balls wins you 10 000 units, matching five balls and the bonus wins you 250 000 units and matching all six balls wins you 10 000 000 units.

Write a program that will ask the user for their choice of six numbers and how many games they want to play. It will then report the results of playing those games with the user's choice of numbers.

You can enhance this program by providing graphical rewards such as loading appropriate files into a Playpen window. You can also add features such as tracking the number of times each number is chosen and displaying a graph of those frequencies in the Playpen.

There are many other enhancements you could add; how far you go is up to you.

The following is a brief summary of the rules for the game of craps played with a pair of six-sided dice:

The shooter rolls the dice. The first roll can have any of the following outcomes: 2, 3 or 12 (craps) which is an immediate loss, 7 or 11 which is an immediate winner, or a ''point'' number which can be 4, 5, 6, 8, 9, or 10. When a point is rolled the dice are repeatedly rolled until either a total of seven results or the total matches the point. If a total of seven is rolled you lose, if point is rolled you win.

Write a computer version that rolls the dice when you press a key and otherwise follows the rules above. So your first roll will give you a win (total of 7 or 11), a loss (total of 2, 3 or 12) or a point. If you have a point the computer will roll the dice on each key press until either you lose (because the roll totals 7) or you win (because you make your point).

When you emulate this game it is important that you actually emulate each of the pair of dice. Using a spinner with the numbers 1 to 12 would be a quite different game.

Other program possibilities

There are many other games of chance that you could emulate. For now, limit yourself to ones that use dice (possibly with more or fewer than six sides) and ones that use spinners. Games involving cards and other materials are probably better kept until we deal with displaying graphical images of such materials.

Sending Hidden Messages

In this section we will be looking at two ways that we can use a PRNG to send hidden messages and pictures. I should warn you that neither method would be secure against modern advanced code-breaking programs, but both of them work well for fun messages.

Using a PRNG as a one-time codebook

A fairly old form of cipher takes the form of combining the letters of the message with the letters from a book. Each letter of the message is combined with the next letter from the codebook. The usual way of combining them was to treat letters as if they were numbers, treating ''A'' as 1, ''B'' as 2 . . . ''Z'' as 26. The next letter from the message is added to the next letter from the codebook. If the total was greater than 26, 26 was subtracted so that we always finished with a number from 1 to 26 which was then written as a letter.

Decoding was done by reversing the process. One advantage of one-time codes was that ordinary books could be used. The two people wishing to communicate agreed where they would start and after that, as long as no messages were lost, they could communicate secretly. The trouble with one-time codes is that they are slow to do manually and a single lost message means that the two people get out of sync.

Now I am going to show you a variation of the idea that uses a PRNG instead of a codebook, together with the C++ **bit-wise exclusive or** operator (usually written as **xor**). The special characteristic of an exclusive or is that applying it twice restores the original. You have already used exclusive or by another name when you plotted pixels using the `disjoint` plot mode in a Playpen. C++ uses the ^ symbol (on the ''6'' key on most keyboards) for the bit-wise exclusive or operation.

To produce our coding/decoding program we write a function that will generate a random letter. You may remember that we use the `char` type to store letters. That type is capable of storing 256 different values. Some of those values will represent punctuation marks, non-printing characters such as codes for tabs and newlines, etc. But as we are going to deal entirely with electronic data we do not need to concern ourselves with whether the result can be printed. The idea will be to read in a file and write out a new coded version. The recipient will read in the coded file and write out a decoded version.

Here is a function to generate the next character value by using `rand()`. We must not use a true random number generator such as my `spinner()` function because the recipient needs to be able to generate an identical value for decoding.

```
char pseudo_rand_char(){
  int const next(rand());
  return char(next % 256);
}
```

In fact we could write that even more simply:

```
char pseudo_rand_char(){
  return char(rand() % 256);
}
```

The reason for the use of `char` just after the return is that I want to tell the compiler that I know that I am turning an `int` into a `char` and that doing so is OK. If I did not do that a good compiler would whinge because it would realize that, in general, I risk losing information (so-called truncation) because there are many more `int` values than there are `char` ones. The process of telling the compiler to change a value to a value for a different type is called casting. You should always treat the process with great care because you are taking responsibility for the consequences. In this case we are just suppressing a warning that we know is unnecessary, but NEVER use a cast to suppress an error or warning unless you truly know what you are doing.

Encoding a file

And here is the program that does the job but has a flaw that I will explain in a moment.

```
// Written by F.G. 08/03/03
#include "fgw_text.h" // for file opening functions
#include <cstdlib>
#include <fstream>
#include <iostream>

char pseudo_rand_char(){
  return char(rand() % 256);
}

using namespace std;
using namespace fgw;

int main(){
  string infilename;
  cout << "What file do you wish to code? ";
  getdata(cin, infilename);
  ifstream infile;
  open_ifstream(infile, infilename);
```

```
    string outfilename;
    cout << "What file do you want to use for the result? ";
    getdata(cin, outfilename);
    ofstream outfile;
    open_ofstream(outfile, outfilename);
    int const key(read<int>("What is the code key? "));
    srand(key);
    while(true){
        char const(infile.get());
        if(infile.eof()) break;
        outfile << char(c ^ pseudo_rand_char());
    }
    cout << "Finished\n";
}
```

All the interesting stuff happens in the `while`-loop. First notice that it is the special form of a loop often called a forever loop because `while(true)` (like `do...while` but with the `while` moved up to the beginning) will not stop unless something internally breaks us out. We know that means that there must be some way out buried inside the body of the loop. That is the task of the `if`-statement. It uses a special `istream` member function called `eof()`. That stands for ''end of file'' and it returns the value `true` when the last operation performed on an `istream` object tried to read beyond the end of the file. The combination of a forever loop with a check for end of file ensures we process the whole file. The `break` keyword in the context of the body of a `while`-loop forces an exit from the loop. This is an ideal example of using it correctly.

The next point is that I use the `get()` member function of `istream` to collect a single character. My reason for doing this is that I want to process every character in the file including special ones. I do not want to skip spaces, tabs, etc. My `read<char>` function will skip whitespace.

Lastly, the reason for my use of `char` in the output instruction is to force the numerical result of `c ^ pseudo_rand_char()` to be interpreted as a character. Try leaving that out and see what happens.

The interesting feature of this mechanism for coding text is that it is symmetrical; exactly the same program will decode a file; just as successive plotting of the same pixel in `disjoint` mode returns the pixel to its original value.

The above was the program I originally wrote and on a couple of early tests it worked OK. Further testing revealed that it often truncated the file when decrypting. I eventually realized that the problem is that both MS Windows and Unix systems interpret one of the possible characters in a text stream as an end-of-file marker. Worse is that they use different characters for this. Of course our original text file will not contain such a character but the encrypted one might.

We need to stop the intermediate processes that happen when data is written to or read from a text stream. Experts have a number of tools available but we only need a couple of simple ones. The first of these is to open the files in binary mode. This means that the contents of the file are to be treated literally rather than translated into human readable form as is done when you either read a file in your text editor (such as Quincy or Microsoft's Notepad) or extracted by a text stream (which we have been using till now).

My library includes two functions, one for input streams and one for output that force the file to open in binary mode. These functions are:

```
open_binary_ifstream(istream & stream, string const & filename);
open_binary_ofstream(ostream & stream, string const & filename);
```

Only some of the functions for streams will work as you expect when you are using binary streams. For any purpose you will need in this book (and until you become an expert programmer) you will only need get() to read a character from a binary input stream and put(char) to write a character to a binary output stream.

Here is the corrected program:

```
int main(){
  string infilename;
  cout << "What file do you wish to code? ";
  getdata(cin, infilename);
  ifstream infile;
  open_binary_ifstream(infile, infilename);
  string outfilename;
  cout << "What file do you want to use for the result? ";
  getdata(cin, outfilename);
  ofstream outfile;
  open_binary_ofstream(outfile, outfilename);
  int const key(read<int>("What is the code key? "));
  srand(key);
  while(true){
     char const c(infile.get());
     if(infile.eof()) break;
     outfile.put(c ^ pseudo_rand_char());
  }
  cout << "Finished\n";
}
```

There is another flaw (other than the absence of a try-block) in the above that will only bite if the user gives the name of a file that does not exist when responding to the first question. If they do that the program will never end because the infile stream will be in a fail state and so it will do nothing until the problem is detected and corrected. But I have made no effort to do this, so the program will spin forever doing nothing.

I left this flaw to give me an excuse to remind you about the need to test that a stream is working (the fgw::read<> functions do that for you) and also so that I could remind you what to do if you get a program running wild.

To recover control first close Quincy to avoid losing any work. Then hold down the Ctrl key and press C. That combination forces the program to abort.

Create a short text file. Type in the source for the coder–decoder program. Do not forget the ancillary function. Compile and execute it. Look at the new file that has been created. You should see complete junk. Now run the program again giving it the junk file as input and a new file for output. Examine that third file. It should be a carbon copy of the first. If it isn't you must have changed the coding key.

As I mentioned there are a few warts in my code. Before you put the code away (and perhaps use the program for some fun) smarten it up so that it will handle missing input files, exceptions being thrown, etc. In other words, add some polish.

By the way, this program can be used to encode any file because it handles the raw data. That means you could use it to encrypt/decrypt picture files, data files, etc.

Encoding a message as an image

Another way to hide messages is to treat them as a graphic image and then hide that image. In Chapter 12, I will cover the basics of writing text to a Playpen window but even without that you can create a message with your favorite graphics application and then save it as a .PNG (portable network graphics) file. This can be imported into the Playpen as long as the image is 512 by 512 pixels and has been saved with a 256-color palette (refer back to Chapter 9 if you are uncertain about doing this).

When we have got our message into the Playpen we are going to scribble all over it so that the original message is obliterated. However we are going to scribble using the `disjoint` plot mode. The key feature is that by using the `disjoint` plot mode we can "unscribble" over our message by repeating the same scribble again.

There are many ways that we can provide such scribbling functions. That is a positive feature because it means that it will be much harder for those trying to read our message illicitly. Here is one.

```
void random_pixel(playpen & paper){
  int const x(rand() % Xpixels);
  int const y(rand() % Ypixels);
  hue const shade(rand());
  playpen::origin_data const offsets(paper.origin());
  paper.plot(x - offsets.x(), y - offsets.y(), shade);
}
```

`Xpixels` and `Ypixels` are constants defined in playpen.h. They provide the width and height of the Playpen in raw (unscaled) pixels. We saw `playpen::origin_data` in Chapter 6. It is a small type whose sole purpose is to allow us to package up the position of the origin used by a `playpen` object.

The result of calling `random_pixel()` is to plot a single random "blob" on the screen. The size of that "blob" is determined by the current scale of the `playpen` object. If you want to you can enhance `random_pixel()` so that it also randomly changes the scale, and then restores the original scale after it has plotted a pixel. To do this you will need to use the two versions of the `scale()` member function of `playpen`; the one that returns the current scale and the one that changes the scale.

We can now plot a large number of "random" pixels in Playpen that will obliterate whatever was previously there. Here is a function that does that:

```
void many_pixels(playpen & paper, long many){
  long const howmany(abs(many));
  for(long i(0); i != howmany; ++i){
     random_pixel(paper);
  }
}
```

When you use this function you will have to supply a very substantial number for `many` because a Playpen consists of over a quarter of a million pixels (surprised?). I guess that about a million random pixels will about do the job. The `std::abs()` function is defined in the `cmath` header and converts negative numbers to the corresponding positive ones; using it here protects against silly arguments being passed to `many_pixels()`.

`long` (synonymous with `long int`) is another whole number type. It provides the largest range of whole numbers. I have used it here to ensure that the function will handle values in the millions (remember that C++ only guarantees up to 32 767 for an `int` even though most systems actually provide much larger ranges).

TASK 33

Write a program that will load a .png graphics file (see above) and write a million random pixels over it before saving it. You will need to ask for a key so that you can seed the pseudo-random number generator.

Now test that running the program a second time using the output file from the first run restores the original image.

My crude solution is at the end of this chapter. It shows you how to do it basically, but you need to add exception trapping, etc. before you have a good program.

Over to You

I have introduced you to both true random number generation and pseudo-random number generators. We have seen that both these methods have their uses in programming. I chose lotteries for random number generation and encryption for PRNGs because in my experience these applications fascinate many people.

There are a multitude of things you can do with them. It is up to you to come up with ideas that you find interesting. As always, if you write a program that you feel you would like to share with others please contribute it to this book's website. By now you should realize that a program does not have to be big in order to be interesting.

As a side effect of writing a genuine random number generator (i.e. one whose results are entirely unpredictable) I introduced you to another of my library's minimalist types, `keyboard`. While this is not part of Standard C++, many C++ implementations provide a similar functionality. Even the simple ability to test if the keyboard has been used provides a powerful resource. Later we will find out what else can be done with the `key_pressed()` function. For now, think about what else you can do with what is, in effect, a simple press type switch. For example, you have a tool to measure your reaction time to displayed material.

ROBERTA'S COMMENTS

At the moment many of my own programs contain subtle flaws and serious errors and I can't see them so I didn't feel competent to write a critique of the "very bad lottery program." However, I did find the example very useful and have included one of my own "very bad" programs (Exercise 4) to show how easy it is to create one.

In Task 30 I made a simple error in typing in the code, which played havoc with performance. The program compiled and ran but did not work. Francis was not available so I tried various things to get it to work. I eventually got it partly working by moving `choices.erase` and then realized my real mistake.

I had typed `&` instead of `%` in function `int select()`. What really threw me was the fact that it compiled OK. Why did it?

FRANCIS

The trouble is that the compiler cannot read minds. All it can do is check that the source code can be translated into object code. Anywhere that % is valid in C++, & is also valid, as a bitwise and operator (we will learn more about that in the next chapter). It does not work in reverse because & has several meanings in C++.

I didn't have any problems with Exercise 1 and so I decided to reward myself by buying a couple of lottery tickets using numbers generated by newly-written programs. I would like to be able to say I won the lottery but unfortunately I only got one correct number from the two tickets. So the programs may be good for generating random number selections but they are useless for winning.

I felt even better about completing Exercise 2 because it was labeled as challenging and it actually worked first time. My grandson aged 11 was interested in this program but he commented that it didn't work properly because the numbers came out in the correct order (I had used the `sort()` function). I ran the program without `sort()` and he was more impressed then.

I encountered major problems with Exercise 3. I had been so keen to get on and complete the exercises that I hadn't paid sufficient attention to how `rand()` works. I got a working program of sorts but it was then I discovered that `rand()` always selects the same number unless you have first used `srand()` to select a different sequence.

So I rewrote the program to use a spinner but also included a "serious flaw". When I eventually got it working properly (with the help of Francis) my granddaughter aged 8 enjoyed playing it. So I felt very pleased that I was able to impress the children with my programs.

I enjoyed writing the lottery programs and decided to tackle Exercise 4 because it might amuse my grandson. However, while it was under development I encountered another erratic problem. The program sometimes seemed to work but sometimes closed without warning. I assumed I'd done something terrible in the code to upset the operating system again. So I sent the code to Francis who identified the problem.

You confused the number on a ball with its position in the container. Of course these are initially the same but once you start taking balls out of the container it will not be. Imagine that the fourth ball chosen was 49. There isn't a 49th element in the container so you cannot erase the 49th entry, what you want to do is to erase the one with 49 on it which will actually be the last of 46 (three balls have already been removed) which will be number 45 (containers count from 0). When you try to remove a non-existent element from a vector the OS wakes up and throws your program out for trying to do the impossible.

I obviously felt a bit silly when he pointed it out. Francis corrected my code and commented on it as follows:

```
void load_numbers(vector<int> & choices,int first, int last){
  for(int i(first); i != last + 1; ++i){
     choices.push_back(i);
```

```
  }
}
```

This is where things come unstuck and partly bad choices of names are hindering your following your own code.

```
int spinner(vector<int> const & choices){
  keyboard kbrd;
  do{
     for(vector<int>::const_iterator iter(choices.begin());
                         iter != (choices.end() - 1); ++iter){
        if(kbrd.key_pressed()) return *iter;
     }
  }while(true);
}
```

This function simply spins through the available choices until you hit the keyboard and then it returns the value of the selected item (i.e. instead of returning the ball, it tells us what is written on it). And it is in the next function that the problem manifests itself:

```
int spinner_select(vector<int> & choices){
  int const choice(spinner(choices));
     choices.erase(choices.begin() + choice); // Error
  return choice;
}
```

That line marked as an error tries to remove the item in position `choice` rather than the one with `choice` "written" on it. If there is no such item the operating system gets suspicious of your program and kicks it off before it does any damage. You need to replace that line with the following code:

```
  vector<int>::iterator which(find(choices.begin(),
                choices.end(),choice));
  choices.erase(which);
```

which finds the item with the `choice` value "written" on it and then removes it.

I am not going to show you the rest of Roberta's code because I do not want you all copying her. She worked hard to produce a very respectable program for a far from easy problem.

SOLUTIONS TO TASKS

Task 31

The secret to this one is to realize that `select()` is the only function you need to change. Here is the modified form:

```
int select(vector<int> & choices){
  int const choice(spinner(0, choices.size));
  int const value(choices[choice]);
// now erase the choice so that it cannot be used again
  choices.erase(choices.begin() + choice);
  return value;
}
```

This is another aspect of avoiding repetition. With experience you learn to write functions that encapsulate single objectives. That way when you change the way an objective can be achieved you only change one function. The function might have been better named `random_select()`.

Task 33

```
int main(){
  playpen paper;
  paper.setplotmode(disjoint);
  int const seed(read<int>("What is the code key? "));
  srand(seed);
  cout << "What is the input graphics file? ";
  string picture;
  getdata(cin, picture);
  LoadPlaypen(paper, picture);
  paper.display();
  many_pixels(paper, 1000000);
  paper.display();
  cout << "What is the output graphics file? ";
  getdata(cin, picture);
  SavePlaypen(paper, picture);
  cout << "Press RETURN to end.";
  cin.get();
}
```

You will need to add the relevant functions and details such as including the necessary header files, checks for successful file opening and proper encapsulation in a `try`-block.

When you want to find out what is part of my library rather than the Standard C++ library, omit the ''`using namespace fgw;`'' directive. The compiler will give you error messages for everything in my library because it will not be able to find the names you use.

Summary

Key programming concepts

- A random sequence of events (specifically numbers in this chapter) is one in which there is no rule to predict the next event. A random event (number) is a member of such a sequence.
- A pseudo-random number generator is a mechanism to generate a sequence of numbers in which the generating rule is sufficiently opaque so that, without knowing the rule or something about the way the sequence is generated it is effectively impossible to predict the next number in the sequence.
- Genuinely random numbers require some effectively random event. We have to be careful when creating a mechanism to create random numbers from an external event to ensure that successive uses are completely independent.

C++ checklist

- The `%` operator (read as modulus) in C++ provides the remainder when you divide one whole number by another. E.g. 47 % 6 is 5 because 6 goes into 47 seven times with a remainder of five.
- `srand()` is used to seed (provide a starting point) for the pseudo-random number generator provided by C++.
- `rand()` returns the next number provided by the currently active pseudo-random number generator.
- `unsigned int` is a variation of the `int` type. While `int` values are balanced between negative and positive ones `unsigned int` values are always positive or zero. C++ programmers use `unsigned int` in situations where negative values would be a mistake.
- `long` or `long int` is the C++ integer type with the largest available guaranteed range. The guaranteed minimum range for `long` is greater than –2 000 000 000 to +2 000 000 000.
- The `std::vector` container has a member function `erase()` that takes an iterator as an argument. The result of calling it is to remove the item identified by the iterator from the container.
- There is a second (i.e. it is overloaded) version of `erase` that takes two iterators. That version removes all the elements from the first iterator up to but not including the element identified by the second one.
- `remove()` is a poorly-named member of `std::vector` that does not do what its name suggests. When we need it I will go into details, but for now just be careful that you do not confuse it with `erase()`.
- `eof()` is a member of the `istream` classes. It returns `false` until some action on the `istream` attempts to read beyond its end marker.
- `break` can be used to exit any loop. It is one of two useful ways to exit a loop that is designed to run forever or until some event occurs.
- In addition to streams that handle text type data (suitable for creating files in a human readable form) there are binary streams that deal with raw (computer type) data. If we want to work on the actual codes that represent symbols we must use a binary stream.
- Reading a binary stream file as a text file can generate surprises such as early closure of the file.
- `put(char)` is a member function for `ostream` objects that sends a `char` to the object using it (the one whose name will be before the dot). It works correctly for binary streams as well as text streams.
- C++ has a large number of "compound" assignment operators which are composed of an operator followed immediately by an "=" symbol. They are instructions to modify the object on the left by applying the operator and the value on the right to it. For example `i *= 3;` will result in the value stored in `i` being trebled. `x op= y;` is equivalent to `x = x op y;`

Extensions checklist

- The keyboard class from fgwlib.a has a member function key_pressed() that determines if a key is pressed on the keyboard. It ignores key presses unless they happen while one of the windows (console or Playpen) has the focus (is the active window). keyboard objects require an active playpen object. If no key is pressed key_pressed() returns zero (i.e. false).
- There are two functions that allow you to open binary files to read and write raw data. They are:

```
open_binary_ifstream(istream & stream, string const & filename);

open_binary_ofstream(ostream & stream, string const & filename);
```

CHAPTER 11

Keyboards and Mice

In this chapter you will learn about the final pieces of hardware support provided by my library. I will provide the details of the `fgw::keyboard` type that you used in the last chapter and introduce the `fgw::mouse` type, which provides minimal support for a mouse.

This chapter focuses mainly on the technology rather than on programs. When you understand what `fgw::keyboard` and `fgw::mouse` provide you will quickly see how they can enrich your programming.

You should want to revisit some of your earlier programs and rework them to incorporate these new facilities. By doing this you will learn more about the process of software maintenance. Programmers working on commercial software have the same problem when new hardware becomes available. Those whose source code was well structured and designed for change will find their task relatively easy; those who took the view of getting their code to work by trial and error will find the cost of change is high.

A Keyboard Type

You had a brief introduction to `fgw::keyboard` in the last chapter. We used it to check the keyboard to see if any keys had been pressed. Your first reaction might be to wonder why we needed a special type to handle this. Why doesn't `std::cin` manage this?

Let me answer your question with another; why do you think that `std::cin` gets its data from a keyboard? In fact it does not; it gets its input from the operating system (a version of Windows, Linux, etc.). I can almost hear you arguing that I am splitting hairs. Let me tell you about a little device I bought about a year ago called a C-Pen. It is a small hand held device to scan text into a computer (it does several other things as well). It converts what it scans into letters and symbols before sending it to a serial port on my computer.

The software support for C-Pen takes that input and hands it to the operating system *as if* it has come from a keyboard. That is fantastically useful. I can scan a program from a book directly into Quincy. More, I can scan printed material directly into a program that is using `std::cin` to acquire input because the source of data is hidden by the layers of supporting software between the hardware and my program.

However there is a price to be paid for this versatility; my program must avoid things that require a real keyboard. C-Pen does not have keys so it is meaningless to ask what keys have been pressed. If you understand this you will understand why `std::cin` does not support direct access to a keyboard. You will also recognize how much we gain by having decoupled our program from the actual hardware. However there are times when our objectives need more direct access to the hardware.

The `fgw::keyboard` type is designed to provide that. It is not perfect. There are times when mixing direct access to the keyboard with indirect access through an input stream such as `std::cin` may cause problems. The `fgw::keyboard` implementation tries to clear out input so that it will not get sent to `std::cin`. Unfortunately after many hours of trying various possibilities for automatically cleaning up the input I have had to resort to some assistance from the user of the program.

There is a small special purpose function called `fgw::flush_cin()` declared in fgw_text.h that provides an ugly solution to an ugly problem. It first prints an explanation to the user

```
***Clearing keyboard input***
If you do not see 'DONE' press RETURN once.
```

It then attempts to flush out everything up to the next "`\n`" that is waiting for processing by `std::cin`. Finally it prints the message "DONE". The problem is that there must be a next "`\n`". If there isn't one, the program will wait (and not print DONE). We have no option but to prepare for this possibility before it happens hence the message that asks the user to press Return if they do not see "DONE". Sometimes we have no nice options and have to resort to functions like this one.

To summarize: `std::cin` on desktop systems gets data from a high level facility of an operating system such as Windows 98 or Windows XP. The actual device provides the data to the operating system through one or more layers of software that hides the data source from the program. `fgw::keyboard` gets access to the keyboard by asking the operating system for special privileges so that it "sees" the raw data provided by the keyboard's software support.

The fgw::keyboard type

This type's public interface (the member functions that your source code can use) is very limited. You can create a `keyboard` object by defining one. You can then ask that `keyboard` object to report on the status of the keyboard. Just as all `playpen` objects connect to a single Playpen, all `keyboard` objects connect to a single keyboard. However a `keyboard` object requires a Playpen, so it will create a Playpen (i.e. the graphics window on the screen) if there isn't one currently in use.

That is it. All the complexity of getting access to the raw data from the keyboard is hidden away. As users of `fgw::keyboard` we do not need to know anything more about how it works. I left that detail to an expert at that kind of programming. What we do need to know is how to interpret the raw keyboard data because what we will get back is not the symbols but encoded information about which keys have been pressed.

The keys on a modern keyboard form three groups. There is a small group of keys that just do things. For example a keyboard designed for Windows has a special key that pops up the MS Windows start menu. It always does that (which can be useful when we need to regain control of our computer). The Print Screen key is another of those special keys.

The second, slightly larger, group comprises the modifier keys such as Ctrl, Alt, Shift and two of the three locking keys – Caps Lock and Num Lock (not Scroll Lock, it is another of the keys with direct action). The modifier keys divide between those that only act while pressed and those that have persistent behavior (the lock keys). The modifier keys have no effect until the user presses a key from the remaining group, which largely consist of characters. At that time the modifier key affects the value of the main key.

One small warning, my `fgw::keyboard` type does not distinguish between the left and right side modifier keys. If you have never used a keyboard mapped for natural languages that use many accented letters you might not even know that there is a distinction. However if you know that the distinction is possible, you will have to ignore it because my software is not clever enough to notice.

Ignoring modifier keys

You will find complete details of the values returned by `key_pressed()` in Appendix D on the CD. For now we are going to ignore the modifier keys by masking them out with this function:

```
char without_modifiers(int keycode){
  return char(keycode & character_bits);
}
```

That function uses a couple of powerful programming tools. The first of these is the concept of a mask. Remember that internally computers represent data as binary numbers (strings of ones and zeros). We want to extract just those **bits** (derived from **binary digits**) from the `keycode` that represent the main key that is being pressed. The value `fgw::character_bits` provides the binary pattern that selects only the bits that represent the main key being pressed.

What we want to do is to take the pattern of bits (i.e. ones and zeros) that make up the `int` value of `keycode` and limit our interest to the right-hand eight bits.

First we need to write a mask (think of the way a stencil is used) with ones where we are interested and zeros where we are not. The full mask for an `int` in the system we are using is twenty-four zeros followed by eight ones: `...0000011111111`. It is easy to miscount the number of ones if we write it that way so we compress them into 'hexadecimal' digits. That word refers to encoding patterns of bits, four at a time, according to the following table:

0000 = 0	0001 = 1	0010 = 2	0011 = 3
0100 = 4	0101 = 5	0110 = 6	0111 = 7
1000 = 8	1001 = 9	1010 = A	1011 = B
1100 = C	1101 = D	1110 = E	1111 = F

We need to tell the compiler that this is what we are doing. The special number code for that is "0x". The leading zero confirms that we are writing a number and the following "x" tells the compiler that we are using hexadecimal. So `0xFF` (the value I have named `character_bits` in the above) represents an `int` value whose last eight bits are all ones and all the other bits are zeros. In other words it is a mask that will select only the last eight bits (binary digits) from an `int`.

The & operator when placed between two numbers tells the compiler to create a new number with zeros everywhere except where both binary numbers have a one in the same place. Do not worry too much about understanding this in detail yet. The upshot of the application to the code above is that it takes the argument (`keycode`) and removes the modifier codes which happen (by careful design) to be represented by bits that are further to the left.

Finally we need to reassure the compiler that we know we have truncated the `int` we were given in order to return it as a `char`. So the function says: "Take an `int` value, ignore all but the last, right-hand, eight bits of its binary representation and use those to create a `char` value."

TASK 34

I want you to try some code so that you will get a feel for what is happening. I have labeled it as a task because I think it is important that you do it. Compile and run:

```
int main(){
  keyboard keyb;
  int key;
  int const repetitions(30);
  for(int i(0); i != repetitions; ++i){
     while(not (key=keyb.key_pressed()));
     char const result(without_modifiers(key));
     cout << result << '\n';
  }
}
```

The `while`-loop has an empty controlled statement (i.e. there is a semicolon immediately after the closing parenthesis of the `while`). That is a simple and very useful

device to idle until some event occurs. In this case it is the user pressing a main (i.e. character) key. Until such a key is pressed, `key_pressed()` returns 0 regardless of any modifier keys that are pressed. That kind of `while`-loop is a programming idiom. Shortly we will see the same idiom used with a mouse to ensure that we wait for a mouse button to be released as well as waiting for one to be pressed.

The statement `(key=keyb.key_pressed())` saves the current return from `keyb.key_pressed()` in `key` and makes that value available for testing. As long as there is no main key pressed `key` will hold zero, and `(not zero)` behaves as `true`, so the `while`-loop keeps looping. As soon as `key` stops being 0 (i.e. a key has been pressed) the overall value becomes `false` and the `while`-loop stops.

When you experiment with this program you will find that the codes for the numerical keys are those for the symbols 0 to 9 (i.e. the decimal values 48 to 57) and the letter keys give the codes for the uppercase letters (65 to 90). Other keys may seem surprising. That is because we are using the raw data about which keys are pressed. Some of the numbers match those used to represent the symbols on the keys being pressed, but some of them bear little if any relationship to the symbol on the key. This is an important idea. Computers work with numbers; what those numbers mean depends on the context. If we want to process the data, we will have to do the work to process it (taking account of the modifier keys and converting from raw key-codes to the codes of the symbols we want those keys to represent).

Now that you can read the keyboard directly you can change your menu programs so that they use the value of a raw keyboard input to control them. That way your users will not be irritated by having to press the return key after the letter that selects the menu entry; they will just press the key and the selected action will occur.

As a reminder, here is the final version of `get_choice()` from Chapter 8 (with comments about changes stripped out):

```
char get_choice(){
  cout << "Action: (Press letter followed by Return): ";
  while(true){
     string input;
     getdata(cin, input);
     char const letter(toupper(input[0]));
     int const choice(choices.find(letter));
// Check that choice is valid
      if(choice < choices.size()){
         return letter;
      }
// Note you can only get here if the choice was not valid.
     cout << '"' << letter << '"'<< "is not an option.\n";
     cout << "Please try again: ";
  }
}
```

Modify that function so that users do not need to press Return to signify that they have made a choice. They should be able to simply press the appropriate key. You may need to look back to remind yourself about such details as what `choices` is.

When you have made this modification to `get_choice()` your menu program should work exactly as it did before with the exception that the user now needs to press only the key that indicates their choice.

TECHNICAL NOTE

Environmental dependencies

That was my intention, and the way `key_pressed()` was designed to work. Unfortunately the combination of MS Windows and MinGW means that if we follow a use of `key_pressed()` with a use of `std::cin` the last key pressed finishes up in the input. That leaves us with the problem of ignoring it. When the context of your program allows you to be sure that the unwanted key will be there you can simply use a `cin.get()` to remove it. That is fine, except that other combinations of OS and compiler will not put that unwanted key into the input stream. I wish it were otherwise, but welcome to the real world where programs have to be adjusted for different environments.

Dealing with modifier keys

The following diagram illustrates how the raw keyboard data is encoded in the `int` value returned by the `key_pressed()` member function of `fgw::keyboard`:

```
0 0 0 0 0 0 0 0 0 0 0 0 0 0 0 N C A L S X X X X X X X X
```

The eight Xs are a binary representation of the key code for the main key that is currently pressed. If more than one main key is pressed then all the Xs will be set to one (i.e. the character code will be 0xFF). If no main key is pressed all the bits will be set to zero including those representing modifier keys. If a main key is pressed then the five modifier keys have the following effects:

S = 1 if the Shift key was pressed else 0 (mask `fgw::modifier_shift = 0x100`)

L = 1 if the Ctrl key was pressed else 0 (mask `fgw::modifier_control = 0x200`)

A = 1 if the Alt key was pressed else 0 (mask `fgw::modifier_alt = 0x400`)

C = 1 if Caps Lock is on else 0 (mask `fgw::modifier_caps_lock = 0x800`)

N = 1 if Number Lock is on else 0 (mask `fgw::modifier_num_lock = 0x1000`)

I have added the hexadecimal mask (and the name used for it in my library) for each of the five modifier keys. This means that you can write a simple test for a modifier key. For example, if `keycode` is a value returned by `key_pressed()` then `(keycode & fgw::modifier_control)` will be zero unless the control key was pressed.

Dealing with case

Having access to the modifier keys allows us to use a keyboard in a variety of different ways. Some of those cannot be managed through std::cin. As an example of using the modifier keys I am going to show you a small set of functions that determines if a letter key was intended to be upper or lowercase.

First I need a function that determines if a raw key-code represents a letter:

```
bool is_letter(int keycode){
  int const character_code(keycode & character_bits);
  if(character_code < 'A') return false;
  if(character_code > 'Z') return false;
  return true;
}
```

In other words if the character_bits part of keycode is for less than "A" or more than "Z" it does not represent a letter, otherwise it does.

Now let me write the function that will return the character code for a letter adjusted for the intended case. If keycode does not represent a letter this function will just return the unmodified input.

```
int letter_with_case(int keycode){
  if(not is_letter(keycode)) return keycode;
  bool const caps_lock_on(keycode & modifier_caps_lock);
  bool const shift_key_pressed(keycode & modifier_shift);
  int const letter(keycode & character_bits);
  if(caps_lock_on != shift_key_pressed) return letter;
  else return tolower(letter);
}
```

Walk carefully through that source code. We first eliminate all the codes we are not interested in by immediately returning the unmodified keycode value. Now we are left with codes that represent letters possibly with some modifier keys. At this stage I choose to ignore modifier keys that do not change the case of a letter. That leaves me with Caps Lock and Shift. Those two bool definitions rely on the automatic conversion of an int to a bool where zero results in a false and anything else results in a true.

Both Caps Lock and Shift change lowercase letters to upper, but if both are selected they cancel each other out. Hence (caps_lock_on != shift_key_pressed) will only be true if exactly one of the two values is true. As the raw code represents an uppercase letter, we have to convert it to lowercase if neither or both the relevant modifier keys are active.

If you want to eliminate cases where other modifier keys have been pressed with a letter key then you can add in statements such as:

```
if(keycode & modifier_alt) return keycode;
```

to the above function to filter out such cases. Note that it would be normal practice to ignore the status of Num Lock when processing letters.

One extra point to note is that letter_with_case() (like the std::tolower() and std::toupper() functions) has an int parameter and returns an int value. That means that if you simply send the result to an output stream it will be treated as a number. In order to get the result as a character you need to convert it to a char. Storing the answer in a char variable will achieve this. The other way is to tell the compiler that the number is to be used as a char as in the following line:

```
cout << (char)letter_with_case(65);
```

will display the letter "A" in the console window whilst:

```
cout << letter_with_case(65);
```

will display 65. That process (casting) should be avoided unless you are absolutely certain that it is the correct thing to do. A cast overrules the compiler and effectively tells it to do what you say because you know what you are doing. Never use a cast to simply make code work. If you are unsure about why your code is producing unexpected results, check with someone who you can trust.

TECHNICAL NOTE

Casting values

The two forms `type(expression)` and `(type)expression` have the same meaning in C++: they are both ways of writing a cast. So the following statements are identical:

```
cout << (char)letter_with_case(65);
cout << char(letter_with_case(65));
```

Sometimes other factors favor one way over the other. For example, parentheses have to be used round a compound type such as `(int const)` when casting to it. Also parentheses have to be placed round an expression which includes an operator, such as `(x + 1)`, when you want to cast the result to some other type.

EXERCISE 2

Write a program that ignores (does not even display) keys other than the letters, the space bar and the return key. Keys that it does not ignore should be displayed in the console window, with the correct case. Input should terminate when the user presses the Return key twice in succession.

The purpose of this exercise is to help you with the idea of providing controlled input. In other words arranging that a program will accept only certain keys. I would hope that you have noticed that `get_choice()` with raw keyboard read naturally limits choice to the valid keys only.

Using a Mouse

The purpose of this section is to introduce you to the basics of using a mouse as an input device. The introduction of a mouse type input mechanism was one of the major steps forward in computing. The point and click concept was first publicly demonstrated on 9th December 1968 by its inventor Doug Engelbart of Stanford University. Much of the early work was done at Xerox's Palo Alto Research Center. Steve Jobs (one of the co-designers of the Apple computer) saw one there and recognized the potential. In 1983 the mouse finally became available on consumer machines with the birth of what was to become the Apple Macintosh. That is enough history. Let us get on with learning the minimum that will allow us to use a mouse in our programs by means of the `fgw::mouse` type.

This type provides two facilities. The `button_pressed()` member function allows us to ask if any mouse button is currently pressed and returns `true` or `false` as appropriate. If the mouse cursor is outside the Playpen, our program does not own the mouse and `button_pressed()` returns `false` regardless.

cursor_at() returns a value of the mouse::location type. The mouse::location type packages the x and y coordinates of the mouse cursor so that we can get the one we want via the x() and y() member functions of mouse::location. These coordinates are in system standard form so that (0, 0) is the top left corner of the Playpen and (511, 511) is the bottom right corner. If the mouse cursor is outside the Playpen, cursor_at() returns the special value (−1, −1).

The only way that either of the coordinates returned by cursor_at() can be negative is if the mouse cursor is not currently located in the Playpen window. This means that testing whether either coordinate is less than zero identifies when the mouse cursor is outside the Playpen and is not owned by our program.

Converting raw mouse coordinates to playpen coordinates

It is all very well working with raw screen coordinates and there are times that it is the right thing to do but mostly we want to work with playpen coordinates based on an origin, left to right for x values and bottom to top for y values. We will also want to take account of the current scale that our playpen object is using. Just as we wrote conversion functions in Chapter 5 so that we could think in degrees while using a math library that uses radians, we need conversion functions that will convert raw window coordinates to our playpen ones.

Here is a function playpen_x() that, given a playpen object and a mouse::location object, returns the x-coordinate relative to the origin and scale of the playpen object.

```
int playpen_x(playpen const & paper, mouse::location const & loc){
  playpen::origin_data const org(paper.origin());
  double temp(loc.x() - org.x());
  temp /= paper.scale();
  return(int)floor(temp);
}
```

This code may seem more complicated than you expected (indeed my own first attempt was simpler but I then discovered a nasty bug in it). The problem is that integer division has some compiler-dependent behavior. When division involves negative numbers, compilers have a choice of answers when the division has a remainder. For example (-8)/3 can result in either -3 (with a remainder of 1) or -2 (with a remainder of -2). This kind of behavior that is allowed to be different for different compilers is called **implementation-defined** behavior. We have to learn how to cope with it so that our code will work when compiled with a different compiler.

The above code forces floating point division (no remainders involved) by defining temp as a double. That means that when we divide by the current scale of our playpen we get a decimal answer. The last line uses std::floor() which is a standard function that removes the fractional part of a double (i.e. forces rounding down). We then cast that to an int to silence the warning the compiler otherwise gives for converting a double to an int. That warning is reasonable because a double can represent a value far too large to store in an int. We know we are safe in this case because the way we calculated temp cannot provide an answer that is too big to convert to an int value.

Write a program to test playpen_x(). Make sure you test it for various scales. You may find fgw::Wait() useful in writing this program in order to slow it down to a reasonable speed (note the uppercase first letter to avoid conflict with system functions called wait). The value of the argument passed to Wait is a time delay in thousandths of a second. For example, Wait(500) causes a half second pause.

EXERCISE 4

Write a function `playpen_y` that given a `playpen` object and a `mouse::location` object will return the y-coordinate relative to the origin and scale of the `playpen` object. Be careful because Windows' y-coordinates are measured down whereas `playpen` ones are measured upwards. Modify the test program you wrote for Exercise 3 to test your solution to this exercise.

Using the mouse buttons

The ability to query the mouse for its location is the basis for using a mouse. The ability to ask about whether a mouse button is pressed gives us the ability to select a location. First a small utility function to get a new mouse-button click:

```
void new_click(mouse & m){
  while(m.button_pressed());
  while(not m.button_pressed());
}
```

Look at the code carefully. Make sure you understand what it is doing and why it works. It continually queries the mouse until no mouse buttons are pressed. Then it queries the mouse until one has been pressed. That way we are sure that the user has released the mouse button and pressed it again. That is another example of the use of a `while`-loop that waits for a change of condition.

Now a small function to get the location of the mouse when a button is pressed:

```
mouse::location where_on_button_click(playpen const & paper){
  mouse m;
  new_click(m);
  return m.cursor_at();
}
```

Now we are ready to write a function to draw a line between two points that have been selected with the mouse.

```
void drawline_with_mouse(playpen & paper){
  mouse::location const start(where_on_button_click(paper));
  point2d begin(playpen_x(paper, start), playpen_y(paper, start));
  mouse::location const finish(where_on_button_click(paper));
  point2d end(playpen_x(paper, finish), playpen_y(paper, finish));
  drawline(paper, begin, end);
}
```

Write a program to test the `drawline_with_mouse()` function. Consider what enhancements would make it easier to use. Try some of them out.

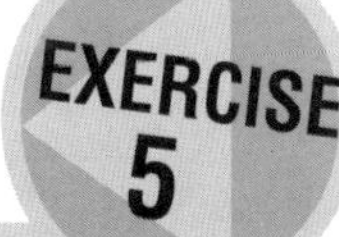

Updating the display continuously

You probably felt that the line drawing function provided in the previous section would be much better if you could see what line would be drawn before making the second mouse click. What we need is a temporary line that is displayed for a short time and then updated. You already have all the tools to do this, but probably do not realize it. If you want to try for yourself, break off from reading because I am about to show a solution.

The secret to drawing temporary lines is to use the **disjoint** plotting mode, because you can draw a line once to see it, wait a short time and then draw it again to remove it. By itself that is not hard, but we do need to remember to restore the plot mode to what it was before going on.

```
void temp_line(playpen & paper, point2d begin, point2d end,
              int wait_time){
  plotmode const oldmode(paper.setplotmode(disjoint));
  drawline(paper, begin, end, white);
  paper.display();
  Wait(wait_time);
  drawline(paper, begin, end, white);
  paper.display();
  paper.setplotmode(oldmode);
}
```

When you read through this code you may wonder why I have elected to plot the temporary lines in white. The answer is that the result of plotting white in **disjoint** mode is to invert the existing color and so guarantee that whatever the screen color may be the temporary line will be visible.

Here is a little program that demonstrates this function in use:

```
int main(){
  playpen paper;
  keyboard keyb;
  while(not keyb.key_pressed()){
     temp_line(paper, point2d(0, 0), point2d(256, 128), 250);
     Wait(250);
  }
}
```

EXERCISE 6

Write a function to select a start point for a line and then repeatedly call `temp_line()` to draw a line from the start to the current mouse cursor position. When you click the mouse button the second time it draws a permanent line and returns to the caller.

CHALLENGING

EXERCISE 7

Write a program that displays a palette of 16 colors across the top of your Playpen window and then allows you to choose a color by clicking on it. Then draw a 10 by 10, colored square at a point selected by pointing and clicking the mouse button.

This exercise leaves you room to design a simple solution that does just enough to complete the task or you can go for more complete solutions which, for example, will not draw over the palette, will allow you to choose the size of the square to be plotted, etc.

CHALLENGING

EXERCISE 8

Write a program that provides a menu of shapes across the top of the Playpen window. Make one of the shapes an "X" – when the user selects that shape, the program exits. Your program should repeatedly prompt the user for a color and a scale and then plot the correctly scaled shape selected with the mouse at a point on the screen selected with the mouse.

(I have not provided a sample solution for this exercise because you should be able to build on the ideas from doing Exercise 7.)

Refactoring Code

This term means taking code and extracting parts of it into functions to make it easier to modify and adapt the code in the future. We often develop code interactively and patch up faults as we go along. Sometimes we have put too much in a function because we did not realize that we were dealing with distinct concepts. I am going to illustrate this with Roberta's solution to Exercise 7. Before I show you her code here is what she had to say about the exercise.

ROBERTA

I had to do some revision to achieve Exercise 7. I knew that I had read somewhere about displaying all the colors but I couldn't remember where. I finally tracked it down as an exercise in Chapter 2. However, the latest Chapter 2 is not the one I originally worked through and I hadn't actually done any of the exercises. So, glutton for punishment that I am, I did them for revision.

I had been struggling with Chapter 11 and it was encouraging to discover how easy I found the exercises in Chapter 2, except for Exercise 5 which contained the solution I was after. I realized that I had progressed in understanding and recalled how I had really struggled with `for`-loops when I started. I'm glad I tried the earlier exercises and was secretly rather pleased when I discovered a couple of errors in the model answers.

I couldn't see an instant solution for Exercise 5 in Chapter 2 and thought how much more difficult it might seem for a beginner. To be honest I couldn't be bothered to think too hard so I just used the solution as a basis for the first part of Exercise 7. Although I knew that there was a solution at the end of the chapter I was determined to solve this one myself. (I had been a bit lazy on the others.)

The most difficult part was trying to decide how to translate the chosen location into color. I had two ideas in mind; the first was to use a `switch` and the second to `push_back()` the colors into a vector. I phoned Francis to ask whether I could use negative numbers in `switch` (apparently yes) and to probe which was best to use, vector or `switch`. He seemed to think vector was better.

I had two main parts to the program: displaying and selecting colors and drawing the square. I got both parts working quickly but had some interesting problems getting it together. At one point the square required a click to plot each and every point and it produced a different color depending where I clicked. It was a good effect and could form the basis of an interesting art program – but it was not what I wanted at that moment. I also got a square with the same color each time.

At this point I decided to look at the solution for clues and discovered that Francis had used *hue* as an argument to *drawsquare()*. I did something similar and mine worked. At the end I was rather impressed and could see the possibilities with the mouse once I had grasped how to do things.

```
int hue_choice(playpen & paper){
  vector<int> hues;
  for(int i(0); i != 16; ++i){
     paper.scale(32);
     paper.plot(i - 8, 7,i*16);
     paper.display();
     hues.push_back(i*16);
  }
  mouse::location const click(where_on_button_click(paper));
  return hues[playpen_x(paper,click)+ 8];
}

void draw_square(playpen & paper, hue h){
  mouse::location const click(where_on_button_click(paper));
  for(int row(0); row != 10; ++row){
     for(int col(0); col != 10; ++col){
        paper.plot(row + playpen_x(paper, click),
                         col + playpen_y(paper, click), h);
        paper.display();
     }
  }
}

int main(){
  playpen paper;
  hue const shade(hue_choice(paper));
  draw_square(paper, shade);
  cout<<"Press return to finish";
  cin.get();
}
```

FRANCIS

Roberta's `draw_square()` function is effectively the same as my `square_at()` but more interesting is her `hue_choice()` function and this is where I want to focus and illustrate the process of refactoring.

`hue_choice()` does three things:

- It selects and remembers the colors that will be used.
- It displays the selected colors.
- It uses the mouse to identify which color is chosen.

Rather more confusingly it interweaves the first two of these things. The process of refactoring will provide a separate function for each of the above. That will mean that we can use different ways of choosing the colors without having to interfere with the display routine. We will also be able to make several choices without repeating the process of selection and display.

I will need a way to pass information between the functions because they will all need access to the chosen colors. However my refactored code will still be based on Roberta's design, which is fundamentally a good solution to the problem as set.

```
vector<hue> select_16_hues(){
  vector<hue> palette;
  for(int i(0); i != 256; ++i){
    palette.push_back(hue(i));
  }
  random_shuffle(palette.begin(), palette.end());
  return vector<hue>(palette.begin(), palette.begin() + 16);
}
```

There are many ways of selecting the colors for the palette. Here I decided to have a little fun by pushing all 256 possibilities into a vector and then shuffling them with a C++ Standard Library function called `random_shuffle()`. I then returned a copy of the first sixteen entries in the shuffled container. At some stage I might decide to replace this function with one that would select fewer or more hues.

Next I need a function to display the selected hues.

```
void display_selected(playpen & canvas, vector<hue> const & selection){
  int const oldscale(canvas.scale());
  canvas.scale(32);
  for(int i(0); i != selection.size(); ++i){
    canvas.plot(i - 8, 7, selection[i]);
  }
  canvas.display();
  canvas.scale(oldscale);
}
```

This function assumes that we will display 16 hues. It would need considerable reworking if we wanted to use it to display more hues. It also assumes that the origin of the Playpen is still in its default position in the center. Notice that I first save the current scale before changing to a scale of 32. I restore the existing scale before the end of the function. I could do something similar for the origin and for the plotting mode. It is adding in those details that would change this function from just being part of a specific solution into a more generally useful function.

Next I will deal with choosing a hue for the ten-by-ten square:

```
int get_shade(playpen & canvas, vector<hue> const & selection){
  int const oldscale(canvas.scale());
  canvas.scale(32);
  mouse::location const click(where_on_button_click(canvas));
  int const choice(playpen_x(canvas, click) + 8);
  canvas.scale(oldscale);
  return choice;
}
```

This function also assumes that there are 16 hues displayed. It also assumes that it can ignore the vertical mouse position. I wrote the code this way because I wanted to show how the implementation can be changed easily because we have separated out the three things that were done by Roberta's original `hue_choice()`. My library includes a couple of functions that handle the Playpen in its raw mode (i.e. using system coordinates rather than Playpen ones). One of these functions is `getrawpixel()` which returns the `hue` of the pixel whose system coordinates are provided. So, for example, `getrawpixel(0, 0)` will give you the `hue` of the pixel at the extreme top left of the Playpen. Remember that the mouse's `cursor_at()` function returns the system coordinates for the mouse's location. Putting these together allows us to write:

```
hue get_shade(playpen const & canvas){
  mouse m;
  mouse::location const click(where_on_button_click(canvas));
  return getrawpixel(click.x(), click.y());
}
```

An interesting feature of this is that we do not have to check that the coordinates are in the Playpen (and not $(-1, -1)$) because mouse button clicks are only recognized if the mouse cursor is in the Playpen. This way of getting a `hue` is more general because, like the eye-dropper of many commercial graphics applications, it gets the `hue` of the pixel at the mouse cursor.

Finally here is my version of `main()`:

```
int main(){
  try {
     playpen paper;
     vector<hue> const hues(select_16_hues());
     display_selected(paper, hues);
     for(int i(0); i != 16; ++i){
        hue const shade(hues[get_shade(paper, hues)]);
        square_at(paper, shade);
        paper.display();
     }
     cout<<"Press RETURN to finish";
     cin.get();
  }
  catch(...){cout << "An exception occurred\n";}
}
```

More Practice

I hope that you now recognize how many professional programs achieve their results. If you combine what you have learnt in earlier chapters with the mouse facilities provided here you can write a very professional drawing program. If you store the points you select in a vector, you can then reflect, rotate, translate and enlarge your mouse driven shapes.

Writing a complete graphics program takes time, lots of it. However you should now realize that they are not based on advanced programming and complicated techniques but on perseverance and careful use of simple tools.

You should spend time studying this chapter, absorbing the ideas in it, thinking about how you can use the mouse and keyboard to enhance your own programs and generally considering how these devices can contribute to the feel of quality for your programs. Working through this chapter should have increased your programming skills and helped you to understand how many of the effects in commercial programs are achieved.

How much more you do before moving to the next chapter is your choice. Please do enough so that you feel comfortable with the ideas. The combination of reading the raw keyboard and the mouse is powerful. Achieving great looking and easy to use programs is largely a matter of spending the time to get your source code working properly.

Please share both your ideas for programs and your finished work with others by sending them in for inclusion in this book's website.

An exercise from Roberta

Write a program for young children to use a mouse and a palette of colors to color in a black and white drawing. Both the drawing and the available colors will be provided as a portable network graphics file. Imagine that you have a .PNG file that contains a Playpen image with sixteen colors across the top (or bottom) like the Playpen for Exercise 7. The rest of the screen is a black and white drawing like those found in children's coloring books.

Now you can use the mouse to select a color and then click in the area you want to color in with that color. The `seed_fill()` function Francis told us about in Chapter 8 will do the work.

ROBERTA'S COMMENTS

*The explanation of how a keyboard works is quite interesting. I didn't assume that **`std::cin`** gets data only from a keyboard because it was explained in Chapter 1 that **`std::cin`** represents console input. If it had meant keyboard input, 'kin' would be more suitable.*

The program for Task 34 built and compiled perfectly. I wasn't quite sure what I was expecting but it wasn't very exciting. Number keys returned numbers, letter keys returned uppercase letters and symbols produced interesting little blobs and things. I can't say that I was overly impressed with the program.

*On my first reading of the mouse section I found it rather difficult. It seemed such a long time since I had used Playpen and I had great difficulty understanding coordinates in the first place but now with two sets of coordinates to contend with it was worse. Once I had struggled through the exercises, I could see that **`cursor_at()`** gives window locations and **`playpen_x()`** gives Playpen coordinates. But I wasn't sure what the point of this was until I came to use the **`drawline()`** function and realized that because it uses **`point2d`** it has to be converted to Playpen coordinates.*

Exercise 5 was remarkably easy compared to the previous two. I didn't actually run it. I wrote it down and checked the solution and was pleased to discover I had it exactly the same.

*When I came to Exercise 6, I phoned Francis because I wasn't sure what a 'caller' was. I also mentioned that I didn't quite understand how the **`while`**-loop works. The examples in function **`new_click()`** and the C++ checklist at the end of the chapter seemed to be different. He explained that **`while(not m.button_pressed());`** is an example of a null or do nothing loop. There is nothing (i.e. no statement) between ")" and ";", therefore it does nothing. If I want to continually call **`temp_line()`**, I need to include that in the **`while`**-loop, e.g. **`while(not m.pressed()) temp_line();`**.*

*I then realized it worked in a similar way to an **`if`**-statement. So if there is more than one statement I assume it is treated in the same way by placing statements in curly braces.*

I sent my code for Exercise 7 to Francis because I thought my solution was simpler than his and I was rather pleased with it. So I was a bit upset when he reworked it and sent it back without explanation. However, as I write this, Francis has just refactored another of my functions – the unintelligible function to produce stars for my US flag in Chapter 8 – that I had written so badly that neither of us could understand how it placed the stars. This really brought home to me the importance of clear code and separate functions and so I will now forgive him for adulterating my simpler code in this exercise.

SOLUTIONS TO EXERCISES

Exercise 1

```
char get_choice(){
  cout << "Action: (Press letter of your choice): ";
  keyboard keyb;
  do{
     char const choice(keyb.key_pressed());
     if(choices.find(choice) < choices.size()){
        return choice;
     }
  } while(true);
}
```

This is much nicer (and simpler) than the original version however you will need to look at other parts of the code that prompt for further data to deal with the problem of mixing raw keyboard input with uses of `std::cin`.

SOLUTIONS TO EXERCISES

Exercise 2

```
char get_alpha(){
  keyboard keyb;
  while(true){
    char const choice(keyb.key_pressed() & character_bits);
    if(choice == key_space) return choice;
    if(choice == key_enter) return choice;
    if(is_letter(choice)) return choice;
  }
}
```

There are many alternative ways to deal with this problem. Here I set up a forever loop that spins until a key is pressed. `character_bits` is a mask that removes any modifier keys. `key_space` and `key_enter` are defined in keyboard.h. This function strips the modifier bits so it will not provide distinct upper/lowercase values.

Exercise 3

```
int main(){
  try {
    playpen paper;
    paper.scale(5);
    mouse m;
    keyboard keyb;
    cout << "Press any key to end program.\n";
    while(true){
      if(keyb.key_pressed()) break;
      mouse::location const here(m.cursor_at());
      cout << here.x() << ", " << here.y() << '\n';
      cout << playpen_x(paper, here) << '\n';
      Wait(100);
    }
  }
  catch(...){cout << "Exception caught. \n"; }
}
```

Note the `while(true)` loop. This is an idiom used by many programmers to highlight loops that run until some internal event breaks out of the loop. The two common ways to break out of this kind of loop is with `break` or with a `return` statement. `while(true)` is exactly equivalent to `for(;;)` and it is largely a matter of personal style which you use.

Exercise 4

```
int playpen_y(playpen const & paper, mouse::location const & loc){
  playpen::origin_data const org(paper.origin());
  double temp(org.y() - loc.y());
```

SOLUTIONS TO EXERCISES

```
    temp /= paper.scale();
    return (int)floor(temp);
}
```

The reversed order of the subtraction compared with the `playpen_x()` deals with the change of direction between screen and Playpen y-coordinates.

Exercise 5

The following is the minimal test program for `drawline_with_mouse()`:

```
int main(){
    try{
        playpen paper;
        drawline_with_mouse(paper);
        paper.display();
        keyboard keyb;
        cout << "Press any key to end.\n";
        while(not keyb.key_pressed());
    }
    catch(...){ cout << "Exception caught.\n"; }
}
```

Notice that now we have a raw keyboard scan we can use a `while`-loop to wait until the user wants to end. When you use this program you will probably wish that selecting a start point would leave a marker on the screen. And what about some color?

Exercise 6

```
void line_with_preview(playpen & paper, hue h){
    mouse::location const start(where_on_button_click(paper));
    point2d begin(playpen_x(paper, start), playpen_y(paper, start));
    mouse m;
    while(m.button_pressed());
    while(not m.button_pressed()){
        mouse::location const finish(m.cursor_at());
        point2d end(playpen_x(paper, finish), playpen_y(paper, finish));
        temp_line(paper, begin, end, 100);
    }
    mouse::location const finish(m.cursor_at());
    point2d end(playpen_x(paper, finish), playpen_y(paper, finish));
    drawline(paper, begin, end, h);
    paper.display();
}
```

SOLUTIONS TO EXERCISES

If your function worked first time out apart from typing errors, congratulations. I had to have three shots to get it to work correctly.

Exercise 7

Please note that the following solution is by way of helping a struggling reader to get the basics working. You should read through it, decide what assumptions are being made and then try to rewrite it to remove the magic numbers and make the assumptions clear.

Step 1: Display a palette

```
void show_palette(playpen & paper){
  int const oldscale(paper.scale());
  paper.scale(16);
  playpen::origin_data const oldorigin(paper.origin());
  paper.origin(0, 0);
  for(int i(0); i != 16; ++i){
     paper.plot(i+8, -1, i*16);
  }
  paper.scale(oldscale);
  paper.origin(oldorigin.x(), oldorigin.y());
  paper.display();
}
```

Step 2: Select a color

```
bool in_palette(int x, int y){
  if(y != -1) return false;
  if(x < 0) return false;
  if(x > 15) return false;
  return true;
}
```

The above helper function makes a lot of assumptions about its input parameters. When writing a function like this, be careful that you clearly identify it as a function that will need rewriting if the function it is helping is changed. Helper functions belong in an unnamed namespace.

```
hue get_color(playpen & paper){
  int const oldscale(paper.scale());
  paper.scale(16);
  playpen::origin_data const oldorigin(paper.origin());
  paper.origin(0, 0);
  mouse m;
  hue shade(black);
```

SOLUTIONS TO EXERCISES

```
  while(true){
    new_click(m);
    mouse::location const where(m.cursor_at());
    if(in_palette(playpen_x(paper, where)-8, playpen_y(paper, where))){
      int shade((playpen_x(paper, where)-8) * 16);
      paper.scale(oldscale);
      paper.origin(oldorigin.x(), oldorigin.y());
      return shade;
    }
  }
}
```

Step 3: Plot a 10 × 10 solid square in the selected color at the selected place

```
void square_at(playpen & paper, hue h){
  mouse m;
  new_click(m);
  mouse::location const where(m.cursor_at());
  int const x(playpen_x(paper, where));
  int const y(playpen_y(paper, where));
  for(int i(0); i != 10; ++i){
    for(int j(0); j != 10; ++j){
      paper.plot(x+i, y+j, h);
    }
  }
}
```

Step 4: And finally, a test program

```
int main(){
  try{
    playpen paper;
    show_palette(paper);
    while(true){
      hue const shade(get_color(paper));
      square_at(paper, shade);
      paper.display();
      if(shade == 0) break;
    }
  }
  catch(...){cout << "Exception caught."; }
}
```

Summary

Key programming concepts

- An important aspect of programming is to organize work into well-defined compartments so that when new technology comes along you can incorporate it without having to rewrite everything.
- Do not try to anticipate the future, just write source code so that tasks are compartmentalized and so can be adapted to new technology.
- One way to wait for a change of state that your program needs is to enter an idle loop that continually checks to see if the required condition has occurred.
- The invention of a mouse allowed another form of communication between a program user and the program. It is useful when dealing with positional data.
- Modern machines run multiple programs simultaneously. This is called multi-tasking. It requires that such pieces of equipment as the keyboard can be "loaned out" to whichever program needs them.
- A mouse can be used to select which program currently has the focus and can use such things as the keyboard.

C++ checklist

- C++ provides a number of operators that combine values of integer types on a bit (binary digit) by bit basis. One of these is the '&' operator. When this operator is placed between two integer values the result is an integer value that contains zero bits in all places where there is a zero bit in at least one of the given values. For example (using only eight bits to keep values simple):

  ```
  131 is represented by  10000011
  87 is represented by   01010111
  So 131 & 87 is         00000011
  ```

  which is a binary representation of 3.
- We do not have a wait... until command in C++ so we simulate it with the idiom of running an empty `while(not required_condition)` loop. As long as what we want is not true the loop continues running. As soon as what we are waiting for happens, the loop ends. For example:

  ```
  fgw::mouse m;
  while(not m.button_pressed());
  ```

  results in the program waiting for the user to press a mouse button.

Extensions checklist

- `keyboard` is a type provided by `keyboard.h`. It requires a Playpen (which it will supply if it has not yet been created). The functionality of keyboard objects is supplied by a single function: `key_pressed()`. `key_pressed()` returns 0 if no "value" key has been pressed and 255 if two or more value keys are pressed. Otherwise it returns a value that identifies the status of the five state keys (Shift, Alt, Ctrl, Num Lock and Caps Lock) and the value key pressed.
- The value keys and the codes for them are listed in Appendix D on the CD.
- `flush_cin()` will attempt to flush all data in the keyboard buffer up to and including the first newline. It will issue a warning and report success. If it does not succeed it will wait till the user presses Return.

- `mouse` is a type provided by `mouse.h`. It requires a Playpen as its actions are based on the Playpen. It has two member functions: `mouse_button_pressed()` returns true if one or more mouse buttons are currently pressed; `cursor_at()` returns a `mouse_location` value that gives the x and y window coordinates of the current mouse cursor or (−1, −1) if the mouse cursor is outside the Playpen.
- `fgw::Wait()` pauses a program for a number of thousandths of a second. So, for example, `Wait(500)` pauses for half a second.
- `getrawpixel()` is a member function of `playpen` that returns the color of a pixel at the system (raw) coordinates provided in the call.

CHAPTER 12

A Pot Pourri Spiced with Bitset

In this chapter I introduce the special container `bitset<n>` that is provided by the C++ Standard Library. This is a fixed size container of n bits (binary digits). The size, `n`, is chosen by the programmer and the value must be provided in the source code.

As well as introducing you to the `bitset<>` container, this chapter is designed to show you how a simple programming tool can be useful in a variety of different ways. You will see `bitset<>` being used for three very different purposes. The possibilities are only limited by your imagination and interests. As you gain understanding of more components of C++ you will have to spend time choosing the right ones for the job you want to do.

Each of the three example programs in this chapter rely on some domain knowledge which I will provide. Even if the subject does not inspire you, working through the design and development of the program will improve your programming.

Computing a List of Primes

What is a prime number?

Prime numbers are whole numbers greater than one that have no factors other than themselves and one. A moment's thought should convince you that every whole number can be divided by itself and by one. What makes prime numbers special is that no other number will divide them exactly. By general convention we exclude one as a special case. The first few primes are 2, 3, 5, 7, and 11. Finding extraordinarily large prime numbers is an important field of modern computing because they can be used in advanced cryptography. Using prime numbers with hundreds of digits is fairly common these days. Nonetheless proving that a specific number is prime usually involves very large amounts of computation because we have to show that it has no factors other than the obvious two. There are many ways of trimming the work but it is practically impossible, for example, to list all 100-digit prime numbers.

We are not going to look at the general problem of determining whether a specific number is a prime, but we are going to tackle a more limited problem of listing all prime numbers less than some upper limit. I will initially aim at an upper limit of 1 million. It would be sensible to deal with something smaller until we have a working program.

The Sieve of Eratosthenes

This is an ancient mechanism for finding all the prime numbers less than a certain value without using division. It needs nothing more advanced than counting. You start with a marker for every number up to the limit. You set all the markers to true (i.e. until you know better you treat them all as prime). You set the first to false (because 1 is treated as a special case that is defined as not-prime). Starting at 2, you leave its marker set to true because it is a prime number. Then you proceed to flip every second marker to false (no even number greater than 2 can be prime). When you have finished this you repeat the exercise for 3 but this time change every third marker to false (apart from 3, no number divisible by 3 can be prime).

The next number is four, but you have already marked that as not-prime so its multiples will also be not-prime but they will already have been dealt with when we removed multiples of two (all multiples of four must also be multiples of two). Next we come to 5: it is still marked as prime so we leave it but mark every fifth number from then on as not-prime. We continue repeating this process using the next prime (i.e. the next number that still has its marker set as true) and eliminating all its multiples.

How long do we have to repeat the process? Here we can make use of a feature of non-prime numbers that at least one of the divisors of any non-prime will be not larger than the square root of that number. For example all non-prime numbers less than 100 have a factor that is less than 10, all non-prime numbers less than 1 000 000 have at least one factor less than 1000. And so on.

It may help you to get the idea if you draw a 10 by 10 grid to represent the numbers from one to a hundred, cross out the first square (one is defined as non-prime) then go through crossing out every second square starting with the fourth, cross out every third square starting with the sixth, cross out every fifth square starting with the tenth and finally cross out every seventh square starting at the fourteenth.

Notice that some squares get crossed out several times, that does not matter. What does matter is that all the squares that remain represent prime numbers. You may also notice that at each step the first new square crossed out by this process is the square of the number you are currently processing (4, 9, 25 and 49).

A special container: bitset<n>

The smallest amount of storage that we can allocate in C++ is a `char`. In general this is eight bits (i.e. it can represent all values that can be represented by not more than eight binary digits). Eight bits is sufficient to store eight `bool` values, one for each bit. Unfortunately a `bool` variable has to be at least the size of a `char` (because that is the smallest amount we have available for use on its own). It would be nice if we could pack eight `bool` values into a single `char`. There are two ways of doing this. One is to use `std::vector<bool>` which is a sadly flawed design (the designers of C++ messed up and do not know how to clean up the mess, but let us say no more about it here). The other is `std::bitset<n>` where `n` has to be replaced by the number of bits we want.

ROBERTA

But what are the contentious areas? I am concerned because I have already used a `vector<bool>` in one of my own programs.

FRANCIS

The biggest problem to professional programmers is simply that `vector<bool>` is not what it says it is. All other `vector` types contain actual objects. For example `vector<int>` contains actual `int` objects. `vector<bool>` does not contain `bool` objects but collections of bits that represent `true/false` values. This difference can matter. For example it is possible to use individual elements of most vectors as arguments for a function with a reference parameter. We cannot do that for `vector<bool>` because there are no `bool` objects in it that can be referred to.

`vector<bool>` stands as an excellent example of a group of exceptional experts being seduced by their own brilliance and making assumptions that are not valid (e.g. that no one would ever want to use an element of a `vector<bool>` as an argument to a function). That could have been fixed had they not also added some special behavior for `vector<bool>` objects that is not available to other `vector` types. Isn't it reassuring to know that even the best can get it wrong?

`std::bitset` has many advantages and one big disadvantage. The disadvantage is that you must know how many bits you want at the time you write the source code. Waiting till runtime and asking the user is too late. That requirement limits the places we can use it but in return we get a great deal of extra performance. It is swings and roundabouts. If we know how many bits we want when we write a program, `std::bitset` is the way to go, otherwise we might use `std::vector<bool>` and carefully avoid contentious areas.

Here is a program that uses a `std::bitset<32>` to determine the number of ones in the binary representation of a positive integer.

```
// written by FGW 14/03/03
#include "fgw_text.h"
#include <bitset>
#include <iostream>

using namespace fgw;
using namespace std;

int main(){
  try{
     int const bits_per_int(32);
     while(true){
        int const value(read<int>(
                 'type in a whole number, or zero to end. "));
        if(value == 0) break;
        bitset<bits_per_int> bits(value);
        cout << "the number of ones in the binary "
             << "representation of "
             << value << " is " << bits.count() <<'\n';
        cout << "the bits representing " << value
             << " are: \n";
        for(int i(bits_per_int); i != 0; --i){
           cout << bits[i-1] << " ";
        }
        cout << "\n\n";
     }
  }
  catch(...){cout << "An exception was caught\n";}
}
```

TASK 35

Study the code. Now type it in and test it. If you enter some negative numbers you may be surprised. C++ uses one of three special mechanisms for dealing with negative binary numbers. The one used on Windows systems uses the left-hand bit to signify whether a value is negative (1 if it is and 0 if it isn't). To get the remaining bits for a negative value all the bits for the corresponding positive value are flipped and then one is added to the result. The above program will allow you to explore this if you want to. However it is not something that is essential for you to know in order to program.

On modern PCs an `int` is usually represented by 32 bits (equal to four `char`s back to back).

Make sure you understand why the inner for-loop starts at `bits_per_int` and counts down. Why `bits[i-1]`? [Hint: we start counting at 0, not 1.] We can index a `std::bitset` object the same way that we index a `std::vector` object.

The above code uses one of the ways that a `std::bitset` can be initialized. In this case we initialize it with the value of an `int`. Other ways include initializing it from a `std::string` that is composed of zeros and ones. So I can write such things as:

```
std::bitset<12> dozen_flags("000110111000");
```

The designers have ensured that initialization with a `string` value will always work. As soon as the program finds a character that is neither a "0" nor a "1" it stops using the `string` and sets all the remaining bits to zero.

Program for the Sieve of Eratosthenes

It is time that we set about using what we have learnt about `std::bitset` to write a program to deal with the Sieve of Eratosthenes. I am going to build up this program piece by piece (and please accompany me by typing in the code yourself). First I will write some code that will create a `std::bitset` with a bit for each of the whole numbers up to 100 and set all the bits to 1 (representing our starting position where we mark all the numbers as prime before we start sieving out the ones that are not).

```
#include <bitset>
#include <cmath>
#include <iostream>

using namespace std;

int main(){
  try{
     int const max_number(100);
     bitset<max_number + 1> numbers;
     numbers.set();
  }
  catch(...){cout << "An exception was caught in main.";}
}
```

I do not want to fuss around with counting from zero, so I have arranged that my `std::bitset` goes from 0 to 100 (101 bits) and I am going to ignore `numbers[0]`. This is a common trick used by programmers who want to deal with whole numbers but it is important to realize that we have to add 1 on to our requirements to cope with the ignored zero element.

Make sure you understand this code. Try removing the `const` from the definition of `max_number`. Notice that the compiler now refuses to compile the code. `std::bitset<n>` requires a `const` value for `n`. In fact it needs even more than that, it needs a `const` value that is provided in the source code. Our trick of initializing `const` values by using `read<>` will not work here.

The `set()` member function of `std::bitset` sets all the bits (to 1, i.e. to `true`).

Next I will add code to set `numbers[1]` to 0 or `false` (i.e. it is not a prime) and start a loop that will look for the next prime that needs to have its multiples sieved out. I have highlighted the new code.

```
int main(){
  try{
```

```
      int const max_number(100);
      bitset<max_number + 1> numbers;
      numbers.set();
      numbers[1] = 0;
      for(int i(1); i != sqrt(max_number); ++i){
        if(numbers[i]){
          // filter out the multiples
      }
     }
  }
  catch(...){cout << "An exception was caught in main.";}
}
```

When you try to compile this code you will get an error. Look at the message. The compiler will be complaining that it can find several versions of `std::sqrt()` and does not know which one you want as they all seem equally good.

We need to help the compiler choose. To do so we need to force `(max_number)` to be one of the three types the compiler expects to use with `std::sqrt`. The easiest way to do that is to tell the compiler which one we want by using a cast. In this case write `(double(max_number))`. However there is a second problem that needs to be dealt with; `std::sqrt()` returns a floating point type (in this case a `double`). It is very dangerous to compare values of different types, the compiler will do some behind the scenes adjustments. For example, the square root of any number that is not an exact square will not be an exact whole number. We have to force the value returned by `std::sqrt(max_number)` into being an `int` so that we can compare it with `i`.

The tidiest way to do that is to use that value to initialize an `int`. Here is the above code improved to handle the problems raised by using `std::sqrt()`. Note that the critical evaluation has been hoisted out of the loop. This is often a good coding technique.

```
int main(){
  try{
      int const max_number(100);
      int const max_test((int)sqrt((double)max_number));
      bitset<max_number + 1> numbers;
      numbers.set();
      numbers[1] = 0;
      for(int i(1); i != max_test; ++i){
        if(numbers[i]){
          // filter out the multiples
        }
      }
  }
  catch(...){cout << "An exception was caught in main.";}
}
```

Those two items in bold type face, `(int)` and `(double)`, are called casts. We have met them before; they instruct the compiler to convert a value to another type. In this case it tells the compiler that the result of calling `std::sqrt()` must be converted to an `int`, and that the argument, `max_number`, must be converted to a `double` before being used to select the correct version of `std::sqrt()` (from the three that are available).

Because the simple casts I have used are easily missed when code is being reviewed for correctness, C++ has uglier but more visible forms that are more selective and help to limit the potential for errors.

There are four of these. The only one appropriate to your level of programming is the `static_cast<>`. Using that in the critical line above we get:

```
int const max_test(static_cast<int>(sqrt(
            static_cast<double>(max_number))));
```

I think you may understand why I have bent the guidelines for good coding by not using `static_cast<>()`. I think it is one of the compromises we sometimes make when writing for publication. Line wrapping often makes code harder to follow. For example, there is no good place to split the above line.

Now it is time to deal with the guts of the program: eliminating all multiples of a prime starting with two times the prime in question. Here it is:

```
for(int j(i * i); j < max_number + 1; j += i){
   numbers[j] = 0;
}
```

(See the summary of Chapter 10 for an explanation of +=.)

Look carefully at that `for`-loop. It has a couple of features that are different from those we have used before. We are not iterating across all numbers but leaping by an amount equal to `i`. That means we cannot use our normal != test. Why? Well we might overshoot and then the loop would get into deep water because it would try to modify elements of `numbers` that did not exist. However we have to be careful to get the test right. We must make sure we continue till we pass `max_number`.

The other characteristic is that we must increment `j` by the value of `i`. The C++ way to write that is `j += i` – read as increment `j` by `i`.

Why did I initialize `j` to `(i*i)`? Remember that when you tried using the Sieve of Eratosthenes by hand that the first new number eliminated was the square of the next prime? Well that sets the start value to the square of `i`. When we insert those three lines in the right place, that will be the square of the next prime.

Drop that into the code, and add some output to give:

```
int main(){
  try{
     int const max_number(100);
     int const max_test(static_cast<int>(sqrt(
             static_cast<double>(max_number))));
     bitset<max_number + 1> numbers;
     numbers.set();
     numbers[1] = 0;
     for(int i(1); i != max_test; ++i){
        if(numbers[i]){
          for(int j(i * i); j < max_number + 1; j += i){
                  numbers[j] = 0;
          }
        }
     }
     cout << "the number of primes less than " << max_number + 1
          << " is " << numbers.count() << ". \n\n";
     for(int i(1); i != max_number + 1; ++i){
        if(numbers[i]) cout << i << ", ";
     }
```

```
    }
    catch(...){cout << "An exception was caught in main.";}
}
```

I have added a little extra output so that we can check that the program really does calculate all the primes less than 101.

Now we have the program running we can change the value of max_number to count the number of primes less than 1 000 001. We just have to replace max_number(100) by max_number(1000000). I tested the above program (without the output of the primes themselves) using 10 000 000 as the limit. On my old AMD Duron 850 machine it took 4.23 seconds.

FOR MATHEMATICIANS

The process of sieving numbers has some interesting features in number theory. Another sieve starts as for the Sieve of Eratosthenes but this time sieves only numbers that have not been eliminated. It starts very much the same: you remove every second number after two. Next you remove every third number that is left apart from three itself. Next you look for the next number (let us call it n) that has not been eliminated so far and then eliminate every nth still un-eliminated number and so on.

Try to write a program to carry out this process. Be warned that it is considerably less elegant than the one for primes.

A Weaving Simulation

There are many places where we use binary information; often without even realizing that we are doing so. As you may not know anything about weaving (why should you?) the following is a short introduction to the subject so that you will be able to follow the program I will then develop.

A brief introduction to weaving

Pick up a piece of cloth and look closely at it. You will see that it is made from two sets of threads that run at right angles to each other. The terms for the threads in the two directions are **warp** for the threads going lengthwise and **weft** for those going across.

These days much cheap cloth is woven from threads of a single color and then a pattern is printed on the result. However the traditional method for producing patterned cloth is by using threads of different colors. Perhaps the commonest examples are seen in things like Tweed jackets and Tartan kilts.

If you look closely at woven cloth made from colored threads you will see that the pattern is produced by passing the weft threads over some of the warp ones and under others. The simplest pattern is to alternate "over, under, over, under, etc." However more interesting patterns are produced by more complicated rules such as "over, over, under, over, under, under, etc." and having successive weft threads follow different rules.

From our perspective the important issue is that for each thread in the warp the weft thread has only two choices, it either goes over or under. While it is possible to thread the weft entirely by hand this is very tedious, slow and often produces a poor texture. There are various ways to automate the selection of over and under. One of the most common is by using two or more **heddles**. The threads of the warp are held by the heddles. Each thread is assigned to exactly one heddle, each heddle will "own" many threads in the warp. A heddle can be in one of two positions, up or down. In the up position they raise the threads they own forming a tent-like gap between those threads and the ones whose heddles are in a down position. Now a shuttle carrying the weft thread can be passed between the up threads and the down ones. In this way the weft passes under the threads belonging to heddles that are up and over the threads belonging to heddles that are down.

If you want to find out more about weaving and looms have a look in your local library or bookshop. There is also a wealth of information available on the Internet. Doing an advanced search with Google for the exact phrase "table loom" will throw up a reasonable assortment of suitable sites to start from.

Setting up the warp

There are several different elements that need to be set up if we are to emulate a loom. I am going to use vertical lines for my warp. 512 threads is a bit much to work with so I am going to use a scale of 2 for my `playpen` object and place the origin at the bottom left corner. Here is a function to set that up:

```
void set_for_weaving(playpen & loom){
  loom.scale(2);
  loom.origin(0, 511);
  loom.setplotmode(direct);
}
```

If we want to change the set-up we can do so by changing that function. Of course, if you were writing an all-singing all-dancing commercial loom emulator both this and the other functions I will give would have to be more sophisticated, but this a programming exercise not a commercial production.

A scale of 2 gives me up to 256 threads. As I am only setting out a simple example I will block those threads into sets of the same hue. Here is a function that will do a simple fixed set-up:

```
void setup_warp(playpen & cloth){
  for(int i(0); i != 4; ++i){
        lay_warp_threads(cloth, i*64, 16, red4);
        lay_warp_threads(cloth, i*64 + 16, 16, blue4);
        lay_warp_threads(cloth, i*64 + 32, 16, green4);
        lay_warp_threads(cloth, i*64 + 48, 16, red4 + green4);
  }
}
```

Now we need a function called `lay_warp_threads()` that will set up a number of adjacent threads with the specified hue.

```
void lay_warp_threads(playpen & loom,
           int from, int threads, hue shade){
  for(int i(0); i != threads; ++i){
     vertical_line(loom, from +i, 0, 256, shade);
  }
}
```

Create a suitable project and type in the above code. Make sure you include the necessary headers. Now create the following test program to ensure that it works:

```
int main(){
  try{
```

```
        playpen loom;
        set_for_weaving(loom);
        setup_warp(loom);
        loom.display();
        cin.get();
    }
    catch(...){cout << "An exception was caught in main.";}
}
```

If you do not like the colors, you can change them in `setup_warp()` or you can write an entirely different `setup_warp()` function. However keep it simple.

Implementing heddles

Our next task will be to provide for the concept of a heddle. Remember that each heddle must be able to own any of the warp threads and there are exactly 256 of these. Ownership is another binary property, you either do or do not own something. This suggests a `bitset<>` to me so:

```
typedef bitset<256> heddle;
```

I am going to emulate a four-heddle loom so I will have a `vector<heddle>` containing four heddle items. We have not used it before but we can construct a `vector` with a given number of items already in place with code like:

```
vector<heddle> heddles(4);
```

It is the (4) which sets us up with four default items to start with. The default for a `bitset<>` is every bit set to zero. Add the `typedef` for `heddle` and the definition of `heddles` to the code you prepared for Task 36.

Next we need to assign all the warp threads to `heddles`. What this means is that each thread must have a corresponding bit in one of the heddles set to one. Again there are many ways of doing this, and each one will produce a different pattern but I am just going to hardcode a simple pattern:

```
void thread_heddles(vector<heddle> & heddles){
  for(int thread(0); thread != 256; ++thread){
     int const use_heddle(thread % heddles.size());
     heddles[use_heddle][thread] = true;
  }
}
```

If you follow that code through you will see that I have just rotated through the choice of heddles, 0, 1, 2, 3, 0, 1, 2, 3, etc. till all 256 threads have been assigned to a heddle.

Implementing a weft thread

A single pass of the shuttle carrying the weft thread needs to know which warp threads it is to go under and which it is to go over. The ones it goes under will hide the weft thread's color, the ones it goes over will be hidden by the weft thread. In other words we need to draw a horizontal line in which only some of the pixels are plotted. It will need the **bitset<>** that determines when it is hidden. That **bitset<>** will effectively be a heddle (though often made by combining two or more of our heddles). This is what we want:

```
void weave_one_row(playpen & cloth,
            heddle const & up, int row, hue shade){
  for(int i(0); i != 256; ++i){
     if(not up[i]) plot(cloth, i, row, shade);
  }
}
```

Which is very like our horizontal line function from Chapter 3 except that it is fixed length and selects which points to plot.

Add that code to your project. Note that unlike the other code this is always the way to weave a row. You can alter and improve the other functions but this one has only a single point of potential improvement – removing the magic number (256).

Test all the code with:

```
int main(){
  try{
     playpen loom;
     set_for_weaving(loom);
     setup_warp(loom);
     vector<heddle> heddles(4);
     thread_heddles(heddles);
     weave_one_row(loom, heddles[0], 0, white);
     weave_one_row(loom, heddles[1], 1, white);
     weave_one_row(loom, heddles[2], 2, white);
     weave_one_row(loom, heddles[3], 3, white);
     loom.display();
     cin.get();
  }
  catch(...){cout << "An exception was caught in main.";}
}
```

This code only uses one heddle at a time. In practice heddles are usually combined. Using a **bitset<>** makes combination easy because we can use the | operator which combines two **bitset<>** objects by creating a new **bitset<>** whose bits are set (to one) wherever either of the originals is set. The | symbol is usually on the same key as backslash and is sometimes represented by a broken vertical line.

If we want to weave a row with heddles 0 and 3 up we can write:

```
weave_one_row(loom, heddles[0] | heddles[3], 0, white);
```

In practice you would not weave rows one by one but store patterns of rows (in a **vector**) and a function that will use that pattern to produce a short section of weaving.

For fun

I hope that the above section has given the artistic and the designers among my readers enough of a start so that they can develop some interesting weaving simulations. I am not setting exercises because this subject is not for everyone. However I think it is a rich ground for those with a particular turn of mind.

Dr Conway's Game of Life

Dr Conway is a mathematician with a great sense of fun as well as one with a profoundly creative insight into the fundamentals of mathematics. Among his inventions is the pencil and paper game called "Sprouts" that went from being the rage at Cambridge University through a period of popularity in many schools. During the 1960s he invented an automata game.

Strictly speaking automata games are not games in the common use of the term. An automata game in mathematics is provided by a set of rules that govern the way in which a pattern will develop through a number of generations. Dr Conway's *Life* game is an outstanding example of such games. It has deep mathematical significance but it is also great fun to those who find mathematics fun. However you do not need to understand the mathematics to have the fun.

Life is an example of a new genre of problem that became fun because of the power of computers. While we could play it with paper and pencil or with counters and a board, it would be very tedious. Here are the basic rules for *Life*:

The "universe" consists of a theoretically infinite square grid of cells. In practice we limit ourselves to finite grids and deal with the edges with special rules. Each cell can be in one of two states: dead (represented by 0) or alive (represented by 1).

We set up an initial state for all the cells in our grid. Normally we make them all dead except for a few that we choose to set as alive. After that we sit back and observe the consequences of the following rules, which govern how the cells change their state at each tick of our clock. That is we look to see how each generation begets the next.

The state of every cell after the next tick depends on its current state and the state of the eight cells that are adjacent to it (see diagram).

neighbor	neighbor	neighbor
neighbor	**cell**	neighbor
neighbor	neighbor	neighbor

- Rule 1 is that any cell with exactly three live neighbors will be alive at the next tick.
- Rule 2 is that any cell with exactly two live neighbors will stay the same at the next tick.
- Rule 3 is that all other cells will be dead at the next tick.

Here are a few examples (assume that all other cells in the grid are dead):

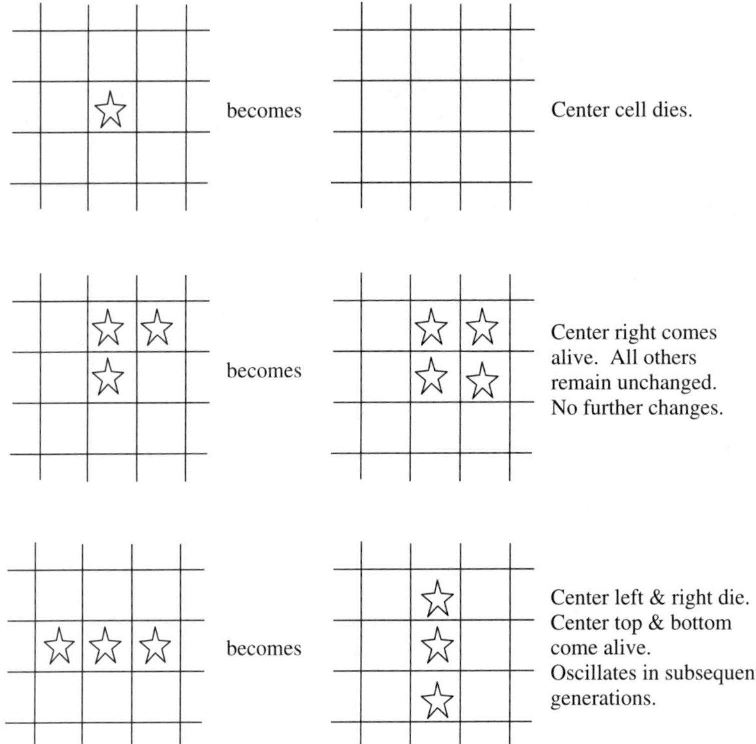

Some *Life* patterns die out, either immediately or over time. Some stagnate, such as the second example above in which each live cell now has enough live neighbors to continue its existence indefinitely. Some go into oscillation. The last example above shows the simplest oscillating pattern.

More intriguing is that there are patterns that move across the grid as time goes by and ones that replicate themselves (though those are extremely complicated). Over the first ten years after Dr Conway published *Life*, investigators discovered that the simple rules provided a staggeringly rich set of results. This book is not the place to go into all that has been discovered. There are many interesting websites covering the subject. At the time of writing, http://psoup.math.wisc.edu/Life32.html is a good starting point. In general, search for a combination of "Game of Life" and "John Horton Conway".

Determining the future state

At the core of any program to generate successive generations of *Life* is the function that determines the state of a cell in the next generation. In order to do this the function will need two pieces of information; the grid representing the current state and the cell we are interested in. We should note that the function will need to extract information about the current state but must not change it. That suggests that access should be provided by a `const &` parameter (see but not change the original). We will also need the x and y coordinates of the cell whose future state we are determining. The following does the job:

```
bool will_be_alive(life_universe const & data, int x, int y){
  int const upper(data[x-1][y+1] + data[x][y+1]
                             + data[x+1][y+1]);
  int const middle(data[x-1][y] + data[x+1][y]);
  int const lower(data[x-1][y-1] + data[x][y-1]
                      + data[x+1][y-1]);
```

```
  int const live_neighbours(upper + middle + lower);
  if(live_neighbors == 3) return true;
  if(live_neighbors == 2) return data[x][y];
  return false;
}
```

Notice how the last three statements of this function exactly mirror the three rules of *Life*. The first four statements just allow us to calculate the neighbors of the cell (x, y) in a tidy fashion rather than with a long rambling expression. Remember to break down calculations into parts that are easy to understand and get right. Not only does that make it easy to write correct code but it also helps the compiler to generate efficient code.

Before we can compile that function we will need to decide what the life_universe type will actually be. We can make a provisional decision by using a **typedef**. That will allow us to check the syntax of the function while reserving the right to change to any suitable type we may find. For the moment I am going to use:

```
int const height(128);
typedef std::bitset<height> column;
typedef std::vector<column> life_universe;
```

So the life_universe type is provided as a container of columns that in turn are implemented with a bitset<>.

Type the above code into Quincy, add the necessary #include statements (remember to add relevant comments) and then compile will_be_alive().

Creating a *Life* universe

The next step is to write the code that will allow us to create the array of cells. I am going to build my array out of columns of cells. Each column is going to be a bitset<height> object. I am going to store these in a suitable vector to build the whole array. Look at the following function:

```
void make_universe(life_universe & array,
                          column const & col, int width){
  for(int i(0); i != width; ++i){
      array.push_back(col);
  }
}
```

Note that this time the life_universe object has to be provided by plain reference because we are changing it. On the other hand we have a const & sample column that can be copied multiple times into the array to create the necessary array of cells.

In case you are wondering why I did not use the constructor for a vector<> that creates a vector<> with the right number of copies in place (as I did for heddles in the weaving program) the answer is that this way I keep control over how I create a life_universe. I can create a *Life* universe in other ways such as reading a specific version in from a file.

Building a program

We need to start writing code that can be compiled into an executable program. By now you should be able to provide your own infrastructure of header files to hold the declarations of functions and implementation files to provide the definitions. At the end of this chapter I will provide a suitable header file for the complete program to allow you to check that you put the right things into yours. Here is my starter program:

```
// Written by F Glassborow 14/04/2003
#include "playpen.h"
#include "life.h"
#include <iostream>

using namespace fgw;
using namespace std;

int main(){
  try{
     life_universe universe;
     make_universe(universe, column(), width);
     playpen paper;
     display_universe(universe, paper);
  }
  catch(...){cout << "An exception was caught.\n\n";}
}
```

The second argument of the call of `make_universe` may surprise you. It is a way to provide a temporary `column` object that can be used to create the array that we are calling `universe`. It tells the compiler to make an anonymous instance of `column` that can be handed over to `make_universe`. This only works because the second parameter of `make_universe` is a `const &` so the compiler knows that we are not going to try to change this temporary object (such changes would be lost because temporary (i.e. unnamed) objects disappear at the next semicolon).

Write an implementation of `display_universe()` that will update the Playpen to show the current universe with live and dead cells in contrasting colors.

Copying the universe

We need somewhere to store the results for the next generation of our universe because all the changes must happen at the same time. We can do this easily by adding:

```
life_universe copy_universe(universe);
```

after we have made the original. This will create a second array of dead cells.

We can pass both the original and the copy to a function that iterates across the cells calling `will_be_alive()` for each cell and using the return value to set the state of that cell in the copy. We must be careful when we write this `next_generation()` function that we do not try to use cells that are at the very edge of the array because these cells do not have a complete set of neighbors. The `for`-loops we use to iterate through the cells must start at 1 (not zero) and finish at `(height-1)` and `(width-1)`.

TASK 39

Implement `next_generation()`. It will take two parameters of type `life_universe`. This is the function that needs changing if you decide to use other strategies to handle the edge of the universe problem.

When we have finished computing the next generation we want to replace the current one with the next. There is a very useful function for many containers called `swap()` that swaps the contents between two containers of the same sort. Swapping in this kind of situation can be done very efficiently because each container takes responsibility for the other container's data.

Playing the game of *Life*

Here is my final version of `main()`. Of course there are many refinements that can be added but you would not want me to do all the work.

```
// Written by F Glassborow 14/04/2003
#include "playpen.h"
#include "keyboard.h"
#include "life.h"
#include <iostream>

using namespace fgw;
using namespace std;

int main(){
  try{
     life_universe universe;
     make_universe(universe, column(), width);
     life_universe working_copy(universe);
     playpen paper;
     paper.origin(0, 512); // move the origin to the bottom left
     initialise(universe);
     keyboard keyb;
     int key;
     cout << "Press the 'End' key to stop. \n\n";
     while(true){
        next_generation(universe, working_copy);
        display_universe(universe, paper);
        universe.swap(working_copy);
        key = keyb.key_pressed();
        if(key == key_end)break;
     }
  }
  catch(...){cout << "An exception was caught.\n\n";}
}
```

Note the way I have used the keyboard. You could add other tests that allowed you to pause the program, change the scale of the display, re-center the display if the life_universe is bigger than the display area and so on.

What you will get depends on the implementation of initialise(). The following fixed initialization (for a pattern Dr Conway calls a Puffer Train) provides an interesting result and shows how simple patterns can have very complex consequences:

```
void initialise(life_universe & universe){
  universe[29][161] = 1;
  universe[30][160] = 1;
  universe[31][160] = 1;
  universe[32][160] = 1;
  universe[33][160] = 1;
  universe[33][161] = 1;
  universe[33][162] = 1;
  universe[32][163] = 1;

  universe[30][166] = 1;
  universe[31][167] = 1;
  universe[31][168] = 1;
  universe[31][169] = 1;
  universe[30][169] = 1;
  universe[29][170] = 1;

  universe[29][175] = 1;
  universe[30][174] = 1;
  universe[31][174] = 1;
  universe[32][174] = 1;
  universe[33][174] = 1;
  universe[33][175] = 1;
  universe[33][176] = 1;
  universe[32][177] = 1;
}
```

Your initialise() function can utilize one of a number of different ways of setting up the starting pattern. For example you could – using what you learnt in the last chapter – write code that uses a mouse to select the initial live points. One way of doing that is to write some code that allows you to point and click to switch pixels on or off (look at the way we used a mouse to draw a line to get some ideas). When you have the pattern you want you would then need to use a function to read the Playpen into the life_universe object. The get_hue(int x, int y) member function of fgw::playpen would be useful here. That function returns the hue of the pixel denoted by the x and y values provided. It takes account of the current origin and scale. In other words it is the inverse of the plot(int x, int y, hue) member function.

Another possibility is to store patterns and part patterns in files that can be restored when needed. After you have worked through Chapter 14 you will have some ideas that will help you with this strategy.

Modifying the *Life* game

Another interesting idea is to change the way that display_universe() works. For example you could arrange that live cells continually increase the intensity of their representation the longer they live. Or you could take blocks of cells and provide them a single shared representation on the screen.

I could suggest many more ideas, but really it is up to your creativity. While there are many implementations of *Life* on the web, very few do more than just implement the basic rules and show little imagination when it comes to how the results are displayed.

Finally you can explore various ways of dealing with the edges. For example if each edge was a copy of the cells adjacent to the opposite edge you would get the effect of playing on a torus (doughnut). This is just one of many ways that you can handle the edges.

No exercises

I am not setting any exercises here because either you are one of those that find automata games fascinating or you will want to hurry on to something new. In the former case it is going to be hard to drag you away, in the latter it will be impossible to keep you here.

ROBERTA'S COMMENTS

I'm afraid I didn't enjoy this chapter much. I'm sure it will be of great interest to those who are interested in math but I don't count myself in that number. Actually I would like to know more about math because it would be so useful for programming. I wish someone would write a book on math that would convince me that I can do that too.

I tried the code in this chapter and was a bit impressed with the Sieve of Eratosthenes when thousands of numbers scrolled down the screen at a quite amazing pace. But Life didn't really affect me at all and I am one of those who can't wait to get onto something more interesting.

Francis added an entire new section (on emulating weaving) after I had worked through the first draft and I have not had time to try that section.

This is a chapter that I will return to in the future when I have more time to check out Life on the Internet and discover whether more information inspires me to go further.

SOLUTIONS TO TASKS

Task 38

```
void display_universe(life_universe const & universe,
                              fgw::playpen & paper){
  for(int x(0); x != width; ++x){
     for(int y(0); y != height; ++y){
        if(universe[x][y]) paper.plot(x, y, black);
        else paper.plot(x, y, white);
     }
  }
  paper.display();
}
```

Task 39

```
void next_generation(life_universe const & current,
                                  life_universe & next){
  for(int x(1); x != width-1; ++x){
     for(int y(1); y != height-1; ++y){
        next[x][y] = will_be_alive(current, x, y);
     }
  }
}
```

Header file for *Life*

```
#include "playpen.h"
#include <bitset>
#include <vector>
```

SOLUTIONS TO TASKS

```
int const height = 256;
int const width = 512;

typedef std::bitset<height> column;
typedef std::vector<column> life_universe;

void make_universe(life_universe & array,
                               column const & col, int width);
void display_universe(life_universe const &, fgw::playpen &);
void initialise(life_universe &);
void next_generation(life_universe const &, life_universe &);
```

If you are puzzled by the absence of a declaration of `will_be_alive()` notice that it is only needed by `next_generation()` and so does not need to be declared here.

Summary

C++ checklist

- `std::bitset<n> is the` C++ container for a collection of n Boolean (or bit) values. The value of n must be known by the compiler and so cannot be supplied by user input at the time the program is running.
- `bitset<>` can be initialized in a number of ways, these include initialization from an integer type and from a `std::string` composed of zeros and ones.
- `bitset<>` supports a number of operators, including &, | and ^, that combine the corresponding bits of two bitsets. & makes all values in the result 0 except for those places where both the originals had ones. | makes all values in the result equal to 1 except for those places where both the originals had zeros. ^ places a 0 where the originals had the same value (both ones or both zeros) and places a 1 everywhere else.
- `for`-loops that skip items must use a test that avoids the possibility of running off the end of a collection. In these circumstances we often use the < (less than) operator to test and the += operator to increment.

Extensions checklist

- The `fgw::playpen` type has a member function `get_hue(int x, int y)` that returns the `hue` of a `playpen` pixel. It takes account of the current scale and origin. It returns the `hue` of the screen pixel that is at the bottom left of the `playpen` pixel.
- The hue of all pixels outside Playpen is treated as black.

CHAPTER 13

How Many...? in Which Set and Map Lend a Hand

In this chapter, you will learn what an associative container is. I will introduce two of C++'s associative containers, `std::set` and `std::map`, and show you ways they can be used. We will use these two types to handle a number of typical small problems that can prove quite demanding without the appropriate tools.

What Is an Associative Container?

An associative container is a kind of container that supports the concepts of insertion and removal of elements. It is different from a sequence container (such as `std::vector<>` or `std::string`) because the order of the elements in an associative container is a property of the specific container. In other words, when we create an associative container we specify the rule for ordering the elements and that rule is fixed.

In general we access an associative container by part of (or the whole of) the element. We call the part used for this purpose **the key**. In some simple associative containers the key and the element are synonymous.

Unless we say otherwise an associative container in C++ is ordered "naturally" so that if `elem1.key < elem2.key` (where the notation `e.key` is used to mean "the key of element `e`") then `elem1` comes before `elem2` in the container. This implicitly requires that "<" must be applicable to the type of the key values. I will confine my uses of associative containers to ones where the keys meet this requirement.

C++ associative containers support **bi-directional iterators**. A bi-directional iterator is one that supports both increment (++) to find the iterator to the next element and decrement (−−) to find the iterator to the previous element. The iterators for associative containers do not support random access (the facility for going directly to the nth element) and those that use the subscript or index operator do not use it the way that sequence containers do. In this book I am going to confine myself to two C++ associative containers: `std::set` and `std::map`.

What Is a Set?

Mathematically a set is a collection of objects in which each object is unique. A hand painted tea-set in which every cup, saucer and plate is distinct might be a mathematical set but a mass-produced one where the cups were indistinguishable would not be. (Please do not start a philosophical argument about this we are only trying to get the idea.)

In computing we refer to a collection as a set if every member has a unique key according to some criterion determined by the user. The simplest criterion is that all the objects in the set are different. In other words if we choose any two elements from a set, say `elem1` and `elem2`, then (`elem1 != elem2`) is required to be true.

As we are restricting ourselves to simple uses in this book that is the rule we will use; we can only add a new element to a set if it is unequal to all the elements that are currently in it. In ordinary English terms a set is a collection of objects that are all different from each other.

How does std::set work?

`std::set` is another collection (half-)type (properly called a class template) like `std::vector`. It is a half-type because we need to know what type of thing we are collecting before it becomes a complete type. We can have a `std::set<string>` or a `std::set<int>` or even a `std::set<point2d>`, etc. But for that last one we would have to provide an implementation of the < operator or another ordering rule.

`std::set` has two very useful member functions; `insert(key)` and `erase(key)`. If you attempt to `insert` an element (key) into a `std::set` collection, nothing will happen if the element is already in it otherwise the new element will be copied into the collection at the right place. If you try to `erase` an element nothing will happen if the element is not found, but if it is found it will be removed.

In order to use a `std::set` we need a suitable iterator type. That is we need a way to refer to elements even when we do not know their value or key. We need a way to refer to the first element of a set, a way to get the next element or the previous one, etc. We have used iterators before but in the case of `std::set` they are essential for doing useful work.

Here is a program to illustrate using a simple `std::set`:

```
// Example program by FGW, written 02/05/2003
#include "fgw_text.h"
#include <iostream>
#include <set>

using namespace std;
using namespace fgw;

int main(){
  try {
     set<int> numbers;
     cout << "Enter some integers.\n";
     while(true) {
        int const value(
           read<int>(
                "Next number (enter -9999 to end input)"));
        if(value == -9999) break;
        numbers.insert(value);
     }
     cout << "You entered " << numbers.size()
           << " unique numbers.\n";
     cout << "they were (in numerical order): \n";
     for(set<int>::iterator iter(numbers.begin());
                iter != numbers.end(); ++iter){
        cout << *iter << ", ";
     }
     cout << "\n\n";
     cout << "Enter some integers to remove from the set.\n";
     while(true) {
```

```
      int const value(read<int>(
              "Next number (enter -9999 to end input)"));
      if(value == -9999) break;
      if(not numbers.erase(value)){
        cout << value << " wasn't in the set.\n";
      }
    }
    cout << "the remaining numbers in order are: \n";
    for(set<int>::iterator iter(numbers.begin());
              iter != numbers.end(); ++iter){
      cout << *iter << ", ";
    }
  }
  catch(...) {cout << "Caught an exception.\n"; }
}
```

Try this code and test it to see that it works even in the awkward cases such as when you type −9999 immediately. Note the use of `while(true)` to manage a loop where the test for ending the loop logically comes in the middle. Whenever I see `while(true)` I look for `if(test) break;` or `if(test) return;`. Standard mechanisms like these are called idioms. Sometimes an idiom is personal, sometimes it is widely used, in both cases consistent use of idioms helps others understand the code.

TASK 40

Write a program that opens a text file, reads it in word by word, builds the set of words used and then writes this list of words to a new file.

You should find it fairly easy to write the basic program, however you should not be satisfied until you have a program that handles punctuation (by ignoring it). That means that you will need to take each raw word of input and trim off any leading and trailing punctuation. Be careful because such things as apostrophes can be used internally and would then constitute part of the word.

For a bonus, consider whether you should count words that start with an uppercase letter as distinct from those that do not. For example should "Smith" and "smith" be counted as different words? Do not expect to solve this problem completely because the rules of English make it far from trivial. For example, "White is not a color." and "White is a science fiction author." both contain "White" but with different reasons for the uppercase "W".

The C++ Standard Library contains a function `isalpha()` that is declared in <cctype>. It returns `true` or `false` depending on whether the `char` you pass to it is or is not an alphabetic character. So `isalpha('a')` returns `true` and `isalpha(';')` returns `false`.

Write a program that collects a list of items from the user and writes them out to a file in alphabetical order.

EXERCISE 2

Read the names of twenty objects (such as "cat", "chair", etc.) from a file into a `std::set<string>` container one by one. Display each object in the console window scrolling the screen up by five lines between each object and allowing an interval of half a second between each line scroll (`fgw::Wait(500);` will provide a half second pause). Continue scrolling after the last object until the console is blank. Ask the user to type in the names of the objects. Remove each correct answer from the container. Allow two minutes for their answers. At the end, print a list of any remaining items.

For this exercise you will need the `clock()` function that is declared in the `<ctime>` header. It returns a value that depends on how long a program has been running. The return type is `clock_t` and, for MinGW, it measures time in thousandths of a second. So the following statement outputs the time the program has been running, in thousandths of a second:

```
cout << clock() << '\n';
```

The following statement saves the program time in the variable called `start`:

```
clock_t const start(clock());
```

Do not confuse this with facilities you may read about to extract and manage calendar time. `clock()` is entirely to do with measuring time since program start.

There are many ways that you can polish this program. You could store the user's answers in another container and display them at the end. You could tell them when they have got one right (one way to detect that is by checking the return value of `erase()` which will be `true` if an element was removed).

Keep the objects simple so that typing errors are not going to be a problem.

EXERCISE 3

Modify your program for Exercise 2 so that it displays 20 pictures from .png files (remember 512 by 512 pixels in a 256-color palette) whose names (without the .png suffix) are provided by reading the file objects.txt. The names of the files are also the names of the objects. Display each picture for a fixed time. Complete the program as before.

Try one or more of your programs on a friend, colleague or relation. Get some feedback from them and try to improve the program in response to the user comments.

What Is a Map?

You know what a map is but the term has a special meaning in mathematics and computing. In mathematics, a **map** is a relationship between two sets called the **domain** and the **range**. Every value of the domain corresponds to a value in the range. Several values of the domain may have the same range value. If every value of the range has a *unique* value in the domain (and vice versa) the map is described as a one-to-one map.

Road maps, travel maps, etc. are mathematical maps because every point on the map corresponds to a point in the real world.

In computing terms, a map is an associative container of *pairs* of items. The first member of each pair is a value from the domain. It is called the **key**. The second member, called the **value**, comes from the range. All the keys must be unique. A map is an associative container because the keys are stored in a pre-determined order.

`std::map` is a powerful C++ container (half-)type that implements the general concept of a map. We need to specify the types of both the key (i.e. the type of domain objects) and the value (the type of range objects) when we create a map container.

Some common examples of the map concept are:

- Dictionaries: words are keys and definitions are values.
- Price lists: items are keys and prices are values.
- Book indexes: an entry is a key and the list of page numbers is the value.

Sometimes we want containers where a key can have multiple entries (think of a phone book where a name like John Smith will appear many times). C++ has a container for these as well called a `multi-map` but we will not be using it in this book.

How does std::map work?

`std::map` is like `std::set` but with some extra features. Here is a program to start creating an electronic telephone book. It shows some of the features of `std::map`.

```
// Map example written 30/04/2003 by Francis Glassborow

#include <iostream>
#include <map>
#include <string>

using namespace std;

int main(){
  try {
     map<string, string> telephone_book;
     string name;
     string number;
     while(true) {
        cout << "type in next name"
             << (type END to finish this section.)\n";
        getdata(cin, name);
        if(name == "END") break;
        cout << "What is their telephone number? ";
        getdata(cin, number);
```

```
        telephone_book[name] = number;
    }
    while(true) {
        cout << "\nWhose telephone number do you want?"
             << "(END to finish this section. \n";
        getdata(cin, name);
        if(name == "END") break;
        cout << name << "'s phone number is: "
             << telephone_book[name] << '\n';
        }
        cout << "Here is your phone book:\n";
        for(map<string, string>::iterator
                                iter(telephone_book.begin());
          iter != telephone_book.end(); ++iter){
          cout << iter->first << '\t' << iter->second << '\n';
    }
  }
  catch(...) { cout << "An exception was thrown. \n";}
}
```

ROBERTA

In the *while* loop there is no *string const terminator("END")* which you used elsewhere. Does this mean that a name without a number isn't stored?

FRANCIS

Thanks for pointing that out. In my earlier code I used best programming practice and named my termination literal (`terminator`). I got lazy here and just used the literal value "END". I have left it as it is here so that I can make the point that this works though the earlier code was better quality. However as to your second question, the **`getdata()`** function ensures that something will always be used as a number (even if that happens to be the next name, so you will need to make sure that every name has a number).

Notice that we can put items into a `std::map` by using index notation and the key. There are other ways of putting new items into a `std::map` but this one is enough for now. If we try to put a second item into our telephone directory that has exactly the same key as one already there, it just updates the corresponding value. The second `while`-loop demonstrates accessing data stored in a map by indexing with the key.

ROBERTA

Does index notation mean e.g. *telephone_book[name] = number* where *name* = key?

FRANCIS

Yes, the key goes in the square brackets and is used to determine which item the value belongs to. For example, if I write *telephone_book["John Smith"] = "020 123 3412";*, the key is "John Smith" and the value is the string "020 123 3412".

`std::map` is not a sequence container and so we cannot access it by placing a number in square brackets. As a result we need some other way of listing all the members. In other words we need a suitable iterator. The `for`-loop declares a suitable iterator, calls it `iter` and initializes it to refer to the start of the container.

The output statement in the `for`-loop illustrates both a new operator and the way we get hold of the key (which C++ calls `first`) and the value (which C++ calls `second`) of each item in a `std::map`. This operator (`->`) is called **arrow** and is the way to use an iterator to get a feature from an object that the iterator identifies. Its use here is equivalent to writing `(*iter).first` and `(*iter).second`. Most programmers find arrow a tidier and more intuitive way to provide this access.

Notice that your telephone book is kept in alphabetical order. This is a characteristic of associative containers. By default they store data in its natural order. There is a way to provide a different ordering rule but natural order is sufficient for our purposes.

TASK 41

Type in the above program, compile it and use it.

EXERCISE 5

Modify the program for Task 41 so that your telephone book is written out to a file. Then write a program that will read the telephone book in from a file.

CHALLENGING

Write a menu-driven telephone-book program. Your program should eventually provide for reading and writing the data to a file, looking up someone's phone number, adding new people, adding more data from another file, removing someone and updating a telephone number. The `erase()` member function may be useful for removing entries.

CHALLENGING

EXERCISE 7

Create a file that contains the titles of pictures and the names of the files containing them. The files will have to be ones that are suitable for loading into the Playpen window (i.e. they will have to be .PNG files of 512 by 512 pixels with a 256-color palette).

Write a program that reads the file into a `std::map<string, string>`, displays the picture titles and then invites the user to choose one, which is then displayed.

Checking if an item is already in a std::map

We need a way to test if an item is in a collection, not just in a `std::map` but in any collection. We could write a function that iterates through a collection testing to see if an item is there. We could make our function simply return `true` or `false`. However, if the answer is `true` the most likely next question is ''Where is it?'' Indeed our general problem is to find an object in the expectation that it is in the container while allowing for the possibility that it is not.

The designers of the C++ containers came up with a neat trick to deal with both questions in one go. They specified that `find()` functions would return an iterator that locates the object found when searching a range (commonly from `begin()` to `end()`). Then they dealt with the special case that the item wasn't found by defining that a return of the end iterator would represent that the object had not been found. Remember how we always use half-open ranges in which the first iterator points to the first item in the range whilst the second iterator marks that the preceding item was the last. (An empty container has its start and finish iterators equal.)

They applied this principle to the special cases of `std::set` and `std::map` so that you can search the whole of such a container for a particular key. If it is found you get an iterator that identifies the item, if it isn't you get the `.end()` iterator. This might sound complicated, but it is simple in practice. Here is a small section of code that will test our `telephone_book` for an entry:

```
string name;
cout << "What name do you want to look up? ";
getline(cin, name);
if(telephone_book.find(name) == telephone_book.end()){
  cout << name << " is not in the book.\n" ;
}
else {
  cout << name << "'s telephone number is "
       << telephone_book[name] << '\n';
}
```

EXERCISE 8

Improve your telephone-book program so that it checks that a name you try to add isn't already there (which could lead to accidental overwriting of data if two people have the same name). If the name is already there, the program should ask you how to proceed.

EXERCISE 9

Write a program that uses a `map<string, int>` and reads words from a text file which it stores in the map, updating the value part to keep track of how many times the word has been used. It then outputs an alphabetical list of all the words used in the file together with a count of how many times each word is used. The output should be a word followed by the number of times it was used.

[Hints: `words[word]++` will increment the count associated with `word` used as a key. You will also find my helper function from Task 40 useful in this exercise.]

EXERCISE 10

Think of at least one more example of a map and implement it. If you think of an idea that is not already listed on this book's website please write the program and then send both the idea and the program in and get yourself credited with it.

ROBERTA'S COMMENTS

This is a very deceptive chapter. It not only introduces two new containers but the exercises involve many of the things covered in previous chapters. Of all the chapters so far I think this took the longest to complete but I think it was worth doing all the exercises because, after all the revision, I felt more competent at the end of this chapter than I did at the beginning.

It was also in this chapter that I finally learnt how to create *.png* files and once I had mastered this I could see endless possibilities for games for children. (It's a marvelous way of learning spelling lists especially when rewarded with a favorite picture or a new one. I also thought it could be useful for creative writing.)

Earlier in the book, there was an exercise similar to Exercise 1 but using a `vector`. I found using a `set` easier because it is not necessary to sort the items. It was also possible to eliminate the word "END" from the list. But I was not sure why I needed to record the number of items.

In Exercise 2, I assumed that `clock()` was some kind of stop watch but on checking the solution I realized that `clock()` shows something that is already being timed. When I looked at the solution I was pleased to discover that I had used a very similar function to scroll five lines.

The thought of creating 20 *.png* files put me off doing Exercise 3 at first – but I am glad to say I came back to it later. It took quite a while to create 10 files let alone 20 but I probably spent more time on this than necessary because I was creating pictures that would appeal to my grandchildren (my chief program testers). I did suggest to Francis that he include some *.png* files on the CD.

I had already been doing what Exercise 4 asked.

Exercise 6 involved a major revision session and is quite a long exercise especially when you consider that a similar exercise was the only task in Chapter 6. I couldn't see that there would be much difference between adding a new name and updating a number at this stage because adding the same name will overwrite an existing entry won't it?

FRANCIS

Exactly, but you really do not want to do that without some warning. When you say you are adding, the program should stop you if the name is already there. If you say you are updating, the program should warn you if it cannot find the name.

Exercise 7 also used *.png* files. I asked Francis how to create some *.png* files so that I could complete the exercises. I had difficulty in getting them to work but was very pleased with the results when I did. (You will find a folder of *.png* files included in the *Chapter 13* directory.)

SOLUTIONS TO TASKS

Task 40

First, a helper function to get a word (defined in this context as being a sequence that starts with a letter and finishes with a letter and has no internal whitespace).

```
string word(string const & data){
  int begin(0);
  int end(data.size());
  while((begin != end) && (not isalpha(data[begin]))) ++begin;
  while((end != begin) && (not isalpha(data[end-1]))) --end;
  string const result(data.begin() + begin, data.begin() + end);
  return result;
}
```

Each of the two `while`-statements first tests that there are symbols left to use. The part after the "&&" operator will be skipped if there is no symbol to test. This is a useful characteristic of "&&". In

SOLUTIONS TO TASKS

the second `while`-statement I have to be careful to remember that I am working backwards and that `end` marks the finish and does not locate anything.

The definition of `result` relies on the fact that you can create a new `std::string` (or any collection) by providing iterators into an existing `std::string`. It works for empty sub-strings so we do not have to treat that as a special case.

And here is a program that uses the above function to achieve the required result:

```
int main(){
  try {
     set<string> words;
     ifstream in("textfile.txt");
     if(in.fail()){
       cout << "no such file" << '\n';
       return 1;
     }
     while(true){
        string input(read<string>(in);
        if(in.eof()) break;
        words.insert(word(input));
     }
     ofstream out("words.txt");
     for(set<string>::iterator iter(words.begin());
                                iter != words.end(); ++iter){
        out << *iter << '\n';
     }
  }
  catch(...){ cout << "An exception occurred." << '\n';
}
```

Remember that placing an "*" before the name of an iterator provides the value the iterator is pointing at. So `*iter` successively becomes each of the words in the `words` set.

We have to be careful with identifying the end of a file that we have not explicitly marked with an end sentinel (such as making the last entry "END"). The `eof()` member function of the stream types will return `true` once you have attempted to read *beyond* the end of the file. That is why I have to try to extract the next word from the file and then test if I have gone off the end (in other words, there wasn't another word to get).

SOLUTIONS TO EXERCISES

Exercise 2

This sample solution uses the `word()` function from Task 40. The solution could certainly be improved, not least because `main()` is beginning to get rather long for a single function. It would be a

SOLUTIONS TO EXERCISES

useful exercise for you to break the program up so that `main()` calls separate functions to get and display the items, to get and process the user's answers and finally to output the results. This refactoring of the code makes it easier to understand and modify.

```
void display_object(string const & obj){
  cout << obj << '\n';
  for(int i(0); i != 5; ++i){
     Wait(500);
     cout << '\n';
  }
}

int main(){
  int const number_of_objects(20);
  int const time_allowed(120000);
  int const lines(24);
  try {
     ifstream in("objects.txt");
     if(in.fail()){
       cout << "no such file" <<'\n';
       return 1;
     }
     set<string> objects;
     string input;
     for(int i(0); i != number_of_objects; ++i){
        getdata(in, input);
        input = (word(input));
        objects.insert(input);
        display_object(input);
     }
     for(int i(0); i != lines; ++i) cout << '\n';
     clock_t const start(clock());
     while(objects.size()){
        cout << "Next item: ";
        getdata(cin, input);
        if((clock() - start) > time_allowed){
          cout << "times up.\n";
          break;
        }
        input = word(input);
        if(objects.erase(input)){
          cout << input << " found and removed. "
             << objects.size() << " left.\n";
        }
```

SOLUTIONS TO EXERCISES

```
        else {
          cout << input << " was not one of the items left.\n";
        }
      }
      if(objects.size()){
        cout << "You missed: \n";
        for(set<string>::iterator iter(objects.begin());
                                iter != objects.end(); ++iter){
          cout << *iter << '\n';
        }
      }
      else {
        cout << "Congratulations, you named all the items.\n";
      }
    }
    catch(...){ cout << "An exception occurred." << '\n';}
}
```

Note that you could rework this program with the items stored in a `vector<string>`. That would give you the option of shuffling the items before you display them. The disadvantage is that you have to find the item to be removed because `erase()` for a `std::vector` uses an iterator.

Exercise 9

If this basic solution looks much like the solution to Task 40, that is because it is. There is little merit in trying to make programs different. Learn to reuse ideas and basic structures.

```
int main(){
  try {
    ifstream in("icon.txt");
    if(in.fail()){
      cout << "no such file" << '\n';
      throw problem("File did not open");
    }
    map<string, int> words;
    while(true){
      string entry(read<string>(in));
      if(in.eof()) break;
      entry = word(entry);          // from task 40
      words[entry]++;
    }
    for(map<string, int>::iterator iter(words.begin());
              iter != words.end(); ++iter){
      cout << iter -> first << "  " << iter -> second << '\n';
    }
```

SOLUTIONS TO EXERCISES

```
  }
  catch(...){ cout << "An exception occurred." << '\n';}
}
```

Summary

Key programming concepts

- An associative container is a container in which items are held in a defined order. The ordering rule is part of the definition of the container.
- Associative containers are powerful tools. Two particular containers are set and map. A set has the property that each item is unique (there are no copies). A map contains (key, value) pairs where each key is unique.

C++ checklist

- The set and map containers are provided in C++ by the `std::set` and `std::map` container types.
- All C++ containers have special iterator types whose values are used for locating items in a container.
- C++ associative containers, like the sequence containers, have member functions `begin()` (to locate the first item) and `end()` which identifies the finish and is not an item.
- `std::set` and `std::map` have special versions of `erase()`, `insert()` and `find()` where the argument passed to the function is the item (in the case of a `set`) or the key (in the case of a `map`). `erase()` returns 1 or 0 in accordance with whether an item was erased or not. `find()` returns the iterator for the object if it is found or the value of the `.end()` iterator if it isn't.
- A `std::map` container can be indexed by a key. The result will be the corresponding value. For example, if `dictionary` is a `std::map<string, string>` then:

  ```
  cout << dictionary["help"];
  ```

  outputs the value corresponding to "help" (i.e. you get the definition of help).
- You can use the result of indexing a map in any way that would be an appropriate use of the value type. So given

  ```
  std::map<string, int> stats;
  ```

  `stats["the"]++;` will increment the value associated with "the". If there is no entry for "the" in `stats`, one will be created, with a starting value of 0 which will be incremented immediately to 1.
- C++ has a special operator -> (arrow) that is used to select a member from an object that is identified by an iterator.
- The C++ Standard Library provides a number of functions in the <cctype> header that classify `char` values. These include `isalpha(char)`, which returns `true` if the argument is a letter

otherwise it returns `false`; `isdigit(char)`, which returns `true` if the argument represents a decimal digit; `islower(char)` and `isupper(char)`, which return `true` if the argument represents a lower/uppercase letter.

- The `<ctime>` header provides support for various time concepts.
- The function `clock()` returns a `clock_t` value that measures the time since program start in units that depend on the computer system you are using. `time_t` for the combination of MinGW and MS Windows measures time in thousandths of a second.

Extensions checklist

- `fgw::Wait(n)` causes your program to pause for n thousandths of a second.

CHAPTER 14

Getting, Storing and Restoring Graphical Items

In this chapter I will introduce you to further details of implementing and using persistence. I will show you how to write code to get and save a rectangular part of a Playpen. You will also learn how to write code to restore a saved area to a location of your choice.

I will tell you something about fonts and how to add text to the Playpen. During the process you will learn about two-dimensional `vector`s and make further use of `std::map`.

This chapter gives further examples of developing new types (called user-defined types to distinguish them from the fundamental types provided by the C++ language). I will walk you through the thinking processes I went through while achieving my objectives. This is deliberate. You need to learn by example rather than just see the end product.

Preparing to Program

I wonder how you feel when you prepare to write a program from scratch. I know how I feel: a sense of trepidation, a feeling of anxiety that it will prove difficult and take me a lot of time to get it right. Many programmers I know feel similarly. Even though we know we are competent or even very good programmers we still have these feelings with each new project we start. Each time we make an act of faith that we will have enough skill and knowledge to complete the task.

The reward comes at the end when our program works. For me, at least, it does not matter how small the program is I still get a sense of pleasure the first time a program runs successfully. Even when writing the little programs for earlier chapters I was anxious when I started and experienced a sense of joy when they worked as intended. I also experienced a sense of profound irritation every time I found that the code was not quite correct even though it had worked for the test cases.

The reason that I am sharing this with you is because sometimes that sense of initial trepidation stops (or, in my case, seriously delays) us doing the job. You will probably experience anxiety when preparing to work on a new program. You need to know that this is normal. You should also experience a sense of elation when the program finally works. And unless you are very lucky there will be moments of despondency (sometimes close to despair) when things do not work and you cannot see why.

Many years ago I spent a great deal of time writing a program that could only be compiled as a complete item. The first time it went through a compiler the computer operator (this was in the days before desktop machines) returned with an entire box (1000 sheets) of fanfold computer paper with 60 error messages per sheet. He added that these were just the first few but they had decided not to waste paper printing out the rest. I had misunderstood a feature of the computer and had to rewrite almost my entire program. That moment was a very bad one for me, but the moment, six months later, when the final program passed all its tests was a great high spot.

If programming never gives you a sense of achievement, elation, or pride in work well done then you probably should think about doing something else. Even a job should reward you with positive feelings, and a hobby certainly should.

I hope by now that you have become part of the broad programming community even if you have yet to meet others. I hope you are continuing to study this book, not because you have to but because your experience so far motivates you to learn more.

Icons, Sprites and Related Items

You should be familiar with the concept of an icon as it relates to computing. It is the term for those little pictures that are often scattered across a computer screen and are used to identify programs and activities.

I once had a pupil who spent two months creating a beautiful set of ''icons'' for an illuminated alphabet (the kind of thing you see in medieval manuscripts where the first letter of a section is a large rectangular area with elaborate detail encapsulating the letter). He first had to write the program that allowed him to manipulate the pixels. These days we could ''cheat'' by using a graphics application such as Paint Shop Pro.

A **sprite** is like an icon but has the added feature that it is designed to be movable (and sometimes animated). Some computers have special hardware facilities to handle that movement and animation and add something called collision detection to detect if the sprite hits a barrier or another sprite. If you get serious with your graphics programming and want to write games and other animation-based material you will need to find out about the special support libraries that are provided for your machine. As you are still learning the basics I will provide code to implement primitive sprites in the next chapter.

The fundamental resource we will need to achieve our objectives is a primitive graphical object. It is time we revisited the process of creating a new type in C++. I am going to call this type `icon`.

Designing an icon type

Recall from Chapter 5 that types must be designed. The first element of design is to specify what we want the type to do. Only then can we think about how we can make that work (implement it). Here is a first shot at designing the `icon` type:

```
class icon {
public:
  void display(fgw::playpen &, int x, int y)const;
  bool load(std::istream & in);
  bool load(std::string const & filename);
private:
// data
};
```

The three member functions are an overloaded pair of functions to load an icon's data from a stream or file and a single function to display an `icon` in a `playpen`. The `load()` functions return a `bool` so we can determine if they succeeded or not, which might be important at a later stage. Remember that `const` at the right of the declaration of `display()` means the function will not alter the internal data (or state) of an `icon`.

There are many ways in which we could store the data for an `icon`. I am going to keep things simple even though the result is extravagant use of memory. In the past that would have been a serious issue because memory was a scarce resource so you would have had to worry about keeping data compact. Nowadays we can focus on getting ideas working first and then consider ways to make them more compact if we need to.

For the time being we will keep the data for an `icon` as a container of `columns` of graphical data. A `column` will be a container of `fgw::hue` data for the pixels in a column. This information is private to the `icon` object, nothing else needs to know about how the data is organized internally in an `icon` object.

Using a `std::vector<fgw::hue>` for the column type seems reasonable to me so I will add this `typedef` in the `private` part of the definition of `icon`:

```
typedef std::vector<fgw::hue> column;
```

I am going to make the data for an `icon` a container of columns so I add this as well:

```
typedef std::vector<column> icon_data;
```

I place those `typedef`s into the `private` part of the definition of `icon` because I am applying the ''need to know'' guideline. The concepts of `column` and `icon_data` are for use within the implementation of the `icon` type and unless or until I discover otherwise, I do not want code outside the `icon` implementation to use them. This means that if I later decide to change the way I store the data for an `icon`, I can do so without having to worry about whether some other code outside the implementation of `icon` depends on the current choice. As a general guideline, the less you expose your data to general use the more freedom you have to make changes in the future.

My definition of `icon` now looks like this (with the additions in bold):

```
class icon {
public:
  void display(fgw::playpen &, int x, int y)const ;
  bool load(std::istream & in);
  bool load(std::string const & filename);
private:
  typedef std::vector<fgw::hue> column;
  typedef std::vector<column> icon_data;
  icon_data data;
};
```

Loading data into an icon

Before we can use an `icon` we will need to load some data. We need to deal with one of the `load()` functions. Here is my code which does that:

```
bool icon::load(istream & in){
  try{
     string column_data;
     icon_data new_data;
     while(true){
        getline(in, column_data);
        if(in.fail()) break; // input failed, possibly EOF
        if(column_data.size() == 0) break; // blank line read
        new_data.push_back(extract_column_data(column_data));
     }
     data.swap(new_data);
     return true;
  }
```

```
    catch(...){ return false;} // I do not care what went wrong
}
```

This function checks that the input line is not empty (that would mark the end of the icon data). It also checks that something was successfully read in. The most likely reason for failure is that it has tried to read past the end of the input stream. Note that I need to use std::getline() and not fgw::getdata() because the latter skips blank lines and we will use a blank line to mark the end of an icon's stored data.

If an exception is thrown during the processing of the try-block, I do not care what it was, just that the load failed and so I catch all exceptions and return false.

If you try to compile this function you will get an error; it calls the function extract_column_data() which has not even been declared. That function is intended to help the implementation of icon::load(). Nothing outside the implementation of the icon member functions needs to know about it. That tells me that I should place it in the unnamed namespace in the icon implementation file. Here is the definition for you to add to icon.cpp (or whatever you called it):

```
vector<hue> extract_column_data(string const & data){
  stringstream source(data);
  vector<hue> a_column;
  while(true){
     hue const value(read<hue>(source));
     if(not source.fail()) a_column.push_back(value);
     else return a_column;
  }
}
```

Even though the motive for writing this function is to support icon, it does not have access to the private typedefs of that class so I have to use the actual type of icon::column which is vector<hue> (check the typedef). This function keeps extracting hue values until there are none left. Each one that it successfully extracts gets added to the vector<hue> we are building. Note that I need to #include <sstream> because I am using a stringstream object to help with data extraction.

Do you remember that we should be testing early and often? It isn't enough that our code compiles, we need to start executing it as soon as possible. Create a test source file (call it icon_test.cpp) and start it with the following code:

```
#include "icon.h"

using namespace fgw;
using namespace std;

int main(){
  icon test;
  cout << "Type in some numbers."
       << " To finish enter a blank line.\n";
  test.load(cin);
}
```

Now compile and build the program. It won't do anything exciting but it will test that our `load()` function is working.

ROBERTA

That program does not do anything? How do I know if it works?

FRANCIS

Yes, programs without output are not very useful. If you do what the prompt says the program keeps collecting input until you hit enter without typing in any more numbers. That is all you can do by way of testing at the moment because I am yet to implement `icon::display()`.

Displaying data from an icon

Now let me focus on implementing the display function so that we can do something with the data we can now load into an `icon` object. You might try this for yourself before looking at my solution. Your first instinct is probably that it is hard but if you think it through carefully you may decide that it isn't that difficult. I will simply work through the columns stored in the `icon`. For each column I will work through its stored `hue` values using them to display pixels in the Playpen.

```
void icon::display(playpen & paper, int x, int y)const {
  for(int i(0); i != data.size(); ++i){ // the columns
     for(int j(0); j != data[i].size(); ++j){ // the hues
        if(data[i][j]) paper.plot(x+i, y+j, data[i][j]);
     }
  }
}
```

This implementation of the `display()` function treats the zero `fgw::hue` (`black`) as invisible – that is the effect of `if(data[i][j])`. Having an invisible `hue` will prove useful elsewhere. Now change your test program as follows (and add some prompts):

```
int main(){
  try{
     playpen paper;
     icon test;
     test.load(cin);
     paper.scale(4);
     test.display(paper, 20, 20);
     paper.display();
     cin.get();
  }
  catch(...) { cout << "An exception occurred.\n"; }
}
```

ROBERTA

This program does even less than the previous one.

FRANCIS

It waits for you to type in some numbers. If you just hit return at once, that is a blank line and your `icon` *will be an empty one. Add a prompt before* `test.load(cin)` *to remind you that you need to provide some data. The one in the previous program will do.*

Note that we often keep code to the bare minimum when writing these very early test programs. This kind of early test is largely written and then discarded or absorbed into more permanent tests (which are used to check behavior when code is changed perhaps months or years later).

Have you noticed that our `icon` objects do not actually have to be rectangular? A column extends upwards for as many pixels as there is data.

Now you are probably getting pretty tired of typing in test data and would like to get the data from a file so it is time I implemented that second version of `icon::load()`.

Loading data into an icon from a file

Most of the work has been done because the version of `icon::load()` that we already have extracts information from any `istream`. All our alternative version needs is to use the filename provided to open an `ifstream` and then use the other version to finish the job (remember how programmers hate repeating themselves?). This is another example of delegation, where we make something else do most of the work. Again, you might try this for yourself before looking at my solution.

```
bool icon::load(string const & filename){
  ifstream in;
  open_ifstream(in, filename);
  if(in.fail()) return false;
  return load(in);
}
```

To test this function we need a file with some data in it. Use Quincy to create a text file with several rows of numbers in it (separated with spaces, no punctuation). Now modify the test program to load the data from that file instead of from `std::cin`.

Adding icon constructors

Do you remember that when I designed and implemented `point2d` I added things called constructors. Their job was to allow a new object to be created with relevant data already in place. It would be nice to add the same kind of functionality for the `icon` type. What is more we can do so cheaply.

We have three cases: create an empty `icon` (which is what happens at the moment, because the compiler does that if we do not provide any constructors), create an `icon` with data from a stream or create an `icon` with data from a named file. These are the declarations we need to add to our definition of the icon type:

```
icon();                             // from nothing
icon(std::istream &);               // from a stream
icon(std::string const & filename); // from a named file
```

And here are the implementations:

```
icon::icon(){}
icon::icon(std::istream & in){
  if(not load(in))
     throw fgw::problem("Stream input failed in icon.");
}
icon::icon(std::string const & filename){
  if(not load(filename))
     throw fgw::problem("File input failed in icon.");
}
```

Remember that the `icon::load()` functions returned a `bool` which is `false` if they failed? Here is an example of using that information. The last two constructors are examples of delegation because they make the `icon::load()` functions do the work.

I have to provide the trivial ''do nothing'' constructor because once I start writing constructors the compiler stops doing so. I still want to be able to create empty icons so I must provide the empty constructor.

Storing icon data in a file

Storing data in a file is an improvement to typing it in each time. It would be even better if I could use images from an existing Playpen to create files of data. This is what I am going to do in this section. This is a typical example of writing an auxiliary tool to support something we are doing. The tool is not a direct part of `icon`, but having it will make it much easier to develop icons for use.

I need an implementation of:

```
typedef std::vector<fgw::hue> column_data;
typedef std::vector<column_data> area_data;

area_data get_area(fgw::playpen const &,
                        int x, int y, int width, int height);
```

coupled with an implementation of a function that will write the result to a file:

```
void save_area(std::string const & filename,
                  area_data const & area);
```

TASK 42

It's time you did some work instead of just following me. Write and test the above function to save an area_data object to a file. The file format should have each column on a new line and the individual pieces of data separated by a space.

Now you have that working you need the other function so that you have some real data to test it. This implementation does the basic job:

```
area_data get_area(fgw::playpen const & paper,
                        int x, int y, int width, int height){
  area_data result;
  for(int i(0); i != width; ++i){
     column_data column;
     for(int j(0); j != height; ++j){
        column.push_back(paper.get_hue(x+i, y+j));
```

```
        }
        result.push_back(column);
    }
    return result;
}
```

Remember that `fgw::get_hue()` extracts the `fgw::hue` from a Playpen using `fgw::playpen` coordinates (allows for origin and scale).

When you have tested this function and corrected the unwarranted assumption (you did notice that it fails if either `width` or `height` is negative? See the end of the chapter for the corrected code) you will surely wish you could select the area you are interested in with a mouse.

TASK 43

Look back at Chapter 11 where we used a mouse to draw lines. We used an ''elastic'' temporary line to show what we would get if we clicked the mouse button. Write a similar function that will draw a temporary rectangle from the first place you clicked a mouse button to the present location of the mouse. If the mouse cursor leaves the Playpen it should cancel the currently selected anchor point and wait for you to select another point.

The function should return a `vector<int>` that contains the x-coordinate and y-coordinate of the first mouse click followed by the x-coordinate and y-coordinate of the second mouse click. You will need to use some of the utility functions we wrote for the mouse in Chapter 11.

TASK 44

Use the function you wrote for Task 43 combined with the `save_area()` function to implement the following function, which uses the mouse to select an area and then saves it to the file:

```
void select_and_save_area(fgw::playpen &, std::string const &
    filename);
```

EXERCISE 1

There are various transformations that we can apply to a block of pixels such as rotating the block, inverting or reversing it. Write and test functions to do some of those things to an area whose data is stored as an `area_data` object.

The `<algorithms>` header in the Standard C++ Library includes `std::reverse()`, which reverses the order of elements in a sequence container. Given `cont` is a suitable container the following reverses the elements:

```
reverse(cont.begin(), cont.end());
```

Using your answers to Exercise 1, add some other member functions to `icon` so that you can rotate and reflect the stored image. Note that an `icon` does not have to be rectangular, so you will need to add a function that levels up all the columns to the same height. That leads to the question as to what hue should be used for filling out short columns. Use `black` (0) which `icon::display()` treats as invisible.

Further practice

Now that you have working code for icons or images, experiment with it. One thing to try is to load a graphic from a .png file with `LoadPlaypen()` (remember that the file must be one containing a 512×512 pixel image using a 256 – or less – color palette). Now set the scale to 2 (or 3, etc.) before extracting part of the image. Clear the Playpen window and display the extracted image with the scale set to 1.

Try other ideas. You have a set of tools for simple image manipulation so do not be afraid to have fun experimenting with them.

I have provided a complete implementation of `icon` on the book's website if you do not want to type in the source code for yourself. You will find a butterfly.icon file on the CD that you can use as a basis for your initial experiments. I provided a guide to using Paint Shop Pro 7 to create the .png files in Chapter 9.

Making a Font

There are two kinds of font that we use in computing: bitmap fonts provide a pattern of pixels or dots for the different letters and outline fonts provide instructions to a font utility that draws the letters rather than just plotting them.

Bitmap fonts were popular in the early days for use on screens and for dot-matrix printers. They tended to be fairly ugly and did not scale well. These days we like our screens and printers to display high quality text at many different scales. Bitmap fonts are poor for this, so outline fonts are now the preferred ones. However they do need sophisticated design and special tools to display them.

For our purposes we need something simple so I am restricting myself to showing you how to produce a bitmap monochrome font. Our first problem is to find a way to get a sample of each symbol we want to use.

There are many ways of achieving this objective. For example:

- You could write a program that allows you to use a mouse to meticulously design each letter pixel by pixel. Imagine that you are working black on white. You could write a small function that simply reverses the color of the pixel under the mouse cursor each time you press the mouse button. Add in some keyboard control and a menu that allows you to move on from designing a letter on the screen to extracting it and saving it as an icon.
- You could use a graphics application such as Paint Shop Pro to generate a 512 by 512 screen with the letters you want. Save it as a suitable .png file. Now load that file into the Playpen window and use the tools we developed in the first part of this chapter to save each symbol in `icon` format.
- A third choice would be to use your text editor to create a suitable data file of **glyphs** (the technical name of the graphical representation of a symbol).

We are going to develop a fixed height but variable width font. That is, all the glyphs will be the same height but the number of columns making up a glyph will vary in accordance with the natural width of the symbol ("i" will have fewer columns than "m").

I am going to make my font 13 dots high. That is enough to produce a reasonably readable font. Each dot will either be in background color or in the current selected color for writing. In other words it is in one of two states. This suggests to me that a column of dots can be held in a `std::bitset<13>`. As I want to use a variable number of columns I will package them into a `std::vector`. A couple of `typedef`s and an `int const` will make it easier to talk about these components:

```
int const symbol_height = 13;
typedef  std::bitset<symbol_height> dot_column;
typedef std::vector<dot_column> glyph_data;
```

As the data for a font (composed of the `glyph_data` for a number of symbols) will be stored in a file I need to consider the format of that file. When I read the data from the file I will need two things for each symbol:

- What the symbol is.
- The actual data, with one line of data for each `dot_column`.

A typical entry might be:

```
E
0000111111111
0000100010001
0000100010001
0000100010001
0000100000001
```

Designing a glyph type

Let us take a break from the problems of acquiring and storing data for glyphs and work on the design of code to use the data. For now I will use hand-coded data for a couple of letters. You will find these in a file glyph.data in the Chapter 14 directory.

Here is my design for a class that will represent a single glyph. Notice that it has no knowledge of what symbol the glyph will represent; we will get to that eventually.

```
class glyph {
  public:
     void display(fgw::playpen &, int x, int y, fgw::hue)const;
     bool load(std::istream & in);
     bool load(std::string const & filename);
     int width() const{return data.size(); }
  private:
     glyph_data data;
};
```

It is time to start up another project, add the definition of `symbol_height` and those two `typedef`s I gave earlier to glyph.h and then add the definition of the `glyph` type.

A `glyph` object can obtain data from a stream or a file (in a very similar way to an `icon` object). It can display the glyph in the Playpen. That is it.

I have provided a `width()` member function so that functions to display strings in the Playpen can know how much space a glyph takes. That allows them to calculate where to start the next glyph. As `width()` delegates all its functionality to the `size()` member of a `vector` type, I have used an option of C++ that allows the definition of a member function to be included in the class definition. You should only consider providing in-class definitions for member functions where the entire functionality is delegated to another function.

Implementing the glyph member functions

TASK 45

Try to implement the member functions for `glyph`. The code will be similar to that for `icon`. However using a `dot_column` (`bitset<13>`) for the innermost container does simplify things a bit for the `load(std::istream)` function. The `load(std::string)` function delegates the main work to `load(std::istream)` after successfully opening a file.

There is not a lot more that can be done for our glyph type but you might decide to provide some constructors. These will be much the same as those I provided for `icon`. If you want to go the extra mile, please do so.

Creating a font

A font for our purposes is a collection of glyph data for all the letters, digits and symbols that we want to use. In this book I will stick with simple fonts for the normal (unaccented) English letters, digits and symbols. However if you follow the general principles, you will be able to create elaborate bitmapped fonts for yourself.

Now that we have a way to read data for a glyph from a file we need to have a way to create glyph data for many symbols and store it in a file.

Here is how I did that. There is no programming in this process other than writing short programs to use the tools I provided earlier for extracting icon data from the Playpen. Programming isn't just a matter of writing source code; it also involves using any tools that are available to create the data your programs need. I am lucky in that Paint Shop works very well with `playpen` generated .png files. If you are using some other graphics editor to supplement your compiler you will have to depend on your expertize with it.

Step 0 I created an empty, black playpen and then used `SavePlaypen()` to create a file for use with Paint Shop. That way I could pass the basic palette encoding to Paint Shop in a suitably-dimensioned file.

Step 1 I loaded my prepared image into Paint Shop and used the text feature to write a sample of all the letters and symbols I wanted. I selected the Arial typeface and size 10.

One piece of helpful serendipity is that the above process leaves the background encoded as 0 and whatever color is chosen for the text encoded as 1. Had my image included any other colors I would have lost that lucky result (lucky because it encodes symbols in strings of zeros and ones, exactly the kind of string data that `std::bitset` can use). I next saved the result as arialfont.png (there is a copy on the CD for your use).

Step 2a I loaded arialfont.png into the Playpen and used this little program to fix up the palette so that it is more usable. I will say something about `setpalettentry()` in the next chapter.

```
int main(){
  try{
    playpen paper;
    LoadPlaypen(paper, "arialfont.png");
    paper.setpalettentry(255, HueRGB(0,0,255));
    paper.setpalettentry(0, HueRGB(255,255,0));
    paper.setpalettentry(1, HueRGB(0, 0, 0));
```

```
        paper.updatepalette();
        paper.display();
        SavePlaypen(paper, "arialfont.png");
        cin.get();
    }
    catch(...) { cout << "An exception occurred.\n"; }
}
```

After running the above program the type will be black on a bright yellow background. The outline box that identifies the selected area in Step 2b will be bright blue.

Step 2b Now I used `select_and_save_area()` to grab the entire row of uppercase letters into a file called uppercase.font.

Step 3 I loaded uppercase.font into a text editor (MS Word works well for this). I stripped out all the spaces. Then I replaced all lines that contained only zeros with blank lines. This step isolated the images for each letter. Next I made sure that the baseline for the font was in the right place. I happen to know that some lowercase Arial 10pt fonts extend 3 pixels below the base line and that all uppercase letters in Arial sit on the base line. This means that I had to edit my file to ensure that the bottom of the uppercase letters was in the right place (in this case adjusting the lines so that the first line for ''A'' starts with 0001). I also had to trim off trailing zeros so that every line was exactly 13 zeros and ones in length.

Step 4 Still in the editor I added the uppercase letter being represented immediately before each block of glyph data. I also made sure that each block of data was followed by a single blank line (to mark the end of the data for a glyph). I removed any other blank lines so that the resulting file is the one on the CD named uppercase.font. Have a look at it and I think things will be clearer.

Designing a font type

A font is a map from characters to glyphs. When I try to display a particular character I want the corresponding glyph displayed in Playpen. In other words I want to be able to write something like:

```
int font::display(char, fgw::playpen &, int x, int y, fgw::hue);
```

The parameters should be self-explanatory. The function returns an `int` which is the width of the glyph. This can be used to calculate where to start the next glyph.

When I consider what else I need for a font object I get:

```
class font {
  public:
    int display(char, fgw::playpen &,
                              int x, int y, fgw::hue)const;
    bool load(std::istream &);
    bool load(std::string const & filename);
  private:
    typedef std::map<char, glyph> font_data;
    font_data data;
};
```

The reason for the `typedef` being declared in the `private` section is that it is an implementation detail that I do not want to leak out into the source code of programmers who use my `font` type. This is different to the problem with a `glyph` type where users may need details so that they can write their own functions for such purposes as preparing data files. Later on we might want to add other functionality, but this will do for now.

Implementing the font member functions

Try to write the implementation code for the member functions. Do not spend too long trying to get your version of `font::display()` to work because there is a nasty C++ problem and you are unlikely to find the solution for yourself.

Apart from that, the biggest trap is to forget that a font might not have a representation for some characters and your `font::display()` function must handle that gracefully. In my solution I am just going to display some blank space, but you might add a glyph to represent a "missing" character.

Here are my definitions for the two `font::load()` functions:

```
bool font::load(istream & in){
  try{
     insert_space_glyph();
     while(true){
        char const symbol(read<char>(in));
        if(in.fail()) break; // no char read, possibly eof
        if(symbol == '\n' or symbol == ' ') break;
          // read a newline or space; end of data
        string garbage;
        getline(in, garbage); // discard rest of line
        glyph representation;
        representation.load(in);
        data[symbol] = representation;
     }
     return true;
  }
  catch(...){return false; } // just report failure
}
```

There are three ways that a file (or stream) of font data might end: with an end of file symbol, with a newline character or with a space character. I will come to that `insert_space_glyph()` shortly but here is the other `font::load()` member function.

```
bool font::load(string const & filename){
  ifstream in;
  open_ifstream(in, filename);
  if(in.fail()) throw fgw::problem (
                  "Could not open file in font::load\n");
  return load(in);
}
```

Notice the `insert_space_glyph()` function. Every font will need a representation of a blank space but there is not a sensible way to code that in a file of font data. When I realized that I would always need a glyph for a blank space (which did nothing) I added an extra member function to my font type, but made it a `private` member because it is an implementation detail. Functions like this one are often called "helper functions". Here is the definition of this one:

```
void font::insert_space_glyph(){
  stringstream space_rep;
  space_rep << "0000000000000\n";
  space_rep << "0000000000000\n";
  space_rep << "0000000000000\n";
  space_rep << "0000000000000\n";
  space_rep << '\n';
  glyph space(space_rep);
  data[' '] = space;
}
```

This creates a `stringstream`, loads it with the representation for a blank space and then uses it to create a glyph which can be loaded into the font map.

Displaying a font object

This is what I wanted to write for the `display()` function. Displaying a symbol should not alter the `font` object. That means that it should be a `const` member function (as signified by the `const` directly after the closing parentheses of the parameter list):

```
int font::display(char c, playpen & paper,
                           int x, int y, hue shade)const {
  if(data.find(c) == data.end()) c = ' ';
                                  // no representation for c
  data[c].display(canvas, x, y, shade);
  return data[c].width();
}
```

The above implementation would have been clean and elegant. Unfortunately the behavior of the index feature of `std::map` causes problems. Remember that when we use an index on a `std::map` object, it adds a new element if the key is not found. That is generally very helpful behavior, but it means we cannot use `[key]` on a `const` qualified `std::map` object because doing so might change the map by adding a new element. We have to find another way to write this code that will keep the compiler happy.

The solution is that we will have to use an iterator but not a plain iterator. We use one that promises not to allow changes. Such iterators belong to a special type called `const_iterator`. The `const` is part of the type's name and is not a qualifier.

Here is the rewritten `font::display()`:

```
int font::display(char c, playpen & paper,
                    int x, int y, hue shade)const {
  font_data::const_iterator iter(data.find(c));
  if(iter == data.end()) iter = data.find(' ');
  (iter -> second).display(paper, x, y, shade);
  return (iter -> second).width();
}
```

Make sure that you check this code through and understand it. We first try to find the character we want to display, if it isn't there we use a blank space instead (and we know that is always there because it is the first thing we load when we load a font). You should note that `iter` refers to a `(char, glyph)` pair of values, so `iter->second` is a `glyph` value; the one that corresponds to the symbol we want to print. That means the calls of `.display()` and `.width()` will be the ones that apply to `glyph` objects.

Write a program to test the `font` type. It will need to read a font from a file (uppercase.font) and display a couple of letters in the Playpen.

Displaying a String in the Playpen

We are very nearly done. We have all the tools we need and can write the final bit.

Write an implementation of:

```
void display_string(std::string const &, fgw::playpen &,
                    font const & type, int x, int y, fgw::hue);
```

When you have written your own, look at my solution at the end of this chapter. My solution may look easy, but writing it takes hard thought or lots of experience.

Write a program that asks the user to type in a message that you display in the Playpen.

CHALLENGING

The arialfont.png file contains lowercase letters, digits and quite a number of punctuation marks. Use the tools and the methods described in this chapter to produce a more complete font.

CHALLENGING

Write a program that displays a menu in the Playpen and uses the mouse to select an item. You actually know enough to write a menu program where the item under the mouse cursor is highlighted. However if you succeed in doing that you are far above average as a programmer and have an understanding of how modern programs work.

EXERCISE 5

ROBERTA'S COMMENTS

My very first impression of Chapter 14 and, in fact, the following chapters was that they seemed far more difficult than the others or at least had very complicated things in them. It was almost as if at this stage we were to be treated more like real programmers and less like beginners.

I had problems with the code that tested the icon *load()* function and complained to Francis when nothing seemed to happen when I ran it. He said that this was raw basic code and at this stage we are expected to fill in any gaps ourselves. I was not sure that I wanted to be a real programmer just yet.

But, as is usually the case, I ended up enjoying most of the exercises and I'm looking forward to creating my own font.

Task 46 showed that even now I'm still making silly mistakes. The first problem I had was that the characters I selected were undeclared. I didn't realize that it was necessary to write 'C' for the *char* argument in *font.display()*. Then when I tried to compile the project I got the error message "undefined reference to font." I had forgotten to include *glyph.cpp*.

I worked Task 47 out in principle and then looked at the solution which I couldn't understand at first. I didn't recognize the operator (I haven't had the luxury of appendices) and only when I went back over the chapter did I realize that *font.display()* returns an *int*.

I had a few problems with Exercise 4 which I hope will be resolved by the time you do it. However, problems are sometimes useful and I gained more understanding through struggling.

I was determined to be "above average" and tackled the hard bit of Exercise 5 too. However, I will have to admit to having a slight advantage without which I doubt I could have done it. In an earlier version of this chapter, Francis included his solution to Task 43 which included a highlight function using the *disjoint* plot mode function as follows:

```
void highlight_block(playpen & paper, int x, int y, int width,
                                   int height, int wait_time){
  plotmode const oldmode(paper.setplotmode(disjoint));
  fill_rectangle(paper, x, y, width, height, white);
  paper.display();
  Wait(wait_time);
  fill_rectangle(paper, x, y, width, height, white);
  paper.display();
  paper.setplotmode(oldmode);
}
```

Having got the basic functions working, I proudly sent the *.exe* file to Francis. He replied saying the program didn't work. We tried various things and in the end I reluctantly sent him my *.cpp* file.

He then reminded me that the program needed two external files: a *.png* file, which I had told him about, and a font file, which I had forgotten. So if you send programs to friends, be sure to include all the necessary files along with the program.

SOLUTIONS TO TASKS

Task 42

```
void save_area(string const & filename,
                area_data const & image){
  ofstream out;
  open_ofstream(out, filename);
```

SOLUTIONS TO TASKS

```
  if(out.fail()) throw fgw::problem(
                        "file did not open in save_area");
  for(int i(0); i != image.size(); ++i){
     for(int j(0); j != image[i].size(); ++j){
        out << int(image[i][j]) << ' ';
     }
     out << '\n';
  }
  out << '\n';
}
```

Task 43

Before you look at the solution you should know that this is not my design but Roberta's. I had a poorer design to a slightly less well-defined task. Roberta came up with a good design but there were problems with her implementation. After discussing it we provided a working version. I have since applied some polish to the code but that should not detract from her contribution. Why am I telling you this? Because teachers should give credit to their students and because I want you to see that you really can do it.

The repetition in this code suggests that it could be further polished but I am not sure it is worth the effort at this stage.

```
void temp_rectangle(playpen & paper, int beginx, int beginy,
                        int endx, int endy,int wait_time){
  plotmode const oldmode(paper.setplotmode(disjoint));
  vertical_line(paper, beginx, beginy, endy, white);
  horizontal_line(paper,endy, beginx, endx, white);
  vertical_line(paper,endx, endy, beginy, white);
  horizontal_line(paper, beginy, endx, beginx, white);
  paper.display();
  Wait(wait_time);
  vertical_line(paper, beginx, beginy, endy, white);
  horizontal_line(paper,endy, beginx, endx, white);
  vertical_line(paper,endx, endy, beginy, white);
  horizontal_line(paper, beginy, endx, beginx, white);
  paper.display();
  paper.setplotmode(oldmode);
}
```

The following part of the solution makes use of `where_on_button_click()`, `playpen_x()` and `playpen_y()` from Chapter 9. It also has quite a tricky little play with `while` loops to allow us to restart our selection by moving the mouse outside the Playpen. I suspect quite a few experts would look very askance at this code but at this stage in your programming it makes excellent use of the tools you have at your command.

SOLUTIONS TO TASKS

```
vector<int> rectangle_preview(playpen & paper){
  while(true){
     cout << "Click mouse button to start.\n";
     mouse::location finish;
     bool restart(false);
     while(true){
       mouse::location const
                       start(where_on_button_click(paper));
       point2d begin(playpen_x(paper, start),
                        playpen_y(paper, start));
       mouse m;
       while(m.button_pressed()); // clear button
       while(not m.button_pressed()){
          finish = m.cursor_at();
          if(finish.x() < 0){ // mouse out of Playpen
             restart = true;
             break;
          }
          temp_rectangle(paper, playpen_x(paper, start),
                                playpen_y(paper, start),
                                playpen_x(paper, finish),
                                playpen_y(paper, finish),100);
          }
          if(restart) break; // cancel mouse click-
          vector<int> coordinates;
          coordinates.push_back(playpen_x(paper, start));
          coordinates.push_back(playpen_y(paper, start));
          coordinates.push_back(playpen_x(paper, finish));
          coordinates.push_back(playpen_y(paper, finish));
          return coordinates;
       }
    }
 }
 void select_and_save_area(playpen & paper,
                                     string const & filename){
 vector<int> coords(rectangle_preview(paper));
 save_area(filename, get_area(paper, coords[0],
                              coords[1],
                              coords[2]-coords[0],
                              coords[3]-coords[1]));
}
```

SOLUTIONS TO TASKS

Task 44

All the hard work of Task 43 bears fruit in this nice little solution to Task 44:

```
void select_and_save_area(playpen & paper,
                                  string const & filename){
  vector<int> coords(rectangle_preview(paper));
  save_area(filename, get_area(paper, coords[0], coords[1],
                            coords[2]-coords[0],
                            coords[3]-coords[1]));
}
```

Task 45

I wonder how much of a problem you had with this code. I know that it eventually turned out to be a lot simpler than I expected. Here is my code:

```
void glyph::display(playpen & paper, int x, int y, hue shade)const{
  for(int i(0); i != width(); ++i){
     for(int j(0); j != symbol_height; ++j){
        if(data[i][j]) paper.plot(x+i, y-j, shade);
     }
  }
}
```

The above code iterates through the columns. Within each column it plots a pixel (dot) if the corresponding bit is set. If you think that because the code is simple that writing it should be easy then you are not counting the hours and the experience that go into producing a design that can be implemented easily. If your solution is anywhere near mine then you can feel justly proud of yourself. Personally I get much more joy from writing simple code than from writing complicated stuff. I always feel that inside complicated code there is simple code trying to escape.

```
bool glyph::load(istream & in){
  try{
     string column_data;
     glyph_data new_data;
     while(true){
        getline(in, column_data);
        if(column_data.size() == 0) break; // no more data
        if(in.fail())break; // abandon, probably end of file
        dot_column const dots(column_data);
        new_data.push_back(dots);
     }
     data.swap(new_data);
     return true;
  }
  catch(...){ return false;} // I do not care what went wrong
}
```

SOLUTIONS TO TASKS

The core of this function is very simple; it just uses an input line to initialize a `dot_column` variable before copying it into a `glyph_data` object. The rest of the code deals with incorrect input and determines when all the data for a glyph has been extracted from the file.

For completeness here is the `load(std::string const &)` version:

```
bool glyph::load(string const & filename){
  ifstream in;
  open_ifstream(in, filename);
  if(in.fail()) throw fgw::problem(
            "Could not open file in glyph::load\n");
  return load(in);
}
```

Finally, here is a test program that will demonstrate that the above code works:

```
int main(){
  try{
     playpen canvas;
     glyph letter;
     ifstream in("glyph.txt");
     if(in.fail()){
        cout << "file did not open.\n";
        return 0;
     }
     char symbol(read<char>(in));
           // get the letter that precedes the data
     cout << symbol << '\n';
     letter.load(in);
     letter.display(canvas, 0, 0, black);
     canvas.display();
     cout << "Press RETURN to finish";
     cin.get();
  }
  catch(fgw::problem & e){cout << e.report() << '\n';}
  catch(...){cout << "\n***An exception was thrown.***\n" ;}
}
```

You might be wondering about that first `catch`. We have been throwing messages when we detect a problem. This is the way to catch them on the basis of what type they are. The `fgw::problem` type has a member function `report()` that will return the message that was provided when the exception was thrown. I will leave more detailed handling of exceptions to another book.

Task 46

Here is a possible program that would meet the requirements of the task. Note that the requirements are so loose that there are many possibilities. However you should test both with characters that are in the font and ones that are not.

SOLUTIONS TO TASKS

```
// written by fgw 24/05/03
#include "myfont.h"
#include <iostream>

using namespace fgw;
using namespace std;

int main(){
  try{
     playpen canvas;
     font test;
     test.load("uppercase.font");
     cout << test.display('A', canvas, 0, 0, green4) << '\n';
// now test for use of a character that is not provided
// should output 4
     cout << test.display('a', canvas, 0, 0, green4) << '\n';
     canvas.display();
     cout << "Press RETURN to finish";
     cin.get();
  }
  catch(fgw::problem & e){cout << e.report() << '\n';}
  catch(...){cout << "\n***An exception was thrown.***\n" ;}
  return 0;
}
```

Task 47

```
void display_string(string const & message, playpen & paper,
                font & type, int x, int y, hue shade){
  for(int i(0); i != message.size(); ++i){
     x += (1 + type.display(message[i], paper, x, y, shade));
  }
}
```

SOLUTIONS TO EXERCISES

Exercise 1

The existence of a function called `std::reverse()` makes two of the suggested problems very easy: one of them simply delegates directly to `std::reverse()`, while the other delegates to it for each of the constituent `column_data` elements (but note that it assumes the block is rectangular, i.e. that all the columns are the same height).

SOLUTIONS TO EXERCISES

```
void reflect_horizontally(area_data & block){
  reverse(block.begin(), block.end());
}

void reflect_vertically(area_data & block){
  for(int i(0); i != block.size(); ++i){
     reverse(block[i].begin(), block[i].end());
  }
}
```

Mathematicians will recognize that 180-degree rotation can be done simply by reflecting both horizontally and vertically:

```
void rotate_180_degrees(area_data & block){
  reflect_vertically(block);
  reflect_horizontally(block);
}
```

A 90-degree rotation is harder because we have to move pixels from columns to rows. It also requires that the pixel array is a rectangular array. Calling this function for a block with columns of mixed heights will result in bad things happening.

```
void rotate_90_degrees(area_data block){
  area_data result;
// note the following assumes all columns are the same
// height, and just uses the height of the first
  for(int i(0); i != block[0].size(); ++i){
     column_data temp;
     for(int j(0); j != block.size(); ++j){
        temp.push_back(block[j][i]);
     }
     result.push_back(temp);
  }
  block.swap(result); // swap the data for the two arrays
}
```

Combining this with other transformation functions will provide more transformations.

Exercise 2

The following function forces an icon's image to be rectangular (i.e. all columns the same height) by adding zeros to any short columns until they are the same height as the tallest:

```
void icon::normalise(){
  int height(0);
```

SOLUTIONS TO EXERCISES

```
  for(int i(0); i != image.size(); ++i){
     if(image[i].size() > height) height = block[i].size();
  }
  for(int i(0); i != image.size(); ++i){
     for(int j(image[i].size()); j != height; ++j){
        image[i].push_back(hue(0));
     }
  }
}
```

Now you can reuse the code from Exercise 1 by using `normalise()` to ensure that the icon's data is rectangular. For safety, it would be best to add a call to `normalise()` at the start of the definition of `rotate_90_degrees()` because that function doesn't just work wrongly for non-rectangular arrays but does bad things by trying to write data to non-existent places.

Exercise 3

```
  // written by fgw 26/05/03
#include "glyph.h"
#include <iostream>

using namespace fgw;
using namespace std;

int main(){
  try{
     playpen canvas;
     font test;
     test.load("uppercase.font");
     cout << "What message? ";
     string message;
     getline(cin, message);
     display_string(message, canvas, test, -100, 0, red3);
     canvas.display();
     cout << "Press RETURN to finish";
     cin.get();
  }

  catch(fgw::problem & e){cout << e.report() << '\n';}
  catch(...){cout << "\n***An exception was thrown.***\n" ;}
  return 0;
}
```

Summary

Key programming concepts

- Avoid magic. It isn't only literal numbers that should be named. Good type and function names make code self-explanatory.
- If a type is composed of several components, make those components explicit by giving them names.
- If you need to do a complicated piece of arithmetic, write a function whose name will document what it does. Structure the function so that the various steps are named.
- With modern fast machines the programming priority is for clear code that is easy to understand and easy to modify when necessary.

C++ checklist

- C++ containers have a special (nested) type `const_iterator` that is used as an iterator when the container is `const` qualified. It is necessary when handling a `const std::map` because we cannot use the map's subscript operator (it might result in adding a new item to the map).

CHAPTER 15

Functions as Objects and Simple Animation

In this chapter I will introduce you to the idea that a function is just another kind of object. Just like other objects, they have types, references to them can be stored in variables and they can be passed as arguments to functions with suitable parameters. Some people think that treating functions as objects is very difficult and cannot be of much use. They are wrong on both counts.

You will find that handling functions as objects is actually straightforward. I will also show you one way of using them that by the end of the chapter will allow you to produce animated images in the Playpen. These will include both animation on the spot and objects that move around the Playpen.

Functions that Remember

Programming applies a special meaning to the word ''state''. When we say that something has **state** we mean that it has some property that endures. In a sense, state is akin to having memory. The commonest things that have state in programming are variables. In C++ functions can have state. By that I mean that as well as doing things (the normal view of a function) we can write functions that remember things from their last use. This may seem odd when you first come across it. It may also seem to be of very little use. Let me first try to give a non-programming example to help you understand the idea.

You are in the process of reading this book. We could express that in pseudo-programming terms as applying a function `read_this_book()`. However the process isn't a continuous one, you read a bit, do something else, read a bit more and so on. You have to remember where you are in the book so that you do not repeatedly start reading at the beginning. There are two ways of keeping track, you can remember or you can make the book remember (e.g. by using a bookmark). The first way might be represented like this:

```
int read_this_book(int page);
int page_of_this_book(0);
while(alive){
        // do many things
        if(study_time){
                page_of_this_book = read_this_book(page_of_this_book);
        }
        // many other things
}
```

I know this is silly code but the purpose is to highlight one of the costs of externally remembering your place in a book. Among other things you have to allocate it a variable in your life program. Compare with the following code that we could write if our `read_this_book()` function could remember where we were:

```
void read_this_book();
while(alive){
        // do many things
        if(study_time){
                read_this_book();
        }
        // many other things
}
```

In other words, delegating the responsibility for remembering where we are to the `read_this_book()` function simplifies the code that uses it. The data must still exist somewhere but by hiding it inside the function we restrict it to the place it is needed.

I hope this helps you understand why functions with internal state (i.e. memory) could be useful. Now let us see how we can do it in C++. Like much in this book this is a simple version. Professional programmers and experienced users of C++ would use more advanced features of the language.

Implementing a function with memory

Look at the following function declaration:

```
void multihued_plot(playpen &, int x, int y);
```

The idea of the function is that each time it is called it will use the next `hue`. The first time it is used it plots in hue 0 and then progressively increments the value till it hits 255, at which stage it will return to using 0 and on through the `hue`s again. If we had such a function we could use it to plot a multi-hued horizontal line with:

```
void multihued_horizontal_line(playpen & canvas,
                       int yval, int start, int end){
  if(start < end){
     for(int x(start); x != end; ++x){
        multihued_plot(canvas, x, yval);
     }
  }
  else {
        // handle right to left
     for(int x(start); x != end; --x){
        multihued_plot(canvas, x, yval);
     }
  }
}
```

How can we implement a function with memory so that `multihued_plot()` can remember what hue it should use next? The secret lies in a special kind of "local" variable; a `static` one. In computer science we say that something is **static** if it is done by the compiler, the opposite is **dynamic** which means that it is done at the time that the program runs. We need to tell the compiler to allocate storage for a variable even though it is defined inside a function. That means that that piece of memory will remain (and hold its contents) for the life of the program and not just for the time the function takes to run (which is what happens for normal variables).

Here is the definition of `multihued_plot()`:

```
void multihued_plot(playpen & canvas, int x, int y){
  static int shade(0);
  canvas.plot(x, y, shade);
  ++shade;
  shade %= 256;
}
```

The first time this function is called, `shade` is initialized (to 0 in this case). That does not happen for subsequent calls (that is the way C++ is designed to work), instead `shade` retains its value from one call of the function to the next. The last lines of the function increment `shade` each time the function is called and then hang on to the remainder when it is divided by 256 (the number of entries in our palette).

TASK 48

Write, compile and execute a test program for `multihued_plot()` and `multihued_horizontal_line()`.

EXERCISE 1

Write a function (call it `plot_every_third()`) that plots a black point only if it did not plot a point the last two times it was called. Use that function to write a function that draws a dotted horizontal line. Test the result. You can assume that it is OK to always draw left to right.

TASK 49

Look at `multihued_plot()` and `multihued_horizontal_line()` and compare them with the functions you wrote for Exercise 1 (or, if you skipped that, use the end of chapter solutions). Try to extend the idea so that you can describe a way to produce functions to draw special lines (colored, dashed, dotted, etc.)

Passing functions around

Remember how programmers hate repeating themselves? I hope you decided that there were some suspicious similarities between the functions that drew multihued lines and the ones that plot dotted lines. Indeed the main difference is that they have different names (though they have identical parameter types).

The other difference is in the implementation details of the plotting functions: the only difference in the line drawing functions is in which plot function they call.

I could have asked you to try a whole bundle of other special kinds of line but I am crediting you with enough sense to realize that they would all be variations on a theme. Wouldn't it be nice if you could simply plug in a plotting policy (change color, only plot some points, etc.) to a line drawing function? Programmers designed C++ and programmers hate repeating themselves, so C++ has such a mechanism. To use it we have to learn that functions are objects and have types like any other object. Unfortunately, function types have complicated names made up from their parameter and return types. The result is that defining a variable of a function type has obscure syntax.

While function types will prove easy to use (otherwise they would not be in this book) writing their names is fiddly. Here is a way that will work.

Start with the declaration of a function that you would like to pass around such as:

```
void multihued_plot(fgw::playpen &, int x, int y);
```

Replace the function's name with a general name for functions of this kind (this will become the name for the type of this function):

```
void Plot_policy(fgw::playpen &, int x, int y);
```

Now put parentheses round that name:

```
void (Plot_policy)(fgw::playpen &, int x, int y);
```

That line reads as (starting with the name we are declaring) "`Plot_policy` is the name of a function whose parameters are a reference to `fgw::playpen`, followed by two `int`. parameters. The function returns `void` (i.e. nothing)."

The next step is to convert that into the general type name functions of that kind. For that we use a `typedef` and write:

```
typedef void (Plot_policy)(fgw::playpen &, int, int);
```

The result of the above is that we have declared that `Plot_policy` is the name for the type of simple plotting functions (i.e. functions with a `fgw::playpen` parameter followed by two `int` parameters and returning nothing).

ROBERTA'S COMMENTS

Why the capital "P"? You hardly ever use uppercase letters in your names.

FRANCIS

That is to avoid a collision with an almost identical name in my library. It saves having to add namespace qualifications when you come to use it over the next few pages.

At this stage in your programming it is probably sensible to treat the above as a recipe for creating a name for a **function type**. I think this is one of the places that you should be pragmatic and be satisfied, for now, with a method that works.

I am going to use this type to create and use a general horizontal line function that can be adjusted by telling it how points will be plotted by giving it a `Plot_policy` function.

```
void horizontal_line(playpen & canvas,
        int yval, int start, int end, Plot_policy plotter){
```

```
      if(start < end){
      for(int x(start); x != end; ++x){
         plotter(canvas, x, yval);
      }
   }
   else {
            // handle right to left
      for(int x(start); x != end; --x){
         plotter(canvas, x, yval);
      }
   }
}
```

It really is that simple: one extra parameter to hold the **function object** provided by the caller (i.e. the calling function). The parameter name is then used as a function name. That is it.

Using this function is also simple. Rather than trying to describe the details in words, here is an example:

```
int main(){
   try{
      playpen canvas(blue4 + green4);
      canvas.scale(2);
      horizontal_line(canvas, 20, -10, 100, multihued_plot);
      horizontal_line(canvas, -20, -10, 100, plot_every_third);
      canvas.display();
      cout << "Press RETURN to finish.\n";
      cin.get();
   }
   catch(...){cout << "An exception was caught.\n";}
}
```

Please try the above code. Make sure that the declarations of `multihued_plot()`, `plot_every_third()` and `horizontal_line()` are available to the compiler. The definitions of those three functions will be needed by the linker so must be provided by a file in the project.

When I want to pass a function to another one I use the name of the function that I want to pass with *no parentheses* after it. That is how the compiler recognizes that I want the function as an object rather than the result of calling the function.

There is one problem; we can only use functions of exactly the right type. For example, we cannot use the `plot` function from `fgw::playpen` because it is a member function – and so has a different type. Even if we had a free (non-member) plot function the parameter list and return type must match that of the type of the function parameter.

```
void plot(fgw::playpen &, int, int);
```

is fine but:

```
bool plot(fgw::playpen &, int, int);
```

fails because it has the wrong return type and

```
void plot(fgw::playpen &, double, double);
```

fails because it has the wrong types for the second and third parameters.

Where this becomes problematical is when we want to add a parameter. For example, `plot_every_third()` always plots black pixels. How can we get it to use different colors without changing the number or type of the parameters?

Using a default argument

If we think about the general form for plotting pixels we will notice that we need four, not three pieces of information: ''on what shall we plot'', ''where'' (two coordinates) and ''what color''. Some plotting functions such as `multihued_plot()` provide the color information internally; some such as `plot_every_third()` do not. However function variables require that all the functions we use with them have identical types of parameters and return type.

As I started with `multihued_plot()` I found myself declaring a function type that did not include a parameter for the color. When you moved on to `plot_every_third()` you found that we had to pick a color rather than letting those using the function do so. This does not seem satisfactory because we finish up with only being able to plot black lines. We can always ignore superfluous data but we cannot provide data for which our function does not have a parameter. Logically, `plot_every_third()` needs an extra parameter so that we can specify the color. However if we add that parameter, our line drawing functions based on `Plot_policy` will not be able to use it.

We could change the declaration of `Plot_policy` to:

```
typedef void (Plot_policy)(fgw::playpen &, int, int, fgw::hue);
```

That would allow us to change the declaration of `plot_every_third()` to:

```
void plot_every_third(fgw::playpen &, int x, int y, fgw::hue);
```

and the definition of `horizontal_line()` to:

```
void horizontal_line(playpen & canvas, int yval, int start,
                int end, hue shade, Plot_policy plotter){
  if(start < end){
     for(int x(start); x != end; ++x){
        plotter(canvas, x, yval, shade);
     }
  }
  else {
            // handle right to left
     for(int x(start); x != end; --x){
        plotter(canvas, x, yval, shade);
     }
  }
}
```

Now the problem is that this version of `horizontal_line()` does not work with `multihued_plot()` because that lacks a `hue` parameter (it does not need one). We can fix that by simply adding another parameter so that the declaration becomes:

```
void multihued_plot(fgw::playpen &, int x, int y, fgw::hue);
```

That is fine, except that programmers using our code are going to find providing an argument that is never used rather weird and irritating. C++ has a mechanism, a default argument, which deals with that problem. We can provide a value in the declaration of the function, which will be used if the caller of the function does not provide a value. We add a default argument (i.e. what the compiler is to use if the caller does not provide a value) by adding it as an assignment-like statement in the function declaration. In the above case we change the declaration to:

```
void multihued_plot(fgw::playpen &, int x, int y,
                                        fgw::hue = fgw::black);
```

Now those using this function in their code can write something such as:

```
multihued_plot(canvas, 10, 20);
```

and the compiler will treat it as if they had written:

```
multihued_plot(canvas, 10, 20, black);
```

In this way we can ensure that the function declaration has the right form to be compatible with other plotting functions that need a color, and keep those using the function happy because they do not have to provide a useless value.

Note that default arguments can only be provided for the right-hand parameters. In the declaration, once you give a parameter a default all the parameters to its right must also have defaults. Similarly, once a caller relies on a default argument for a parameter they have to let the compiler use the defaults for any subsequent parameters. In other words when you switch to values provided in the declaration of a function you cannot switch back to providing later ones.

You do not have to use default values, you can provide a value for parameters that have defaults:

```
multihued_plot(canvas, 10, 20, red2);
```

However, in this case, providing your own value serves no useful purpose because the function does not use the value of the fourth parameter. It ignores it and uses the value it has remembered from its last use.

We have not quite finished because in this case we are getting the compiler to fill in a default argument that has no purpose other than to make the function have the right pattern of parameters to match some other similar functions. In general if we provide information, compilers expect us to use it and will start issuing warning messages if we do not. C++ has a mechanism to deal with this. If we do not provide a name for a parameter when we write the *definition*, we have no name to use it by and the compiler understands that. It will not warn us about unnamed parameters. It recognizes that the data provided for an unnamed parameter is to be ignored. We rewrite the definition of `multihued_plot()` like this:

```
void multihued_plot(playpen & canvas, int x, int y, hue){
  static int shade(0);
  canvas.plot(x, y, shade);
  ++shade;
  if(shade == 256) shade = 0;
}
```

Now everyone should be happy: the user does not have to provide unused information (because the declaration provides a default value as a dummy); the compiler can treat the called function as if four arguments had been provided; and the compiler can confidently ignore the dummy argument (provided by the default value) in the definition.

Modify the declarations and definitions of `horizontal_line()` and `plot_every_third()` to match this requirement that all `Plot_policy` functions will have a final parameter to pass the plotting color, even if it is defaulted to `fgw::black` for functions that provide the plotting color internally. Add a version of `vertical_line()` to draw lines based on `Plot_policy` up the screen.

Note that when you come to test these you may get an ambiguity error. If you do you will need to use the elaborated names to resolve the ambiguity (because almost identical functions exist in my library). Assuming that the declarations for the lines in this chapter have been placed in global space (i.e. not in a namespace) precede the function name with `::` (two colons) at the places that the compiler complains about ambiguity. For example modify:

```
vertical_line(canvas, 20, -10, 200, red4, plot_every_third);
```

to:

```
::vertical_line(canvas, 20, -10, 200, red4, plot_every_third);
```

Using a namespace to pass information

`plot_every_third()` breaches the principle of not repeating ourselves because if we want to plot at some other interval we have to write almost identical code, except that we change the frequency of the plots. If we generalize to `plot_every_n()` we have a problem because that function will need a value of `n`. The solution we used for color will not work this time because the extra data is too specific to the function. We need another mechanism to provide supplementary data. When you progress to using more advanced C++ you will find that there are some excellent ways of meeting this need but at this stage in your programming I am going to show you a simple way that will work.

By analogy with my earlier example of `read_this_book()`, a third way to remember your place is that you can write it in your private diary.

This is how to do that in C++: encapsulate the necessary resources and functionality into a `namespace`, hide as much of the detail as possible in an implementation file, and bury anything that the user does not need to know about in an unnamed `namespace` (like hiding information in your personal diary). Here is an enhanced version of `plot_every_n()` that allows you to select the frequency for plotting.

Create a header file (remember the header sentinels) and place the following code in it:

```
namespace pf_ns {
  typedef void (Plot_policy)(fgw::playpen &, int x, int y,
                                               fgw::hue);
  void horizontal_line(fgw::playpen &,
             int x, int y, int length, fgw::hue, Plot_policy);
  void plot_every_n(fgw::playpen &, int x, int y, fgw::hue);
  void plotting_frequency(int);
}
```

Now create a test such as:

```
int main(){
  try{
     playpen canvas(blue4 + red4);
     canvas.scale(2);
     pf_ns::plotting_frequency(2);
     pf_ns::horizontal_line(canvas, -128, 0, 256, 34,
                                    pf_ns::plot_every_n);
     canvas.display();
     cout << "Press RETURN to finish\n";
     cin.get();
  }
  catch(...){cout << "An exception was thrown.\n";}
}
```

Finally create an implementation file and insert the following code:

```
namespace pf_ns {
  typedef void (Plot_policy)(fgw::playpen &, int x, int y,
                                                fgw::hue);
  namespace {
     int frequency(1);
  }
  void plotting_frequency(int n){
     if(n > 1) frequency = n; // ignore silly data
  }

void horizontal_line(playpen & p, int yval, int start, int end,
                              hue shade, Plot_policy plotter){
  if(start < end){
     for(int x(start); x != end; ++x){
        plotter(canvas, x, yval);
     }
  }
  else {
           // handle right to left
     for(int x(start); x != end; --x){
        plotter(canvas, x, yval);
     }
  }
}

void plot_every_n(playpen & canvas, int x, int y, hue shade){
  static int count(1);
  if((count % frequency) == 0){
    canvas.plot(x, y, shade);
  }
  ++count;
}
```

We have squirreled away a variable, `frequency`, to hold the plotting frequency for plotting functions that need it. We do not want the variable out there where users can accidentally abuse it or find it conflicting with their own choice of names for things. Globally visible variables are considered to be very poor style though expert programmers sometimes use them when there are very special reasons for doing so. By hiding `frequency` in an implementation file and wrapping it in an unnamed `namespace` that is itself encapsulated in the `plotting_functions namespace` we ensure that it will not leak out and do damage to other code. Please make sure you understand this code.

TASK 51

Add a `plot_n_every_n()` function to the plotting functions that will plot dashes separated by an equal amount of space. Do not forget to test your code (modifying the test provided is fine).

First Steps to Animation

A moving point

Write a plotting function that remembers internally the last point it plotted and erases it before it plots the next one. It will also need to call the `playpen::display()` member function before it returns so that the user will see the result.

You will almost certainly need to use `fgw::Wait()` to insert a delay as well because on all but the slowest computers the point will streak across the Playpen.

The most obvious mechanism is to use the `disjoint` plotting mode, however a better solution would be to use a method that restores the previous pixel regardless of the plotting mode. (Hint: `fgw::get_hue()` along with another `static` variable could be part of a solution.)

If you completed this task you should be able to use `horizontal_line()` to get a single point to move from left to right across your screen. If you give some extra thought to it you should manage to control the speed at which it moves.

If you have trouble with writing this please check my solution at the end of the chapter. The code is not difficult but there are several things you need to keep balanced. Note that my solution takes into consideration more things than yours is likely to.

Now we have the basics for moving-ball type animation. In other words we have a mechanism for making an image move across the screen. When I provide a more general line-drawing function that has a `Plot_policy` parameter we will have the essential tool for handling both fancy lines (multihued, dotted, dashed, etc.) and linear motion between any two points in our Playpen.

EXERCISE 2

Write a function, using a `Plot_policy` parameter, that draws a square given the bottom left corner and the length of the side. Use it to draw a variety of different squares, including the case where a single point moves round a square.

Been there before?

Does this give you a sense of having been there before? It should do because the functions are much like those we were doing in Chapter 3. If you remember what you did then you will recall that we built an entire set of tools for drawing shapes.

There was one thing that I contributed which was a function called `drawline()` to draw general straight lines, not just vertical and horizontal ones. The reason was that the general case requires some careful management and unless you have done it before or have a great deal of experience in the problem domain you would find the task depressingly awkward even if I explained the algorithm to you.

Even with all the extra experience you have gained you would still find it difficult to write a general line-drawing function with policy-based plotting. However having such a function will prove to be immensely useful. In fact it has been sitting quietly in my library and is available by including the line_drawing.h header file. All the line drawing functions provided by my library and declared in line_drawing.h are policy-based functions with the last function defaulted to a simple plot point function. The only thing you need to do is supply suitable plotting functions.

In this context, a suitable function is any one that has exactly four parameters of types `fgw::playpen &`, `int`, `int`, `fgw::hue`. The function is also required to have a void return type. This means that, for example, the following code produces an oblique dotted line in medium red using the scale determined by `paper` (assuming that is the name of an active `fgw::playpen` object).

```
drawline(paper, 20, 20, 100, 100, red4, plot_every_third);
```

At this stage you might have a look at the source code for `drawline()` (in line_drawing.cpp) and see if you can understand it (do not worry if you cannot yet, I know quite a few people who make a living out of programming who would struggle because they would lack the domain knowledge). The basic idea is to start at one end of the line and then make repeated small increments (or decrements) both horizontally and vertically. After each pair of changes check to see if you have moved close to a new pixel. If so plot it with the plotting function provided (which defaults to a simple function that delegates to `playpen::plot()`). This process is repeated until you reach the point at which you can finish by going straight across or straight up. At that point it hands over to the special functions that deal with the vertical and horizontal cases.

Please return to Chapter 6 where you did various exercises with `vector<point2d>` being used to store the vertices of a polygon. Rework that part of the chapter using `drawline()` called with a plotting policy as the last parameter.

My intention is that you should both refresh your memory of that earlier work and gain an appreciation of how powerful the policy-based plot mechanisms are. This should consolidate your understanding before we go on to the next section, which uses these tools to provide moving objects.

A moving object or sprite

For this next part you will need to use ideas you learnt and perhaps code that you wrote while studying the first part of the last chapter. Please refresh your understanding of the `icon` type. The key point is that nothing in our plot policy concept specified that we would only plot a single pixel. In this section we are going to design and implement a small extension of the icon concept. We are then going to use that to write one more plot policy function.

Designing a sprite *type*

The extension is that the new type will have modified display properties so that the call of its display function will save the area of the Playpen window that you are about to write to. This means that it will need a second object in which to store data.

We will also provide a `restore_area()` function whose sole purpose is to replace the saved data. However, it would be a mistake to try to restore when we have nothing saved so we will add a single flag (a `bool` variable) that will indicate if the object has saved data waiting to be restored. `restore_area()` will check that flag and do nothing if it is `false`. Here is my draft definition of my sprite type. (I have included the `typedef`s from the last chapter to remind you what we mean by `area_data`.)

```
typedef std::vector<fgw::hue> column_data;
typedef std::vector<column_data> area_data;

class sprite {
  public:
     void display(fgw::playpen &, int x, int y)const;
     void restore_area(fgw::playpen &)const;
     void load(std::istream & in);
     void load(std::string const & filename);
  private:
     area_data image;
     mutable area_data saved_image;
     mutable bool saved_image_available;
     mutable int last_x;
     mutable int last_y;
};
```

What do you think `mutable` does? It solves an awkward problem; displaying a `sprite` does not conceptually change the `sprite` (i.e. it does not care whether it is being displayed or not) so we want to qualify `display()` (and `restore_area()` which reinstates what was on the screen before we put a sprite there) as `const`. However, as a result of calling `display()` we want to cache the overwritten area. `mutable` warns the compiler that even `const` qualified member functions can change these items. Note that we also need to cache the coordinates of the block we have saved so that we can restore it correctly. There is a hidden assumption that neither the `playpen`'s scale nor origin has been changed. We will need to use the `direct` plotting mode when we do the restoration.

A `sprite` assumes that its data is stored in an `istream` object. We can use the same data files that were used by `icon`. And we can use the same tools to create new data files. I have provided a suitable file for your use in testing code (butterfly.icon).

Implementing the sprite *member functions*

We have to provide four functions for the `sprite` type to work, including two `load()` functions that are similar to those for `icon`. To save you hunting for them, here they are amended for `sprite`:

```
bool sprite::load(istream & in){
  try{
     string column;
     area_data new_data;
     while(true){
        getline(in, column);
        if(in.fail()) break; // input failed, possibly EOF
        if(column.size() == 0) break; // blank line read
        new_data.push_back(extract_column_data(column));
     }
```

```
        image.swap(new_data);
        return true;
    }
    catch(...){ return false;} // I do not care what went wrong
}

vector<hue> extract_column_data(string const & data){
    stringstream source(data);
    vector<hue> a_column;
    while(true){
        hue const value(read<hue>(source));
        if(not source.fail()) a_column.push_back(value);
        else return a_column;
    }
}

bool sprite::load(string const & filename){
    ifstream in;
    open_ifstream(in, filename);
    if(in.fail()) return false;
    return load(in);
}
```

The second version simply opens the file, checks it succeeded and then passes over to the first version. This is the delegation idiom that we have already seen several times.

What do you think we should do if we call `load()` when there is already a saved block that has not been written back? My answer this time is that that is the problem of the writer of the code that uses my `sprite`. I am going to trust him to decide when he loads `sprite` data whether to restore the saved block first or not.

Next we can write `restore_area()` because that is functionally the same as `display()` for `icon`. Well almost, we have to check we have something to restore and mark it as restored when we finish.

```
void sprite::restore_area(playpen & canvas)const {
    if(saved_image_available){
        plotmode old(canvas.setplotmode(direct));
        for(int i(0); i != image.size(); ++i){ // the columns
            for(int j(0); j != image[i].size(); ++j){ // the hues
                if(image[i][j]) paper.plot(x+i, y+j, image[i][j]);
            }
        }
        saved_image_available = false;
        canvas.setplotmode(old);
    }
}
```

Note that we have to save the current plot-mode so that we can restore it at the end. This kind of attention to detail is important if you are to become a programmer whose work can be used by others.

All we have left to do is to write the function `sprite::display()`. This time we have to do some extra work because we have to save the existing pixels before writing over them.

```
void sprite::display(playpen & canvas, int x, int y)const {
// ensure that image and saved image are the same shape by
// making one a copy of the other
  saved_image = image;
  for(int i(0); i != image.size(); ++i){
     for(int j(0); j != image[i].size(); ++j){
        saved_image[i][j] = canvas.gethue(x+i, y+j);
        if(image[i][j]) canvas.plot(x+i, y+j, image[i][j]);
              // treat color 0 - black - as transparent
              // and do not plot those pixels
     }
  }
  last_x = x;
  last_y = y;
  saved_image_available = true;
}
```

I only set the position and availability at the end. It is a small thing but if something goes wrong in the reading and writing to the canvas, the jumbled mess in saved_image will not be used by restore_area(). I doubt that it much matters here but as a matter of style, if possible, I do the parts that can go wrong first.

Preparing to use sprite

That is it, we have our sprite class and all we need to do to activate it is to write a plot policy function that uses it. I am feeling generous (actually I want you to use what I am building here so that you can write programs that will give you pleasure) so here is a function that will do that:

```
void display_sprite(playpen & canvas, int x, int y, hue){
  active_sprite.restore_area(canvas);
  active_sprite.display(canvas, x, y);
}
```

What, you may ask, is active_sprite? Remember the trick we used to remember what n to use when we wrote plot_every_n()? We are going to use the same trick to remember what sprite is available for use by display_sprite(). In the relevant header file, the one where we define sprite would do well, add:

```
void display_sprite(fgw::playpen &, int x, int y,
                                     fgw::hue = fgw::black);
void set_active_sprite(std::string const & filename);
void set_active_sprite(sprite const & );
```

The last of those is so we can copy a sprite we have already created as an alternative to loading new data from a file. In the implementation file add the definition:

```
sprite active_sprite;
```

in an unnamed namespace. Add these definitions to the general namespace (in which you have encapsulated sprite and its ancillary functions):

```
void set_active_sprite(std::string const & filename){
  active_sprite.load(filename);
}
void set_active_sprite(sprite const & source){
  active_sprite = source;
}
```

If you have been following carefully you will realize that we also need a function to remove the `sprite` when we have finished with it. Here it is:

```
void remove_sprite(playpen & canvas){
  active_sprite.restore_area(canvas);
}
```

When you have typed in the code, debugged your typos and tested it to your satisfaction you will be ready to try this program:

```
int main(){
  try{
     playpen canvas(white);
     set_active_sprite("butterfly.icon");
     canvas.display();
     drawline(canvas, -90, 10, 200, 10, black, display_sprite);
        cout << "Press RETURN to remove sprite.\n";
        cin.get();
        remove_sprite(canvas);
        cout << "Press RETURN to finish.\n";
        cin.get();
     }
  catch(...){cout << "\n***An exception was thrown.***\n" ;}
  return 0;
}
```

If you combine the tools from the last chapter that allow you to grab blocks of the Playpen and save them as `icon`s with the tools you now have to turn them into `sprite`s you have the basis for simple movement of objects in the Playpen. Please try to appreciate how each individual bit of code is relatively simple, but when we combine them we can produce results that will surprise.

At the moment you only have a single sprite because my active sprite mechanism assumes that we have just one. However if you want more and want to be ambitious you can now modify the code so that active sprites are held in a `std::map<std::string, sprite>`. Then you can select the sprite you wish to make active by name.

Enhance the `sprite` type by adding functions to reflect and rotate sprites in the same way that you did for an `icon`. Then use these to write a program that results in the butterfly sprite traveling round a square with the position and size of the square selected at run time (see Chapter 14).

Add a speed control to the sprite implementation. Note that there are two ways to do this, you could make the speed a property of a sprite by adding another data member that can be set by calling a member function, or you can do it the same way that we controlled the speed of a moving point (with a hidden variable and a `set_speed()` function).

A Matter of Palettes

Up until now I have avoided the issue of different palettes. If you have been using another application to prepare graphics that can be loaded into the Playpen with `LoadPlaypen()` you might have discovered that using `LoadPlaypen()` changes the active Playpen's palette so that, for example `paper.clear(white)` may produce a Playpen of some other color than white. If you have not yet experienced this, try adding:

```
LoadPlaypen(canvas, "background.png");
```

into the program listed above to test the sprite code. You should find that the butterfly is completely different in color. Actually it is now using the colors from the original photograph I used to get the data for a butterfly.

Adding `canvas.rgbpalette()` after we have displayed the butterfly will restore the colors to our default palette. The difference should be quite dramatic. Loading `background.png` loads the palette of the graphic from which I originally created my butterfly sprite data. By loading it I reset the palette to the one that renders the butterfly in its original colors. Calling `canvas.rgbpalette()` restores the standard palette we have been using through most of this book.

How can we save and load a particular palette? To do this you need three more of the member functions for `playpen` objects. They are:

```
playpen&  setpalettentry(hue, HueRGB const &);
HueRGB getpalettentry(hue) const;
playpen const & updatepalette() const;
```

You will also need to know a little about `fgw::HueRGB`. This is one of my library types that packages up three numbers each in the range 0 to 255, that represent the intensity of red, blue and green for a pixel on your monitor. If you want to mix a new shade to assign, for example, to entry 27 of the 256 palette entries you write something such as:

```
canvas.setpalettentry(27, HueRGB(150, 200, 50));
canvas.updatepalette();
```

where I am assuming that `canvas` is the currently active `playpen` object. That mix would be 150 parts red, 200 parts green and 50 parts blue. On my screen that is lime green. The second function – `updatepalette()` – passes the new data to Windows so that it will be used wherever the pixels are in `fgw::hue(27)`.

`HueRGB getpalettentry(hue)` allows us to ask what the mix is for a specific item of the current palette. In order to use it you will need to know how to unpack the data packed in a `HueRGB` variable. Here is a bit of code that demonstrates that process:

```
int main(){
  try{
```

```
      playpen canvas(white);
      HueRGB const mix(canvas.getpalettentry(30));
      cout << "Red:    " << int(mix.r) << '\n';
      cout << "Green:  " << int(mix.g) << '\n';
      cout << "Blue:   " << int(mix.b) << '\n';
   }
   catch(...){cout << "\n***An exception was thrown.***\n" ;}
   return 0;
}
```

The way the intensities have been encoded means that we have to tell the compiler that we want the results printed as numbers. I do not want to go into the low-level details of the implementation because all you need is to use them. If a `HueRGB` variable is called `x`, then `int(x.r)`, `int(x.g)` and `int(x.b)` are the three intensities (red, green and blue).

EXERCISE 4

Write a function, `save_palette()`, that will extract the red/green/blue intensities of the whole palette (256 entries, 0 to 255) and write the answers to a file. The format of the file should be one line per triplet with space separating the three values.

Write a program to use the function and store the results in a file called basic.palette. Check that you can read the results in your editor.

EXERCISE 5

Write a function, `restore_palette()`, that can read back a file of palette data and use it to reset the current `playpen` to that palette.

EXERCISE 6

Create some palettes for yourself. For example create a palette that is entirely shades of red. Now try one where 0 is black, 255 is white, 1 to 85 are reds, 86 to 170 are greens and 171 to 254 are blues.

Instead of loading the background.png file to make sure that the colors match those originally used, you can load the butterfly.palette that I have also provided. You can only have a single palette active at a time, so trying to fly a butterfly across your favorite seascape will not work unless you do a large amount of extra work or choose which palette is loaded.

More Advanced Animation

At last we are ready to tackle animation in which objects change their shape as well as their position. Surprisingly we have very little more to do. In order to animate a sprite we need to add one extra feature: the sprite must hold a container of images rather than a single one. It must also track which image is the next one to display.

We need to change the data so that the single image of our `sprite` is replaced by a container of images. We might as well use a `std::vector<pixel_array>`. We must also add a `mutable int` to keep track of which image is the next one to display. Here is the redefined **sprite**:

```
class sprite {
  public:
     void display(fgw::playpen &, int x, int y)const;
     void restore_area(fgw::playpen &)const;
     void load(std::istream & in);
     void load(std::string const & filename);
  private:
     std::vector<pixel_array> film;
     mutable int next_frame;
     mutable pixel_array saved_image;
     mutable bool saved_image_available;
     mutable int last_x;
     mutable int last_y;
};
```

I have highlighted the necessary changes in the definition. Now if you check back you will find that only two of the member functions have implementations that touch the changed data: `display()` and the version of `load()` that does the work.

Let me deal with the easier one first; `display()` simply has to track which image to use:

```
void sprite::display(playpen & canvas, int x, int y)const {
  if(saved_image_available) restore_area(canvas);
// always replace saved area first
   saved_image = film[next_frame];
// prepare correct cache shape
   for(int i(0); i != film[next_frame].size(); ++i){
      for(int j(0); j != film[next_frame][i].size(); ++j){
         saved_block[i][j] = canvas.gethue(x+i, y+j);
         if(film[next_frame][i][j]){
            canvas.plot(x+i, y+j, film[next_frame][i][j]);
            // treat 0 - black - as transparent
         }
      }
  }
  ++next_frame;
  next_frame %= film.size();
  last_x = x;
  last_y = y;
  saved_image_available = true;
}
```

If you compare this with the earlier code you will find that it is structurally identical, but where we had `image` in the earlier code we now have `film[next_frame]`. I have also added two lines of code to manage which frame is next. I have highlighted the differences for you. I hope you will agree that that is very little change for a lot of gain.

To deal with the process of loading I have to repeatedly use the code that I wrote earlier for a single frame type sprite. To do that I take that code (from `load()`) and use it to create a helper function called `get_frame()` that I will place in an unnamed namespace in the implementation file for `sprite`:

```
bool get_frame(area_data & frame, istream & in){
  try{
     string column;
     area_data new_data;
     while(true){
        getline(in, column);
        if(in.fail()) break; // input failed, possibly EOF
        if(column.size() == 0) break; // blank line read
        new_data.push_back(extract_column_data(column));
     }
     frame.swap(new_data);
     return true;
  }
  catch(...){ return false;} // I do not care what went wrong
}
```

Which allows me to implement this advanced sprite-loading function with:

```
void sprite::load(ifstream & in){
  vector<area_data> new_film;
  area_data image;
  while(get_frame(image, in)){
          new_film.push_back(image); // loop till no more images
  }
  film.swap(new_film);
  next_frame = 0;
  saved_image_available = false;
}
```

That is it. The `display_sprite()` plot-policy function we wrote earlier now provides you with animated motion and a suitable `for`-loop will provide you with static animation. You can add frills such as rotating and reflecting a sprite – I hope you will – but we now have a fully-mobile animated object and all we need to do is spend time creating suitable data to see just how much we have achieved. Here is a demonstration program using a rotating stick.

```
int main(){
  try{
     playpen canvas(white);
     sprite image;
     image.load("stick1.txt");
     cout << "rotate in place.\n";
     canvas.scale(3);
     for(int i(0); i != 800; ++i){
        image.display(canvas, 0, 0);
```

```
      canvas.display();
      Wait(5);
    }
    canvas.scale(1);
    set_active_sprite(image);
    drawline(canvas,-100, -100, -100, 50,
        black, multihued_plot);
    drawline(canvas,-100, 50, 150, 50,
        black, multihued_plot);
    drawline(canvas, 150, 50, 150, -100,
        black, multihued_plot);
    drawline(canvas, 150, -100, -100, -100,
        black, multihued_plot);
    canvas.display();
    drawline(canvas,-100, -100, -100, 50,
        black, display_sprite);
    drawline(canvas,-100, 50, 150, 50,
        black, display_sprite);
    drawline(canvas, 150, 50, 150, -100,
        black, display_sprite);
    drawline(canvas, 150, -100, -100, -100,
        black, display_sprite);
    canvas.display();
    cout << "Press RETURN      to finish";
    cin.get();
  }
  catch(char const * message){cout << message << '\n';}
  catch(...){cout << "\n***An exception was thrown.***\n" ;}
  return 0;
}
```

That is it. Because we are using a plot-policy function to manage our animation we can send our sprites anywhere that we can draw lines. The limit is your imagination and the time you have for preparing data.

ROBERTA'S COMMENTS

This was the hardest chapter by far, partly because the material seems to be the most advanced in the book but also because I found myself working against a deadline. The publisher needed this comment and I had had to take a break from my study because family illness had required my attention.

I discovered that programming with deadlines is not fun. Francis says that this is an important lesson to learn because it is one of the differences between programming for personal interest and programming as work.

A second discovery was that taking a few weeks off, as I had before trying this chapter results in losing fluency with the skills I had just acquired. I think if you take time off during your study of programming you should expect to have to spend time refreshing some of the skills you learnt before. I don't think you can work through the first 14 chapters, take four weeks off and then expect to dive straight into Chapter 15.

Another thing I discovered in this chapter is the difference between solving the immediate problem and writing code with more general use. I wrote a program that produced the visual result required by Task 52 and felt that Francis' solution was far too complicated. I was pretty sure that he was going to criticize my solution as my program moved a point across the Playpen but assumed that the only thing being displayed was the point. Here is my plotting function. What do you think of it?

```
void plot_and_erase(playpen & paper, int x, int y, hue shade){
  static int savex = x;
  static int savey = y;
  paper.plot(x, y, shade);
  paper.display();
  Wait(100);
  paper.clear();
  ++x;
  ++y;
}
```

FRANCIS

The purpose of publishing this piece of code is to let you see that working under pressure can result in a marked deterioration in code quality. I am not going into detail here but note that this function does not meet the requirement because it does not remember the last point plotted. The first time the function is called it remembers the values of `x` and `y` but then it never uses `savex` and `savey`.

The final point that this chapter highlighted was a problem with the way I had been writing my code. I had got into the habit of putting all my functions in the unnamed *`namespace`* of the file where I was writing *`main()`*. That way I avoided having to write separate header files and implementation files. I was relying on the definition of a function also being a declaration. In this chapter that did not seem to work because the declaration had default arguments and the definition had unnamed parameters. Later Francis explained that I could have provided a default argument to an unnamed parameter, but it was probably a good thing that I had a problem here because it made me think more carefully about the value of separating code into header files and implementation files.

This is certainly a chapter that I will be revisiting after the pressure of meeting publication deadlines has gone away.

SOLUTIONS TO TASKS

Task 49

The purpose of this task is to make you stop and realize that we are back to the old problem of repeating ourselves. The code for all the special horizontal lines is almost identical with the solitary exception of which plotting function is called.

Task 50

```
void horizontal_line(playpen & canvas, int x, int y,
                int length, hue shade, Plot_policy plotter){
  if(start < end){
     for(int x(start); x != end; ++x){
         plot_every_third(canvas, x, yval, shade);
     }
  }
  else {
          // handle right to left
    for(int x(start); x != end; --x){
        plot_every_third(canvas, x, yval, shade);
    }
  }
}
```

Notice that we now have the problem of specifying a `hue` even when we do not need it back again. This time we cannot fix it with a default argument because it isn't the last parameter (and making it the last parameter might not work if we wanted to default the `Plot_policy`. The fix this time is to use delegation and keyword the `inline` keyword:

```
inline void horizontal_line(playpen & p, int yval, int start,
        int end, Plot_policy plotter){
  return horizontal_line(p, yval, start, end, fgw::black, plotter);
}
```

The reason for using `inline` is that it allows us to place the function definition in a header file without risking redefinition errors. You should only do that for cases like this where all the work is delegated to another function but we want to tweak something such as supplying an argument to a parameter which has not been provided with a default argument. Officially `inline` has another meaning, but in practice it means that a function definition can be placed in a header file.

To work as expected you need to ensure this definition is after the declaration of the version it is delegating the work to.

```
void vertical_line(playpen & canvas, int x, int y, int length,
                              hue shade, Plot_policy plotter){
  if(length > 0){
     for(int i(0); i != length; ++i){
        plotter(canvas, x, y + i, shade);
     }
  }
```

SOLUTIONS TO TASKS

```
  else {
     for(int i(0); i != length; --i){ // handle negative length
        plotter(canvas, x, y + i, shade);
     }
  }
}

inline void vertical_line(playpen & p, int x, int y,
       int length, Plot_policy plotter){
  return vertical_line(p, x, y, length, fgw::black, plotter);
}
```

Here are the modified plotting functions. Notice that the default arguments are not shown in the definitions. Default arguments should only be in a declaration (because that is where the compiler will need the information to fill in any values that the programmer using the function has left out).

```
void plot_every_third(playpen & canvas, int x, int y, hue shade){
  static int skip_it(0);
  if(not skip_it){
     canvas.plot(x, y, shade);
  }
  ++skip_it;
  skip_it %= 3;
}
```

Task 51

We can reuse the frequency mechanism from `plot_every_n()` so I will not repeat it here.

```
void plot_n_every_n(playpen & canvas, int x, int y, hue shade){
  static int count(0);
  static bool plotting(false);
  if(count == 0) plotting = not plotting;
  if(plotting) canvas.plot(x, y, shade);
  ++count;
  if(count == frequency) count = 0; // reset to flip switch
}
```

Effectively, `plotting` is used as a switch that is reversed every time you count through n.

Task 52

First a few helpers and declarations for the header file (use the one you used for Task 51).

```
void start_motion();
```

The `start_motion()` function sets a hidden variable that can be used to start a new motion. Without this hidden variable second and subsequent uses of functions like `horizontal_line()` will

SOLUTIONS TO TASKS

remember where the last use ended and not realize that we are starting a new line. We may want an end_motion() function to clear up the last plot when we get into more advanced uses.

```
void set_speed(int speed);
```

The set_speed() function sets a hidden variable that can be used to control the speed of a moving object (a point for now). Low values will give high speed. Negative values are ignored. Zero will give the highest speed.

```
void moving_point(fgw::playpen &, int x, int y, fgw::hue);
```

The moving_point() function is going to do most of the work. Notice that its declaration conforms to the needs of the Plot_policy function type.

Here are the definitions from the implementation file. In the unnamed namespace:

```
bool new_motion(true);
int motion_speed(10);
```

In the pf_ns namespace:

```
void set_speed(int speed){
  if(speed > -1) motion_speed = speed;
}
void start_motion(){
  new_motion = true;
}
```

And the main workhorse:

```
void moving_point(playpen & canvas, int x, int y, hue shade){
  static int last_x;
  static int last_y;
  static hue last_shade(0);
  if(new_motion) new_motion = false;
  else{
// restore previous point
     canvas.plot(last_x, last_y, last_shade);
  }
  last_x = x;
  last_y = y;
  last_shade = canvas.get_hue(x, y);
  canvas.plot(x, y, shade);
  Wait(motion_speed);
  canvas.display();
}
```

SOLUTIONS TO TASKS

This function first sets up static storage for remembering its state, in this case what it last plotted. Then it checks if it is doing a new run, in which case it will not have a point to restore. If this is the first use for a new run it flips the flag, otherwise it restores the last point it plotted.

Next it saves the data to restore the next time, plots the new point, waits a short time then updates the display.

Once we have this function running we can make a small change to allow us to test if we should just restore the previous point and not write a new one. For that we would need a control variable similar to `new_motion`. Indeed we could remove `start_motion()` and replace it with `finish_motion()` which could both set a flag to stop the current motion and update the `new_motion` flag. We would need to give some thought about what we wanted to achieve before electing to make that design choice.

SOLUTIONS TO EXERCISES

Exercise 1

```
void plot_every_third(playpen & canvas, int x, int y){
  static int skip_it(0);
  if(not skip_it){
     canvas.plot(x, y, black);
  }
  ++skip_it;
  skip_it %= 3;
}
```

The result of the last two lines is that `skip_it` will cycle through 0, 1, 2, 0, 1, 2, etc. Remember that 0 is treated as `false` and all other values for a whole number (such as an `int`) are treated as `true`. Yes, I chose that name for the static variable carefully so that the source code is effectively self-documenting. It is always worth taking a few moments choosing variable names so that they will explain their uses.

```
void dotted_horizontal_line(playpen & canvas, int yval,
                                               int start, int end){
  if(start < end){
     for(int x(start); x != end; ++x){
        plot_every_third(canvas, x, yval);
     }
  }
  else {
          // handle right to left
     for(int x(start); x != end; --x){
```

SOLUTIONS TO EXERCISES

```
        plot_every_third(canvas, x, yval);
      }
    }
  }
```

Exercise 2

```
void square(playpen & canvas, int x, int y, int side,
             hue shade, Plot_policy plotter){
  horizontal_line(canvas, y, x, x+side, shade, plotter);
  vertical_line(canvas, x+side, y, y+side, shade, plotter);
  horizontal_line(canvas, y+side, x+side, x, shade, plotter);
  vertical_line(canvas, x, y+side, y, shade, plotter);
}
```

Here is a sample test program:

```
int main(){
  try{
    playpen canvas(blue4 + red4);
    canvas.scale(4);
    pf_ns::plotting_frequency(2);
    pf_ns::square(canvas, -25, -25, 50,
                  green4, pf_ns::moving_point);
    canvas.display();
    cout << "Press RETURN to finish\n";
    cin.get();
  }
  catch(...){cout << "An exception was thrown.\n";}

}
```

Exercise 4

```
void save_palette(playpen const & canvas, string filename){
  ofstream out;
  open_ofstream(out, filename);
  if(out.fail()) throw problem(
              "Could not open file for save_palette.");
  for(int i(0); i != 256; ++i){
    HueRGB const mix(canvas.getpalettentry(i));
    out  << int(mix.r) << " "
         << int(mix.g) << " "
```

SOLUTIONS TO EXERCISES

```
        << int(mix.b) << '\n';
  }
}
```

Exercise 5

```
void restore_palette(playpen & canvas, string filename){
  ifstream in;
  open_ifstream(in, filename);
  if(in.fail()) throw problem(
              "Could not open file for save_palette.");
  for(int i(0); i != 256; ++i){
     int r(read<int>(in)), g(read<int>(in)), b(read<int>(in));
        canvas.setpalettentry(i, HueRGB(r, g, b));
  }
  canvas.updatepalette();
}
```

Summary

Key programming concepts

- The term "state" in computing refers to a property of something that has some permanence. For example, variables have state.
- The terms "static" and "dynamic" are used to distinguish between things that a compiler can provide and those that have to be provided when a program runs.

C++ checklist

- The C++ keyword `static` is loosely related to the computing concept of static but is not identical. When used to qualify a variable it means that the memory for storing the variable's state (or value) is provided by the direct actions of the compiler. Values assigned to static variables are retained until they are changed. This contrasts with normal variables that are destroyed at the end of the block of code in which they were created.
- A function variable (usually a parameter of a function) stores information about which function has been chosen. This allows us to select the exact behavior of other functions by our choice of function object.
- Function objects allow us to reuse general methods, even methods that are provided long after the original code was written. Their use for this purpose is often called a "callback".
- Default arguments are a way to provide default values for parameters that will be used if the programmer does not supply a value when the function is called.
- Once the declaration of a function provides a default argument for a parameter there must also be default arguments for all subsequent parameters.

- Once the caller of a function relies on a default argument (i.e. does not supply an argument) they must rely on defaults for all subsequent arguments.
- If a parameter is not actually used in the definition of a function no name should be provided for it in the definition.

Extensions checklist

- `fgw::playpen::rgbpalette()` is a function that resets the palette of the Playpen to the default version set at the time a `playpen` object is created.
- Palettes are properties of the Playpen and not of the individual `playpen` objects so you can only have one palette at a time.
- There are three member functions of `fgw::playpen` that allow us to manage the palette data of the Playpen window. They are:

```
playpen& playpen::setpalettentry(hue palette_entry,
          fgw::HueRGB const &);
```

  which sets the red/green/blue proportions of a specific palette entry which will be updated the next time the screen is updated or when specifically updated by calling `fgw::playpen const & fgw::playpen::updatepalette() const;`. The latter is a `const` member function because it does not change the data; it just activates it by passing it to the operating system.

```
fgw::HueRGB fgw::playpen::getpalettentry(fgw::hue entry)
   const;
```

  supplies the red/green/blue mix for a specified palette entry.
- `fgw::HueRGB` is a simple type with a limited purpose, that of packaging the red, green and blue values for a palette entry. Each value has a range of 256 values (0 to 255). The package is created with a function-like cast such as `fgw::HueRGB(24, 183, 42)`. You can also create variables of this type with a simple declaration such as:

```
fgw::HueRGB mix(0, 0, 0);
```

  which would make `mix` the representation of black. Given an `fgw::HueRGB` variable such as `mix` you can select the individual color data (either to read it or to change it) with `mix.r`, `mix.g` and `mix.b`.
- All the line drawing functions in line_drawing.h include a final parameter of type `plot_policy` which is defined as:

```
typedef void(plot_policy)(fgw::playpen &, int x, int y,
   fgw::hue)
```

This means that they can have their behavior adjusted by providing the name of the function that defines what is to be done at each point along the line.

CHAPTER 16

Turtles and Eating Your Own Tail

In this chapter I introduce you to an entirely different way of viewing graphics. I will tell you about Seymour Papert's Turtle Geometry, which formed a part of the programming language LOGO. He designed LOGO for teaching children to program. As a side effect of learning about Turtle Graphics you will learn about recursion, another way to repeat some action.

Some History

Sometimes it helps when we learn why something was invented. Turtle Graphics was invented by Seymour Papert for a very specific reason. Just as I decided to provide a graphics library for you to use because it would provide a more colorful journey into the world of programming, Seymour Papert wanted something that would make a child's early experiences of programming better fit a child's view of the world.

He wanted to provide some form of interaction with the real world. The mythology (I have no idea how much truth there is to it) says that he looked around and found that the Artificial Intelligence labs at the University of Edinburgh had a device they called a turtle. This device was programmed to investigate its environment looking for electricity sockets. When it found one it would plug itself in to charge up its batteries so that it had power to go looking for electricity sockets. This is a very simple model of life: work to find the energy (food) to support work to find energy...

Papert recognized that he could use the basic mechanism. He removed the search program, provided a pen that could be raised and lowered and put it under the control of a computer. The computer could be programmed to give the turtle simple instructions. The basic instructions would consist of:

FORWARD n:	go forward n steps
LEFT n:	turn left through n degrees
PENUP:	raise the pen, so it does not leave a trace
PENDOWN:	lower the pen, so that movement leaves a written trace.

He added other features to the programming language to allow variables, loops, functions, etc. and then continued to develop LOGO for use by children, most specifically children who suffered from cerebral palsy. The basic philosophy of LOGO is that people control computers and that this must be made absolutely clear in the programming language. He wrote a book (*Mindstorms: Children, Computers and Powerful Ideas* that was published in 1980 with a second edition in 1999) about this work which is well worth reading.

Actual "turtles" are relatively expensive devices because of the number of mechanical parts in them. This resulted in an early move to simulating a turtle on a graphics screen. These days some schools have mechanical turtles but many just use electronic simulations. These are powerful tools for investigating both programming and geometry.

One of the more interesting aspects of using a turtle is that its view of the world is centered on its current position. That is, a turtle is self-centered. For example, getting a turtle to draw a square consists of:

REPEAT 4 [FORWARD 40 LEFT 90]

You could draw a hexagon with:

REPEAT 6 [FORWARD 40 LEFT 60]

That last example emphasizes the difference between a turtle-centric view and a classical view. In the classical view we focus on the interior angle (120° for a regular hexagon) but the turtle view looks at the angle it must turn through to change direction for the next side. If you wrote:

REPEAT 6 [FORWARD 40 LEFT 120]

you would find that your turtle goes twice round an equilateral triangle. This turtle-centric view is closer to a child-centric view. Indeed you can experiment by issuing simple turtle commands to a child:

repeat four times (forward 4 steps, turn left ninety degrees)

There is much more to LOGO. http://www.papert.org/ is a good place to start if you would like to learn more about it. However its concepts are more general and can be used in other forms of programming.

Designing a Turtle Type

As with the last two chapters I am going to encapsulate required behavior in a class. We will declare a number of member functions that provide the basic behavior of a turtle. I will also design a `private` data structure that will act as a turtle's memory of its state.

Implementing turtle behavior

```
class turtle {
  public:
     turtle(double x, double y);
     turtle();
     turtle & forward(fgw::playpen, double distance);
     turtle & left(fgw::playpen, double angle);
     turtle & penup();
     turtle & pendown();
  private:
    // data
};
```

You should be becoming familiar with designing a new class type though you have some way to go before doing that for yourself (something that I will cover in my next book). The constructors for `turtle` give it an initial state. A `turtle` knows nothing about the outside world; the primitive instructions are relative to where it is now and which way it is pointing. That means that I must give it a starting point when I create (construct) a new `turtle`. I could have created all `turtle`s at the origin but that seems a little too restrictive. Starting them all pointing in some default direction seems fine to me, but I want to choose *where* they are created.

I have, however, provided a second (default) constructor so that the programmer can create a `turtle` object – called, for example, `francis` – at the origin by writing:

```
turtle francis;
```

As for `fgw::playpen`, you must *not* add empty parentheses if you want the default version. If you do so the compiler will read it as a function declaration rather than as a definition of a default object.

I am using `double` for the values of direction, position and movement so that data can be provided to a very high degree of accuracy. By the way we are going to find out why we have those `turtle &` return types in this code (I promised to give an example of this idiom when I introduced it in Chapter 5). In this type the difference matters and is not just a matter of personal style.

The two functions that might make some visible change have to know about what `playpen` they are using.

Create a suitable header file and place the above, provisional, class definition in it. Now create a test_turtle.cpp file and write a test program to test each of the functions. Note that you should be able to compile it (F5) but not run it (F9) because we have not yet implemented the member functions.

TASK 55

Implementing turtle state

The next design concern is to decide what data a turtle will need about itself. While the turtle does not publicly know where it is (all places look the same to a turtle) we will need that information privately so we can determine where to show it on the screen. `fgw::point2d` would seem to be a good way to store the data about the turtle's position.

We will also need to keep accurate track of the direction the turtle is facing and whether it is currently leaving a trail or not (i.e. is its pen down?). Possibly we would like to store what the turtle looks like but that is a refinement so let me leave it for now.

That gives us the minimal specification for our turtle:

```
class turtle {
  public:
     turtle(double x, double y);
     turtle();
     turtle & forward(double distance);
     turtle & left(double angle);
     turtle & penup();
     turtle & pendown();
  private:
     fgw::point2d position;
     double direction; // in degrees
     bool drawing;     // pen down?
};
```

Update your header file and check that the test program still compiles.

TASK 56

Implementing turtle member functions

Four of these are easy; one takes more thought (and if your mathematics is weak, you probably need to get some help – or just use my solution).

Create an implementation file for the `turtle` type and implement the constructors, `left()`, `penup()` and `pendown()`. Provide a stub function for `forward()` (i.e. a function that does nothing except say that it hasn't been implemented). While you can do something to implement `left()`, that also will not yet be complete so make it print a message to that effect.

Making the turtle visible

The problem with finishing the `left()` member function is that the turtle does not show itself. We need to add a mechanism for the turtle to show itself in the Playpen.

How should a turtle display itself? For now I am going to keep it simple and use an arrowhead with the tip at the `turtle` object's current location. Here is a function that draws a small arrowhead pointing in the direction of future travel.

```
void turtle::display(){
  plotmode const oldmode(world.setplotmode(disjoint));
  int const size(8);
  int const sharp(30);
  double const x1(position.x() -
              size*cos(radians(direction - sharp)));
  double const y1(position.y() -
              size*sin(radians(direction - sharp)));
  double const x2(position.x() -
              size*cos(radians(direction + sharp)));
  double const y2(position.y() -
              size*sin(radians(direction + sharp)));
  drawline(world, position, point2d(x1, y1), white);
  drawline(world, position, point2d(x2, y2), white);
  world.display();
  world.setplotmode(oldmode);
}
```

There is one large problem with this definition and a personal issue. The personal issue is that if you are not fluent at trigonometry those calculations of `x1`, `y1`, `x2` and `y2` are going to be daunting. Remember that is why you get hold of domain specialists to help with such code. Even an expert programmer would be unreasonable to expect to know all the areas of technical knowledge that are needed to write programs.

The large problem is that we have used `world` (in context, a `playpen` object) without defining it. This highlights the need for a turtle to know what Playpen it is using. To solve that issue we have to add an item of data and alter the constructors to initialize that data. The extra data will have to be a `playpen &`. Sadly, by doing that we lose the ability to create a default turtle because we must now always supply it with a reference to a `playpen` object.

Before we make that change let us look at a minor problem. It would be nice if turtles could use color for drawing. Black would be fine for a default, but we should be able to change the color, and that means we will need an `fgw::hue` piece of data and a member function to change it.

Here is the new definition of a `turtle` type with the changes in bold typeface.

```
class turtle {
  public:
     turtle(fgw::playpen &, double x, double y);
     turtle(fgw::playpen &);
     turtle & forward(double distance);
     turtle & left(double angle);
     turtle & penup();
     turtle & pendown();
     turtle & penshade(fgw::hue);
  private:
     fgw::point2d position;
     double direction;
     bool drawing;
     fgw::hue shade;
     fgw::playpen & world;
};
```

TASK 58

Amend the files for the turtle project so that the header, implementation and test reflect these changes. Do not forget to ensure that the test project still compiles.

The next question is where to put the function that displays the turtle. This is an implementation detail and so does not belong in the `public` part of a turtle's behavior. Perhaps at some later stage I will think of an alternative way to represent turtles. For example, I might decide to use a sprite. That is the clue that the declaration of the `display()` for `turtle` should be made a `private` part of the definition of `turtle`.

TASK 59

Amend the turtle project to include `display()` and add its use to the implementation of `left()` and `forward()`. You will need to alter the constructors so that a newly created `turtle` immediately displays itself.

Note that moving a turtle requires that you call `display()` before you move, to remove the current image, and after the move to restore the image.

We now come to a little problem; we need to be able to kill our turtles. That is, when they cease to exist they must disappear from view. In other words the dying action of a `turtle` is to call `display()` for one last time so that it will remove itself from view (we do not want our Playpen littered with dead corpses).

C++ has a special function, a destructor, which is called at the end of an object's life. The destructor's job is to clean up any debris. The name of a destructor is similar to that of a constructor; it is the name of the type preceded by ~ (tilde). In the case of our `turtle` type we need to add a destructor whose sole action will be to remove the image of the turtle from the Playpen window. (In case you are wondering, the compiler makes up a destructor for us if we fail to provide one – but it will only do things that are obvious to the compiler.)

In the header file for `turtle`, add the declaration:

```
~turtle();
```

immediately after the two constructors (it is customary to keep all the constructors and the destructor together). Then add:

```
turtle::~turtle(){
  display();
}
```

to the implementation file and rerun your test program.

Moving the turtle forward

We now have just one thing left to finish the implementation of our basic `turtle`. No doubt there are many other things that you would like to add and there is nothing to stop you doing so, but once we have a working `forward()` function we have the essentials. I am doing this for you because it calls on some knowledge of trigonometry that you may not have (though there is no reason why you should not try for yourself before reading on).

```
turtle & turtle::forward(double distance){
  double const x(position.x() +
             distance * cos(radians(direction)));
  double const y(position.y() +
             distance * sin(radians(direction)));
  point2d const new_position(x, y);
  display();
  if(drawing) drawline(world, position, new_position, color);
  position = new_position;
  display();
  world.display(); // ensure you can see the results
  keyboard keyb;
  if((keyb.key_pressed()& character_bits) == key_escape)
                                throw problem("turtle aborted");
  return *this;
}
```

You may be wondering about that use of the keyboard; it is to give us an emergency way out in case we lose control of our turtle (which is always a possibility when you start to explore the world of turtle graphics). Basically it gives us a panic button. We can hit the escape key and the `forward()` function will finish its current action and then `throw` an exception. What happens then depends on what we do at the place where we `catch` the exception. We could add this feature to other actions such as `turtle::left()`.

As well as having a panic button, it would be nice to be able to pause when we wanted to interrupt the turtle but not actually abandon the process. One of the keys on a standard keyboard is actually marked as "Pause Break". By testing for that key as well as ESC you could arrange for the program to idle until you press that key again.

Exploring Turtle Graphics

Now that we have a turtle we can start to explore the rich world of turtle graphics. To get you started here is a little function that draws a regular polygon:

```
void polygon(playpen & canvas, double x, double y,
        double direction, int sides, double side, hue shade){
  turtle artist(canvas, x, y);
  artist.left(direction).penshade(shade);
  for(int i(0); i != sides; ++i){
     artist.forward(side).left(360.0/sides);
  }
}
```

Notice how I can chain instructions together. That is the benefit of having the member functions end with `return *this;` with `turtle &` as the return type. It isn't to save typing time: it allows us to write our code so that we can see its structure more clearly.

To give you an idea about the power of turtle graphics try this little program that uses nothing but the above function:

```
int main(){
  try {
     playpen paper;
     for(int i(0); i != 360; i += 5){
        polygon(paper, 0, 0, i, 6, 70, i*3);
     }
     cin.get();
  }
  catch(...){ cout << "An exception occurred. \n";}
}
```

Here is another little program to show how things can get out of control if you are not careful. When you run this program remember that the ESC key will halt the turtle.

```
int main(){
  try {
     playpen paper;
     turtle runaway(paper);
     try {
        while (true){
           runaway.forward(5).left(3);
        }
     }
     catch(problem & p){ cout << p.report();}
     cin.get();
  }
  catch(...){ cout << "An exception occurred. \n";}
}
```

That program also demonstrates how we can catch a particular kind of exception. In this case it is a simple type from my library that does very little other than report the message it was given to deliver. Try the program and see how easy it is to regain control. Here is another example of a program where you will need the ESC key to regain control:

```
void spiral(turtle & pencil, double angle,
                              int step, int increment){
  while(true){
     pencil.forward(step).left(angle);
     step += increment;
  }
}

int main(){
  try {
     playpen paper;
     turtle runaway(paper);
     runaway.penshade(red3 + blue3 + green2);
     double const angle(read<double>("What angle? "));
     try {
        spiral(runaway, angle, 5, 3);
     }
     catch(problem & p){ cout << p.report();}
     cin.get();
  }
  catch(...){ cout << "An exception occurred. \n";}
}
```

If you have never tried turtle graphics before please spend some time experimenting. Even simple things such as feeding in different numbers to the above program can result in a remarkable range of results. Programming should have its light moments when we can just enjoy the fruits of our hard work.

What else can a turtle do?

Because you have control of the definition of `turtle` you can add functionality. For example, adding a function that will hand out the position information for a turtle and a second one that allows you to set a turtle's direction (rather than just change by turning left a given number of degrees) would allow you to simulate predator–prey chases.

If you want ideas about what you might do with a simple `turtle` try reading *Turtle Geometry: The Computer as a Medium for Exploring Mathematics* by Harold Abelson and Andrea diSessa. This book starts simply but gets very deep before the end. It may take some work to understand how to convert the code of the book into C++ but the results can be very rewarding if you have the time and inclination.

Here is a little example based on an early item from that book:

```
void branch(turtle & walker, int length){
  if(length){
     walker.forward(length).left(45);
     branch(walker, 2*length/3);
     walker.left(-90);
     branch(walker, 2*length/3);
```

```
    walker.left(45).forward(-length);
  }
}

int main(){
  try {
    playpen paper;
    paper.scale(2);
    turtle bunny(paper);
    bunny.left(90);
    try {
      branch(bunny, 40);
    }
    catch(problem & p){ cout << p.report();}
    cin.get();
  }
  catch(...){ cout << "An exception occurred. \n";}
}
```

If you run this program you will probably realize that the turtle is spending most of its time drawing and "undrawing" itself. Even if you are happy with the speed, the constant flickering may irritate. But this is your code so you can tackle that by adding a couple of extra member functions, a piece of data and a modification to the implementation.

Hiding and showing the turtle

Here is the modified definition of the turtle type:

```
class turtle {
  public:
    turtle(fgw::playpen &, double x, double y);
    turtle(fgw::playpen &);
    ~turtle();
    turtle & forward(double distance);
    turtle & left(double angle);
    turtle & penup();
    turtle & pendown();
    turtle & hide();
    turtle & show();
    turtle & penshade(fgw::hue);
  private:
    void display();
    fgw::point2d position;
    double direction;
    bool drawing;
    bool visible;
    fgw::hue color;
    fgw::playpen & world;
};
```

We need to modify just three functions: the two constructors, to initialize `visible` to `true`, and the `display()`. All the changes are easy. Add `visible(true)` into the constructor initializer lists and wrap the actions of `display()` in an `if`:

```
void turtle::display(){
  if(visible){
     // all the old code
  }
}
```

Implement `hide()` and `show()` before you look at my solutions. It would be fair to warn you that there is a little trap waiting to catch you out. However that is enough of a hint.

Recursion

Look at the definition of `branch()` above. Do you notice anything? No, not the simple use of negative values for `forward()` in order to go back and for `left()` in order to turn right. The special feature of that function is that it calls itself in its implementation. That is called recursion. It is a powerful but highly dangerous computing technique.

It is dangerous because every time a function is called without an intervening return some of the computer's memory resources are consumed. Badly-written recursive functions can quickly consume all the available memory and your machine grinds to a halt. If you are lucky, it issues a message telling you that it has run out of resources.

This means that we need to be careful that a recursive function has some way to detect that it should stop calling itself. In the above function that is when the length parameter gets a zero value (and if you keep on reducing a number to two-thirds of its current value (using whole number arithmetic) you will soon get to zero.

Here is an example of lethal recursion. Please do *not* try it unless you are ready to restart your machine. Alternatively, add a panic button the way I did for `turtle::display()`.

```
void recurse(){
  cout << "...\n";
  return recurse();
}
```

There are some clever compilers that can spot that particular type of recursion (called tail recursion because the function calls itself on its way out) and convert your program into a slightly less dangerous form:

```
void recurse(){
  while(true){
     cout << "...\n";
  }
}
```

That version runs forever (or until you do something to stop it) but it isn't consuming ever more machine resources. You should not rely on the cleverness of a compiler to keep you out of serious trouble.

Unfortunately many books give you very bad examples of recursion, cases that are quite unnecessary and just lead the innocent into bad habits.

Any function that calls itself either directly or indirectly (e.g. a function calls a second function which in turn calls the first one) must have a way to stop the process. One common way is to use some form of level count which will limit the number of levels of recursion. Here is an example:

```
void nestedtriangle(turtle & worker, double size, int level){
  if(not level) return;
  for(int i(0); i != 3; ++i){
     nestedtriangle(worker, size/2, level-1);
     worker.penshade(level*30).forward(size).left(120);
  }
}
```

Here is a small program to use that function. If you want you can go as high as nine levels instead of the six in the demonstration program. More than nine is pointless because the size for the smallest triangle becomes too small to show on the screen.

```
int main(){
  try {
     playpen paper;
     paper.setplotmode(disjoint);
     turtle bunny(paper);
     bunny.left(90).penup().forward(-200).pendown();
     bunny.left(-30).hide();
     try {
        nestedtriangle(bunny, 512, 8);
     }
     catch(problem & p){ cout << p.report();}
     cin.get();
  }
  catch(...){ cout << "An exception occurred. \n";}
}
```

Did you notice the hidden assumption in that program that `level` would be positive? See how easy it is to make these assumptions. Have a look at the code and see how you could block the disaster (yes, it would be) if someone wrote:

```
nestedtriangle(bunny, 512, -1);
```

Finally, here is an example of mutual recursion that produces a dragon curve.

```
void rdragon(turtle & worker, int size, int level);
// we need to declare this function because the following
// definition uses it.
void ldragon(turtle & worker, int size, int level){
  if(not level){
     worker.forward(size);
     return;
  }
```

```
  ldragon(worker, size, level-1);
  worker.left(90);
  rdragon(worker, size, level-1);
}

void rdragon(turtle & worker, int size, int level){
  if(not level){
     worker.forward(size);
     return;
  }
  ldragon(worker, size, level-1);
  worker.left(-90);
  rdragon(worker, size, level-1);
}
```

And the driving program:

```
int main(){
  try {
     playpen paper;
     turtle dragon(paper);
     dragon.hide();
     try {
        rdragon(dragon, 3, 12);
     }
     catch(problem & p){ cout << p.report();}
     cin.get();
  }
  catch(...){ cout << "An exception occurred. \n";}
}
```

Wrapping It Up

Another chapter with no exercises though quite a few tasks. I hope that the ideas that you find in this chapter are ones that you want to pursue. I think that the simple `turtle` type I have provided here is an example of the power of programming in C++ and similar languages. `turtle` has opened up an entirely different form of graphical programming. Because you have control over the type you can add new features when you want to.

If you read books about LOGO you will find all kinds of ideas that you can now implement in C++. Some of them are going to require more skill than you have currently but not skill that is out of your reach.

All those tasks that we did earlier with our `shape` type can be done with a turtle instead. Some of them are easier with a turtle, some harder. For example, drawing circles with a `turtle` is easy:

```
void circle(turtle & me, double circumference){
  int const steps(circumference/2);
  for(int i(0); i != steps; ++i){
     me.forward(circumference/steps).left(360.0/steps);
  }
}
```

which works quite nicely in the following demonstration program:

```
int main(){
  try {
     playpen paper;
     turtle pencil(paper);
     pencil.hide();
     try {
        for(int i(0); i != 30; ++i){
           circle(pencil,400);
           pencil.left(12);
        }
     }
     catch(problem & p){ cout << p.report();}
     cin.get();
  }
  catch(...){ cout << "An exception occurred. \n";}
}
```

Please share the developments you make to the `turtle` class with others by posting them to this book's website. Of course you will get credit, which should add to the pleasure you get from taking control and making your computer do things you want to do.

ROBERTA'S COMMENTS

I tried this chapter out of sequence. I had been having problems with the previous two chapters and Francis suggested I leave them till he had time to do some reorganization and that I try this chapter instead.

My first reaction was that it seemed odd to end a book by introducing material from an entirely different programming language. I then felt unhappy about the need to clean up the "dead" turtles. However I enjoyed this chapter with its different perspective on graphics.

I visited the website Francis suggests. Following the links from there provided me with insight and new ideas for programming.

After the mind-challenging tasks of the last few chapters this one is more direct. I found it easier to do while providing plenty of opportunity to experiment.

SOLUTIONS TO TASKS

Task 57

```
turtle::turtle(double x, double y)
          :position(x, y), direction(0), drawing(true){}

turtle::turtle()
          :position(0.0, 0.0),direction(0.0), drawing(true) {}

turtle & turtle::forward(double distance){
  cout << "Not implemented yet\n";
  return *this;
}
```

The above is a simple stub function that reports itself as unimplemented and then returns the correct value (i.e. the object that has been instructed to move forward).

```
turtle & turtle::left(double angle){
  cout << "No display yet\n";
  direction += angle;
  return *this;
}
```

The above is a partial stub function that reports itself as missing a display facility then returns the correct value (i.e. the object that has been instructed to turn left).

```
turtle & turtle::penup(){
  drawing = false;
  return *this;
}
```

Neither this function nor the following one have any problems because it simply changes the way that the turtle object behaves in future.

SOLUTIONS TO TASKS

```
  turtle & turtle::pendown(){
     drawing = true;
     return *this;
  }
```

Task 58

Here are the changes you need to make to your implementation file (again, with the changes highlighted in bold):

```
turtle::turtle(playpen & p, double x, double y)
      :position(x, y), direction(0.0), drawing(true),
         color(black), world(p){}

turtle::turtle(playpen & p)
     :position(0.0, 0.0),direction(0.0), drawing(true),
        color(black), world(p){}

turtle & turtle::penshade(hue shade){
  color = shade;
  return *this;
}
```

Task 61

The trap is that you have to time the call of `display()` carefully to either remove or replace the image. You also have to remember that the program may try to do an action that is already done, and it might be an error to do it again.

```
turtle & turtle::hide(){
  if(visible) display(); // remove image
  visible = false;
  return *this;
}

turtle & turtle::show(){
  if(not visible){
     visible = true;
     display();
  }
  return *this;
}
```

Summary

Key programming concepts

- Turtle graphics is an object-centered view of geometry that was first developed by Seymour Papert.
- Imperative programming refers to a program style in which the machine is given instructions rather than asked for information.
- Programs, particularly imperative ones, sometimes need an escape mechanism to either interrupt or abandon a process.
- Recursion is the term used to refer to a function that calls itself either directly or indirectly (it is indirect recursion when one of the functions it calls, calls it in return).
- Recursive functions need a way to stop calling themselves.

C++ checklist

- A C++ class can have one defined destructor per class. The job of a destructor is to clean up at the end of an object's lifetime. The destructor for a class is referred to by the class name preceded by ~ (tilde). If you do not provide a destructor the compiler will provide a trivial one that does nothing except ensure that any data objects clean themselves up.
- A C++ class can have many (overloaded) constructors, one for each way that an object of that type might be created, but it can have only one destructor.

CHAPTER 17

You Can Program

If you have got here by studying the previous 16 chapters you have discovered that you can program and that somewhere inside you there is a programmer. I hope you have also experienced the high spots of a tremendous kick when it all goes together and works. Unless you are unusually talented you will certainly have experienced low moments when the code just refuses to work. I hope the high points have more than compensated for the low ones. I know that has been true for me. There have been times while writing this book when I have been hitting my desk and shouting at my computer when source code simply would not behave itself. However there have also been plenty of times when I have felt overjoyed and even surprised at how well some code has worked.

If you have the patience it is probably worth going back and reworking the early chapters. I think you will be amazed at how much easier they are second time round. Much more important is that I think you will find that you are writing more elegant code second time around. The first time, your priority was to get the code working and to try to understand what you were doing. The sample solutions are not intended to be definitive, just examples of a way of solving the problems you have been given. Again you probably had to work quite hard at understanding the solutions Roberta and I provided. I know she had to work very hard understanding some of mine, but you should also know that sometimes she produced essentially better solutions than mine even if her code sometimes lacked polish.

What Use Is What You Have Learnt?

You still have some way to go before you become a master programmer but that is not a reason to assume that there is nothing useful you can do. Programming can be fun in itself but it is not an end in itself; it is a tool for achieving things. I often hear people opine that there is not much use in learning to program because all the useful stuff has either already been done or is too hard.

To me that is rather like saying that there is no purpose in learning to compose music or to use oil paints because all the good music and beautiful paintings have already been written or painted. When put like that you can see how stupid the statement is.

You also know that an inexperienced musician or artist is not going to produce a masterpiece, but at the same time that does not make a student piece valueless. The same applies to programming which is one reason that I have encouraged you to do more than just the tasks and exercises I have provided. The problem that newcomers to programming often have is appreciating what they can attempt and what is likely to be beyond them. In the next part of this chapter I am going to look at some problem areas and suggest things that you could tackle even though the obvious task requires more expertize than you yet have.

Most of the rest of this chapter is just ideas. They are the tiniest tip of what can be done and they should mainly serve to set you thinking. It was always time to write programs that you found useful or interesting but now you are a programmer the balance changes so that this is mostly what you should do. When I started writing this book several of my expert colleagues told me that animation in C++ was way too hard for novices and that something as simple as Playpen was not nearly enough. Were they right?

Games-Based Problems

Chess

In the days when I taught programming to teenagers there would always be the one who wanted to write a program to play chess. That is an unreasonable ambition for a first time programmer but that does not mean that they cannot write programs for the keen chess player. More to the point, some of these programs have yet to be written (as far as I know). Here are a few ideas, some hard, some moderate and some largely a matter of careful work.

Electronic chessboard

Most programs to support the chess player will benefit from a visual display starting with a basic chessboard. While it is very easy to turn the Playpen into a chessboard (change the scale to 64 and use a pair of nested loops to alternately plot black and white pixels), it would be nice to have something more elegant.

First it would be nice if the chessboard were scaled so that it did not take over the whole Playpen. That is easy; just change the scale in the above to something less than 64. But look for more elegance such as adding a rim to the board that will scale appropriately.

Being able to relocate the board so that it is not centered in the Playpen just requires changing the origin, but try adding texture and coloring for both the board and the rim.

Providing perspective so that the board can be viewed from an angle is harder. You will have to abandon the simple use of large pixels. You will also need some skill in the maths of perspective (vanishing points and lines, etc.) or you will need to find sources for that information (either books or domain experts).

The final touches are to provide both a zoom facility (easy when handling just an overhead view) and the ability to rotate the board.

Identifying squares on a chessboard

Write a function to highlight a selected square with some suitable visual mechanism. For program purposes I would probably reference the squares of the board in a coordinate-like form so that `board[0][0]` would identify the near left corner square, `board[7][0]` the near right, `board[0][7]` the far left and `board[7][7]` the far right.

There is then the need to convert the internal representation to the representations used externally. There are two common mechanisms for naming the squares on a chessboard. That leads to four functions, each of which converts to or from the internal representation and one of the external representations.

There is also the idea of writing functions that convert between the two human mechanisms (external representations). Consider writing a program that could read a game from a file in classical notation and save it in modern algebraic notation (or vice versa). Unless you are a reasonably expert chess player you will need a domain expert to explain the details of the notation of games in the two formats.

In computing environments we also have the option to use a mouse to point to the square we want. This suggests functions that will highlight a square identified with a mouse, and output the name of the square in either classical or algebraic format.

Chess pieces

The first problem with chess pieces is to provide a graphical representation of them. I would keep it simple for starters and just use symbols that get displayed on a board viewed vertically (i.e. like the diagrams you see in newspaper chess columns). You will need to consider the issue of there being two sets of contrasting colors (light and dark) and that these must be visible and distinct on the two tone board.

The problem of displaying pieces in three dimensions with perspective and possible rotation is tough because it calls on a lot of specific domain knowledge (the mathematics of three-dimensional visualization). You know enough programming to do it but you are unlikely to have the domain expertize. However if you want to acquire that expertize, tackling this problem might be a good way of doing so.

There are various aspects of the movement of pieces that lend themselves to programming. The first is providing a visually elegant method for moving a piece (the `sprite` type springs to mind as a possible solution).

The second issue with moving pieces is determining legal moves for a specified piece. Your program needs to be able to determine if a specified piece can move legally from its current location to another one that has been specified.

Once you have a "legal move" function (or set of functions to cope with the different pieces) you have the potential to write a function that will highlight all the squares that a specified piece can move to from its current location. There is also the inverse problem of identifying all the pieces that can legally move from where they are to a selected square.

Strategy support

You can build on the final functions of the last section by developing functions that will assist a player by identifying weak points. That is pieces that are inadequately defended for the number and type of pieces that are attacking them.

Game study support

With all the above you have the tools to write a program that will read in a game from a file move by move and allow you to study the positions by asking about apparently weak squares (under-defended), the legal moves for a piece, the pieces that can move to a specified square, etc.

Solving problems

This is one that I would consider close to cheating, but you certainly could write a program that takes a chess problem (typically problems of the form: "White to mate in three") and solves it by meticulous analysis of all possible moves.

While it removes the challenge of such problems it would be a good program to work on if you wanted to study the area of general strategy analysis.

Conclusion

There are many other kinds of program that you could write based on various aspects of chess without even starting to write a program that allows the computer to play. That is a program that I am happy to leave to experts.

Other forms of chess

There are many other forms of chess, each with its own challenges for both the player and the programmer. Both China and Japan have chess-like games that differ substantially from International Chess. Indeed Japan has many forms of Shogi (its national chess-like game) each with its own challenges.

At the time of writing a good starting point if you are looking for the rules and details of boards and pieces is http://www.chessvariants.com/index.html. Unfortunately the Internet is not a stable organism, people lose interest, move on to other things and pages disappear. However you can be sure that information on most subjects is there somewhere.

If you want a substantial source of programming problems for a chess variant try looking at http://homepages.ed.ac.uk/rjhare/shogi/tai-shogi/intro.htm where you will find details of Tai Shogi (or Grand Shogi).

Other board games

There are a vast number of other board games that you could use as material for programs. However I must give you a warning; do not write programs for commercial games such as Monopoly. The owners of the intellectual property rights (copyrights and patents) get upset if you start providing computer versions of their games. As there is a vast wealth of non-commercial games available there is no need to risk annoying them.

Indeed it seems that game playing is a fundamental part of human nature. There is an extraordinary wealth of games going back thousands of years. One of the greatest strategy games (the Japanese game of Go) traces its origins back to China some 4000 years ago. We have written records of games from circa 1000 BC that clearly demonstrate that the essential rules of the game have not changed in three millennia.

I have no problem with all the multitude of computer-based games that are invented these days, indeed I thoroughly enjoy adventure games and god games (ones where you are responsible for managing the development of civilization) but I regret the erosion of knowledge of the many great classical games. Computing gives us the chance to revive those games because we can play with other enthusiasts over the Internet. Even if only one in ten million people are interested in a game, we can find plenty of opponents to play electronically.

Card games

An ordinary pack of playing cards can be used to play a vast range of different games. There are thousands of card games available using an amazing range of different types of game play. Most people are familiar with trick-taking games, such as the various forms of Whist, and collecting games, such as Rummy (in all its variations). Then there are gambling games such as Blackjack and Poker. But there are also many other games both old and new.

If you want some ideas about newer ones go to www.google.com and do an advanced search for "Robert Abbott" as a complete phrase. That will give you some interesting material to fire your imagination, not least the material you will find on logic mazes.

Before you start writing programs to play card games there are some fundamentals that you can program:

- Create a pack of cards with suitable ways to represent the cards both as text output (on the console or in the Playpen window) and as graphical images.
- Functions to produce a shuffle of one or more packs (some games use multiple packs and some games use part packs).
- Functions to deal cards into hands.
- Functions to sort a hand of cards by suit, denomination or both.
- Functions that can handle various trick-taking rules (some games rank cards in quite different ways from the one that we are most used to (AKQJ...32).
- Functions to display groups of cards.

I could go on but you should get the idea by now.

When you have got the basic components working satisfactorily it will be time to try to write a program to handle the mechanics of a simple game played over a network. Of course such play relies on either a high degree of trust (that the players do not cheat) or the use of a non-playing intermediary (a computer acting as a games server).

The basic idea of playing a card game over a network on an informal basis with trusted opponents is that the players all have copies of the program which on start up prompts to know which player you are (e.g. dealer, left of dealer, etc.) and is fed a large number to start the pseudo-random number generator. The program then tells each player about the cards they receive. It manages the play with each individual telling the others what they are doing (e.g. which card they wish to play next is fed to each individual's copy of the program which validates the action and keeps track).

As a starter try a simple two-person game such as Cribbage. That game has the added challenge of providing an electronic board and pegs to emulate the traditional way of keeping score.

Other games

My problem here is where to stop, so perhaps I should not start. Every society of which we have records has invented competitive games. In fact, games-playing and games invention seems to be a fundamental attribute of being human.

While the Internet is a source of a horrific amount of rubbish, it is also a rich repository for seeking out details of games that you might use as the basis for some programming practice.

On my first computer (circa 1979), I started to develop my own "dungeons and dragons" game. This was nothing to do with today's trademarked games of that name. My idea was to create a maze with various monsters each with its own characteristics. I will not go into the details here except to say that it was very popular with my pupils at that time and that it was never finished.

However one requirement of the game was building a maze. Mine created a grid of square cells. It then removed at random a percentage of the internal walls. I then generated a random exit cell that took you down to the next level and a random starting point for the player. The program then checked that it was possible for the player to reach the exit; if it wasn't it removed the minimum of walls to ensure that it was possible. The player also had a number of "spells" they could use which included one of last resort called "earthquake", which created a new random maze.

I think I have said enough to point those who want to try a little games programming in a direction worth pursuing. As always the ultimate limit is your imagination and creativity. Not only are current computers many orders of magnitude more powerful than the ones I was using in the late 70s but the programming tools you already have are far more powerful than those I was using 25 years ago.

Analytical Problems

I am not referring to mathematical analysis but the process of taking some data and trying to extract information from it. Alongside inventing and playing games human beings have a common desire to find patterns in the world around them. In this section I am going to suggest a few areas where you might write a program to help with the search for pattern.

Lexical analysis

It seems that every one of us has personal patterns in our writing. These are not quite as permanent as our fingerprints or the irises of our eyes but there are a lot of ways in which our writing is distinctly ours.

Analyzing text for authorial signatures is very tedious if we try to do it by hand but once text is in a computer-readable form we have the ability to look at the text in many different ways. Here are a few:

- The distribution of word lengths. For example, what percentage of a piece of writing is two-letter words, three-letter words, etc. Some people tend to use shorter words; some use longer ones more often.
- The distribution of sentence lengths. Like words but now we are concerned with the number of two-word sentences, etc.
- The complexity of sentences. This one is harder but one simple measure can be the proportion of commas to full stops.
- The use of punctuation such as the ratio of exclamation marks to question marks.
- The use of specific words. Many people have words that they use significantly more often (or less often) than the average use for the population as a whole.
- The distribution of an individual's use of the most common ten, twenty, hundred, etc. words.

There are many more ways that you can analyze a piece of text. Collecting the results of a number of these for a piece of writing will create a profile of that writing which you can then compare with the profiles of other pieces of writing.

Language analysis

As well as profiling a piece of text to try to identify authorship, you can also profile a piece of text to try to automatically determine which language it is written in. Word length and letter frequency are good indicators unless the sample text has been deliberately manipulated. For example, there is a short French novel that has been written without one of the vowels (I think it was "a"). Even more remarkable (to me at least) is that it was translated into English with the identical restriction. I mention that to illustrate how it is possible to manipulate the letter frequencies given time and skill.

Even without noting accented letters, human languages have fingerprints that allow identification without the aid of word recognition. For example, given a big enough sample (a couple of thousand words) it is possible to distinguish Spanish from Portuguese with a high probability of success simply by using a couple of profiling measures

Writing a program to automate the counting process is well within your programming ability.

Looking for hidden messages

Take any large piece of writing such as an English dictionary or the works of Shakespeare that you have available in electronic form. Now take the nth word of each paragraph and look to see if there are any hidden messages. You are unlikely to come up with anything if you use the first word but using something such as the fifth or sixth word can turn up surprises (but do not take them seriously).

You can do the same using the nth letter of each paragraph, sentence, page, etc. Again you might be surprised by how prophetic such texts can be. However remember that if you analyze any text in enough different ways you will get patches of accidental sense in a sea of nonsense. However it can be fun and baffle your friends. And some books actually do have such hidden messages deliberately written into them.

Sporting analysis

Many people like to try to find patterns in sports results, either for fun or because they want to bet. They try to determine if there is something that acts as a predictor for specific results. For example, does a horse run better in certain weather conditions, does a sports team perform better on certain days of the week, and so on.

Without casting any judgment on the value of such analysis, you have enough programming skill to relate a horse's success to the humidity or temperature on the days it races.

You can also write programs to calculate various sporting statistics, such as a baseball batter's averages or a cricketer's bowling average. Of course there are already programs that will do these things but the fun of having your own program is that you can look at the data in different ways.

Visualization tools

One of the tools of analysis is to help our insight when looking for patterns by displaying the information in some way. Histograms, pie charts, distribution curves and scattergrams are just a few of the ways used to help find patterns by creating visual representations of data.

You have the programming facilities to write your own programs to create visual representations of sports data (or any data that interests you).

I once knew a statistician who claimed that if you gave him any two sets of figures that he could provide a visual representation that appeared to relate one to the other. He would take great delight in plotting a couple of curves showing that the death rate for 20-year-olds in England in the 17th century was similar to the cost of sugar in New York during the 20th century. I mention that as a warning against thinking that seeing is believing.

Mathematical Problems

There are plenty of opportunities for writing programs to deal with mathematical problems from the byways of mathematics. I do not mean profound problems from the cutting edge of modern mathematics; I mean the many curious aspects of mathematics that can be entertaining to those who have not been trained to believe that all mathematics is beyond their intellectual resources.

I am not going to give you an interminable list because that would do little to break down a lifetime's aversion to mathematics. However those without such an aversion may still need a little help in seeing how their newly acquired programming skill could allow them to explore new ideas.

I am going to outline four problems that can be explored or solved with the help of computer programming. There are many more but four will be enough for here.

Managing an oil company

I want you to imagine that you are the manager of an oil company that owns four oilfields and four oil refineries. Each refinery can exactly process the production from any one of the oilfields. However the costs of transport from oilfield to refinery plus the costs of refining the oil vary. Your job as manager is to select the cheapest assignment of oilfields to refineries.

The costs are represented in an array:

	Easy	Final	George Town	Home Central
Able Field	2832	1356	5278	8956
Baker Field	4326	2471	3189	9342
Cork Field	9534	4127	8437	8575
Denton Field	8645	5623	7523	6729

So how good a manager are you? Perhaps you start by assigning Able Field to Final. That seems reasonable because that is much the cheapest combination. Next you assign Baker Field to George Town as the best option from what is left. Next you assign Denton Field to Home Central. That leaves Cork Field being processed by Easy.

That last choice might make you a little uncomfortable because that is the most expensive combination possible. It seems that the policy of making the "best" choice of what is left traps us into a bad final choice. Can we do better?

Well, yes. Try A->E, B->G, C->F and D->H. That is certainly better, but is it the best? Well you are the manager so write a program that will determine the best overall choice for this grid. Now generalize it to cope with different size grids and different values.

If you are not already familiar with the algorithms for solving this kind of optimal assignment problem it is time to find a domain expert or a relevant book. You are a programmer; do not let that trap you into believing that you can be an expert on everything.

I used to present this problem to my pupils as a paper and pencil exercise. The lesson had a hidden message. At the end of the lesson I used to point out that there are many places where a manager has to make such assignments. For example as the Head of Mathematics in the school I had to assign teachers to classes that took place simultaneously. The lesson was that giving one class the very best teacher for them might result in another class getting the very worst one. But it might be possible to arrange that everyone got the second best.

And the programming point is that the program you write isn't about managing an oil company but is one of optimizing interacting choices.

Solving equations graphically

In my youth, I had to learn how to solve simultaneous equations by pure mathematical methods. Graphical solutions had their place but were considered inferior because they had very limited accuracy.

In the 1980s, I came across a program that would plot any reasonable mathematical function. It had a zoom facility that allowed you to zoom in (i.e. use an ever larger scale). You could also select a point with your mouse and the x and y coordinates would be displayed. The further you zoomed in the more decimal places would be given. This meant that you could solve simultaneous equations graphically to considerable accuracy by zooming in on the points of intersection. These were not simple simultaneous equations but ones that involved complicated mathematical functions for which there are no exact methods of solution.

This was an impressive program at the time. One day, two of my sixth-formers tried to break the program by zooming in further and further. They gave up when the program was working to twenty places of decimals (and they checked that it was still giving ever more accurate answers).

You cannot duplicate this phenomenal program without writing special high-precision arithmetic functions, but you can duplicate the idea and get answers up to about a dozen decimal places.

An added feature is to work out a way for the user to input the mathematical functions in something approximating normal mathematical format.

If you have not already realized, this one is definitely just for the mathematicians in my readership.

Hamiltonian Paths

Given a network of lines connecting various points a Hamiltonian Path is a route that visits every point exactly once. (The similar problem of going down every connection exactly once is called an Eulerian Path.)

Given a file which contains pairs of letters defining paths between points (so AB means that there is a direct path from A to B, BA means that there is also a direct path from B to A, etc.) write a program that will determine if there is a path between a pair of points provided as input. A typical use might look like:

Where do you wish to start? : D

Where do you wish to end? : E

Route: D->A->G->H->E

Some pairs of start and end points may be impossible. Enhance the program so that it will list any impossible combinations of start and end points. Finally write a program that will determine if there is a path that visits every point exactly once.

This program might have prevented the disastrous time when a road planner introduced a new one-way traffic plan to a city. Unfortunately it was not obvious that you could reach points from which there was no way out (having got there you just went in long tedious paths that brought you back to the same place). The morning the new one-way signs were uncovered is not one the local police force wish to remember.

Double polar coordinates

I was teaching mathematics to a very bright group of 17-year-olds when one of them commented that there was a missing system of two-dimensional coordinates. I asked her what she meant. She explained that Cartesian coordinates located points with the distances from two axes. Polar coordinates located points with a distance from a fixed point and an angle from a fixed direction. However what about locating points with two directions measured from a pair of points that also defined the zero direction.

She wondered what a linear relationship between the two angles would look like. Had the question been asked a year earlier it would have died on the spot because plotting such a relationship would have been tedious in the extreme. But the school had just acquired a computer so a group of my students set out to write a program to explore the question.

Perhaps you would like to repeat it (note that these students knew very little about programming).

Conclusion

The above math problems are all relatively tough ones but can be tackled with the programming tools you now have as long as you have sufficient domain expertize. There is an extremely rich field of problems available for attack with computer programming. You do not need sophisticated programming techniques but you do need understanding and insight.

Conclusion

Every area of interest has opportunities for writing both simple and complicated programs. The best place to look for problems is in your own areas of interest and knowledge. The main caveat in choosing a problem is to avoid those for which you do not have a clear idea about how to solve the problem.

The suggestions I have made above are very far from exhaustive and the most important thing to understand is that despite common belief, programming is not mathematics. Being good at mathematics can help with some kinds of problems but there are many problems where math, in the narrow sense of what is taught in schools and colleges, will be of little use.

Now that you can program you have an immensely powerful set of tools for capitalizing on the power of the modern computer. Computers never have been just about numbers. From the earliest days, those with imagination have used them as creative tools. In the very early days of computing (the late 1950s) students at MIT started exploring what they could do with the crude (by our standards) tools they had available. With the encouragement of their instructors (who had more imagination than most) they set about writing the first version of Space War. Their tools were a teletype machine and a barely useable cathode ray tube as a primitive VDU. That was the first great motivator. Many versions of Space War were written and played in the dead of night on employers' lumbering mainframes.

A few years later, a couple of Fortran programmers (Fortran was a language specifically designed for mathematics) wrote the very first adventure game. That game has continued to be played over the years, polish has been added but the original game is as good as it ever was even though it was pure text.

A few years later, programmers working on early Unix systems (the precursor of Modern Linux, BSD Unix, etc.) wrote a game called Net Hack. That game also entertained and inspired a whole generation (and was written in the precursor to C++, a language called C, which is still widely used today).

The point I wish to make is that all those things were done with far cruder tools than you have on your desk, and with far less program language support than you have now. Great programs are written by people with creativity. Learn to use your tools simply but well and you may amaze both yourself and those around you. There is no virtue in complexity; the skill is in doing complicated things in simple ways.

Computers are good at repetitive tasks, so problems that you know how to solve but which take tedious amounts of work are ideal material for a computer program. The tedium may be that producing one solution involves a great deal of repetitive work or it may be that you will naturally want to apply the program to a large number of instances.

Make sure you understand the problem and have thought carefully about a good way to solve it. It is easy to be blinded by the awesome power of a modern computer and waste time writing a program to apply some brute force solution to a problem that you could have solved much more quickly by applying some intelligence to it.

Many years ago I had just become the proud owner of an expensive programmable mathematical calculator (the modern generation would be aghast at both its lack of power and its cost) when a colleague of mine who was a woodwork teacher pounced on me and asked if I would calculate the spacing of the frets on a guitar for him because one of his students was making a guitar for his coursework. I asked him to explain how the fret spacing was calculated. He described how he would do it on paper and I simply keyed in a program to emulate that process. The calculator took almost an hour. In the meantime I had thought about the problem, correctly identified the mathematical function involved and produced the figures Andy needed by using a simple four-function calculator.

That was an important lesson: think before you program. Understand the problem and apply your human intelligence to it. And finally remember that different devices change the optimum way to tackle a problem.

Where Next

You have come a long way to reach this point but there is much still to learn if you wish to become a master programmer. Some people reading this will feel happy with what they have so far achieved and will not want to go further, or at least not yet. Others will want to go on and learn about such things as object-oriented programming and then generic programming followed eventually by the new kid on the block, metaprogramming.

Each of those topics will be covered by subsequent books in this series but for now enjoy what you have achieved and spend some time producing a programming sampler that you can use to demonstrate to others that you are a programmer even if you still have much more to learn.

Remember that programming is best pursued as a shared task, both sharing the work and the results. Good luck with your programming endeavors and thanks for taking this journey through my world of programming.

I hope to meet you again in my next book, in the meantime have fun and improve your skills.

APPENDIX

Some Common Errors

This appendix just lists a few of the things that tend to be the cause of errors. Any new ones will be added to the website. If you have a consistent problem that is dealt with neither here nor on the website, please email me at you_can_do_it@robinton.demon.co.uk and I will help if I can. I know that everything works if used as expected, but identifying all the ways something can fail is, at best, difficult. I can remember an old game (for a Sinclair ZX Spectrum) that had difficulties when the player picked up the room they were in. The game designer had never envisaged that a player would try to do that and so had done nothing to make it impossible. The same will apply to learning to program; some of you are going to try things I had never thought of and sometimes that will get you into trouble.

I encourage you to learn by experiment so sometimes your difficulties will represent that you are being a good student and experimenting. If you do not tell me about any difficulties you have and fail to solve for yourself I will not be able to help you. If at some later stage I discover that you gave up because of some such problem I will feel unhappy.

- Forgetting to end a header file with a carriage return results in an error, often in the next file included.
- Forgetting to include a header file. While this is often obvious, sometimes the error messages are obscure. (It seems that forgetting `<fstream>` is particularly bad in terms of the error messages.)
- Forgetting to save an altered header file before recompiling means the compiler will use the old version.
- Forgetting to change the opening brace of a function definition to a semicolon when creating a function declaration in a header file (with cut and paste) results in bizarre errors, usually in some entirely different header file (usually a C++ Standard Library header).
- Leaving off the semicolon at the end of the last declaration in a header file often results in weird errors in some library file from the C++ Standard Library. If the compiler claims to be confused always check that you have not made this mistake because at this level of programming it is the commonest cause of that error.
- The commonest cause for the ''No such file or directory'' error message is that you have not set the include path in the options menu.
- Accidentally saving a file in the wrong directory can also lead to ''No such file or directory'' errors.
- Trying to link a project when you do not have the project file open will result in a raft of missing definition errors.
- Writing `& const` instead of `const &` in a declaration; while there is some allowance for varying the position of `const` in a declaration, it must not come after the symbol that qualifies a type as a reference type.

- If some keywords in your source code are not in the keyword color you have probably forgotten a closing quote for a string literal.
- Forgetting the brackets for a function call without arguments (e.g. writing `cin.get;` when you meant `cin.get();`) may get past the compiler but often generates curious error messages such as "cannot convert..." or "cannot resolve overload ...." If you get such an error message check that you have not left out the empty parentheses at the end of a function that is being called without arguments.

Index